# HISTORY
# OF HUNGARIAN
# LITERATURE

BY

TIBOR KLANICZAY
JÓZSEF SZAUDER
MIKLÓS SZABOLCSI

CORVINA PRESS

PH
3012
K513

EDITED BY MIKLÓS SZABOLCSI

TRANSLATORS:

JÓZSEF HATVANY (PARTS ONE AND TWO),
ISTVÁN FARKAS (PART THREE)

© TIBOR KLANICZAY, JÓZSEF SZAUDER,
AND MIKLÓS SZABOLCSI, 1964

49496

PRINTED IN HUNGARY, 1964

ATHENAEUM PRINTING HOUSE, BUDAPEST

# CONTENTS

5

# PREFACE

There are few English-language works about Hungarian literature. A short book appeared on the subject in 1898 (E. Reich : *Hungarian Literature*) ; 1906 saw the publication of a brilliant essay by F. Riedl, an eminent Hungarian follower of Taine (F. Riedl: *A History of Hungarian Literature*) ; but since these pioneering attempts, only shorter or longer papers and articles about some detail or problem of current interest have come out. The fullest and most modern summary of the history of Hungarian literature is to be found in the Encyclopaedia Britannica, under the entry "Hungarian Literature," but here available space limits detailed discussion.

Our *History of Hungarian Literature* thus represents the first effort for over fifty years to give a comprehensive treatment of Hungarian literature from its beginnings to the most recent developments. We are aware of the difficulties of this undertaking: we had to span a long period of time within relatively few pages; we had to list a large number of names and present a multitude of facts; we had to describe a great many trends and literary works, and at the same time keep our work clear, readable and informative.

*History of Hungarian Literature* is the work of three different authors, each of them an expert on a different period. This division of labour is in itself the source of a certain unevenness and disproportion as each writer would necessarily have a different style and technique of discussion. Actually the reader will find three works dealing with the three different principal periods of Hungarian literature. Nevertheless, the three authors attempted to achieve some kind of harmony: the work of all three is characterized by a consistent Marxist approach, the ambition to use the results of most recent research, and the desire to show the currents which link Hungarian literature with the mainstream of world literature.

We know that our work has shortcomings and we shall welcome any attempts by critics to point out where the greatest need for improvement lies.

PART ONE

# FROM THE ELEVENTH
# TO THE EIGHTEENTH CENTURY

BY TIBOR KLANICZAY

# ANCIENT POETRY

We have no certain knowledge of the origin and formation of Hungarian poetry and are therefore dependent on very indirect evidence. During the centuries of ancient Hungarian history, before the establishment of the Hungarian State (about 1000 A.D.), the cultural heritage of the Hungarians living under a clan or tribal form of organization was completely oral, so that we cannot speak of literature in the proper sense, but only of folklore. This earliest poetry was a communal product, passed down by word of mouth. Though an ancient Hungarian form of writing, the runic, did exist in the eighth to tenth centuries, indications are that its use was confined to inscriptions. The Hungarian runes are of Turkish origin and probably attained their ultimate form in the eighth century when the Hungarians were, in the region of the Black Sea, subjected to Slav and Byzantine cultural influences. Only some late mementoes of the ancient runic script are known, and these only because the Székely people living in Transylvania preserved it for a long time.

The poetic works of ancient Hungarian folklore were not preserved and not a single fragment has come down to us in its original form. Nevertheless, numerous relics testify to their erstwhile existence and popularity. Hungarian folk tales, folk songs and folk customs have to this day preserved motifs whose origin is rooted in the nomadic and pagan period of the Hungarian people. The core of many folk tales could only have been conceived in a society leading a nomadic way of life, and there are also frequent traces of the ancient matriarchal system. The memory of the ancient religion of the Hungarians has been especially bountifully preserved in folklore. In this respect not only some of the motifs of the folk tales and folk songs, but even certain of the artistic forms of Hungarian folklore may be traced back to the pagan times before the foundation of the State as some of the customs and ritual songs linked to the various pagan religious festivities survived in the Christian era, attached to certain Christian holidays and suitably transformed. Two cases in point are the folk custom of shamanistic singing *(regölés)* on the second day of Christmas, and the folk customs attached to Midsummer day. The shamanistic songs and Midsummer-day songs performed on these occasions and recorded in innumerable versions have preserved very many ancient elements. In the sixteenth century some superstitious incantations were noted down, which were also late heralds of a folklore connected with the ancient religion. The survival of ancient traditions may be suspected in the lamentations, and there is also factual evidence for the existence of ancient Hungarian work songs.

The shamanistic songs *(regösének)* have even preserved the name of the most ancient Hungarian singers. The shamans *(regös)*, who were pagan priests and magicians and performed their songs as such, must have been the most important authors of ancient poetry in the pagan era. Tradition moreover considers the shamans to have been the authors and performers of the old Hungarian legends and heroic songs. The Hungarian chroniclers of the eleventh to fourteenth centuries who wrote in Latin, made use of the content of several ancient legends and not infrequently even recorded them. These historical legends are the most valuable tangible relics of ancient Hungarian poetry. Two of them, the legend of the origin of the Hungarians *(Legend of the Miraculous Stag)* and that of their princes' descent *(Legend of Álmos)*, are totemistic legends of ancient origin which were incorporated in the chronicles in considerably altered form. Some of the numerous legends of the conquest of the new country (end of the ninth century) and of the incursions in the more developed countries (tenth century) have survived in their entirety. They are the *White Horse Legend* connected with the acquisition of the land by Prince Árpád the Conqueror, and the *Legends of Botond and Lehel,* two leaders of the incursions. The existence of others may be suspected from references in the chronicles—for example of songs relating the deeds of the various leaders of the conquest in the first person. One of the medieval chronicles, the work of the author known as Anonymus (about 1200 A.D.), has indeed preserved two lines, in Latin translation, of a lost song about the campaign of Chief Töhötöm:

*Omnes loca sibi aquirebant*
*et nomen bonum accipiebant.*

The three legends whose content has been preserved, testify to the artistic merits of ancient Hungarian legend-poetry. The Legend of Botond, for instance, relates a duel between a Hungarian and a Greek knight, making a well-rounded dramatic scene of it, sketching the background, giving a vivid impression of the whole spectacular event and conveying the mood of the attendant crowd that inspired the combatants to heroism. This story could well be part of any of the great epics.

The pagan songsters, the ancient Hungarian bards, did not disappear immediately in the Christian era, but for a long time preserved and spread the heroic songs of the pagan era, incurring contempt and persecution on the part of the Church and State. The successors of the pagan shaman bards gradually fused with the entertainers (jugglers, *Spielmänner*), whose order was also beginning to evolve in Hungary. The Hungarian entertainers of the Middle Ages (the sources either call them by the Latin name of *joculator* or the Slav one of *igric*), similarly to their colleagues of other nations, engaged in the most varied methods of entertainment, of which the recital of songs was only one. In the fourteenth century this order of entertainers began, in Hungary too, to undergo a process of differentiation, with the separation of the so-called *lutanists* and *fiddlers* who henceforth only sang songs to the accompaniment of an instrument. At the time when literature in Latin flourished in this country—right up to the sixteenth century—the Hungarian minstrels ensured the continuity of the songs in the Hungarian language and more or less consciously cultivated the verbal poetry, perfecting and polishing its forms.

Their stock of songs is certain to have included many kinds, but it is only of the heroic songs, the epics they performed, that we have authentic facts. At the beginning of the thirteenth century they still sang heroic songs of the times before the establishment of the State, but while maintaining these pagan traditions they also soon began to sing of those who stabilized the new order of the State. It was especially the struggles around the throne and the wars waged in defence of the country in the second half of the eleventh century that inspired a veritable garland of songs, and even the Latin versions in the chronicles have preserved a reflection of their beauty. Their naive but ingenious composition, the terse but telling characterisation of the main persons of the story, the symmetry of the general arrangement, the similes and metaphors which have retained their excellent illustrative qualities even in the Latin translation, are all so many proofs of the further artistic enrichment of verbal poetry in these songs. The main hero of the songs was mostly St. Ladislas, King of Hungary (1077-1095), and his memory has thus been preserved in folk tradition to this day.

The Latin chroniclers of the Middle Ages showed profound contempt for the songs of the "jugglers," but in as much as the message of their songs or the facts contained in them could be made to fit their ideas and serve their political aims, they did not hesitate to use them as fully valid sources. The work of the scholarly Anonymus even features the verbose style of the songs, with their frequent repetition of stereotyped turns of phrase. This link must, however, have been a reciprocal one—some of the stories recorded by the chroniclers will also have enriched the treasury of the minstrels' songs. Thus did the oral literature in Hungarian and the written literature in Latin permeate and sustain one another during the centuries of the Middle Ages.

# THE MIDDLE AGES

It was in opposition to the ancient, folkloristic poetry, and in a process of continuous struggle against it, that Christian literature in Latin was established in the eleventh century. The formation of the Hungarian feudal kingdom (in 1001) and the organization of the Catholic Church in Hungary necessarily involved the use of writing, at first by few people, but on an ever wider scale as the centuries of the Middle Ages progressed. This also implied the writing of certain literary works. For a long time the only written language was Latin, the official tongue of the Catholic Church; writing was, up to the thirteenth century, tantamount to Latin writing. The first men of letters were the German, Italian and later French ecclesiastics who came to Hungary during the reign of St. Stephen, the first King of Hungary (1001-1038). Especially prominent among them was the Venetian St. GERARD, who wrote his mystical theological work *Deliberatio supra hymnum trium puerorum*, during the course of his residence in Hungary. It must also have been an erudite foreign cleric who, on the basis of the king's instructions, composed King Stephen's *Injunctions* to his son *(De institutione morum ad Emericum ducem)*. However, the eleventh century also saw the appearance of the first writers of indigenous origin, for example, Bishop Maurus, the author of the first Hungarian Christian legend.

The first homes of the new Christian culture were the Benedictine monasteries, the bishoprics and the royal court. It was in the Roman-style cathedrals and monasteries erected in the eleventh and twelfth centuries, and the Royal Palace at Esztergom that the first signs of literary life began to appear. Relatively speaking, the most lively centres of activity developed at the royal and archiepiscopal seat at Esztergom and the headquarters of the Benedictine Order in Hungary at Pannonhalma. By about 1100 a fair circle of literary men had formed of the senior members of the priesthood, who wrote and compiled religious legends, chronicles and codes of law. The Hungarian authors of medieval Latin literature had, from the twelfth century onwards, generally attended foreign universities too, and had thoroughly mastered the rules for the composition of written works, and also the style that was then taught. In Hungary, in full agreement with the trend of European development, the eleventh and twelfth centuries witnessed the use of rhymed, and the thirteenth and fourteenth of rhythmical Latin prose. What is more, in the case of the latter, certain Hungarian chroniclers even established a particular form.

The most important works of the Latin-language literature between the eleventh and fourteenth centuries were the *chronicles* and the *gesta*. Whole series of these were written, because the chroniclers repeatedly revised and supplemented the works of their predecessors, or re-wrote them on radically new lines, in accordance with the interests of the king and the various parties and feudal factions who happened to be in power. Unfortunately only a few of these works have survived—the *Gesta* of Anonymus (about 1200) and Kézai (about 1283), moreover the *Illustrated Chronicle* (1358) and its numerous variations. Due to the close textual correspondences between the existing chronicles, however, scholars have also been able to trace back the lost works and have even succeeded—particularly on the basis of the *Illustrated Chronicle*—in partially analysing their texts. It accordingly appears that the writing of Latin-language histories in Hungary began during the reign of King Andrew I. It was in about 1052 that the history of the origin, migrations, conquests and incursions of the Hungarians and the story of the first kings was set down in writing in the so-called *Prime Chronicle*. In the eleventh and twelfth centuries several others continued and partially revised this ancestor of Hungarian chronicle-writing.

A new chapter in the development of the Hungarian chronicles was opened by the court recorder of King Béla III, whom scholars have called ANONYMUS. By the time Béla III (1172-

1196) ascended the throne, literary life had developed considerably and it was he who organized a Court Chancellery, which made it increasingly necessary to have erudite men of letters trained at the universities. Apart from Hungarians who had been to French and Italian universities, foreign masters of the *Minnesang* and of trubadour poetry *(e.g.* Peire Vidal), also appeared in the splendid court of Béla III at Esztergom. The chivalrous environment left its mark on the work of Anonymus, who had studied in Paris and probably in Orléans and worked to scholarly standards, choosing as his literary model the medieval histories of the Trojan War and of Alexander the Great. We learn, indeed, from the foreword to his *Gesta* that he had himself written a further version of the medieval romance of Troy. In his *Gesta Ungarorum*, written in about 1200, he completely transformed the earlier evolved history of the migrations of the Hungarians and the conquest of their land. He did not confine his narrative to the deeds of the reigning dynasty, but—in close agreement with the prevailing social conditions—ascribed a considerable role to the real or imagined ancestors of the peers of his own age.

A few decades later SIMON KÉZAI, chronicler to King Ladislas IV (1272-1290), set down a new and daring assumption in writing, when he elaborated his theory of the identity of the Hungarian and the Hun peoples, treating the adventures of the Huns and the Hungarians as the history of one and the same people. Although this assumption is completely unfounded, it is so convincing and its literary presentation was so successful that right up to the nineteenth century it played a prominent part in the historical thought of the Hungarians. After further revisions and continuations of old chronicles, it was finally MÁRK KÁLTI who achieved renown in the fourteenth century, not so much as an author but as a clever editor. With the sole exception of the *Gesta* of Anonymus, he edited all the earlier chronicles to form a united one (1358), thus leaving a unified work to form the basis of Hungarian historiography in subsequent centuries. King Louis the Great (1342-1382) had Kálti's work copied and lavishly illuminated. This so-called *Illustrated Chronicle* is the most outstanding masterpiece of medieval Hungarian miniature painting (now preserved in the National Library at Budapest).

Contemporaneously with the chronicles, ecclesiastical literature in the strict sense also began to be written. Liturgical books were copied and new liturgical texts of Hungarian concern were written. Of the works of ecclesiastical literature it is especially the religious legends and the hymns that are worthy of attention. The legends of the Hungarian saints are closely related to the chronicles, even the subjects being frequently identical, for the Kings St. Stephen and St. Ladislas and the Bishop St. Gerard played an important part in both kinds of writing. The oldest Hungarian religious legend, the story of St. Zoorard and St. Benedict, two Slav monks in Hungary, was written by Bishop Maurus of Pécs in about 1060. This was followed in about 1100 by the three legends of King St. Stephen, by one of several about St. Gerard, and one about the Prince St. Emery, then at the end of the twelfth century by the legend of King St. Ladislas. The writers of these legends had occasion to prepare biographies and character-sketches of the most important personalities of early Hungarian history, and thus to write the first successful literary portraits. The authors of the various legends show some variety—the three legends of St. Stephen, for instance, differ considerably from one another. The earlier, so-called "greater legend," written after his canonization in 1083, portrayed a devoted, gentle and gracious king, while the "lesser legend," written a good twenty years later at a time of acute factional strife, shows a militant proselytizer, a monarch who ruthlessly put down his opponents as he organized the state. The legend of St. Ladislas, a king famed for his heroic military exploits, was written at the end of the twelfth century and is coloured by the hues of the Age of Chivalry.

It was also in pursuance of the cult of the Hungarian saints that the Hungarian clerical poets of the Middle Ages enriched the country's hymn-writing. Liturgical hymns were written for the Hungarian saints' days, particularly in the thirteenth and fourteenth centuries. The most outstanding work of medieval Latin poetry in Hungary is the *Planctus* of an unknown ecclesiastical writer, which presents a striking poetic picture of the devastation of the country during the Mongolian invasion of 1241-42. The whole work is permeated by sincere human grief and is tuned to a perfect unity of mood by the patriotism which dominates it. The keynote of the poem is that of the despair felt at contrasting the terrible present with the glorious past, and it is only towards the end that this is resolved in a passionate prayer.

During the last centuries of the Middle Ages Hungary also had significant preachers, especially among members of the mendicant orders. Several notable Dominican collections of sermons in Latin from the fourteenth and fifteenth centuries have come down to us, and at the end of the fifteenth century two highly effective sermon authors appeared among the Franciscans. PELBÁRT TEMESVÁRI (d. 1504) published two voluminous collections of sermons entitled *Stellarium* and *Pomerium*. In his orations he deliberately endeavoured to meet the people's requirements— he made use of legends, historical traditions and not infrequently of elements taken from folk tales, and evolved a colourful style. His third work, the *Rosarium* is a systematic compendium of scholastic learning. His pupil OSVÁT LASKAI, also published several important collections of sermons at the beginning of the sixteenth century.

Under the shadow of the dominant Latin-language literature, writing and literature in Hungarian only began to develop slowly. Yet those who drafted the Latin texts had from the very first not been able to avoid recording some Hungarian words. It was frequently necessary in deeds and chronicles to mention the Hungarian names of persons and places, which could not be translated into Latin and had thus to be inserted into the Latin texts as Hungarian fragments. A text particularly rich in these Hungarian fragment relics is the *Charter of the Benedictine monastery at Tihany* dated 1055. Gradually some kind of usage began to be evolved for spelling Hungarian words, particularly at the Royal Chancellery, and it was recognized that the Latin alphabet was suitable for the notation of Hungarian sounds, too. Thus the technical condition for writing texts in the Hungarian language was established.

The need for the appearance of such texts made itself felt very soon in the practice of the Church. This was the origin of the oldest known Hungarian-language text that has come down

2*

to us—the *Funeral Oration* and the attendant *Supplication*, written in surprisingly fine style and recorded in about 1200.

In the thirteenth century it was the spread of the lay religious movements to Hungary that provided further inspiration for the appearance of Hungarian-language works. Hymns, legends and parts of the Gospel were translated into Hungarian for the *beguines* and nuns who did not know Latin. Such movements were in the thirteenth century mainly formed around the two mendicant orders, the Franciscans and the Dominicans, and it was these therefore—and in particular the nunneries belonging to them—that became the centres of Hungarian-language religious literature in the last centuries of the Middle Ages. However, only one literary work in Hungarian originating with these lay religious movements in the thirteenth century has come down to us. It is the *Ancient Hungarian Lamentation of Mary*, written at the end of the century, which is the oldest Hungarian poem. It was the work of a Hungarian Dominican monk, written after Geoffroi de Breteuil's Latin hymn. Just as the *Funeral Oration* testified to the considerable standard of development achieved by Hungarian prose, so did the *Lamentation of Mary* prove the same with respect to the Hungarian poetic language. We may therefore regard these two earliest relics of the language as the fortunately preserved heralds of a written civilization in Hungarian, which must by then have been fairly widespread. The Hungarian adapter of the *Lamentation of Mary* also had a gift for poetic expression—he entered fully into the content of the poem and interpreted the sorrow of the Mother in tones betokening fervent feeling. The rhythm and rhymes make use of the technique of medieval Latin verse, preparing the way for the greater tests of Hungarian poesy that were ahead.

It was at the beginning of the fourteenth century that a Hungarian translation was made of the *Legend of the Blessed Princess Margaret* (d. 1271), who had strong mystic inclinations and was one of the most outstanding figures of the Hungarian *beguine* movement. The text has unfortunately only been preserved in a copy made at the beginning of the sixteenth century of a version that had undergone several modifications. Even so, we may form an idea of the literary value of the *Legend of Margaret,* and particularly of some of its parts. The Legend is particularly noteworthy for its realistic portrayals. It supplies an authentic, human image of the Princess who voluntarily assumed poverty, abstinence and austerity, and faithfully presents the life of the *beguinage.* Even through its frequently naive description of facts and events, it is able to convey the deeper springs of the deeds and behaviour of the persons involved in the *Legend.* The closed world of the nunnery is shown in such a manner as also to reflect the multitude of conflicts and social tensions in the world outside its walls.

Facts about the Hungarian-language literary activities of the Franciscan order are available from the fourteenth century onward. A report from Jacopo Passavanti permits us to assume that by this time the Franciscans had even translated a part of the Bible into Hungarian. All that has come down to us, however, is a Hungarian translation from about 1370 of the Legend of St. Francis of Assisi, in a book copied around 1440. This so-called *Jókai Codex,* which contains the Hungarian version of the *Legend of St. Francis,* is at the same time the oldest known book to have been written entirely in Hungarian. The Hungarian translation has several passages which, in accordance with the original spirit of the Franciscan movement, express new strivings that could hardly have harmonised with the official Church view. The *Legend* voices the new theory of nature which St. Francis and his companions propagated, and—though for religious ends—the recognition of the beauties of nature also wells up in it.

The great upsurge of religious literature in the Hungarian language took place in the fifteenth century, as an accompaniment to, and partly under the influence of, the Hussite movement. It was the Hungarian Hussite heresy, which spread increasingly from about 1410, and in 1437 matured into a peasant rising in Transylvania, that produced the first Hungarian *translation of the Bible.* The Hussite preachers TAMÁS and BÁLINT in Southern Hungary translated either the whole of the Old and New Testament, or at least a considerable part, into Hungarian in about 1430. Of their translation, the Books of the Prophets, the Psalms and the Gospels have survived. Tamás and Bálint did yeoman work in interpreting the Books of the Bible, for the vocabulary of the Hungarian language was not rich enough to express the finer shades of meaning in the language of the Bible. They therefore had to create and construe new words, which have remained a part of the Hungarian vocabulary ever since. Since the Hussites gave Hungarian Bibles to the masses of the people who did not know Latin, the Church was also forced to translate an increasing number of religious works into the vernacular. This process was hastened by the reform movement within the Church, which had developed in Hungary too by this time, and also by the requirement of the mendicant orders, strengthened by organizational reforms, for religious literature in their own tongue.

However, even in the course of this expansion of religious literature in the fifteenth century, hardly any original works in Hungarian were written. The increasing number of Hungarian-language codices were filled with translations of many excellent items of the medieval universal stock of legends, of the rich parable-literature of the Middle Ages, of prayers, monastic rules, popular hymns, and of the meditations of noted mystical authors (H. Seuse, T. à Kempis, etc.). Further signs of the increasing practice of translation are the growing number of Hungarian glossaries in Latin codices, and also the compilation of numerous Latin-Hungarian word-lists. Religious literature in Hungarian—particularly monastic literature—attained the peak of its development at the close of the Middle Ages, in a period when the Renaissance culture and humanistic literature had struck roots not only in the more developed countries of Europe, but also in Hungary.

This late monastic literature was, though consisting of translations, of great importance for the development of Hungarian literature. It was during this period that the Hungarian language had to cope with the peculiar requirements of the various species of literature, the theological, mystical, etc. and to evolve the terminology and literary style necessary for rendering them in Hungarian. Particularly important from this point of view are the *translations of legends* and *of parables*, which were the first significant stations of Hungarian narrative prose. The translations of many of the famous legends of the Middle Ages and of many of the parts of the *Speculum exemplorum*, the *Gesta Romanorum* and the other famous medieval collections of parables are also noteworthy from the artistic point of view. A codex of about 1520 contains the first Hungarian-language drama, an adaption of the play *Dulcitius* by the tenth-century German nun-authoress Hrotsuitha, entitled *Of the Three Christian Daughters*. The *Legend of St. Catherine of Alexandria* in verse 4000 lines long, was translated from a Latin original which is so far unknown. The Hungarian codices of about 1500 also contain translations of many parts of the Bible, and especially prominent among these is an outstandingly beautiful, poetic translation of the *Song of Songs*. The religious literature at the end of the Middle Ages also played a noteworthy part in the development of Hungarian poetry. Several Latin hymns were recast in Hungarian verse, including an inspired poetic rendering of the Latin *Hymn about King St. Ladislas* written in the fifteenth century. One author whose name we know, ANDRÁS VÁSÁRHELYI, a Franciscan monk in Pest, enriched the literature of the period by writing an original hymn to the Virgin Mary in Hungarian.

Prominent by far among the monastic translators and copyists, all wrapped in a cloak of anonymity, was the so-called NAMELESS CARTHUSIAN, a writer of distinctive character. His work, the *Érdy Codex* of about 1000 printed pages, was the summit of Hungarian-language monastic literature, and at the same time its last station. The volume, which was completed in 1527, is a collection of sermons and legends compiled to a deliberate plan with the aim of making a desperate attempt to halt the decay of the Church. The surging waves of the Reformation were ever present before the writer's eyes, and striving to fight for the interests of the old world with new methods, he urged the publication of the Bible in Hungarian. Thus, despite his intentions, he became a precursor of the Reformation, at least in linguistic and literary respects. His work is artistic prose of a high standard, touched by the breath of humanism, and served to prepare the way for the fine Hungarian prose of the next decades.

The religious literature which set out from the lay movements and spread mainly among the mendicant orders was only one branch of the development of medieval Hungarian-language literature. The beginnings of Hungarian-language temporal literature in all probability also reach back to the thirteenth century. The results of scientific investigations indicate that in this, or the following century, Hungarian translations were prepared of certain chivalrous romances, including the *Romance of Troy* and the *Romance of Alexander the Great*. The original Hungarian text of neither has been preserved, but South-Slav translations prepared from the Hungarian version and other facts prove that they once existed. The increasing prominence of the secular elements, which could be observed from the thirteenth century onward, was also evidenced by the Hungarian chronicles beginning with Anonymus, and this process was only accentuated still further in the fourteenth and fifteenth centuries.

A more favourable opportunity for the development of Hungarian-language temporal literature, particularly poetry, opened in the fourteenth century when schooling for laymen became increasingly widespread. The secular men of letters were mostly employed by noblemen, particularly the aristocracy, and their surviving songs were also intended to serve the interests of their employers. As these songs soon lost their topical value, they were not preserved, and only an occasional example or two has remained from the second half of the fifteenth century and the first part of the sixteenth.

It was in 1476, for instance, that an unknown author wrote his song about the *Battle of Szabács*, in which he tells how the armies of King Matthias took Szabács, one of the important fortresses of the Turks. The finest of these songs was a poem in 1515 by MIHÁLY SZABATKAI in praise of the military and political plans of his master, Bishop Péter Beriszló of Veszprém, who defeated the Turks. In about 1500, laymen who had now graduated from the universities, enriched Hungarian literature with the elements of goliardic poetry. They now established a superior style of poetry with higher standards in matters of form as evidenced by surviving fragments of a few love-songs, as well as by FERENC APÁTI's highly ingenious *Cantilena*, written at the beginning of the 1520's, a witty and caustic mockery of priests, monks, gentlemen and peasants alike.

By the end of the Middle Ages both the religious and the secular literature in the Hungarian language had attained the level of development which was soon to permit independent literary works of real value to follow. This, however, was to be the fruit of the new era, emerging in the course of the Renaissance and the Reformation. The literature of the Hungarian Renaissance, in Latin as yet, had got off to a vigorous start at the end of the Middle Ages, in the second half of the fifteenth century. The literature of the monasteries and the lay songsters was by this time only a part of the whole of Hungarian literature, for now the humanists were in the mainstream of literary development.

# THE RENAISSANCE

Renaissance culture began to strike roots in Hungary in the fifteenth century, and its last waves were to reach to the end of the seventeenth. Its widespread acceptance can be traced from the beginning of the sixteenth century, and it reached its pinnacle in the second half of that century. However, even by the second half of the fifteenth century, considerable results had been achieved. This early stage of the Hungarian Renaissance was represented by learned Latin humanist literature.

By the middle of the fifteenth century conditions in Hungary too were ripe for the introduction of the new humanistic culture, at least as far as a narrow, leading ecclesiastical stratum was concerned. Not only lower schooling was developing swiftly, as shown by the rapid formation of a lay intelligentsia, but in 1367 King Louis the Great founded the country's first university at Pécs, to be followed in 1389 by the foundation of the University of Óbuda. The establishment of universities in Hungary did not decrease attendance at the foreign universities, which continued at the same time to grow. In the fifteenth century, apart from the great attraction exercised by Hussite Prague over ten or twenty years, it was mainly the Italian universities, the attraction of the Italian Renaissance, that drew the young people from Hungary.

Not that it was always necessary to go to Italy to find the new secular culture. The Age of Chivalry in Hungary experienced its last period of brilliance during the reign of the Anjou dynasty (1308-1387) and of Sigismund (1387-1437), and during this time the new, more advanced forms of secular views had begun to appear in Hungary. One sign of this was that King Louis the

Great's historian JÁNOS KÜKÜLLEI no longer wrote in the naive manner and approach of the earlier chroniclers, but in a completely novel way, giving prominence to human personality and the glory of wordly fame in his biography of the King. The Court at Buda of the Hungarian King and Holy Roman Emperor Sigismund saw the appearance of several outstanding representatives of the Italian Renaissance, for instance, Masolino, the great painter of the Quattrocento, and Pier Paolo Vergerio, one of the leading Italian humanists of the beginning of the fifteenth century, who spent a considerable time in Hungary. Decisive in the rapid development of humanism and the Renaissance in Hungary, however, were the political interests of the House of Hunyadi. Regent János Hunyadi (d. 1456), the great hero of the century for his victories over the Turks, expected the humanists to propagate his policies and to accomplish the diplomatic persuasion of the other European states to join in the war against the Turks. His son, King Matthias (1458-1490), was a real Renaissance prince, who maintained a brilliant court, had his palace at Buda rebuilt by Italian architects, and had a new magnificent Renaissance palace built at Visegrád. He established his famous library, the Corvina, founded a university at Pozsony* and a printing press at Buda, invited foreign humanists to his court, maintained contact with Italian Renaissance princes and leading scholars, and extended bountiful aid to such great Italian humanists of his age as Pomponius Laetus and others. He was an adherent of the new Platonic philosophy, and himself an astute letter-writer who knew all the cunning tricks of Renaissance diplomacy. These circumstances make it understandable how, while the translation of legends, prayers and hymns into Hungarian was just beginning to spread to wider circles, and while Hungarian-language temporal songs were only just making their timid debut, not only were polished Hungarian humanists able to appear before the learned men of Hungary and of Europe, but among them was also an excellent poet, Janus Pannonius.

The great humanist poet was the nephew of JÁNOS VITÉZ (1408-1472), the Chancellor and leading diplomat of János Hu-

* Today Bratislava, Czechoslovakia

nyadi, who had first been Bishop of Nagyvárad* and later became Archbishop of Esztergom. Vitéz had acquired his humanist learning from Pier Paolo Vergerio, and he not only collected a marvellous library, but through his humanist *epistles* and *rhetorical works* became the first important Hungarian humanist writer. It was largely due to him that JANUS PANNONIUS (1434-1472), who was of Croatian extraction, had the opportunity to acquire a humanist culture and good fortune in his career.

János Vitéz made it possible for his nephew to attend school in Italy, where he was noted as a child prodigy at the age of 13, for his sparkling epigrams. At Guarino's school in Ferrara, and later at the University of Padua, he worked his way up to become one of the best of the humanists of his time, and his contemporaries, such as Guarino, Marsilio Ficino and Aeneas Silvius Piccolomini indeed considered him to be so. In the world of the Italian Renaissance, with a knowledge of classical Latin and Greek literature, his poetic gifts rapidly developed. His name became particularly known for his epigrams in which he made fun of his fellow-students, praised his friends, mocked at the Popes and particularly the Holy Year of 1450, as well as touching on erotic and obscene subjects *(In Gryllum ; Deridet euntes Romam ad iubilaeum ; Galeotti peregrinationem irridet ; De amatore librorum veterum ; De sua aetate ; Conqueritur, quod se, socii ad lupanar seduxissent,* etc.). During his stay in Italy he was also a successful author of panegyrics, one of which has indeed proved to be of lasting value. His *Panegyric of Guarino* is a rare example among the otherwise not particularly praiseworthy crop of contemporary laudations. In tones of sincere reverence and love, he describes the course of his master's career and his scholarly way of life, giving a faithful and artistic, comprehensive picture of the North-Italian humanism of his age. In this work, Janus Pannonius declared that his own aim was to bring the antique Muses to his country of Pannonia, to the valleys of the Danube and the Dráva.

The time for this came when, in 1458, the year of King Matthias' ascendance to the throne, he returned to Hungary, where he was first a canon at Nagyvárad under his uncle, then shortly

---

* Today Oradea, Rumania

became Bishop of Pécs and Royal Chancellor, one of the chief executives of Matthias' foreign policy. It was after his return home that he became a truly great poet. The place of his earlier epigrams, which were outstanding mainly on account of their ingenuity and his brilliant gift for form, was taken by elegies of rich lyricism. His concern and nightmare visions over the ravages and menace of the Turks, his anxious love for his country, the pain he felt over his mother's death and his ever more overpowering disease, together led to the maturing of the first great Hungarian lyricist with truly deep feelings. (*Blasio militanti Janus febricitans; Threnos de morte Barbarae matris; De se aegrotante in castris; Mathias rex Hungarorum; Antonio Constantio poetae Italo; Ad animam suam; De inundatione*, etc.) His isolation from the educated Italian world, his lack of company in "barbaric" Hungary, the many official duties imposed on him, the iron discipline demanded by the King and the ever more frequent differences of opinion he had with him, conjured forth a poetry of a surprisingly individual and personal tone which seems almost modern. Meanwhile, though ill, he took part in the campaigns against the Turks and wrote his poems when prostrated by disease. In 1465 he led a mission to Rome and was then able again to meet his Italian humanist friends and to receive their applause, but this served only further to deepen the crisis within him and increased his discontent at his situation. He endeavoured to make up for his lack of companions by means of books; he feverishly collected books for his library and translated Plutarch and Demosthenes into Latin. Finally he attempted to make a break with his lot and joined the enemies of the King, becoming with his uncle a leader of the conspiracy against Matthias. Death overtook him at the Croatian castle of Medvedgrad as he fled towards Renaissance Italy from the victorious King.

He proudly proclaimed that he was the first real poet in Hungary and that he had been the first to bring the Muses to the banks of the Danube. He himself best characterized his own great contribution to the development of Hungarian literature, in a magnificent little epigram entitled *Laus Pannoniae* :

*Quod legerent omnes quondam dabat Itala tellus*
*Nunc et Pannonia carmina missa legit.*
*Magna quidem nobis haec gloria : sed tibi major,*
*Nobilis ingenio Patria facta meo.*

Janus Pannonius became an example to all the Hungarian humanists, who copied his verses and later, in the sixteenth century, Hungarian and foreign humanists successively published his works. However, none of his indigenous followers could surpass, or even come anywhere near him. Since Vitéz and Janus Pannonius had in 1471 organised a conspiracy against the King, Matthias lost confidence in the Hungarian humanists for some time, and for this reason such gifted writers as the poet PÉTER GARÁZDA or the letter-writer PÉTER VÁRADI, were relegated to the background. In place of Hungarians, the King in the 1570's and 80's preferred to surround himself with Italian humanists, a process also promoted by his wife, Beatrice of Aragon. Several of the Italian humanists who came to Buda enriched literature in Hungary with valuable works, particularly in the field of historiography.

Matthias could not, with a view to his political and dynastic plans, do without the new historiography in the humanist spirit. It was necessary to undertake a development and partly a revision of the earlier, medievally-minded Hungarian history writing. First a Hungarian temporal nobleman, JÁNOS THURÓCZI, who was only just becoming acquainted with the elements of humanist culture, wrote a new, comprehensive history in glorification of the deeds of the Hunyadis. In respect to the previous centuries he relied on the chronicles, but he wrote independently of the age of Sigismund and the Hunyadis, voicing the interests of his own class—the nobility allied to Matthias. His well-rounded work, concisely assembled, is particularly notable for its colourful, lively style. It was probably on commissions from Matthias that it was printed both at Augsburg and Olomouc in 1488. Thuróczi's works could not, however, suffice to satisfy Matthias, who wanted to see the history of the Hungarians, and particularly of his own reign, written in the full armour of humanist scholarship. He therefore commissioned the Italian ANTONIO BONFINI (1427-

1503), who had come to his court by mere chance, to write a new history of Hungary. The immense work *(Rerum Ungaricorum Decades)* was only completed after the death of Matthias and treats the history of the country from its beginnings to 1496. Bonfini, after the fashion of the humanists, sought to find the casual links between events. He romanised Hungarian history—even had the House of Hunyadi stem from the Romans—and constantly made the protagonists of history utter humanistic speeches of his own invention. The most valuable part is that concerned with the reign of Matthias, which shows the political aims and court of the King in their true grandeur. Bonfini's work exercised considerable effect on the development of Hungarian historiography and literature in the sixteenth and seventeenth centuries and became the main stay of the Matthias tradition, which served to strengthen national consciousness. Beside Bonfini, the most notable among the Italian humanists of Matthias was the itinerant humanist GALEOTTO MARZIO (1427-1497), who was a friend of Janus Pannonius. He wrote a humanist collection of anecdotes about the deeds and wise sayings of Matthias *(De egregie, sapienter, jocose dictis ac factis regis Matthiae)*, in which he gave a very complimentary account of the excellence, greatness and humanistic erudition of the Hungarian King and the brilliance of his court, not stopping short even of ingratiation and exaggeration. The ingenuity of his anecdotes and Galeotto's many valuable observations on contemporary Hungarian conditions render this work highly valuable.

In the age of King Matthias, the humanist literature in Latin was destined to serve the political aims of the King, particularly the consolidation of a strong, centralised monarchy. After his death, under the rule of his successors of the Jagello family (1490-1526), his great plans were brought to naught, the brilliant Renaissance court at Buda disintegrated, the central power was weakened, and feudal anarchy came to dominate the country. Though humanist literature thus lost its main base and guiding beacon, humanist learning continued to spread. Hungarian humanist Church dignitaries and chancellors (Tamás Bakócz, László Szalkai, György Szathmári) vied with one another and with their foreign counterparts in organizing brilliant courts at their seats, where scientific discourse at a high level was carried on and humanist conferences were held.

Humanistic learning at the same time ceased to be a monopoly of the leading Church dignitaries and high-ranking chancellery officials. Young men of the temporal peerage also began to attend foreign universities and an increasing number of noblemen and burghers with a humanist education also appeared on the scene. The spread of humanism was facilitated by the fact that by now the nearby universities of Vienna and Cracow had also caught up with the Italian universities, so that it was no longer necessary to make the pilgrimage to distant Italy at great expense in order to obtain a humanist education.

The humanists of Hungary at the time included numerous people of great learning who were honoured and celebrated, among them the members of the *Sodalitas Literaria Danubiana* organized by Conrad Celtis, correspondents and friends of Erasmus, the publishers of the poems of Janus Pannonius. The humanists of the Jagello era, however, did not produce great literary works. The two most outstanding poets of the period were themselves of middling talent. They were canon ISTVÁN TAURINUS of Gyulafehérvár,* who was of Moravian extraction, and the Benedictine monk MÁRTON NAGYSZOMBATI. They both reacted to the great political events of their time—the Peasant War of 1514 and the menace of the Turks.

That which the humanists of the period feared, soon came to pass. In 1526 King Louis II suffered a catastrophic defeat at Mohács, at the hands of the Turks, and this led to the collapse of the medieval Hungarian empire. The country was now rent into three parts. A large portion was gradually conquered by the Turks, the western and northern regions were dominated by the House of Hapsburg which had been raised to the Hungarian throne, while in the eastern part of the country (Transylvania), a separate Hungarian principality was organized which was to some extent dependent on the Turks. The previous organizational forms of Hungarian literature were also completely transformed, for the great historical changes swept away the centres of both

* Today Alba Julia, Rumania

32

monastic and humanist literature. Humanist literature in Latin was still cultivated by a number of eminent authors, but this whole branch of literature, and soon indeed Latin-language literature in its entirety, increasingly became a peripheral phenomenon.

The most outstanding Latin humanist writers and scholars of the middle of the sixteenth century were obliged for a long time, in some cases permanently, to continue their work abroad. MIKLÓS OLÁH (1493-1568), who belonged to the circle of Erasmus, spent some time in the Netherlands as secretary to Queen Mary, and in his brief treatises entitled *Hungaria* and *Attila* recalled the memory of the quondam greatness of the Hungarian Kingdom. Bishop ISTVÁN BRODARICS (1470-1539) travelled throughout Europe as a diplomatic representative of King John (1526-1540), and at the behest of the King of Poland wrote a history of the Battle of Mohács in an excellent little memoire. JÁNOS ZSÁMBOKI (Johannes Sambucus, 1531-1584) was a scholarly polyhistor of European fame who worked mainly in Vienna and did much to uphold the Hungarian humanist tradition, for he published the works of Janus Pannonius and of Bonfini. ANDRÁS DUDICH (1533-1589), a tireless Hungarian propagator of religious tolerance, spent many decades in Poland and Silesia, conducting a correspondence that enmeshed almost the whole humanist world.

The last products of Latin-language humanism in Hungary to be of significance were in the field of history. FERENC FORGÁCH (1530-1577), the author of one of the most moving humanist historical works, in his *Historia* treated the events of the fifty years following upon the Battle of Mohács, contrasting the struggles of the heroic soldiers who fought against the Turks with the unbridled havoc wrought by the great lords in the prevailing state of anarchy, leading to the destruction of the country. Finally, at the very beginning of the seventeenth century, Latin humanist literature was crowned in the early years of the seventeenth century by the monumental historical work of MIKLÓS ISTVÁNFFY (1538-1615). In this sixteenth-century story he rendered a more colourful, rich, more beautiful and more authentic picture of the struggles against the Turks than any description could furnish. In his work the defence of the small Hungarian castles is virtually transformed into a great epic, and it is from

3

33

their heroic struggle that the author expects the future resurrection of the whole country.

Simultaneously with the last receding waves of Latin-language humanism in the sixteenth century, Hungarian-language literature was already developing in its full breadth. While Miklós Istvánffy was writing his Latin-language history, Renaissance Hungarian-language poetry was flourishing in its best period. After the Battle of Mohács, Hungarian literature also irretrievably became a literature in Hungarian and the sixteenth century is therefore that of the foundation of a national literature in the stricter sense of the word. In the Middle Ages we may in many instances talk rather of literature in Hungary, than of a Hungarian product, since a considerable part of the literary works in Hungary, conceived to serve our domestic development and be a part of it, were written by writers who were not of Hungarian origin. Hungary then was a country of many nationalities, comprising also Croatia and Dalmatia. The writers of German, Croatian or other nationalities who lived here, however, were exponents of the same Hungarian state patriotism as those of Hungarian origin, and what is more, even those who immigrated from foreign countries, either at the beginning of Christianity in Hungary in the period of St. Stephen, or to the humanist court of Matthias, were also at one with them in this. The Hungarians and those of other nationalities, the native- and the foreign-born, all equally served the purposes of the Hungarian King and the Hungarian State, with no particular national trends of their own. The development of the nationality point of view in Hungarian literature began, after sporadic earlier signs, with great force in the sixteenth century.

The assumption of a national character by Hungarian literature first became manifest through the conscious and deliberate efforts made to cultivate the Hungarian language and to let Hungarian-language literature hold equal rank with that in Latin. In the very years immediately following on the Battle of Mohács, it was three Hungarian disciples of Erasmus, all of simple parentage and a humanist education, who pioneered the path that led to this end. BENEDEK KOMJÁTHY, GÁBOR PESTI and JÁNOS SYLVESTER in the 1530's translated parts of the Bible into

Hungarian, no longer with the primitive methods of the Hussite preachers of a hundred years earlier, but according to the scientific standards and pretensions of Erasmian philological accuracy. This required an intensive study of both the Latin and Hungarian languages, and they thus became the first Hungarian writers to pay special attention to the problems of the Hungarian language. Pesti, who translated the *Four Gospels* (1536) was a veritable artist of style. He advocated a program of translating into Hungarian the Latin works of literature, and set an example in this respect too, through his excellent translation of *Aesop's Fables* (1536). With him the cultivation and development of the Hungarian language had become a patriotic duty, and he even published a *Latin-Hungarian Dictionary* (1538). Sylvester, who went as far as to translate the whole of the *New Testament* (1541), compiled Latin text-books, and drew up the first *Hungarian Grammar* (1539), declaring proudly that the system of the Hungarian language was of equal rank to that of the Sacred Tongues (Latin, Greek and Hebrew). It was also he who discovered that the Hungarian language was excellently suited to rendering classical metres in verse. He forthwith proceeded with astonishing success to write the first Hungarian poem in distichs. All three of them published their works in print, and thus they also became the authors of the first printed books in Hungarian. Komjáthy's work was published in Cracow, Pesti's in Vienna, but Sylvester organized a printing press of his own at Sárvár, in Transdanubia, to publish his works. Sylvester was backed in his endeavours by one of the most important leading politicians and aristocratic patrons of the period, Tamás Nádasdy. Another of Nádasdy's protégés was MÁTYÁS DÉVAI BIRÓ, who supplemented the work of the three Erasmian scripture translators and language cultivators, by compiling the first booklet on Hungarian spelling, *Orthographia Ungarica*.

The full triumph of the Hungarian language in literary usage came in the forties and fifties of the sixteenth century, when a new movement, the Reformation had gained ground. The reform of the faith had already begun to spread in Hungary at the beginning of the 1520's, and in the chaotic years following the Battle of Mohács, in a period of constant warfare against the Turks and of armed factional struggles within the country, it rapidly became general. The masses sought in the new religious ideals an explanation and consolation for the suffering they and the country had to endure, as well as strength and faith for the struggles and trials to come. Since they perceived that the reason for their many calamities lay in the peers, who engaged in unbridled looting and plunder and had disrupted the unity of the country, the Reformation in Hungary (and with it the Hungarian literature of the Reformation) came to have a strong social and anti-feudal tendency. The Catholic Church and the peers—many of whom had become Protestants themselves—were both scourged in the songs, dramas, tales and sermons of the preacher writers of the period. The Hungarian Reformation contained all the trends, from the moderate Lutheran to the most extreme Anabaptist and Anti-trinitarian movements, so that the literature of the Reformation could therefore not be homogeneous. In fact, the writers of the Reformation conducted incessant campaigns, not only against the Catholics, but also against each other. By the middle of the sixteenth century not only the country itself, but its literature too, was a theatre of war—the first generation of the writers of the Reformation devoted their work to the service of this strife. The Reformation once more centred people's attention on religion and led its writers to engage primarily in religious propaganda literature. The development of humanist literature was thus temporarily slowed down, in fact, several of the previous achievements of the humanists were now used by the Reformation. The Erasmian Scripture translators had rendered the Reformation a service both by their Hungarian translations of the Bible and also by cultivating the Hungarian language. Late in his life János Sylvester himself became a Protestant, while the author of Hungarian orthography, Mátyás Dévai Biró, was one of the earliest highly effective Hungarian reformers. Since the writers of the Reformation wrote for the widest reading public and even had their works read aloud to the masses of illiterates, they could only use the vernacular and thus greatly promoted the process of the evolution of a homogeneous literary language. The writers of the Reformation naturalized almost every important form of literature, and though they may not have produced great works, the number of fine passages is all the greater, and they thus successfully paved the way for the masterpieces to come.

The most popular form of literature of the Hungarian Reformation was the sung verse. Large numbers of songs in Hungarian were needed for Protestant divine services and numerous translations were therefore made of medieval Latin hymns adapted to the Protestant spirit, of the songs of Martin Luther and other German Protestant authors, and particularly of Biblical psalms. A considerable part of the songs that were thus written may be said to have been fairly liberal paraphrases rather than translations, and their authors incorporated many topical political, social, satirical and subjective elements in their adaptations. Generally the didactic content was particularly stressed, even to the detriment of the lyrical qualities and of a well-rounded finish. It is not infrequent to find entire sermons composed in verse and also spread and popularized by way of song. The lyrical and didactic features were, moreover, often intermingled with the epical. The long songs time and again contained scriptural stories, and in fact several Bible stories were elaborated in separate recitative songs. The great effect of the Bible gave a homogeneous colouring to the otherwise very varied crop of Protestant songs in the sixteenth century. The Old Testament was especially popular, and this was boosted by, and partly due to, the similarity which the writers of the period thought to find between the history of the Hungarians and that of the Jews of the Old Testament. The songs of this era present a veritable Old Testament picture of their world, and this was naturally accompanied by the spread of the terminology, the imagery and style of the Old Testament.

The first in the succession of the more prominent song writers of the Hungarian Reformation was ANDRÁS BATIZI (1530-1550), who frequently evinced a tender lyricism. He wrote Hungarian versions to several hymns, was the author of the first Bible stories in verse and of a world chronicle in verse, based on the Bible. The most striking and original character among them was ANDRÁS SZKHÁROSI-HORVÁT, who was first a Franciscan monk and became a preacher in the 1540's. His sermons in verse and his versified scriptural paraphrases (*On Princedom; On*

*Miserliness ; On the Two Kinds of Creed ; On the Curse,* etc.) are full of passages engaging in murderous satire of the teachings and ceremonies of the Catholic Church and of ruthless castigations of the contemporary aristocracy. He was outstandingly able in the construction of scenes and in presenting one or other facet of the lives of the slovenly priests or monks to the reader, in such a manner as to be realistic, lifelike, and at the same time intrinsically ridiculous. His poems against the peers are permeated by the passion of hatred—the stanzas are grouped so as to become ever more menacing, to fling ever graver accusations and ever more annihilating curses at the heads of his enemies. This plebeian preacher, who not infrequently struck a revolutionary note and spoke in the name of "the poor hoers," was one of the most ingenious song-writers and the best of the old Hungarian exponents of satirical poetry. His works excel in their visual qualities, their rich imagery and also their great linguistic power. MIHÁLY SZTÁRAI (d. 1575), a highly effective Protestant proselytizer and Church organizer, was also very significant as an author of songs. He was the first to translate several psalms in passionate tones and he was also a notable author of Biblical epics. One of the most beautiful psalm adaptations is due to MIHÁLY KECSKEMÉTI-VÉG (1561), who in his interpretation of Psalm 55, has given us a confession of his own individual fate which is of striking lyrical force.

In the second half of the century, however, Protestant song-writing in general declined. In place of the momentous songs of the first period there were ever more stereotyped Church hymns or songs that engaged in lengthy explanations of various dogmas. Two psalm translators were particularly prominent among the song-writers of the second half of the century. One was the Calvinist GERGELY SZEGEDI, who in the 1560's paraphrased several psalms in Hungarian verse, showing a highly developed sense of form. He also wrote an exceptionally beautiful patriotic song about the sufferings of Hungarians carried off into captivity by the Tartars. The Unitarian MIKLÓS BOGÁTI FAZEKAS (1548-c. 1590) produced the first complete translation in Hungarian verse of the psalms and also versified several scriptural and secular stories.

Apart from song, it was the drama that rendered particularly good service to the propaganda of the Reformation. It was to this fact that the evolution of an original dramatic literature in Hungarian was due. At first it was of a rather primitive form, because the plays did not stage real dramatic action, but only religious disputes. The earliest dramatic author, who has already been mentioned among the song-writers, was Mihály Sztárai, the author of two of these religious dispute dramas in the 1550's *(The Marriage of Priests ; The Mirror of True Priesthood)*. Both set out to prove one of the cardinal theses of the Reformation, occasionally engaging in successful mockery of the Catholic adversary, thus testifying that the author had a gift for presenting burlesque scenes on the stage. The religious dispute dramas were, ten years later, developed further by the anti-trinitarian writers. *The Debrecen Dispute* of 1570 was written anonymously and is an important step towards the emergence of real drama. The scope of the religious disputation is here narrower, and there is considerable space for the background to the dispute, for showing the private lives of some of the protagonists. The first two acts are particularly successful—they depict the household of a contemporary village or small-town priest, in the framework of a very apposite piece of satire. The unknown dramatist was here no longer only concerned that those representing the views opposed to his own should be defeated in the course of the dispute within the play, but also that the action itself, and the development of the individual characters should necessarily lead to the defeat of the ridiculed party. Another work by an anti-trinitarian author, which no longer had anything to do with religious disputes, was the *Comedy about the Treachery of Menyhárt Balassi*. Being concerned wholly with the advocacy of the social aims of the Reformation, this is not even a religious work. It presented one of the most ruthless, predatory aristocrats of the period, particularly his conspiracies and treachery. This type of comedy developed from the lampoon put into dialogue form. Here too, the centrepiece was furnished by a dialogue—Menyhárt Balassi's confession to the archbishop. The author managed to characterize both participants in the dialogue excellently, and in the course of the further scenes to provide a broader background to the portrait of Menyhárt Balassi. This comedy also signalled the birth of Hungarian secular comedy-writing, and in several places betrayed the humanist education of its author. Though the play is unbalanced in form, it is one of the important products of Hungarian-language Renaissance literature.

The comedy about Menyhárt Balassi was also an indication that by the second half of the century the literature of the Reformation was tending to adopt higher literary standards, and that apart from the desire to teach, convert, and engage in propaganda, an unconscious or even deliberate striving for artistic merit was also becoming manifest. This was a necessary accompaniment to the ever more frequent appearance of the elements of humanism and the Renaissance in the works of the writers of the Reformation. While the first preachers were mostly former Franciscan monks who had become propagandists of the new faith, the Protestant writers of the second half of the century were educated priests who had even attended foreign universities and were versed not only in divinity, but also in classical culture. It was from among them that the two most outstanding prose writers of the Hungarian Reformation emerged, also to become important representatives of the Hungarian Renaissance. These were Gáspár Heltai and Péter Bornemisza.

GÁSPÁR HELTAI (d. 1574) was a preacher and printer at Kolozsvár,* who probably began his career as a Catholic priest, then became a Lutheran, later Calvinist, and finally, under the influence of Ferenc Dávid, the only eminent theorist of the Hungarian Reformation, ended up as an anti-trinitarian preacher. Despite his German (Transylvanian Saxon) origin, he was the most full-blooded Hungarian prose author of the century. He mostly adapted foreign (German or Latin) works into Hungarian, completely transforming the original texts, spicing them with scenes of Transylvanian life and romanticising history as well as his disputations or moral disquisitions. He transformed the famous treatise of Sebastian Franck on drunkenness into a dialogue, and furnished it with the genuine *couleur locale* of his city Kolozsvár (1552). He supplemented the pamphlet of the

---

* Today Cluj, Rumania

40

Spanish Reginaldus Gonsalvius against the inquisition with Hungarian features (1570), and produced a romanticized Hungarian version of Bonfini's work on Hungarian history (1574). His most important literary feat was the Hungarian adaptation of *Aesop's Fables* on the basis of German texts (1566). His Aesopian fables were no literary translations, like those of Gábor Pesti, but highly colourful, free adaptations with an atmosphere of their own, veritable short stories, which apart from the Aesopian tales also contained entirely independent, original stories. The tales themselves are well-rounded, soundly written works. Heltai was particularly good at conjuring up an atmosphere—he did not go into too much detail in his descriptions, touching only on the characteristic traits and flashing his spotlight on an occasional set, then going on with the elaboration of his plot. His tales support the moral and social teachings of the Reformation and this tendency is further stressed by the interpretations appended to the various tales.

PÉTER BORNEMISZA (1535-1585) was the son of a family of burghers in Pest. After an adventurous youth he became a Lutheran preacher and for some time a bishop in the north-western part of the country. He was distinguished by his superior humanistic scholarship and this itself served to set him apart from all of his fellow preachers. Beside the University of Wittenberg he had also attended the humanist universities of Vienna and Padua, and had in his youth prepared for a secular career. He was in favour of the Reformation from his early youth, but at first he voiced his feelings and views in temporal works. It was only when he had become a preacher, in the 1570's and 80's, that the wrote his main work—a voluminous collection of sermons. He first excelled as a song-writer, with his patriotic *Farewell Poem*, written before he set out for foreign parts. This is one of the finest works of ancient Hungarian poetry. During his student years in Vienna, in 1558, he produced a Hungarian version of Sophocles' *Electra* in which he departed considerably from the original and adapted the plot to Hungarian conditions. His *Volumes of Sermons*, over ten thousand pages in all, serve as a veritable encyclopaedia to sixteenth-century Hungarian life, replete with interesting stories, expressive descriptions and original observations. He increasingly intended his sermons not so much to be spoken as read. In the volume of his collection concerned with the temptations of the Devil, the framework of the sermon has almost completely vanished to give place to a peculiar type of writing—part treatise, part fiction. Here he assembled all the foreign and Hungarian Devil-stories, mental and spiritual life and sexual problems of sixteenth-century man.

By the end of the century the different trends of the Reformation had in Hungary too been organized in various Protestant denominations, and the now rigid and bleak Protestant church life could no longer be such an incentive to literature as the lively Reformation movement of the first half of the century had been. The last great literary feat of the Hungarian Reformation was realized somewhat belatedly, when GÁSPÁR KÁROLI (d. 1591), a preacher of Gönc, translated and published the full text of the Bible in 1590. Károli's Bible was for centuries to come the most widely read book in Hungarian and thus played an enormous part in formulating a homogeneous Hungarian national and literary language.

During the years of the Reformation, secular literature was mainly cultivated by the songsters in aristocratic courts and castles, in the markets and in the inns. These sixteenth-century singers differed in many respects from their medieval predecessors. They disseminated their works not only by word of mouth, but also in writing, not infrequently even in print. Very many of them had had some schooling and were acquainted with the rudiments of music, having only been forced to become songsters by the sorry conditions due to the Turkish conquests. They sympathized with the Reformation and were not averse even to religious themes; nevertheless, apart from satirical verse and drinking ditties, they mainly composed historical songs. The recitative songs about the past and contemporary struggles of the Hungarians played an important part in the life of their period. They frequently served as a substitute for newspapers, and—especially among the soldiers fighting in the so-called outpost fortresses which defended the country against the Turks—they considerably boosted the community and national spirit.

The most outstanding Hungarian songster of the sixteenth

century was SEBESTYÉN TINÓDI (d. 1556), who mainly sang the story of the anti-Turkish struggles of his own age in his many recitals, which he published in printed form under the title *Cronica* in 1554. His songs were written with strong political awareness, sometimes at the behest of one or other of the leading politicians of the century. He was an enthusiastic advocate and faithful chronicler of defence and fight against the Turks and strove for the authenticity of his accounts and facts, rather than for artistic polish. His frequently monotonous songs are, however, suddenly rendered pleasant and artistic in effect by the tunes of his compositions, which have also secured him a prominent place in the history of Hungarian music.

Apart from the historical songs which aimed at strict authenticity, the second half of the sixteenth century saw the increasingly frequent appearance of versified fictitious stories. As a result of increasing secularization and the growing requirements of the reading public, temporal epics for entertainment and lays came to develop. The lay became one of the most important literary forms of Hungarian Renaissance literature, which after modest beginnings in the first half of the sixteenth century really started to flourish in the last thirty years of the century. The writers of lays include authors of the most diverse occupations, such as songsters and preachers, as well as peers, students and schoolmasters. Indicative of the great part played by sung verse is the fact that literature for entertainment consisted almost exclusively of works in verse and that even several of the prose products of foreign literature were translated into Hungarian in the form of verse.

The sources of the Hungarian lays are very varied. Short fictional stories of this type were written on the basis of widely different originals. PÉTER ILOSVAI-SELYMES, one of the celebrated songsters of his day, wrote his romantic story about *Miklós Toldi*, a fourteenth-century Hungarian hero, from an ancient Hungarian legend. It was on the basis of his work that János Arany was later to write one of the masterpieces of Hungarian literature, his Toldi Trilogy. The lay *Szilágyi and Hajmási*, written in 1560 by an unknown author, is attractive reading because of the interesting construction of its story and the conciseness of its presentation. It tells the tale of the liberation of two fifteenth-century Hungarian warriors from Turkish captivity. Another lay, *About King Béla and Bankó's daughter*, written in 1570, is the elaboration of a South-Slav legend. The author created a magnificent character in the part of the young girl who triumphs over the men and makes a fool even of the amorous king. Lays were written of the story of Aeneas; of one of the most interesting stories in the *Gesta Romanorum*, that about *Prince Apollonius;* of the German folk-book about *Fortunatus*, moreover of several of Boccaccio's stories *(Walter and Griseldis, Titus and Gisippus, Gismunda and Gisquardus)*. The adaptor of the story of Gismunda and Gisquardus (1574), the Unitarian preacher György Enyedi, showed considerable resourcefulness. He continued the story beyond the original and used it to advocate certain humanist principles, such as the right to love and freedom of marriage, and to engage in sharp criticism of the nobility.

Their poetic value and pure belletristic merit, free of all didactic elements, render two works prominent, far above the rest of the rich crop of lays. One is the story in verse of *Eurialus and Lucretia* (1577), written after the celebrated Latin story by Aeneas Sylvius Piccolomini. The unknown Hungarian translator showed such skill and refinement in his versification of the erotic story, that several scholars have thought to attribute the work to Balassi, the great poet of the sixteenth century. The other notable lay, *The Story of Argirus*, is based on an unknown Italian *bella istoria* and on elements of Hungarian folklore. Prince Argirus, who becomes the victim of a plot but finally nevertheless finds happiness in fairy-land, became one of the favourite fairy-tale heroes of the Hungarian people and the work itself was published in innumerable editions, to remain a favourite piece of reading for centuries. Albert Gergei, the little-known Hungarian author of Argirus (his name is known only because his acrostics spell it out) accomplished an outstanding feat in the artistic construction of his story, in his style which fully conveys the naive charm of the tale, and also in his verse. It was on the basis of his story that the great romantic poet Mihály Vörösmarty wrote one of his greatest works, *Csongor and Tünde*.

The spread of the lay, and within this the predominance of

in irreconcilable opposition to all the ugliness and inhumanity of the extant world. With Balassi, love was inseparably interwoven with the idea of freedom, as was to be the case later with Petőfi. The main message of the cycle is therefore the longing for happiness and freedom, which he expresses in poems of the most varied themes. *(To the Cranes ; Entreaty to Cupid ; Finding Julia he Greets her Thus ; On the Eternal Nature of his Love*, etc.*)* One of the secrets of Balassi's greatness as a poet is that his great and noble ideals are never abstract, not independent of time and space, but that they contain at white heat one of the most restless and stormy lives of the century. He was imbued with an awareness of his aristocratic descent and of the proud spirit of the nobility, yet he frequently had to eat the bread of a fugitive and refugee. In contrast to the other Renaissance lyricists of contemporary Europe, the poet of the Júlia Cycle did not live at a court, in peace and prosperity, but was always on the go—a soldier-poet, speeding on horseback from one country to the next. His poems are rich with concepts, imagery and similes taken from the soldier's life and the world of battle between Turk and Hungarian. The magnificent descriptions of nature which abound in his verse, similarly combine the joyful discovery of nature that is the trait of a roaming warrior, living winter and summer with the sky for his awning.

It was the danger-laden beauty of military life in the outpost fortresses that inspired Balassi to write some warriors' and patriotic songs of unmatched loveliness *(In Praise of Spring Weather ; In Praise of the Outposts; Farewell to his Homeland). In praise of the Outposts*, which he wrote in summer 1589, became his most famous and most popular poem, a veritable hymn of the struggle against the Turks. As a true poet, Balassi did not embellish the warrior's lot. He stressed the grave sacrifices, the dangers and the suffering, but in such a manner that the life, moral stature and heroic grandeur of the warriors' life was nevertheless made to seem the most beautiful and most desirable vocation, alone worthy of a real man. Beside love and war poetry, he was also one of the greatest masters of Hungarian religious verse. He was born a Protestant and later became a Catholic, but his religious poems bear the mark of neither persuasion—his God was not identical with the one taught by the churches. Even as he wrote his religious poems, he remained a humanist—making a man of God, with whom he quarrelled and argued, not merely beseeching him but demanding that he should help him and wreak vengeance upon his enemies. Just as his warrior's poetry fuses with the lover's, and as both are set in the brilliant frame of nature, so do his songs about God also fit organically into this grand symphony.

Balassi's poetry is distinguished by an extraordinary richness of forms. By developing the earlier Hungarian stanza patterns and applying his own virtuosity in the techniques of rhyme, he produced new verse forms of which the finest became universally known and used as the "Balassi stanza." In obedience to the general tradition of old Hungarian poetry, he too always wrote his poems to a tune, but their text is fully valid on its own and does not require the crutches of music. This was how the sung poem in his work became text verse, and it was this that completed the evolution of Hungarian written poetry as a poetry in its own right.

Beside poetry, he also experimented with other forms of literature—he adapted an Italian pastoral play in Hungarian, thus becoming the founder of Hungarian Renaissance comedy on the subject of love. In the Prologue to this work, he himself declared that his aim had been to naturalize this genre, and at the same time propounded his views on poetry. He took a definite stand in favour of the rights of literature on the theme of love, in fact placing it above all else. His drama, whose complete text has only recently been discovered, attains the same high standards in its composition as his poems—the polish of his language is particularly brilliant. The poet did not deny his former self and the text of the play frequently switches to verse.

The heroic and restless life of this highly erudite poet, who read and spoke eight languages, ended on the field of battle, as did that of the greatest Hungarian lyricist, Petőfi, 250 years later. The fatal bullet struck him during a charge, in the course of the siege of Esztergom, which was then held by the Turks.

During Balassi's life, but particularly in the period following his death, numerous aristocrats and noblemen are known to have written Renaissance poetry in the Hungarian language. They generally wrote on Balassi's subjects—poems of love, religion and patriotism. The poetic works of the majority have, however, been scattered and only a few accidentally preserved poems are now known. In the first quarter of the seventeenth century, the poets of the period wrote an increasing number of moralising, philosophical poems, corresponding to the neo-Stoic interests of the Protestant humanist nobles of the age and the great popularity of this school of philosophy. Balassi's most outstanding follower, János Rimay, continued Balassi's poetic tradition and later became one of the most noted Hungarian representatives of the neo-Stoic trend.

JÁNOS RIMAY (1569-1631) was a well-off nobleman in Northern Hungary who spent all his life in the service of various aristocratic families, and had in his youth entered the orbit of Renaissance culture in the courts of peers. As a young man he belonged to Bálint Balassi's circle and became a friend of the poet, later undertaking to sustain his remembrance and his poetic heritage. After Balassi's death, he paid tribute to him in a cycle of poems, a most carefully composed *epicedium*, celebrating and mourning mainly the hero in his person. He later endeavoured, though unsuccessfully, to publish the collected poems of his late master, and he indeed wrote an introduction to the projected publication, in which he was the first to appraise Balassi's poetic works, setting them in the framework of the European Renaissance. His own poems at first followed closely in Balassi's footsteps, particularly in the case of his early love and religious poems. From the 1600's, however, he found his own independent mode of expression, and produced political, patriotic and philosophical poems of a quite novel kind. As a supporter of the neo-Stoic philosophy, his later poems were completely pervaded by the Stoic approach and moral attitude. He formulated a surprisingly rich poetic language, frequently seeking bizarre novelty, full of startling imagery and with a virtuosity in rhyming that borders on self-centred formalism. Rimay's poetry represents the mannerist tastes of the declining Renaissance, of which he was the most outstanding representative in Hungarian poetry.

The Renaissance taste and spirit emanating from the aristocratic Renaissance centres, and to a smaller extent also from

4

the towns, slowly began to permeate all the poetry of the period. The historical epics of the sixteenth century, that is the songs recounting topical historic events, were also refreshed, and abandoned the monotonous manner of the chronicles in favour of more complex structures with a more developed faculty for description. The so-called Fifteen-Year Turkish War, from 1591 to 1606, as well as the struggle for freedom waged against the Hapsburgs by István Bocskay, Prince of Transylvania (1604-06), provided opportunities for topical poetry to experience a general upsurge. Numerous soldiers' songs, poems to celebrate victories or mourn defeats, etc. were written, including quite a few which were of noteworthy artistic merit (e.g., a poem by JÁNOS S. DEBRECZENI to greet Bocskay, dirges mourning the death of Bocskay, lamentations over the depredations of the Tartars, etc.).

The struggle for freedom led by Bocskay, and even the previous movements, were of especially great significance for the further development of Hungarian literature. This was the beginning of the armed struggle of the Hungarian people against the Hapsburgs, who strove with increasing perseverance from the end of the sixteenth century to subjugate the country. However, the Hapsburg rulers who occupied the Hungarian throne always had a significant number of supporters within the country, too, and this was for centuries to determine the interior political conflicts of Hungary. Beside the open political or frequently even the military arena, the struggle between the pro-Hapsburg and the anti-Hapsburg forces was also present in literature throughout the whole of the seventeenth century. It was from this stage that Hungarian literature became intensely politically minded, while writing with the avowed subject of politics also began to flourish. From the turn of the century one anti-Hapsburg political poem followed the next (including those of Rimay, for instance), and the same was true for publicism. One of the most interesting and in many respects pioneering works of the Hungarian publicistic literature which flourished in the seventeenth century, appeared in 1602—it was a booklet on the reasons for the decay of the country, written by the Lutheran preacher ISTVÁN MAGYARI (d. 1605), at Sárvár. In his work, the national approach was united with the Protestant one, and he availed himself of many of the ideas of the first Reformers. At the same time he also endeavoured to take a political stand, and used the humanist works, including those of Erasmus, as his main sources. His booklet was still a strange mixture of the frequently naive, scriptural views of the previous century, with the modern ideas obtained from the political theory of the Renaissance.

Our treatment of Hungarian Renaissance literature must finally include a prominent group of writers who exercised considerable influence on the literary and cultural status of the country in the first third of the seventeenth century. They were a group of Protestant, or more precisely of Calvinist authors, who, beside Rimay and the other noblemen like him, formed the bourgeois branch of late humanism in Hungary. This group was also closely linked to the national efforts against the Hapsburgs, and gathered mainly around Gábor Bethlen, Prince of Transylvania (1613-1629). Bethlen conducted successful wars against the Hapsburgs in the course of the Thirty Years' War and raised the Principality of Transylvania to the rank of an important political factor. He devoted much attention to the cultural development of the principality and extended considerable support to the Protestant writers not only of his own land, but also of the part of the country dominated by the Hapsburgs. A singular characteristic of this group of writers is that almost without exception they studied at the University of Heidelberg, which flourished with particular intensity at the beginning of the century. Their human and literary traits were thus formed at what was then the most progressive spiritual centre of contemporary Germany. Several of these authors also earned considerable appreciation in foreign scientific and literary circles.

The most outstanding of these late humanist Protestant writers was ALBERT SZENCZI-MOLNÁR (1574-1634), who though he spent a large part of his life in Germany, maintained constant contact with Hungary, paid frequent visits to his homeland and was the recognized spiritual leader of contemporary Hungarian Protestantism. His works were aimed at satisfying the literary, religious and scientific requirements of the Hungarian Protestants. He republished Gáspár Károli's translation of the Bible in a revised edition and appended a song-book to it. He compiled a

*Latin-Hungarian* and a *Hungarian-Latin Dictionary* and wrote a *Hungarian Grammar*, thus continuing and perfecting the work of the Erasmian linguists of the first half of the sixteenth century. He published a *collection of sermons*, a *prayer book* and translated Calvin's famous Institutes of the Christian Religion into Hungarian. His most important work was an excellent *translation of the Geneva psalms*. The translation of the Geneva psalms of Marot and Bèze into the various languages was not only a Protestant, but also a humanist programme, and Szenczi-Molnár accordingly translated the original text with full accuracy, even being careful to preserve the metrical form of the original. His psalm translations rank with Balassi's poems and are among the greatest examples of Hungarian Renaissance poetry. His collection of psalms was published in very many editions and came to be the most popular and most read book next to Károli's Bible. Szenczi-Molnár maintained contact with the most outstanding Protestant scholars and writers of his age, conducting widespread correspondence, both in Hungary and abroad. He was an important disseminator of Hungarian culture abroad, and at the same time spread foreign achievements in Hungary.

A whole series of writers grouped round Szenczi-Molnár also enriched Hungarian literature or scholarship. MÁRTON SEPSI-CSOMBOR (1594-1623), a teacher of Kassa* who had travelled over a great part of Europe, published a very colourful and interesting account of his journeys, entitled *Europica varietas* (1620). PÉTER ALVINCZI, a preacher of Kassa, was a court chaplain to Bocskay and later Bethlen; apart from a collection of sermons and polemical works, he also achieved success in anti-Hapsburg publicistic literature. ANDRÁS PRÁGAY (d. 1636), a preacher of Szerencs, produced a translation of Guevara which is one of the finest works of Hungarian mannerist prose.

The activities of the Protestant writers of late humanism extended to every part of the country during the first thirty years of the seventeenth century. However, during this period the Hungarian counter-reformation also continuously gained strength, and, particularly in the western parts of the country,

* Today Košice, Czechoslovakia

52

successfully ousted Protestantism. By the end of the Renaissance period therefore, the true basis of Protestant literature was Transylvania and the eastern part of the country generally, where Protestant culture was able to continue to flourish under the protection of Gábor Bethlen and later of his successors. The real centre of Hungarian Protestant scholarship also owed its existence to Gábor Bethlen, who at his princely seat of Gyulafehérvár* established an academy to which he invited outstanding contemporary German scholars.

Due to the general triumph of the Reformation in the sixteenth century, the Hungarian Renaissance became well-nigh inseparable from Protestantism. The Catholic counter-attack on the other hand came already with the baroque spirit, at the beginning of the century. In this last phase of the Hungarian Renaissance, so rich in achievements yet nevertheless increasingly on the decline since the death of Balassi, the baroque trend, which was to determine the main features of the next period, appeared with growing intensity in Hungarian literary life.

* Today Alba Julia, Rumania

# THE BAROQUE PERIOD

After a start at the beginning of the seventeenth century, baroque culture became predominant in Hungary towards the middle of the century, and subsisted till the seventies of the eighteenth century. At the end of the eighteenth century it was to be replaced in the ideological field by the Enlightenment and in style by classicism. Even during this period of about 150 years, however, the predominance of baroque learning and art may not be regarded as having been absolute. The baroque only became really general throughout the territory of the country and in all sectors of its population in the eighteenth century, while in the second half of the seventeenth century we may still find very significant trends and works which were foreign to the baroque. One of the main reasons for this was that the baroque had from its beginnings in Hungary become linked to the counter-reformation and the Hapsburg Court, so that the national and Protestant resistance had been reluctant to adopt the baroque spirit and its artistic approach.

As with the spread of Hapsburg domination and of the counter-reformation, so baroque culture too, was pioneered by the Jesuits. The Jesuits had settled down by the second half of the sixteenth century, and the beginnings of the Hungarian counter-reformation date from the 1570's. Miklós Telegdi, the head of the Hungarian Catholic Church of which only the ruins then existed, made the city of Nagyszombat* the centre of the Catholic revival where he established a printing press, organized the training of priests and endeavoured to supply the Church with books. The

* Today Trnava, Czechoslovakia

expansion of Jesuit activities was particularly rapid in the seventeenth century. They founded a succession of monasteries and schools, organized Congregations of Mary, staged their baroque school plays, etc. The country's first baroque churches also owe their existence to Jesuit building activity.

The large-scale development of the counter-reformation is linked with the name of PÉTER PÁZMÁNY who was also the virtual initiator of Hungarian baroque literature. Pázmány (1570-1637) was born of a Protestant family, but having been converted to Catholicism, became a Jesuit and studied in various foreign monasteries, including a fairly long period in Rome under Bellarmin. He became a professor of the Jesuit university at Graz and later (in 1615) archbishop of Esztergom and thus the head of the Hungarian Catholic Church. He was at the same time one of the leading politicians of the country and a firm supporter of the House of Hapsburg against the Hungarian strivings for independence. The foundation in 1635 of the University of Nagyszombat (which later moved to Budapest) was his work, and during the seventeenth and eighteenth centuries this was one of the centres of Catholic baroque culture. He wrote several *polemical religious works*, conducting disputes with István Magyari, and on several occasions with Péter Alvinczi. He translated Thomas à Kempis' book, the *Imitation of Christ*, wrote a *Prayer Book* and published a collection of his sermons. His greatest work was the *Guide to Divine Truth* of 1613, which was an attempt at a systematic and comprehensive refutation of all the teachings that differed from the Catholic Church. Pázmány was one of the most eminent cultivators of Hungarian rhetorical and didactic prose, a master of composition and style. His intricate, but logically crystal-clear periods, the complex and nevertheless monumental structure of his works, ushered in the beginnings of Hungarian baroque literature. He always wrote intelligibly, in a manner that was comprehensible to the people, but his works also bore the marks of the greatest artistic care. His *translation of Thomas à Kempis* is one of the masterpieces of literary translation into Hungarian. His theological and philosophical works in Latin (collections of his university lectures) also earned him a place in the history of baroque scholasticism.

Several outstanding authors of the counter-reformation and of the baroque followed in the wake of Pázmány. The Jesuit GYÖRGY KÁLDY (1572-1634) was the founder of Catholic Bible-translation, while BÁLINT LÉPES, archbishop of Kalocsa, was the author of an interesting item of early Hungarian baroque prose in his book of meditations on death. The first thirty years of the century also saw the appearance of the first baroque poet in the person of Canon MÁTYÁS NYÉKI-VÖRÖS of Győr (d. 1654). The first baroque writers, Pázmány's contemporaries, were without exception Catholic churchmen, and in subsequent times Catholic priests and Jesuits continued to be the main authors of Hungarian baroque literature. An extraordinary number of polemics, sermon collections, school plays, Church songs and many other literary works were written by them in the course of the seventeenth and particularly the eighteenth century. These, however, mostly served only practical purposes and there are few among them that attain to higher literary standards.

Under the influence of Pázmány and his companions, the aristocratic families of the period were successively converted to Catholicism and as a result, the Stoic-mannerist poetry of the aristocracy began to tend towards the baroque style. The converted Catholic aristocratic youth attended the Catholic universities of Nagyszombat, Graz and Vienna, with their baroque approach, and undertook educational journeys to baroque Italy and to the centre of the counter-reformation—Rome. They included the greatest Hungarian poet of the century, Miklós Zrínyi.

MIKLÓS ZRÍNYI (1620-1664) came from a family of Croatian extraction, who had become famous as scourges of the Turks. Having early lost his parents he was given a Jesuit education, visiting Graz, Vienna, Nagyszombat and Italy. His education was directed personally by King Ferdinand II and Péter Pázmány. From the age of eighteen he lived on his estates which bordered on Turkish territory, and was engaged in constant battle against the enemy. His first literary works were amorous idylls written on the pattern of Marino and other Italian baroque poets. It was as a young man (in 1645-46) that he wrote the main work of his life, his fifteen-song epic *The Peril of Szigetvár*. In it, he sang the story of the heroic feat of his great-grandfather of the same

expounding his opinions on topical problems in the form of letters. It was in the very midst of his activities that a tragic death overtook him, interrupting the execution of his great plans—he was killed while hunting on big game by an enraged wild-boar.

Despite its numerous baroque traits and elements, Zrínyi's poetry tenaciously maintained Renaissance traditions. Several other aristocratic and noble poets of the seventeenth century similarly stood at the border between the Renaissance and the baroque.

László Liszti (1629-1663) was Zrínyi's contemporary and, inspired by the example of the latter's epic in 1653, wrote a heroic poem called *Hungarian Mars* on the Battle of Mohács; this poem was, however, of no particular poetic value. More interesting is the work of another poet, Péter Beniczky (1603-1664), who was also a contemporary of Zrínyi's and wrote a volume of lyrical verse in the poetic manner of Balassi, but developing Balassi's tradition in the direction of the baroque. István Koháry (1649-1731), a nobleman in the service of the Hapsburgs, was a characteristically baroque poet, but he lacked really profound literary gifts, being led to write poems mainly by the inactivity of the years he spent in the captivity of Rákóczi's freedom fighters. A more original talent was that of Kata Szidónia Petrőczi (1664-1708), one of the earliest Hungarian poetesses, who poured out her ardent Protestant religious feelings, her life of strains and worries, the grief she felt over being deceived in love and the failure of her marriage, in sincere lyrical confessions.

In the seventeenth century only one important poet apart from Zrínyi emerged from among the mediocre writers of the nobility—István Gyöngyösi (1629-1704). He completed his schooling in Hungary, at the Calvinist Academy in Sárospatak, where he obtained an excellent training in law and became a famous lawyer. He spent a considerable part of his life in the service and courts of various aristocrats and always endeavoured to conform to his employers. Later he even adopted the Catholic religion. He engaged in the lighter and more popular vein of narrative poetry, conforming to the tastes of the aristocratic and noble public. He developed a new type of epic poetry, setting the histories of fashionable marriages to verse, adhering to the actual events but drawing profusely on mythological sources and making prolific use of lyrical and descriptive passages. His works are in the last resort magnified epithalamia, pseudo-epics, containing all the outward features of the epic but describing perfectly ordinary, everyday happenings instead of great and magnificent events that affected the fates of entire peoples. The first and also the most successful of these works was his *Venus of Murány in Conversation with Mars* of 1663, in which he recounted the story of the marriage of his master, the Palatine Ferenc Wesselényi. He endeavoured, in an account which is rich in fine detail and written in a captivating style, to conjure heroism and romance into this well-considered marriage of convenience. His second important work, *Phoenix Risen from his Ashes,* was about the marriage of János Kemény, Prince of Transylvania. Here he vividly and successfully recounted the story of his hero's captivity under the Tartars, with a fine description of the feelings of the aristocratic prisoner and his longing for freedom and for his loved one. The song about *The Marriage of Imre Thököly and Ilona Zrínyi* is shorter than the previous ones, but because of the uneventful story it is also duller. The lyrical passages are, however, again of lasting value, especially in the descriptions of the feeling of love and of the beauty of the heroine. Although Gyöngyösi generally placed his protagonists in a false world, he was able to portray their sentiments with psychological veracity and was an excellent observer of detail. He devoted particularly great attention to the formal aspect of his works. His fluent diction, fine sense of rhythm and gift for rhyme made his works entertaining reading. While the conservative nobility of the seventeenth and eighteenth century failed to understand the grandeur of Zrínyi and his ideas which were ahead of his times, Gyöngyösi was their favourite author.

The works of the aristocratic and nobleman poets and similar authors of whom we have spoken  formed only a smaller part of Hungarian poetry in the seventeenth century. Beside these conscious cultivators of poetry, there was also an enormous multitude of songsters. In the seventeenth century members of the most varied strata of society—not only aristocrats and nobles, but also preachers, teachers, soldiers, scribes and craftsmen—wrote masses of poetry. The majority of these works were not even published in print but spread only as manuscripts, or by word of mouth, and frequently had close mutual links with folklore. Almost every sphere of life was flooded by verse. Poems were written for every occasion and verse became the means for courting in love, just as it was that of bidding farewell to the dead. The codes of law were versified, as were the textbooks and even the New Testament. These verses were of course of no poetic value, although in certain types of occasional poetry, such as poems of greetings, there were frequently very fine descriptive or lyrical passages.

This flood of verse, however, had several branches which are not only interesting for the history of literature but were also able to produce works of high artistic value. Among the love and entertainment songs, the soldiers's marching songs, the political verse, the songs of lamentation over the havoc wrought by Turks and Germans, the plaintive songs of soldiers and persecuted men forced into outlawry—among, that is, the types of verse which opened up a wide field for true lyrical expression, there is a fair number of real masterpieces. This popular poetry, intermediate between written poetry and folklore, was closely intertwined with the anti-Turkish and anti-Hapsburg national struggles of the period. In this respect it was a direct continuation of the trend of development which had its roots in the first decades of the seventeenth century. Anonymous Hungarian Tyrtaeans* inspired their compatriots to fight for their independence and commemorated the heroes who fell. The most valuable of these poems, both historically and artistically, were the so-called *Kuruc songs*\*\* written at the end of the century and the beginning of the eighteenth.

Among the Kuruc poems we may find outlaw poems of striking lyrical qualities, worthy for the pens of great poets *(Song of Jakab Buga,* etc.*)*, soldiers' poems that are almost ballad-like reflections of the exuberant spirits of the Kuruc soldiers *(Come on, Palkó, Transylvanian Heyduck Dance,* etc.*)*, moreover

---

* After the Spartan poet Tyrtaeus noted as a writer of spirited martial and patriotic songs in the seventh century B.C.
\*\**Kuruc* was the name given to the freedom-fighters who opposed the Germans and the Hungarian adherents of the Hapsburgs.

61

laments over the soldier's destitution *(Outlaw's Song)* or over lost battles. Some Kuruc poems were substitutes for publicistic writing and pamphleteering, setting out the aims of the freedom-fighters, though not in terms of dry arguments but with poetic fervour and patriotic sentiment *(Thököly's Council of War)*, etc. Many poems treat the person of Ferenc Rákóczi II, the leader of the great Kuruc struggles for freedom in 1703-1711. Even after the failure of this struggle, during the years of total oppression, songs recalling the memory of Rákóczi were nevertheless born. They include the so-called *Rákóczi Song* which right up to the revolution of 1848 was the banned and persecuted, but secretly all the more cherished, song of the Hungarian people. It is related to the tune which Berlioz later used for his famous "Rákóczi March."

The sung poetry of the seventeenth century that has just been discussed, has mainly been preserved in manuscript song collections, but many songs have also been found attached to letters, or inscribed by hand into printed books. This manuscript poetry presents a very motley picture from the point of view of form, style and prosody. In many cases it perpetuated the forms of the sixteenth century and a considerable part is on the whole reminiscent of folklore to the modern ear, with rather the same forms and rhythm. Other poems again bear the marks of baroque complexity, with a somewhat solemn, bombastic manner and a surfeit of decoration. This rich and varied fund of verse was a veritable melting pot for the later classical Hungarian poetry. Here the steel was still mingled with the slag, but the lasting values were increasingly selected and passed on to the future as valuable traditions.

Although manuscript song-writing flourished in every part of the country, the more notable poets of the baroque period who have so far been discussed all lived in the regions under Hapsburg domination. In the seventeenth century the division of the country was manifested even more sharply than in the sixteenth. Apart from the territory occupied by the Turks, the Kingdom of Hungary under Hapsburg rule and the independent Transylvania were also sharply divided, not only politically and in matters of religion, but also with respect to art and literature. In Calvinist Transylvania the baroque had not yet struck roots in the seventeenth century, but the gates were wide open to the bourgeois trends of the time. While the western part of the country based its orientation on and established links with areas of Catholic, baroque culture in the literary, educational and ideological respects, Transylvania had close ties with the West-European Protestant countries—Holland and England, then fighting their bourgeois revolutions. From the 1620's, instead of going to Heidelberg, which had been destroyed in the Thirty Years' War, the young men of Transylvania and Eastern Hungary began to frequent Dutch universities where they were able to learn about the latest and most progressive currents of thought—Descartes' ideas, the Puritan movement, etc. Many of them, in order to learn still more about the Puritan-Presbyterian teachings, crossed the Channel to England and translated into Hungarian one after another the works of the great English Puritan theologians, such as Perkins, William Ames and others.

In Transylvania and the eastern parts of Hungary the Puritan movement first appeared in the 1630's. Its first highly effective representatives and the heads of the movement were PÁL MEDGYESI (1605-1663) and JÁNOS TOLNAI-DALI (1606-1660). They had both been to England and disseminated their views in numerous theological works. Despite bans by the heads of the official Calvinist Church and the Prince, they initiated a movement for the democratic reorganization of the Reformed Church. They also devoted great attention to the development of schooling. János Tolnai-Dali carried out modern reforms at the Sárospatak College of the Calvinists, which was further developed in the 1650's by the great Czech educationalist Comenius, who taught at Sárospatak for a few years.

The greatest figure of the Hungarian Puritan movement and at the same time the most significant Protestant scholar and author of the seventeenth century was JÁNOS APÁCZAI CSERE (1625-1659). He, too, had studied in Holland, where beside Puritan divinity he had also become acquainted with Descartes' philosophy of which he had become an enthusiastic supporter. On his return he became a professor at the College of Gyulafehérvár, but due to his Presbyterian views he came into conflict with the Prince (György Rákóczi II), who considered him an independent and a revolutionary and therefore had him transferred to the Kolozsvár* school, which was of lower rank. However, he succeeded during his few years there, in raising the Kolozsvár College to a high standard. In the course of his short life he wrote several notable works. It was in Holland that he began writing his main work, the *Hungarian Encyclopaedia*, which he completed in Transylvania. It was the first summary of all the sciences, including the natural sciences, in the Hungarian language. He was impelled to write this work by the realization that the sciences could only be really mastered in the vernacular and he therefore strove for the first time to provide Hungarian students with a Hungarian-language scientific compendium. The *Encyclopaedia* was on the whole up to the scientific standards of the period—it conformed to the views of Descartes and made use of the new results in the natural sciences, *e.g.* it courageously sided with Copernicus. One special merit of Apáczai was that with this work he established the Hungarian scientific language, forming a large number of new words and special terms. In the Latin-language foreword to his work he laid down his views on pedagogy, stressing the need for education in the vernacular. He was above all an educationalist, and the problems of pedagogy and public education also attracted him in his other works. Outstanding among these were his two great speeches delivered as inaugural lectures at the Colleges of Gyulafehérvár and Kolozsvár, entitled *On Studying Wisdom* and *On the Supreme Need for Schools*. In these two excellent rhetorical works in Latin, he advanced a large-scale scientific and educational programme, formulating the fundamental principles of a Cartesian pedagogy. At the same time he exercised sharp criticism with regard to the backwardness of Transylvania, urging that more cultured and urban conditions be established.

During the second half of the seventeenth century Protestant Transylvania, despite the increasing decline of the Principality, produced several more enthusiastic apostles of science and education like Apáczai. One of the most interesting personalities among them was MIKLÓS TÓTFALUSI KIS (1650-1702), the most prominent scholarly printer of his age. He had learnt the printer's craft in

* Today Cluj, Rumania

Holland from the best masters, and it was particularly in letter-cutting that he achieved outstanding results. Brilliant prospects awaited him in Holland, where he worked for the most varied clients, including for instance his cutting of the first printed Georgian letters. In 1689 he came home to Transylvania, there to establish a press and to devote all his energies to the service of Hungarian culture. His press at Kolozsvár was the finest Hungarian print-shop of bygone centuries and his books achieved a very high standard in typography. Tótfalusi also had a deliberate publishing policy of his own, his aim being to flood the country with cheap books and to have his publications raise cultural standards. The same purpose was also served by his spelling reform, through which he strove to unify the hitherto very uncertain practices of Hungarian orthography. Most of the orthographic principles laid down by Tótfalusi are still valid today. However, the Calvinist Church authorities looked upon him with distrust and later hatred, considering him a dangerous innovator. The offended printer opposed them first in Latin, in his *Apologia* (1697), then in Hungarian, in *Excuse*, written in 1698. The latter is a passionate indictment of conservatism and stupidity, full of interesting autobiographical and historical items. It is part memoir, part pamphlet, but is given excellent unity by the author's tremendous temperament and his militant readiness courageously to oppose those in power. Finally, however, his opponents succeeded in breaking him, in frustrating his great designs and ruining his life.

One of the few friends and supporters of Miklós Tótfalusi Kis was FERENC PÁPAI-PÁRIZ (1649-1716), a physician, linguist, philosopher and author. This interesting and highly educated polyhistor was the first to publish a medical book in Hungarian. Hungarian culture and science also owes him a debt of gratitude for a dictionary which was very much more voluminous and up-to-date than that of Szenczi-Molnár. An interesting figure of late seventeenth-century Transylvania was the Unitarian writer GYÖRGY FELVINCZI (d. 1716), whose long works in verse were mainly intended to satisfy practical requirements. He was one of the few people, or indeed the only one, who in this period proposed to make a living through literary activity alone. He therefore wrote occasional works of all sorts, on commissions from various individuals, guilds

and institutions. He also experimented with playwriting and became especially noted for the fact that he was the first in Hungary
to organize an independent theatre company.

From the middle of the seventeenth century, literary activity
among the Transylvanian aristocracy differed considerably from
that of their compeers in Hungary. Here poetry did not predominate, but rather memoirs and historiography. The practical
attitude manifested in the work of the Transylvanian burgher-
authors of the period was also present in that of the nobility, except
that they chose and cultivated forms which served the immediate
purposes not of public education, but of politics. Their memoirs
were in fact always intended as a defence and a justification of
their careers and policies. The first of the succession of great
Transylvanian memorialists was JÁNOS KEMÉNY (1607-1662), a
Prince of Transylvania who wrote his *Autobiography* while in
Tartar captivity, exercising restrained and objective discernment
in his account of several decades of Transylvanian history. It was
at almost the same time that JÁNOS SZALÁRDI (1601-1666) wrote
his *Mournful Chronicle*, in which he recorded the collapse of Transylvanian might in the late 1650's.

The greatest of the Transylvanian memorialists was MIKLÓS
BETHLEN (1642-1716), one of the leading politicians at the close of
the seventeenth century. He completed his studies under the
guidance of János Apáczai Csere, later attended Zrínyi and spent
years in Holland, England and France. He was one of the most
erudite and modern-minded men of his time, who strove for the
peaceful development of Transylvania amid the political intrigues
of the declining Transylvania, suffering prison and risking even his
life, all in vain. When at the end of the century Transylvania also
came under Hapsburg rule, the plan of Transylvanian development
became even more hopeless of execution, and indeed at the beginning of the eighteenth century he spent ten years in the prisons of
the Austrian authorities. It was during this period that he wrote
his memoirs under the title *Autobiography*. His work was simultaneously a confession in the Augustinian sense and influenced by
the Saint, and also a political apologia. He opened up his soul,
endeavoured to confess all his sins in his work, but at the same
time also justified and defended his deeds and political activities.

This autobiography is a mirror of the struggle within a great man which also reflects the exciting image of a period of political turmoil. The last chapter of his work is called "The Tragedy of Miklós Bethlen," and the whole composition is in fact construed so as clearly to show how his life inevitably had to lead to a great tragedy, despite his innocence. Bethlen was also an excellent artist of style and he was the first in Transylvanian prose whose writing unmistakably shows the appearance of the baroque.

Bethlen's memoir was written in the first ten years of the eighteenth century, and it was to be followed by a succession of other noted works of a similar nature. The memoirs of Prince FERENC RÁKÓCZI II (1676-1735), written at the time of his exile, were not actually prepared in Transylvania but fit into the general process of development of the Transylvanian memoir literature. After the failure of the struggle for freedom in 1703-1711, the Prince wrote his vindicatory memoirs while an emigré in France and Turkey. Since he was writing abroad and mainly for foreign readers, he wrote his confessions *(Confessiones peccatoris)* in Latin and his volume on the events of the struggle for freedom *(Mémoires)* in French. Judging by these works, Rákóczi was not only a great politician but also an excellent writer, a master of psychological analysis, character-study and of vivid, colourful narration. While in exile, Rákóczi became a supporter of Jansenism and the Jansenist religious approach also permeated his confession. In his case too, there is a desire to justify himself, as with Bethlen, but he gives more prominence to his own "sinfulness," which he frequently exaggerated to himself. It is only in the French volume on the struggle for freedom that this confessional attitude is relegated to the background. Here the politician speaks, giving a brilliant analysis of the antecedents of the struggle for freedom and the reasons for its successes and its failure. Beside these two great works Rákóczi also wrote several other books which mostly remained in manuscript. They were mainly religious meditations in the Jansenist spirit, which incurred the considerable disapproval of ecclesiastical circles.

KELEMEN MIKES (1690-1761), the most outstanding Hungarian prose author of the eighteenth century, was Rákóczi's companion in his exile. He had entered Rákóczi's court as a young lad during the struggle for freedom and loyally stayed by his master to the end, submitting to exile for the rest of his life. In Paris he learnt French and acquired a modicum of French culture which he continued to develop during his many years at Rodosto (Tekir Dagh) in Turkey, where he maintained contact with French circles at Constantinople. He probably began to write his work, the *Letters from Turkey*, after the death of the Prince, using his earlier notes. In the form of a fictitious series of letters, he in fact wrote a memoir of the lives of the Hungarian emigrés at Rodosto and of his own monotonous life. The backbone of the work is a description of the lives of the Kuruc exiles in Turkey, with the figure of the Prince in the centre. Mikes was an excellent observer and he was able to select the most characteristic from among the everyday events of the Hungarian colony at Rodosto. His descriptions are thus highly vivid and evocative, excellently conveying the mood as well as the concrete facts and events. Some of the finest pages of this book of letters are those concerned with the Prince himself, his way of life and his habits. Even in his descriptions of the Prince amid the boredom of his weekdays, he is able to show his serenity and convey the magic of a great personality. Mikes also gave plentiful indications of his own feelings, the most dominant among which were his love and loyalty to the Prince and his unquenchable longing for his homeland. It was especially of the latter feeling that he was able to write without any sentimentality, but in all the more moving and human terms. His letters are freely interwoven with the experiences of his reading. He tells of events and stories that he has read about and records anecdotal events, taken from life, thus furnishing proof that he had a good faculty for writing minor epics. He, too, was strongly affected by Jansenist religious teachings, but as a result of his reading, an occasional idea of the early Enlightenment also makes its appearance in his work. The varied contents of his letters are related in the language of contemporary educated conversation to their fictitious addressee, a certain Hungarian countess with whom the author engages in gentle banter. He was a perfect master of the Hungarian language and no one before him had been able so brilliantly to express complex moods and feelings in the Hungarian language as Mikes did.

The eighteenth-century memorialists who actually lived in

Transylvania also looked back to the past and complained of oppression and the unfavourable changes of the times, in much the same way as the memoirs written in prison or in exile. Among the more noteworthy was MIHÁLY CSEREI (1669-1756) who in his history surveyed events in Hungary from 1661 to 1711, showing particularly the decline and fall of independent Transylvania. His contemporary, the Transylvanian peer PÉTER APOR (1676-1752), in his *Metamorphosis Transylvaniae* complains with dogged conservatism of the change in the habits and ways of life in Transylvania. Apor lamented the disappearance of the old patriarchal and also more Hungarian-minded Transylvania, and looked with antipathy upon the new, Germanic fashions which were in fact equivalent to the now widespread advance of baroque culture in Transylvania. A specially valuable feature of his work is that it records the intimate aspects of social life, gives us a glimpse of the homes and the kitchens, describes the various forms of entertainment, etc. In the course of an attractively written little memoir he thus provides an extremely valuable picture of the history and development of civilization in his period.

The most excellent of the eighteenth-century Transylvanian memorialists was a woman, KATA BETHLEN (1700-1759). She was an aristocrat and an ardent Calvinist, whose main concern in life was to uphold and defend her religion. Kata Bethlen adhered strictly to her denomination, but was forced to marry a Catholic husband. She was perpetually importuned by proselytizing priests. All this resulted in her becoming more absorbed than ever in her own faith, and she came to be seized by a peculiar kind of Calvinist bigotry. In her autobiography too, she described mainly the story of the way she was pestered on account of her religion. Through this, however, she was able realistically to depict the fate of a lonely woman who was never understood. She describes the torments and upheavals of spiritual life with a highly skilled pen, often almost drawing in advance on the methods of the modern psychological novel.

In Transylvania baroque culture only began to strike roots in the eighteenth century, when the baroque in other parts of the country had already reached its culminating point. The real upsurge of baroque art and literature could take place only after the failure of Rákóczi's struggle for freedom in 1711, when the influence of Vienna and the Catholic Church could develop unimpeded. In the literary field this involved a weakening of the national spirit and the silencing of democratic and bourgeois trends, which was not to the advantage of literature but eliminated the very factors that had been the mainspring of the development of Hungarian literature. Even the Hungarian language was forced into the background. The majority of the Catholic Church authors again wrote in Latin, and the aristocratic families, turning away from the traditions of their ancestors, came to despise Hungarian culture, preferring to read and converse in French or German.

A Hungarian literary life similar to that of the seventeenth century could not be found in the magnificent baroque mansions which were erected one after another, and even Hungarian books and Hungarian speech were scarce there. The very few aristocratic families which nurtured and cultivated Hungarian literature and poetry were almost by way of being an exception.

The most important aristocratic poet in the first half of the eighteenth century was LÁSZLÓ AMADÉ (1703-1764), who wrote mainly love poems. He cultivated the almost rococo-style gallant court poetry which had spread all over Europe by the eighteenth century. There is no particular originality or diversity about his poems, but his virtuosity of form is all the more striking. He was an admirably facile verse-writer, able to put his syrupy, gallant compliments in the most complicated metres without any special effort.

The most versatile writer of the eighteenth-century Hungarian baroque world was the Jesuit FERENC FALUDI (1704-1779). He had been to all the larger monastic houses of Hungary and Austria and those of Italy as well, engaging in swiftly changing intellectual pursuits. Of special significance for his literary work and cultural experiences were the five years he spent in Rome where he functioned as the Hungarian confessor. He proved most original in verse. He too, like Amadé, became subject to the influence of contemporary gallant poetry, but in his case the contents of the poems are more profound and varied. He accepted rather the formal inspiration of gallant rococo poetry and his verses, written in a variety of forms, expressed his own more sensible views on life

70

and his pleasant, inventive and jovial humour. Impelled by foreign prosodies and tunes, he developed new rhythmic patterns, thus promoting the rebirth of Hungarian poetry at the close of the eighteenth century. He liked to draw on popular idiom and the motifs of folk life using, for instance, features observed in contemporary Hungarian shepherd life to enrich the traditional idyllic elements in his pastoral eclogues. His interest in folk elements became the starting point of a process which was to reach its culmination at the time of Petőfi and Arany. A considerable part of his work was in the translation of prose. He translated the works on morals of the English Jesuit Darrel and the Spanish Gracian *(The Noble Man; The Noble Woman; The Noble Youth; The Courtier)*, thus providing his Hungarian readers with a baroque code of ethics for court life. His most important work in prose is a collection of short stories under the title *Winter Nights*, in which, following a Spanish author, he recounts eight stories in a single framework, some of them very vividly. His translations are of special value because he set about them as a deliberate artist of the language. In contrast to the lengthiness and clumsiness of older Hungarian prose, he strove to use brief, snappy sentences, varied modes of expression, also taking pains over the rhythm of his sentences. His only play *(Constantinus Porphyrogenitus)* did not rise above the standards of the average school drama.

In Hungary too, as in other European countries, the age of the baroque could have led to an upsurge in dramatic literature and play-acting. However, except for the efforts by György Felvinczi, which we have mentioned, no independent secular theatre companies were established and no true dramatic literature could thus develop. The brilliant courts of the Hungarian aristocracy in the eighteenth century could also have become the hotbeds of Hungarian secular drama, but due to the estrangement of the aristocracy from the nation, only Italian or German actors were tolerated at the aristocratic palaces, but no Hungarians. Thus Hungarian play-acting could develop only on the school stages, under ecclesiastical supervision and control.

In the seventeenth century and the first half of the eighteenth, school dramatic performances mostly took place in Latin, and it was only at the middle of the century that school dramas began rapidly to turn to Hungarian and at the same time also to become secular. By this time the students of the schools had begun putting on performances for the general public, and this necessarily involved adjustment to the requirements of a bourgeois audience, leading to the predominance of the more temporal features.

It was on the school stages that Hungarian-language adaptations from the works of the foreign masters of seventeenth and eighteenth century dramatic literature (Molière, Metastasio) began to appear. The clerical adaptors, however, carried out fairly radical changes in the various plays, eliminating the love motif wherever possible. Their activities were significant even so for the development of Hungarian-language playwriting and acting. Original Hungarian plays appeared only as so-called interludes to the various dramas. The most interesting and successful of these was a Pauline interlude of 1765 called *On the Marriage of Michael Jelly*. This presented the story of two impoverished village families of the petty nobility in the form of a farce, holding up to ridicule the backwardness and lack of education of the nobility. This was the start in Hungarian literature of the tradition of making fun of the nobility, which was fifty years later to become one of the most popular subjects. True that as yet only the lowest stratum of the nobility was involved, but an important process was nevertheless thus started in Hungarian literature.

Of all the forms of literature it was the development of prose fiction that was most tardy in the baroque period. Those writers who had a feeling and a gift for prose wrote memoirs, which, though they were rich in artistic literary passages, may on the whole not be regarded as purely narrative works. The encouraging development that had begun at the time of the Reformation, mainly through Gáspár Heltai, was interrupted for a long time, and when prose narrative once more appeared at the end of the seventeenth century, it was way below the standard of contemporary literature. Even now, only the translation of old international themes was undertaken, as in the case of the *Triple Story* of JÁNOS HALLER (d. 1697), which contains three works of medieval fiction— the story of the Trojan War, the romance about Alexander the Great and the *Gesta Romanorum*. The same applies to the *Horologium Turcicum* of DÁVID ROZSNYAI (d. 1717), which is an adaptation of the Pancha Tantra on the basis of a Turkish translation. Even as late as the eighteenth century it was mainly the translation of the various internationally well-known subjects into Hungarian that was predominant, while original artistic prose narrative had yet to come.

The real development of Hungarian prose fiction was only to start at the time of the Enlightenment but this period nevertheless saw the appearance of its first important harbinger. He was only a harbinger, because though his book makes excellent reading, it is not a work of fiction in the true sense. This author was JÓZSEF HERMÁNYI-DIENES (1699-1763), Calvinist dean of the town of Nagyenyed* in Transylvania, and his book a collection of anecdotes under the title *Democritus of Nagyenyed*. As a matter of fact, this work of Hermányi-Dienes was a continuation of the Transylvanian memorialist traditions, but he further developed the memoir as a literary form. Just as Mikes had dressed the memoir in the fortunate form of a collection of letters, so the author of Nagyenyed broke it up into separate little stories. Within the various short stories he always sought the features of everyday life, endeavouring to record the lives of average people. Thus, through his minute observations, the scenes and stories taken from real life, he compiled raw material almost sufficient for a realistic novel, providing a masterly image of contemporary Transylvanian society.

The Hungarian baroque literature of the eighteenth century was—even though it witnessed the appearance of important pieces of initiative and though it did give us one great writer (Mikes)—in the final analysis one of the poorer periods of Hungarian literature. Circumstances were not favourable for the development of poetry and fiction. The rich scientific literature of the period, however, provides compensation in many respects. It was after the initiative displayed by Apáczai and his associates that the various branches of science began to assume independence in Hungary in the eighteenth century. Unfortunately this scientific activity again returned temporarily to the Latin tongue, not following the ventures of its seventeenth-century precursors in this respect.

* Today Aiud, Rumania

Up to this time historiography had more or less also been a form of literary activity, in which the writer's artistic presentation played a decisive part—a general feature of humanist history writing. This was now to be displaced by modern historiography based on thorough research and a study of the sources. There was a veritable fever of research for sources in the eighteenth century. Numerous noblemen and ecclesiastics, interested in history, had vast masses of source material copied out. The publication of the old Hungarian chronicles was begun, and based on all these, the first great systematic histories were written. Two Jesuit scholars are especially prominent among the historians of the eighteenth century: GYÖRGY PRAY (1723-1801) and ISTVÁN KATONA (1732-1811). History, linguistics and geography were all cultivated by MÁTYÁS BÉL (1684-1749), a Lutheran of Slovak extraction who was also appreciated abroad as an outstanding representative of the eighteenth-century school of political science.

The most important, however, from the point of view of the history of literature is that this period also saw the start of writing on the history of Hungarian literature. It is true that the history of literature was at this stage still completely intermingled with the history of learning, but at any rate the systematic arrangement of the biographical data of the authors was begun, and so was the search for the ancient mementos of Hungarian literature. Credit for this pioneering work must go to DÁVID CZWITTINGER (1676-1743) who compiled the biographies and bibliographies of almost 300 Hungarian writers, with grave omissions and many errors however. He was followed by the Transylvanian polyhistor PÉTER BOD (1712-1769), a Calvinist preacher who in his *Hungarian Athenas*, published in 1766 and this time in Hungarian, introduced over 500 writers; some of them, particularly the Transylvanians, in great detail and very much more accurately than Czwittinger.

From the middle of the eighteenth century the works of several writers, the interest shown in French literature and the translations of French works, began to betray the first winds of the Enlightenment. The Hungarian Enlightenment began with the appearance of György Bessenyei in the 1770's, opening at the same time a new period in the history of Hungarian literature.

# PART TWO

# FROM THE BEGINNING OF THE ENLIGHTENMENT TO THE END OF THE NINETEENTH CENTURY

BY JÓZSEF SZAUDER

# THE AGE OF THE HUNGARIAN
# ENLIGHTENMENT (1772-1820)

After the failure of the struggle for freedom led by Rákóczi, there was nothing to stop the Hapsburgs from organizing Hungary—which they had conquered with colonial methods—in the form of an actual colony. Under cover of the ostensible "constitutional compromise" of the Peace of Szatmár (1711), where the Hungarian ruling class had, in return for their lives and their fortunes, given up the political and economic independence of the nation, Hungary's colonization by Austria began in the first half of the eighteenth century.

After the middle of the eighteenth century (under the reign of Maria Theresa) fissures began to show in the compromise between the Hapsburgs, who kept Hungary in semi-colonial servitude, and the Hungarian ruling class—the nobility. The repeated outbreaks of serf revolts were warnings to the sovereign and the nobility of the mounting crisis of feudalism. Beyond the feudal services required of them, the burdens of taxation and of maintaining the State also rested on the serfs. It was precisely over the reduction of these burdens (over deciding at whose expense this should take place) that the class interests of the Hungarian nobility again clashed—for the first time since Rákóczi—with those of the Austrian colonising state at the Diet of 1764-65. A spate of protests against the Austrian tariff policies that impeded the development of the nobility's estates, and even more the rising demand for the free use of the Hungarian language, served to broaden the economic and political antagonisms, which came to assume a national character. This was why the middle stratum of the nobility and some of the peers began to turn against the almost omnipresent clerical and legal Latin of the first half of the century, and against its main exponents, the half-Germanised Hungarian aristocracy and the high clergy. This stirring of national and bourgeois trends obtained considerable ideological reinforcement beyond the tradition of developing the national tongue, particularly from increasing acquaintance with the chief works of the French Enlightenment. Some Hungarian authors, drawing encouragement from the example of Viennese reaction which wished to achieve the supremacy of the German language against the earlier cosmopolitan Franco-Italian culture of the Court, proposed a return to the Hungarian national tongue.

These forces together guided the activities of the first nucleus of the Hungarian Enlightenment, formed in Vienna among the Hungarian noblemen who were in Maria Theresa's body-guard and who provided the first vanguard of the rebirth of Hungarian literature.

GYÖRGY BESSENYEI (1746-1811), a native of Szabolcs County and leader of the group, was linked directly to the national tradition by Sándor Báróczy and Ábrahám Barcsay, both of Transylvania, and the senior member of their circle, Lőrinc Orczy, who came from the Great Plains. Apart from the memory of Zrínyi, the greatest Hungarian epic poet of the sixteenth century, this tradition comprised mainly the works of the baroque nobleman-poet Gyöngyösi, among the lyricists the popular, Hungarian-style rococo of Ferenc Faludi, and in prose the same author's moralities, and the more political works of the Transylvanian memorialists. The tasteless folk-books of peasant crudity were popular with the masses of the lower nobility, while the political poetry of Rákóczi's war of independence, though of a high standard, was relegated to manuscript circulation.

LŐRINCZ ORCZY (1718-1789) and GEDEON RÁDAY (1713-1792), who considerably preceded Bessenyei, were aristocratic authors of the old stamp, who had written for their own amusement in the seclusion of their country mansions as early as the middle of the century. These writers never even published their works, but the literary movement which developed under Bessenyei's leadership in the eighties drew both their works and their persons into the main current of public and literary life, through the very features that were related to this trend. In the case of Orczy's work this

78

was typified by his conservative, nobleman's attitude, so characteristic both of his person and his poetry. He strove to defend the patriarchal life from Austrian innovations, was thoroughly Hungarian and popular, and must have nurtured the noblemen's national resistance which was developing in the eighties. In the works of Ráday these features were mainly his West European rhyming and metrical poetry, his naturalization of a new style and taste, and particularly his great educative influence which he exercised as a patron and by organizing a huge library.

The two body-guards SÁNDOR BÁRÓCZY (1753-1809) and ÁBRAHÁM BARCSAY (1742-1806) set out on their careers at about the same time as Bessenyei, at the beginning of the seventies. However, they both confined their literary activities to a narrow circle, and Ábrahám Barcsay, like Orczy and Ráday, was reluctant to publish his works. The classical forms of his poetry were only occasionally suffused with his enthusiasm for the science of the Enlightenment and for knowledge—in this he was more modern than his old friend Orczy—and it was only in some places that his poetry acquired a subjective tint, due to an inner conflict with his military calling and to his sense of shock at the world-wide process of colonization. The enlightened reform efforts of the Hapsburgs, directed against the nobility, led him to fear that Hungary, too, would be reduced to a colony. It was this that ultimately induced him to join the Transylvanian, nationalistic Jacobine conspiracy. His lyricism was rendered authentic by his nostalgic yearning for, and depiction of, the people's life of Rousseauian simplicity.

The prose writer Sándor Báróczy on the other hand published his works immediately after the appearance of Bessenyei. In his translation of Calprenède and particularly of Marmontel he proved to be a deliberate cultivator of the light French *style coupé*. His careful and pure use of the Hungarian language exercised a strong influence on the younger writers, particularly their subsequent leader, Kazinczy. As with Ráday, Báróczy's merit also lies in the introduction of a reform in style and taste.

György Bessenyei became the first great protagonist of the Hungarian Enlightenment, as much through his personality, his eagerly receptive and extremely multi-coloured gifts, his sense of

79

vocation and his gaiety as his love of the grotesque which constantly penetrated the frequent melancholy of his pensive and fretful spirit. From Szabolcs County, and the College of Sárospatak, he brought with him to the Queen's body-guard in Vienna in 1765 not only his patriotism but also the bourgeois tradition of the Reformation. There the political events of those years, the example of the national Enlightenment in Vienna, and particularly of his favourite authors (Locke, Voltaire, Montesquieu, Rousseau), rapidly made him aware of what he was to do. The Hungarian Enlightenment is considered to date from the appearance in 1772 of his first important drama, *The Tragedy of Ágis*. A propagator of the Enlightenment who exerted a great educative influence, he linked in his cultural programme and pamphlets the demand for the cultivation of the Hungarian language with the need to spread modern learning (the enlightened teaching of Locke and Voltaire). It was to serve this purpose that he wrote his French-style classicistic tragedies and comedies, depicting the conflict of freedom and despotism, and his philosophical works *(This and That,* a great collection of essays, 1779), which bear witness to a mind predominantly given to internal strife and inclined to materialism. It was he who raised the Hungarian theatre, then only extant in pseudo-popular school dramas and on the aristocratic stages, to the level of contemporary literature. In his "Patriotic Hungarian Society," under the presidency of Orczy, he was the first to strive to unite the prominent scholars and authors of the period. It was in the wake of this great endeavour, which soon failed, that he prepared his plan for an academy (later published). His militant attitude, advocating the new content of the Enlightenment in face of the outdated feudal Hungarianism of the lawyers and the clergy, led to a host of new undertakings with a great future. They included laying the theoretical foundations for a reform of the language, introducing modern forms of literature, initiating the widespread work of translation, especially the translation of plays, and advancing the demand for a Hungarian Academy of Sciences.

All this took place during the Vienna phase of his life, from 1765 to 1782. From 1782 he lived on his estates in the Upper-Tisza region, in ever greater solitude, continuing to write works which he now had no hope of publishing. His grand satirical and utopian political novel, *The Journey of Tarimenes* in 1804, reflected his own plans, his experiences in life and the great personages and events of his age, in what was almost a distorting mirror, using the weapons of grotesque humour and caustic irony to criticise the sharp contradictions in the social life of enlightened absolutism. This work, in which he made full use of Voltaire's *Candide* and *L'Ingénu*, but with a broader horizon and more reflexion, remained unpublished for 125 years.

The movement which developed in his wake in the eighties, was very many-sided. The extremist reforms of Joseph II, based on doctrinaire principles and carried out in the interests of the Monarchy as a whole, divided the slowly expanding camp of writers. Some—such as many members of the Protestant intelligentsia which he protected—took his side and their Josephinism served as vigorous propaganda for the Enlightenment. Others turned against him in defence of national independence, but this they interpreted in accordance with their diehard, conservative, feudal class mentality as noblemen. Thus in the course of the principal trend which followed Bessenyei and favoured an enlightened programme of education, through hostility to Latin and German, through translations and the vigorous demand for a scientific society and a national theatre, a link was established between the endeavours of both the Josephinists and the national patriots of the nobility. Nevertheless, the acceptance of the radical philosophy behind these demands abated for a time.

The main trend alone was served by the translations from Voltaire and Edward Young of JÓZSEF PÉCZELI (1750-1792), a preacher of Komárom, as well as by his instructive tales and his periodical *Mindenes Gyűjtemény* (Universal Collection) for the popularization of science. The same may be said later of the radically enlightened poetry and periodical editorship of Batsányi and Kazinczy.

The first notable poet serving the efforts of the nobility to preserve its conservative traditions contiguous to this main trend, was precisely a pupil of Bessenyei, PÁL ÁNYOS (1756-1784) whose sentimentalism and despair were coloured in no small measure by the conflict between the ideas of the Enlightenment—which were now being spread by the foreign sovereign to the detriment of the

6

concept of the Hungarian nation as consisting only of the nobility
—and of the class interests of the nobility. Beside the poems of
a suggestive cult of the moon and of death, it is for this reason
that his poetry also includes important motifs of the national
movements of the nobility which were further developed in the
first half of the nineteenth century. They include the images and
the warnings conveyed by the old triumphs, the mementoes of the
fall of the nation (Mohács) and the national language, costumes
and habits. The young Paulite priest soon came into conflict with
his vocation and became the first satirist of the resistance of the
nobility in his great invective against the uncrowned King Joseph II.

Full-flavoured fun was made of the resistance of the completely conservative, patriotic nobility who did not wish to know even
this much of bourgeois aspirations, by JÓZSEF GVADÁNYI (1725-
1801) of Szakolca*, in his apposite satirical-comical narrative verse
*A Village Notary's Journey to Buda*, of 1788-1790. The notary, who
rides across the whole country, is at first the hero of amusing
adventures in the provinces, rescued from trouble by the typical
examples of Hungarian pastoral life, who in Gvadányi's view were
the character portraits of pure Magyardom. Thus he set the earlier
decorative pastoral characters of the rococo period squarely on
their feet, with the full relish of realism. On his arrival at Buda,
the notary sees only the degeneration of the old life of the Hungarian nobility, and the petty figure suddenly becomes a merciless
satirist, engaging in Quixotic attacks against Hungarians dressed
in foreign clothes and speaking foreign languages. The break in
the character of the hero is caused by the duality of Gvadányi's
sound observation of reality and his diehard nobleman's approach.
Later Gvadányi, blinded by prejudice, went so far as to malign
the memory of the Hungarian Jacobines. The ideas, themes,
objects and nationalist atmosphere of the resistance of the nobility
were also the subject of ANDRÁS DUGONICS (1740-1818), a member
of the Piarist Order at Szeged, in his pseudo-historical novel *Etelka*
(1788), which introduced real characters under fictitious names.
The novel, whose patriarchally folky style was deliberately provincial, achieved great success by arousing interest in ancient times, in

* Today Skalica, Czechoslovakia

the period of the first conquering Hungarians. The numerous translations by Dugonics, and particularly his plays and scholarly works, continued to be effective examples for the dissemination of knowledge in Hungarian and for the search for a national dramatic hero.

The career of JÁNOS BATSÁNYI (1763-1845), the greatest politician-poet and periodical editor of the time, also had its beginnings in the nobility's resistance. Batsányi, who came from Transdanubia and was of plebeian extraction, lived at Kassa*, then the cultural centre of North Hungary, with the support of the Orczys. It was here that, together with Kazinczy, he founded a literary periodical, the *Magyar Múzeum* (Hungarian Museum), which he devoted to the service of the national resistance. The periodical engaged all the prominent authors of the day and clearly reflected that Batsányi's path soon diverged from that of the conservative nobility of Gvadányi's kind. His enlightened erudition and his acceptance of the teachings of Bessenyei led him to oppose Joseph II, not in order to restore the privileges of the nobility, but to preserve the leading forces of the nation. His poems show that he closely linked the subjects of the national resistance with the progressive, tolerant, democratic ideas of the Enlightenment. As a realistic politician he aimed ultimately to develop the opposition of the conservative nobility to Joseph II into a struggle of national independence. It appeared, indeed, that the international events of the early 1790's were providing some basis for this endeavour—first the outbreak of the great French Revolution, then its triumphant advance after beating back the interventionary armies. Batsányi's political poetry was inspired almost exclusively by these great events—in 1789 he wrote an epigram showing revolutionary sympathies *On the Changes in France*, and in 1792-93 his great poem *The Seer*, with the verve of an ode, in which he prophetically heralds the coming of freedom to the world.

The national movement of the nobility culminated at the Diet of 1790, which created a hitherto unknown richness of Hungarian journalistic literature and resuscitated the previously latent motifs, songs and attire of Rákóczi's Kuruc fighters. Here Joseph II, who was also threatened on the international arena, was forced to

* Today Košice, Czechoslovakia

withdraw most of his anti-feudal and anti-Hungarian decrees. After this swift and bloodless victory, the Hungarian nobility, frightened by the spread of the French Revolution, which was a threat to its own existence, turned away from the essential ideas of the Enlightenment, abandoned the radical independents and concluded a compromise with the Hapsburgs.

Due to the inhibition of social progress, the defeat of bourgeois ideas and the oppression of free thought and feeling, emergent individualistic consciousness found an outlet in sentimental preromantic works, particularly in the poetry of Gábor Dayka and the narrative prose works of József Kármán.

GÁBOR DAYKA (1769-1796), a plebeian youth of Miskolc who had the secularising reforms of the Church by Joseph II to thank for the fact that he was able to develop his gifts in Pest amid a teeming and wordly cultural life, was cast back by the change which took place in 1790 to Eger, to the bigotry and darkness of a clerical township, where he was obliged to return as a seminarist. The Anacreontic lyricist, who had advocated the freedom of man's emotions, of love and of thought, the right to the joy of life and to happiness, later wrote passionate, sentimental poems full of revolt, to express his thwarted feelings. It was this militant, enlightened emotional awareness that led him to break with the clerical way of life. His place in the reformation of Hungarian taste and style was determined by Kazinczy, the leader of the second phase of the Enlightenment.

The finest representative of sentimental prose was the outstanding narrator JÓZSEF KÁRMÁN (1769-1795). The son of distinguished Lutheran parents, the young man studied in Vienna, and in 1794 founded a periodical in Pest. In this, the *Uránia* (1794-95), where his own works were published anonymously, he provided a forum for the most progressive ideas and literary achievements of his age, immediately before their downfall. His cultural programme was founded on that of Bessenyei, but also went beyond it in demanding a conscious effort to write literary works of artistic value and of an originality that bears the marks of national literature. The great essay containing this demand, *The Refinement of the Nation*, also presented a sharp criticism of the way of life and the cultural ideas of feudal Hungary and implicitly contained the earliest seeds of the principles of literary realism (the illustration of reality and an illusion-free knowledge of oneself). He began to put his programme into practice in his excellent stories—outstanding among these for its differentiated and extremely deliberate psychological portrait, which is related to Goethe's *Werther* without being a copy, is an epistolary novel, *The Posthumous Papers of Fanni*. The description of the moods here, and his *style coupé*, show Kármán to have been a brilliant stylist. In another story, *The Treasure-Digger*, written with great linguistic power, he exercised sanguinary irony in simultaneously exposing both the narrow-mindedness of the nobility and the trickery of Cagliostrian masonic bravado.

The new programme of Kármán would have meant the replacement of the popularization of science and of translated literature initiated by Bessenyei with an indigenous artistic literature and the demand for national originality. In addition to this there would be the establishment of drama and of a theatre, a proposal of which Kármán was also a champion. This programme could not be carried out. The progressive development of the Hungarian Enlightenment was halted by the fear of the French Revolution entertained by the nobility and by their agreement with the Hapsburgs. These events made it impossible to put the most advanced bourgeois ideas in literature and politics into practice.

Kármán himself, it seems, must have been a participant in the Republican, Jacobine conspiracy initiated in 1793 by a small group of intellectuals, after the compromise concluded by the camp of the nobility had isolated equally both the radical independents and the representatives of the Enlightenment from the masses, and forced them to engage in an extremist plot with revolutionary aims. They met in secret societies to overthrow the pillars of reaction, the Vienna government of Francis I and Hungarian feudalism, and they copied and disseminated a revolutionary catechism. Their leaders were IGNÁC MARTINOVICS (1755-1795), an abbot, scientist and philosopher, and JÓZSEF HAJNÓCZY (1750-1795), a prominent lawyer of revolutionary views. In the second half of 1794 the conspiracy was quickly liquidated and some of the participants, outstanding young publicists, were executed at the Vérmező (Bloody Field) of Buda, while the greater part, including highly talented progressive authors, were sentenced to long terms of imprisonment. One of those to die in the prison of Kufstein was the prominent young lyricist LÁSZLÓ SZENTJÓBI-SZABÓ (1767-1795), a friend of Batsányi's, who was renowned for his folk style and Rousseauism. FERENC VERSEGHY (1757-1822), a former monk of the Order of St. Paul, spent almost nine years in prison. He was the author of the Hungarian Marseillaise of the period, as well as of the first poetry with a bourgeois approach and of highly important linguistic works. The later literary leader Kazinczy was also with them and was released from prison in 1801. Batsányi, who has sympathised with the Jacobines, received a shorter prison sentence, but his life henceforth became a barren search for a way out of the dilemma. He could now only have carried out his earlier programme of national independence with outside help, and after his discharge he therefore sided with Napoleon who soon overran Austria; he tried to win support for the French Emperor in the hope of thus promoting the interests of Hungarian independence. Later he emigrated to Paris whence he was transported back by the allies victorious over Napoleon and first jailed, then interned for life, at Linz. Only his faithful and devoted wife, Gabriella Baumberg, a noted Austrian poetess of the period, allayed his suffering. In his moving elegies written at Kufstein, and in his later poetry, several of the main motifs of romanticism (bardic poetry, Ossianism) made their first appearance.

The first period of the Hungarian Enlightenment closed in 1795, with the repressive measure of the reaction, the thinning of the ranks of a young and highly talented generation of writers, and a check on their development.

The introduction of new forms of literature, containing new ideas and emotions, also involved a reforming of poetry, with the establishment, beside the traditional Hungarian stressed verse, of the Graeco-Roman and the rhymed-metric forms which now became generally used. The greatest merit in the introduction and development of the Graeco-Roman metre was that of members of the so-called classicistic school, comprising JÓZSEF RÁJNIS (1741-1812), a former Jesuit and later lay priest of Győr, DÁVID BARÓTI-SZABÓ (1739-1819), a Székely (Transylvanian) Jesuit, later a lay priest and schoolmaster, and MIKLÓS RÉVAI (1750-1807), a Piarist who was one of the greatest Hungarian philologists. In the course of what was known as the prosody struggle of Rájnis and Baróti-Szabó (in 1781-1792), the basic problems of the modernization of the Hungarian poetic language, of the orthography and of the uniform literary language were raised.

The most prominent poet of the school was Baróti-Szabó, a friend of Batsányi and Kazinczy, who participated together with them in editing the *Magyar Múzeum* at Kassa. In his many volumes of verse and translations (the *Aeneid*) in Graeco-Roman metre, the usual motifs of the nobility's national resistance were couched in poetically advanced terms, in odes and elegies. A strikingly modern lyrical sensitiveness and unconscious romanticism of style in his advanced years made him one of the stylistic forerunners of romanticism.

Miklós Révai was more modern and endowed with an unruly temperament. A priest and a poet, he had an eventful career and his enlightened sentiments of life, as well as his national consciousness, brought him into frequent conflict with a public opinion shaped by the compromise concluded by the nobility, and by the atmosphere of the restoration. His Anacreontic and sentimental lay poetry and the publications in which he made available the text of earlier Hungarian authors, especially Faludi and Bessenyei, were in themselves sufficient to establish a reputation for him. It was, however, in the first ten years of the nineteenth century that he obtained especially great influence when—as the professor of Hungarian language and literature in the University of Pest—he finished his vast Latin-language philological synthesis of the Hungarian tongue. In it, he preceded Grimm in applying the historical method to the examination of linguistic phenomena. His principles were brought to triumph by Kazinczy, the leader of the movement for the renewal of the language.

At this stage it was the national language that was the dominant feature determining the *Hungarian* character of literature, and this overwhelmingly linguistic approach did not permit of the differentiation which accompanies originality, the deliberate separation of trends of taste from each other and the independent evolution of belles-lettres as such.

The first brilliant synthetiser of the trends in ideas and styles evolved by the resurgence of the nation and the Enlightenment was MIHÁLY CSOKONAI VITÉZ (1773-1805), who rose above all his contemporaries early in the period following the tragedy of the collapse of the Hungarian Jacobine movement in 1794-95, although he had set out on his career only in 1790. Csokonai was in chronological order the greatest Hungarian lyricist after Balassi, particularly through his unparalleled ability to unite the currents of the Enlightenment, the rococo and the folk style.

His plebeian feelings and approach were the fruits of his poverty-stricken petty-bourgeois background at Debrecen. They were to accompany him to the widely famed College of that city, where he neglected his theological studies to devote himself to poetry, at this stage already enjoying the support of the most important literary men of the period, including Kazinczy and JÁNOS FÖLDI (1755-1801), one of the most erudite innovators of form and an excellent botanist. The successive influences of Metastasio's morbid secular melodramatic poetry and canzonet and the Rousseauian, radically enlightened philosophy of life left their indelible imprint on Csokonai's raw and comic school poetry, nurtured mainly by the old Hungarian manuscript and more recent student poetry. This is evinced in his early translations of Metastasio, his rococo poems, but particularly by his perturbed, subjectively heated lyrical poetry, in which he tries to find an answer to the great social and human problems of the Enlightenment.

His lyrical poetry expresses anti-feudal ideas with emotional colouring. Before him Hungarian poetry had not experienced such richness of thought and feeling, such variety in tone or such a mode of expression that was linguistically so precise and differentiated, and yet so easy-flowing. His great lyrical poem *Constantinople*, written in about 1793, subtly switches over from a mood of mocking laughter at dogmatic religions, to a condemnation, in terms of suppressed passion, of "bat-like superstition," and "owl-like bigotry." From there it changes to a hymn in praise of mankind yearning for the fulfilment of the law of nature and almost within sight of it, finally letting his ardour calm down in the evocation and hope of a "century yet to come" that is to bring fulfilment of these yearnings. Only a poet who found a home in the outcast lives of the peasant folk, who identified himself with them, could have written *The Even*, an indictment full of agonizing Hungarian experiences upon a Rousseauian foundation aimed at class society and private property that deprives men of their all and kills them with wars.

In his plebeian-bourgeois, Rousseauian view, the ideas of the European Enlightenment fused with a recognition of the most urgent Hungarian social and national interests. He was no supporter of the nobility's resistance—this is shown by his animal dialogues in which he mocked the bloated nationalist Hungarian nobility. His poetry and plays were pervaded by the great enlightened aims of the cultural upsurge of the nation. In his drama *Tempefői* (1793), Csokonai colourfully portrayed the struggles and conflicts of a poet wishing to live by his poetry, with the Hungarian noblemen who were opposed to art and indulged in cheap revelry. In this satirical drama, written in the manner of the school drama and the Viennese plays, he already included his folk characters and the hues of folk tales.

It was his awareness of being a poet—an awareness that was a compensation, though a painful one, for all ills—that consoled him for his expulsion in 1795 from the Debrecen College, a measure which had been taken mainly for his enlightened ideas and attitude. He was now forced to undertake a journeying existence which set his way of life back to the level of the itinerant poets of centuries past. The plebeian poet, sent down from his school, could not obtain a post as a teacher, editor or official during the epoch of the nobility's compromise. He remained, in his own words, "the country's poor." It was thus that he wandered all over the country between 1795 and 1799, attempting first to complete his legal studies at Sárospatak, from whence, however, the police advised him to move on. Coming to Pozsony*, the seat of the Diet, he attempted to maintain himself by publishing a poetic periodical, the *Diétai Magyar Múzsa* (Hungarian Muse of the Diet), compiled from his earlier poems. After these unsuccessful experiments, he went to Komárom in 1797 and fell deeply in love with Júlia Vajda —whom he called Lilla in his poems—though social differences

* Today Bratislava, Czechoslovakia

soon parted them. A year and a half of wandering and teaching (1798-99) in Transdanubia saw the birth of a large part of his lyrical cycle entitled *Lilla*, and of his comic epic *Dorottya*. These and his volume of *Odes* were his most important works.

*Lilla* and the *Odes* were the finest volumes of poetry of the Hungarian Enlightenment, in a sentimental rococo style which reveals the initial steps towards a popular form of written song. The poems of the *Lilla* cycle are characterized by an intimate expression of the social awareness of the man and citizen, of the poet's yearning for immortality and of man's simple, amorous and communal sentiments. These classical works are rendered outstanding by their symbolic power and musical qualities *(To the Echo of Tihany, To Hope, To the Butterfly)*. The lyrical expression of his disappointment in love at the same time echoed distress at his social ostracism and his indictment of oppression, of the "tyrant law." The sentiment of love, suffused with rich human content, characteristically enlightened ideas and attitudes, radiates a desire for peaceful creative work, the joy of friendship, the concern felt by simple, working people for their country's fate, and a belief in the consolation of beauty, the immortal refuge of poetry. The porcelain translucency of his poems—particularly of the impressionist-rococo ones—permits only a faint image of suffering, homelessness and disease to appear behind his facile, playful and formally incredibly rich verse. It is, however, just his strange duality, the compelling influence of the oft-repressed complaint, that makes his lyrical poetry so nervously restless, so profuse in swift changes of tone and sentiment. His poems, which resemble the popular song and are yet objective and of the character of confessions, drew, not only for their subjects but also for their composition and the elements of their style, on peasant images—Csokonai indeed compiled a collection of popular songs—so that beyond their brilliant rococo stylization they reveal as their motive not merely the poet's spirits, finding consolation in boundless, playful ebullience, but also an identification of his sentiments with those of the simple people. The volume of the *Odes* contains representative works of his amorous and philosophical poetry, concerned with his world of ideals and his pre-romantic resignation. Beside these, there are pieces of rococo flirtation and popular *genre* songs whose naturalness was to remain unparalleled till the advent of Petőfi *(Peasant Song, Poor Zsuzsi)*. This very diversity shows that Csokonai was able to echo all the trends of taste prevalent in his period, with a susceptibility that verged on the naive. In his comic epic *Dorottya* (for which his main example was Pope's *The Rape of the Lock)*, and even more in his later comedies, he drew a vivid, grotesque, almost invariably satirical picture of the nobility and bourgeoisie, submerging and growing petty as they carouse in the obscurity and solitude of the provinces.

From 1801, the date of his return to Debrecen, severely ill, his only aim was the publication of his works. His last poetic work, great both in merit and length, was concerned with an analysis of the immortality of the soul, permeated by inner conflict and set in the framework of the history of religion and of philosophy. Even in this cheerless, detached and artificial literary form he made use of an ancient and popular Hungarian *genre* (the versified farewell to the dead) which enjoyed a status almost equivalent to that of literary trash, raising it, however, to a high level in his work.

His plebeian, peasant, folk characteristics, his enlightened philosophy of life and even his wanderings through the country, made Csokonai a precursor of Petőfi. His varied life's work, with its original richness of content and mood, its craft in the use of popular language and form and its great artistic awareness, became the forerunner of all the later great efforts in Hungarian literature.

At the time of the compromise with the Hapsburgs, originality in literature had no other representative who was so progressively minded and set such high artistic standards as Csokonai—indeed in this latter respect he became somewhat isolated. His friend MIHÁLY FAZEKAS (1766-1828) was also a native of Debrecen and more ardent in his local patriotism than Csokonai. While his poetry was narrower in its scope, nevertheless it too achieved classical prominence in *Mattie the Gooseboy*, his comic narrative verse in a folk style. Fazekas had also studied at the famous College of Debrecen, then became a soldier and returned home from the Rhine theatre of war in 1796. He had become disgusted with military life, with the bloodshed in futile and unjust wars, and in his poems he also expressed his repugnance in the tones of the enlightened humanism of the petty bourgeois. From 1796 till his death he lived at Debrecen and obviously the influence of the great poet, his friend, helped his own poetry to fruition. In his case the great system of thought of the Enlightenment came close to becoming the small-change of everyday truths, and he advocated wise civic morals, a thrifty and industrious life. As a passionate botanist, he became editor of the first Hungarian scientific herbal, while as a fruit-grower and editor of popular calendars, he stood for the bourgeois trend of development, for "common sense," and against superstition. His lyrical poetry also reveals this practical everyday wisdom, the personality of a passionate gardener, in a highly captivating form. Everything is here in organic unity with everything else, nothing stands by itself, nothing is reduced to a mere piece of decorative scenery. Every syllable underscores the atmosphere of organic life, replete with strength, glowing, breathing and changing and fading in colour. This is the overall effect achieved by Fazekas in the magnificent lyrical poems which depict the environment of independent herdsmen and soil-tilling peasants with a plebeian approach, and with the strange flexibility and musical quality of his language. His special gifts and his love of the people scintillate in his *Mattie the Gooseboy* (1804). The narrative poem, written in a popular tone and in hexameters of marvellous fluency, is the elaboration of the French or Central European version of a very ancient migrant motif: it tells of the revenge taken thrice over by the peasant lad who had been given a beating by the haughty landlord. The humorous and sympathetic account of the adventures and tricks of Mattie in outwitting the nobleman, the psychological portraiture of the boy as he sets out on the path of bourgeois enrichment and is interrupted in his endeavour, the almost dramatic presentation of the ever increasing fear of the landlord who is his antagonist, make *Mattie the Gooseboy* the finest poetic narrative of the older Hungarian literature. The mutinous, ingenious, democratic hero of this short narrative poem competes in popularity with the heroes of the folk tales and is still alive in the nation's realm of fancy.

At the time of the Napoleonic Wars and of the essentially reactionary, feudal compromise of the nobility and the sovereign (between 1794 and 1815), the conservatively patriotic, national approach of the nobility became dominant in literature (with the sole exception of Csokonai who dropped out at the very beginning of the century). It was only after 1810 that a struggle against this trend was begun by Kazinczy and his small circle. This conservative, feudal nationalism wished to continue the cultivation of literature in Hungarian, but in the name of an originality that would adhere to the old traditions and strive to conserve the image and the reality of a feudal Hungary, a Hungary of privileges, obstinately warding off the emulation of all foreign and more advanced bourgeois examples. This nobiliary patriotism had, it is true, turned away from the Enlightenment, but it had become secularized and had by now almost completely abandoned its religious baroque garb. Accordingly, while advocating the superiority of the Hungarian nobleman—which it believed to be legally and historically established—this trend became absorbed in searching the past, in the cult of historical mementoes, not least in order to substantiate the principle of the independence of a nation, but its followers appraised both history and contemporary events in the light by moralising, of universal moral principles. It was in this period that Hungarian literature began to show differentiation according to the various trends of taste; there were these same divergent groups of the feudal-patriotic, conservative writers and those striving for bourgeois development and a reform of the language and of taste.

The establishment in poetry of the early historical school, with its adulation of the ancient glory of the nobility and of the moralist sentiment of life, was linked at the beginning of the century with the name of BENEDEK VIRÁG (1754-1830), a former member of the Order of St. Paul. The "holy old man"—he lived in Diogenes-like poverty—was the first great proponent of patriotism at Buda whose work pointed even beyond the ideals of the nobility. His moralistic verse in Graeco-Roman metre, in which he united the Horatian view of life with the cults of the nobility's glory and of bourgeois diligence, was rendered by its classicism exemplary up to the thirties of the century. Provincials on visits to Buda and the writers who lived in Pest-Buda*, frequently gathered round him.

* The capital of Hungary, originally consisted of two separate towns: Pest and Buda, which united and became known as Budapest in 1872.

It was thus that a fairly significant circle of writers was formed at Pest, who were to play a notable part both in initiating the national movement of romanticism and in making Pest-Buda a literary centre. They included the editor ISTVÁN KULCSÁR, the narrator and lyricist MIHÁLY VITKOVICS, the extremist feudal-nationalist historian ISTVÁN HORVÁT and the pioneer of romantic taste PÁL SZEMERE, who was an intimate friend of Kazinczy and of Kölcsey, the great ideologist and politician of the Reform Age. FERENC VERSEGHY, who lived in Buda and was then working on his poems inspired by Herder and on his great philological works, also maintained contact with them.

However, during the period of the compromise between the nobility and the sovereign, at the time of the economic boom of the Napoleonic age, literature tended to withdraw to the provinces. Provincialism, dispersion, the trammels of the county nobility's way of life, were both the cause and the accompaniment of the domination of a conservative, feudal nationalist approach.

The generally fashionable contents of this conservative, noble-men's approach (emphasis an ancient nobility, loyalty, an exclusive class-consciousness, the illusion of a Hungarian Canaan) were most successfully expressed by a Transdanubian landowner, SÁNDOR KISFALUDY (1772-1844), especially in his two-part cycle *The Loves of Himfy*. Kisfaludy had been to Italy and the South of France in the course of a fool-hardy military career, and rose above the average of the nobility. In his *Plaintive Love*—the first part of the cycle which scored a great success in 1800—he elegized upon the poet's longing for the return of the patriarchal way of life of the nobility, which had become critically endangered by the historic progress of the times. The model for the transfiguration of his cruel, cold-hearted lady was furnished by Petrarca's *Canzoniere*, which Kisfaludy read in Provence (Draguignan), where he spent part of his captivity. By publishing his *Himfy* immediately after his return, he developed the trend of nobiliary sentimentalism. Its verse form, the Himfy stanza, of Hungarian-style rhythm but evolved in pursuance of Petrarca's sonnets, a combination of elegiac and epigrammatic styles, contrib-uted considerably to his success. The historic pride of the nobility was increased and its tastes influenced in the pre-romantic sense by his verse legends, where he recalled the times of the national kings or of the Turkish invasions through love stories. His dramatic poems and patriotic "manorial" dramas also served to propagate the ideals and morals of the loyal, nationalist nobility, careful to safeguard their privileges.

The last great poet of the nobility, inspired by their crisis, was DÁNIEL BERZSENYI (1776-1836). Painful resignation streamed from his odes and elegies. Tied to his Transdanubian estate, he spent most of his life farming in Somogy County, in villages, not even seeking the publicity which he mainly obtained through the mediation of his friend Kazinczy, by means of the volume of his works printed in 1813. Yet he had begun his literary work, his solitary, clandestine verse-writing, during the closing years of the eighteenth century. His was an obstinate, introverted, eccentric poetic character and the appreciative but nevertheless reproachful and wry criticism of Kölcsey, in 1817, came as an almost fatal blow to his early failing health and melancholy humour. Kölcsey was the other great hypochondriac of the period, now writing in the capacity of a critic. Henceforward, in order to be able to hit back, Berzsenyi devoted himself to studying aesthetics.

The order in which his lyrical poetry developed can hardly be established. His main literary forms were the ode, elegy, song and epistle. His retired life and archaic erudition were infused with new colours and content through the friendship he contracted with Kazinczy and Kazinczy's Pest circle, particularly in reinforcing the enlightened ideas that had been part of his scholarship from the first (critique of religion).

In contrast to the idyllic conception which the ruling-class nobility entertained of itself (and which, though with elegiac overtones, was characteristic of Sándor Kisfaludy), Berzsenyi represented the heroic and at the same time elegiac-tragic version. He experienced the existence and meaning of his class not from without, but with the sentiments and dissatisfaction of those living within it with a heroic and tragic verve which also carried the seeds of disappointment, the seeds of elegy. In this respect the poet who strove to regenerate his class and elevate it morally to the great historical task it still had to face, who in his accusations against his class and nation also tormented himself, is a prototype of, and has several points of contact with, Kölcsey, the lyricist who expressed the "pangs of conscience" of the nobiliary nation, and Vörösmarty, who was in his Promethean revolt and inner struggle the national romantic. The ideals of Berzsenyi, the lyricist, were his longing for the antique moral values that could never return, for the erstwhile heroic, patriotic spirit of the Hungarian nobility, for a purified religion to be approached by way of reason, and for a moral awareness that would provide strength to face the universal process of decay. In his heroic odes and elegies which told of manly resignation, and in his lyric poetry he expressed the complexity of his soul, which yearned for some kind of permanent value and then was tormented by the realization of the ugly reality of decay. This accounts on the one hand for the imagination, pathos and ardour, whenever the glory of the nobility stood out at a particular turning point of history *(e.g.* during the Napoleonic Wars, in about 1805-07: *To the Hungarians* 2; *Battle of Ulm),* and on the other hand for the presentient moods—the childhood scene, the autumnal melancholy of declining manhood *(Fragment of a Letter to my Lady Friend),* the memory of a love that still torments his dreams, the image of evanescence conjured up by the approach of winter *(Approaching Winter)*—which are characteristic of the rest of his poetry. The concentration of feeling, the brilliant terseness of expression in the classical metre of his poetry, which he was able to handle magnificently and with novel linguistic power, made his work the summing-up of the old (classicist) school, while his contending sentiments, his search for prowess, his philosophy of life that had been born of turbulence and attained Stoic repose, made him a modern poet, a great lyricist and a pioneer of romanticism. It is no accident that his great poems, like *To the Hungarians* 1 and 2, *The Cemetery,* his ode *To Majláth,* pointing as they do to infinite distances and suggesting eternal repose and death even through the tremors of life, or his moving confession at the end of his career, *Poetry Then and Now,* serve to recall Foscolo and Hölderlin.

These moral ideals of Berzsenyi, which were at the same time his lyrical sources, were especially strongly held between 1800 and 1810. With his as yet healthy and extremely temperamental personality he was able to watch even from his farming solitude the decisive events of his country and of Europe with passionate attention. His power in creating a new style, in which with a richness of language and a balance between pessimism and optimism he demanded the moral and political regeneration of the "nobiliary nation," exercised a very great influence. This was effective not only on his junior contemporaries, such as Kölcsey and Vörösmarty, but also on Hungarian poetry in its rejuvenation at the beginning of the twentieth century, when it burst asunder the conservative bonds and the dullness of the imitators.

The greatest literary personality of this period, the second phase of the Hungarian Enlightenment, was FERENC KAZINCZY (1759-1831). Although not its greatest creative artist, for in this respect Csokonai and Berzsenyi transcend him, he was its greatest organizer, and became a "spiritual experience" for all of his contemporaries. He was the scion of a prominent family of the lesser nobility in the part of the country beyond the river Tisza (Bihar County), who, after thorough and many-sided studies extending also to the sphere of the fine arts, set out on a county and later a state administrative career and through his translations of Salomon Gessner and other sentimental authors (1788-1790) became the first and most effective propagator of the bourgeois concept of the new sensibility. As an active and militant organizer of the secular system of schools which had been decreed by the Emperor Joseph II, he soon earned the disapproval of his Calvinist co-religionists and of the conservatives of Hungary, and this was only deepened by his enlightened philosophical propaganda. Having broken with Batsányi in editing the *Magyar Múzeum* of Kassa, which thus became a paper of the nobiliary-national movement, Kazinczy established a separate short-lived periodical, the *Orpheus*, in which he advocated the teachings of Helvetius, Rousseau and the radical free-thinkers. These extreme views, which served to isolate him, and, in addition, his anti-feudalism brought him into close contact with the Hungarian Jacobines in whose fall he was to share. He served seven years in prison, and it was only after his release in 1801 that he started, at the age of 42, to carry out his real task in life. Széphalom, a small farm in Abaúj County where he lived for the rest of his life, was from 1805 for almost twenty years the centre of Hungarian literary life. The understanding of his wife, with their seven children, alleviated the condition of increasing poverty, due to the spending of all he had on literature and on subsidizing other authors and their books.

The nation-wide linguistic, literary and aesthetic movement of language reform was started by Kazinczy in 1811 by means of epigrams attacking the diehard intellectuals and writers (mainly of Debrecen) who declared that their ideal was to preserve life unchanged, with the unalterable (feudal) forms, the deep-rooted originality of Magyardom and an immunity from European thoughts and forms of taste. The matter went beyond a reform of the language (i.e. the formation of several thousand new Hungarian words and idioms for modern concepts which could hitherto not be expressed in Hungarian), and beyond simply increasing the vocabulary of Hungarian. The reform of the language essentially meant the assertion of the ideas of bourgeois progress in an atmosphere of feudal restoration, when the path of open political activity had been barred. It was thus that literature in Kazinczy's period, as a result of his tremendous organizational and literary labours, became the main instrument for changing the ideology, and the main mode of expression and motivating factor of national progress. The language reform soon divided the country into the purists of Debrecen and Transdanubia (where they were grouped round Sándor Kisfaludy), who opposed Kazinczy, and the Pest and generally urban intelligentsia who supported him.

Apart from the writers of Pest who have been mentioned, Kazinczy was backed in particular by JÁNOS KIS (1770-1846), a superintendent of the Lutheran Church, who was a clever popularizer of the Enlightenment and the author of fine memoirs. Their weapons in the struggle, beyond the pasquinades, parodies, essays and critiques, were mainly the masterly epigrams and epistles of Kazinczy. The struggle for the reform of the language was concluded in 1819 with a classical essay by Kazinczy on the principles of neology and orthology. The reform achieved complete victory.

This reform of the language also implied the stylistic evolution of the literary idiom. Kazinczy had for long striven to raise

Katona drew, however, on the most topical national problems, the hatred of foreign domination and of tyranny and the destitution of the serfs. Ban Bánk, acting as regent in the King's absence, returns from his tour of the country, and with his mind preoccupied by the complaints of the people oppressed by the foreigners surrounding the Queen, discovers two "plots" in the Royal Palace, both on the verge of consummation. The one is directed against the honour of his wife Melinda by the wanton younger brother of Queen Gertrudis. The other, woven by the rebellious middle stratum of the Hungarian nobility, threatens the Queen and the foreigners. In his endeavour to do justice as the custodian of the country, Ban Bánk overcomes the conspiracy but is unable to save Melinda from the lascivious Prince who achieves his aim by trickery. The sight of Melinda, outraged and driven to insanity, and the complaint of Tiborc, the stirring representative of peasant poverty, ripens Bánk's resolve to revenge himself on the Queen, who helped her brother to carry out his despicable deed and is the most guilty of the oppressors of the Hungarians. He triumphs over the Queen in a duel of words when she tries to call him to account, and when the offended, haughty, high-tempered woman seizes a dagger, Bánk twists it from her hand and kills her with it, thus giving vent to his long withheld passion, nourished by repression. His collapse is caused by his profound realization that the Hungarians of the palace revolution, which had broken out in the meanwhile and been quickly crushed, accuse him of murder, and he feels upon his soul the heavy burden of his arbitrary act—due in part to his emotions as an individual—which, however justified, cannot be reconciled with the regent's dignity and his own humanity. The violent death of his wife at the very hands of her tempter and the sentence of the King on his return, complete his spiritual downfall.

The tremendous dramatic tension, and the structure based on conflicts, make the first four acts of Katona's tragedy a perfect work, close to the Shakespearean standard. It is only in the fifth act that a certain decline may be felt owing to the insufficient psychological elaboration of Bánk's breakdown.

The stage qualities and psychological portraiture of Ban Bánk are of extraordinary power. Katona was objective in letting the action develop, excluding from his play everything that would have been the author's explanation and also what would, from the point of view of the action or of the feelings shown, have gone beyond what was absolutely necessary. His language is accordingly that of dramatic speech, which was on the whole still the clumsy Hungarian, previous to the reform of the language, not yet adapted to the classical ideal. For this reason, and even more because of the delay in staging his piece, he was at a disadvantage compared to the plays of Károly Kisfaludy, written in the reformed language and permeated by nobiliary patriotism, and therefore somewhat more to the general taste of the audience. Katona himself appreciated the great difficulties of his own dramatic writing, and of all Hungarian playwriting, in an excellent essay, a critique of the plays of Károly Kisfaludy.

Its brilliant character drawing, which in every detail authenticates the place and movement of figures who are rent by suppressed yet increasing passions, its great romantic power, and not least its patriotic and progressive trend, have made *Ban Bánk* the greatest Hungarian national tragedy. With music by Ferenc Erkel, it has become a national opera.

102

# THE REFORM AGE—ROMANTICISM (1820-1844)

The increasing opposition of the middle stratum of the laity to Austrian domination, the course of bourgeois development in Hungary, the spread of the ideals of liberalism due in part to the influence of the liberation movements in other countries, led from the 1820's to the inception of what was politically an increasingly eventful period of bourgeois reforms. The achievement of national independence and the abolition of feudalism were two inseparable tasks in the interest of the bourgeois transformation, for the solution of which the struggle had hitherto, and particularly at the time of the Enlightenment, been waged along two paths that only rarely met. The resistance of the nobility (on behalf of independence) proved narrow in respect of its democratic content, while the Enlightenment and the reform of the language, which relied on a relatively small part of the population for support, only rendered indirect service to the political cause of national independence. Yet without the fulfilment of the bourgeois programme of emancipation for the serfs, a national front of unity, the basis for the achievement of independence could not be established. The practical, political recognition of these connections, the fact that homeland and progress (Kölcsey) were now mentioned together, serves to differentiate the Reform Age from the earlier phases of the struggle. The serf movements, moreover, particularly that of 1831, gave a great impetus to political life.

Social progress was headed by the liberal nobility with medium estates who—though not without equivocation—stood for reform, representing the interests of the nation as a whole. The first phase of political development, which was also reflected in literature, lasted up to about the beginning of the thirties, to the appearance of István Széchenyi, while the second phase may be taken up to the appearance of Kossuth in 1841. Linking the problems of independence and of the liberation of the serfs with one another, the Opposition of the Diet of 1832-1836 went even beyond Széchenyi in the course he had begun. The bourgeois development and democratization of the nobiliary independence movement now began. This decade saw the birth of the first modern scientific and cultural institutions. In 1830 the Academy of Sciences, founded in 1825, began its work, and in 1836 the Kisfaludy Society, a literary association for the cultivation of Károly Kisfaludy's memory and of the national trend in literature he had set, was established. The National Theatre was opened in 1837. The guidance of literature was in the hands of the writers grouped round the *Tudományos Gyűjtemény* (Scientific Collection—1817-1841), the yearbook *Aurora* (1822-1837) and later the periodical *Athenaeum*. Károly Kisfaludy was followed in the first place by the triad of Vörösmarty, Bajza and Toldi. It was with their admiring support, for instance, that the two giants of Hungarian classical national literature, Petőfi and Arany appeared on the scene. Their names lead to the forties, when Kossuth on his release from prison set about broadening and uniting the camp of those fighting for national independence and a bourgeois transformation. This period witnessed the beginning of the modern development of Hungarian industry, trade and transport, and the formation of banks and commercial undertakings. Railway transport and steam shipping began to operate. All this was promoted by the agitation carried on in the *Pesti Hírlap*, a paper founded by Kossuth in 1841. The trend of an aristocracy being transformed into a class of big bourgeois agrarian capitalists, a trend started by Széchenyi, was replaced by an opposing movement of the lesser nobility, led by Kossuth and striving in the economic field for industrial capitalism. It was thus that there was formed within the Opposition the faction of Kossuth's independents, relying for support on the county nobility and that of the more bourgeois Centralists, based on the intelligentsia, both of which were opposed to the conservatives.

Only in the mid-forties did the democratic approach become separated from the earlier liberal trend of the nobility. The leaders

104

of the plebeian intelligentsia who had advanced beyond the liberalism of the nobles were Petőfi and his associates. They fought together with Kossuth for the triumph of the struggle for freedom, but at the same time primarily for the victory of their consistent bourgeois revolutionary aims. Petőfi's revolution in poetry, of 1844, pointed already beyond the reformist political conception of trying to unite the interests of the nobility and the peasantry. The "Company of Ten," organized in 1846 with Petőfi at its head, was an indication of maturing revolutionary awareness.

It was during this period that the liberal-bourgeois concept of the nation, with its admixture of feudal ideas, was formed. Its basis and its propagators were the middle stratum of the nobility. In contrast to Széchenyi's morally superior but less historical and highly idealistic concept of the nation, feudal nationalism advocated its mechanistic requirement for assimilation against the movements of the Slovaks and Rumanians who were striving to achieve national independence. It was at this stage that the leading ideologists and politicians of these movements (e.g. the Slovak Kollár and Stur and their school) rose with particular force against the Hungarian national policy. Setting their common interests aside, the bourgeois national movements of the Hungarians and of the so-called "nationalities" turned against one another, and their antagonism cast just as tragic a shadow on the Hungarian freedom struggle of 1848 as on the false, nationally prejudiced attitude of many of the excellent Hungarian authors of the period —honour due to the few exceptions: Széchenyi, Kölcsey, Petőfi and Kossuth (the latter in his advanced years).

The romanticism of the twenties and thirties, connected with the national reforms initiated by part of the nobility, developed the romantic national epic and drama as its main literary forms and opened the way for the historical novel. The second phase in development was the popular French-style romanticism of the forties which betokened a revolutionary trend. This phase marked at the same time the gradual evolution of realism in narration and of populism. The latter arouse out of interest in folk life and folk culture and became a peculiar political populism after the collection of folklore had begun. Inspired partly by romanticism and in the spirit of realism and revolutionary democratism, folk poetry had, in the forties, become the basis for Hungarian national, classical poetry (Petőfi, Arany).

It was during this period that the Hungarian literary language was finally evolved and regulated, to become in 1844 the country's official language (in place of Latin), thus permitting the newly developed literature to occupy its place in the modern sense in social and cultural life.

The break-through achieved by romanticism with respect to the earlier traditions took place between 1815 and 1825, with the contemporaneous appearance of the great works of Széchenyi, Károly Kisfaludy, Kölcsey and Vörösmarty.

The highest-level, romantic moral concept of nationhood was advanced by Count ISTVÁN SZÉCHENYI (1791-1860), whose thinking had by his very upbringing, and by his place in the rich aristocracy, been kept untainted by the lesser nobility's rhetorical praise of the "ancient glory" and the complacency of "extra Hungariam non est vita." His father, Count Ferenc Széchényi had founded the National Museum in 1802, and had himself opposed the ideas of the Hungarian nobility who did not look beyond their feudal privileges. The economic difficulties of the landowners of his own class, an appreciation of the general backwardness of the nation and particularly of the situation of the utterly destitute serfs, added to the experiences he gathered in the course of his great journeys in Western Europe (in England), prompted him to write his first great book *Credit* (1830). This book, discussing the obsoleteness of the country's institutions with deadly irony and in a rhapsodic style, had a tremendous effect. In place of the policy of venting grievances* and of the ceaseless repetition of problems in constitutional law, he urged a change in the concepts of civil law; and the nobility's property rights, villein services, etc., which had seemed unchangeable to the feudal mind, now became problems as a result of his writing. Beyond the ideas of domestic consumption based on universal prosperity, of a liberal constitution, etc., this and his following great works: *Enlightenment, Stadium,* formulated the outlines of a great national programme containing an inspired advocacy of self-knowledge and moral improvement,

---

* Grievances over the curtailment of the privileges of the nobility and of the nobiliary constitution.

and bitter contempt for the "Hungarian Fallow"—a symbol of Hungarian backwardness and passivity. The courage of his statement: "Hungary is not a country that has been, but that shall be," was not only daringly novel but also urged rebellion. All this soon led to a split in public opinion and the formation of a Conservative and a Reform party.

At first the centre of gravity of Széchenyi's activities lay in the formation of a public opinion that would be modern, on a European level, and at the same time consciously national. Next, in order to carry out his plans, he engaged in intensive and many-sided activity. The development of horse-breeding (with the concealed aim of boosting social activity), the foundation of social circles and of the Academy of Sciences, the establishment of a society for a permanent bridge between Pest and Buda (the later Chain Bridge, to be built under his auspices), the initiation of the regulation of the rivers Danube and Tisza, the inauguration of steam shipping and the many other ventures he propounded, together provide evidence of his immense energy and fervent devotion. It was for them that his later great opponent, Kossuth, called him the "greatest Hungarian."

His struggle against Kossuth was exacerbated and led to an open break between them after the mid-forties, resulting also in Széchenyi's isolation. He had tried, whatever happened, to avoid a conflict with the Court of Vienna, while Kossuth and the lesser nobility who were now under his influence, increasingly felt that the main ills of the nation could be remedied by achieving political independence. Kossuth's economic policies, demanding the establishment of national industries, were also objectively more advanced than Széchenyi's agrarian capitalist ideas. Thus Széchenyi, who was Minister of Transport in the independent Hungarian government of 1848, considered that settling the dispute through bloodshed was fatal and began to blame himself for having set the nation on the path that had led it to the War of Independence and the revolution. His pangs of conscience intensified in the autumn of 1848 to the pitch of mental disorder.

He spent his last years in the mental hospital of Döbling, near Vienna. It was only after 1856 that he regained his ability to work. In his *Great Hungarian Satire* he attacked mainly the decrees and failures of the autocracy, and when in 1857 Bach published the pamphlet *Rückblick* in adulation of his own policies, Széchenyi wrote *Ein Blick auf den anonymen Rückblick* and had it smuggled out to England and published anonymously, thus striking a blow at the government and exposing its trickery and lies. This book directed the attention of the police to Széchenyi; they pestered him with searches and threatened him, so that having already had difficulty in retaining his mental balance, he broke down and killed himself on April 7, 1860.

Széchenyi's path had been prepared by Károly Kisfaludy, whose activities, lasting hardly more than ten years, led to the victory of the principle of original national literature, to the reorganization of the forms of literature and the establishment both of its institutional foundations and of its main forms of expression.

KÁROLY KISFALUDY (1788-1830) had, in contrast to his elder brother Sándor, quitted the feudal form of life of the middle nobility early in the century and his wandering artist's life was that of a *déclassé* Bohemian gentleman. In 1817, still as a painter, he settled down in Pest. The great success of his drama *The Tartars in Hungary*, performed in spring 1819, was due to the fact that the audience consisted of members of the patriotic nobility. By this time he had also completed his charming comedy *The Suitors*, which also earned great praise. Prominent among his better dramas were *Voivod Stibor*, which, with a romantic plot taken from legend, had as its subject the tragic conflict between the peasantry and the landowner, and *Iréne* (1820), a drama of self-sacrificing patriotism, with a Greek subject. Kisfaludy's talent, his masterly stagecraft and fluent theatrical style, were at their best in his comedies. What made these so up to date, was mainly the conflict of the fathers, of the old, vanishing world of the nobles, comic in its fossilization, with the young, who demanded their freedom both in their professions and in love. The threads of these collisions—ultimately always adjusted—are not infrequently, according to the set patterns of Goldoni and Kotzebue, motivated by adroit young, or conceited old intriguers, the latter always becoming enmeshed in their own schemes. The character sketches, the typical comic features, the language in the dialogues which reveal the personalities of the characters, the atmosphere and the amusing situations, are all ingenuously original and Hungarian. In this theatrical reform the Hungarian language was indeed raised to the level of a stage language, but the idiom of true drama was not created by Kisfaludy, although he had managed after very meagre antecedents, to use a fluent, lively Hungarian conversational speech in his comedies, which could be adapted to the situation and characters of the protagonists. For satirical content—directed mainly against the obsolescent but full-flavoured figures of the noble class—but also for the vivacity of its action and the power of its comic situations and characters, it is mainly his three-act *Disappointments* (1828) which is prominent beside *The Suitors*, as well as a few ingenious one-act plays *(Three at the Same Time)*.

The study of characters revealed in dramatic situations led him to write short stories. These, although he wrote few, were excellent. His character sketch *Simon Ponderweight* of a Hungarian nobleman who can hardly move and is always late everywhere, is with its characteristic little episodes and the bold short-cuts in plot, a brilliant piece of satire. A short story which mocks at provincialism and pettiness *What Does the Stork Do?* is based on an anecdote.

His short stories and poems, including romantic ballads, popular songs and stirring national elegies, such as the famous *Mohács* (1824), were all contributions to the literary almanach which Kisfaludy first published at the end of 1821 and which became the main instrument of the organization of the new literature and for making Pest the literary centre.

The almanach *Auróra* (edited by Bajza after 1830 up to the mid-thirties when it lost its timeliness) was a substitute for the missing literary periodical. It gave equally copious space in the pages of its large, ornate volumes to the work of both the old and the youngest writers (Vörösmarty, Czuczor, Bajza, etc.). The literary forms it published (short stories, ballads, one-act plays, etc.) rendered yeoman service to the modernisation of literature and to the widespread dissemination or original—romantic—Hungarian writing. Later it caused a rift in the writers's camp, thus hastening the formation of a modern, differentiated literature, divided into parties and literary periodicals. It was the *Auróra* circle, headed by Vörösmarty, that eliminated the two previous provincial centres of literature (the circles of Kazinczy and S. Kisfaludy) and finally made Pest the capital of Hungarian literature.

FERENC KÖLCSEY (1790-1838) of Szatmár County was at first the most devoted disciple of Kazinczy and was later to become a great romantic thinker, poet and politician. Part of his poetry, essays and critiques date from before the great turning-point of the 1820's, the closing phase of the Enlightenment, and indeed at the outset of his career the radical basic texts of the French Enlightenment (Bayle, Rousseau, Holbach, Voltaire, etc., later Kant) exercised the deepest impression on him, so much so that he retained much of their heritage even in a later phase. His influence weighed rather in the fields of ideology, aesthetics, philosophy, and a liberal, democratic brand of politics, than in literary life, from whose increasingly more modern forms in the capital he generally remained remote.

Having lost his parents, he completed his schools in Debrecen in solitude and handicapped by his disability (he was blind in one eye). He first went to Pest in 1810, where he became known to the friends of Kazinczy, and to Berzsenyi when on a visit, as an eccentric, fastidious, cosmopolitan young man of a retiring disposition and possessing extraordinary erudition in French and Greek. Like Berzsenyi, he too seemed strange to the common-sense, gay, nationalistic Hungarians of Pest. But even the two great hypochondriac spirits, Berzsenyi and Kölcsey, both equally inclined to romanticism, repelled one another from the very first instant of their acquaintance. Berzsenyi had become obsessed with the ancient beauty of Hungarian nobility, Kölcsey with the chimera of French-style bourgeois progress. The former was an inspired poet, more instinctive in his passions, the latter a scholar and an artist of philology, polished, sensitive and intent on concealing his ego. Indeed the conflict of the two soon came to a head.

Kölcsey, who had at the beginning of the 1810's expressed his longing to quit the "barren Hungarian fallow" in sentimental poems in a halting vein, only very rarely rose to a Goethian purity in his search for an ideal and in disciplining his own grief.

110

FERENC KÖLCSEY (1790-1838)

He first appeared before the public at Kazinczy's side, as a poignant debater on behalf of the struggle for language reform. Later he exercised unjustly biased criticism against the great art of Csokonai, and though he himself had liked it and absorbed it in his own poetry, he now took it to task for its provincial, peasant popularity, which he called vulgarity. Still more disagreeable was his criticism of the severely ailing Berzsenyi, who was about to give up writing and whom he reproached for his grandiloquence and the narrow compass of his emotions, though he had held the lyricist in high esteem and made use of his writing too. His criticisms were to a considerable extent aimed at the conservatives who had taken cover behind those who were their subject. This practice, however, only led to Kölcsey becoming isolated from the general views of his day. His premature criticisms, in which he demanded psychologically based, careful, artistic work and was not content with the sole merit of a work having been written in Hungarian, turned public opinion against him. When he finally also deserted Kazinczy, advocating national originality in place of the programme of translations, he brought upon himself a temporary exclusion from literary life.

From 1818 to 1821 Kölcsey was silent, writing nothing, but savouring the tones of the folk-song in the forlornness of his village of Cseke, visited by the wild floodwaters of the county. He turned away from the aristocratic, Goethian humanism of Kazinczy. With the ending of the compromise between the Hapsburgs and the nobility, he became more disillusioned with the Holy Alliance and more encouraged by the freedom movements of Europe. It was, therefore, a Kölcsey reinforced in spirit by the folk trend who returned to literary life in 1821, with folk-songs which he was the first to introduce in Hungarian literature, and with great political poems. Of these the *Hymnus* (1823) later became the Hungarian national anthem. His *Freedom* ode, with its Jacobine sentiments and its condemnation of cowardice, as well as his great poems of hatred for tyranny and of faith in the poet's vocation, were born side by side with the pessimistic poem *Vanitatum Vanitas*, showing at the same time that deep down he had always appreciated his responsibility in the fight for his bourgeois ideals as part of his own class, shoulder to shoulder with a basically lackadaisical, slow-moving, reactionary nobility. With him the tragic picture of the world entertained in the overall views of the nobility aroused an even more profound crisis of self-torment than in Berzsenyi. It no longer inspired him to elegies, but only to a curse, to prophesying the death of the nation. It was this that he expressed in his great poems written at the end of his life, in the second part of the thirties *(Zrínyi's Second Song)*, after his lyrical writing had again been interrupted between 1827 and 1836.

The reason for this interruption lay in his ever increasing activity in the fields of aesthetics, criticism, philosophy and politics. In 1826, in the high-standard literary and critical periodical *Élet és Literatura* (Life and Literature), which he edited together with Szemere, he published a paper under the title *National Traditions*. This was concerned with matters of principle in cultural and literary philosophy, set a programme, and also analysed the Hungarian national character. Its essence is that original national poetry can only be refreshed and recreated on the foundation and model of folk-poetry, thus spanning the unhealthy gap between the public and the poet. It was also at this time that he wrote his aesthetic treatises on the tragic and the comic, which have remained fundamental to this day, and his great essays on philosophy *(Greek Philosophy)* and the critique of religion, as well as a theoretical disquisition on the tasks of criticism.

By 1829 he had entered the arena of county politics. In two great speeches he treated the problems of the tax-paying people, and of whether the impoverished people could be interested in the defence of the homeland. In order to make them interested, they must be given rights and property.

With the great rhetorical power of a man who has triumphed over his own weaknesses and doubts, he was to develop this conception colourfully at the Diet of 1832-36, in the first two years of which he was the leader of the democratic nobiliary opposition and the target of the Hapsburg and Hungarian noblemen's reaction. It was on his speeches, aimed at achieving full freedom of religion, the introduction of Hungarian as the state language, aid for the oppressed Poles, and above all at the liberation of the serfs, that the young Kossuth and the young people who were to be the leaders of 1848 were reared.

Kölcsey's philosophical and political testament, the *Parainesis*, was composed on the ruins of his shattered hopes, when the reaction in his country forced him to resign from the Diet and had him surrounded by informers. This is the finest democratic Hungarian work on education, uniting in its philosophy the idealism of the romantics with the great lessons of the Enlightenment. Writing in the spirit of the ideals in public life of Greek democracy and the French Revolution, he analysed for his nephew the moral requirements of a life of work ; of the love of virtue, the homeland and the world at large ; of noting organic development and honouring the revolutions.

Shortly after this he died, while writing some short stories of poignant social criticism *(Hunting Lodge)*, and the tremendous legal defence of Miklós Wesselényi, one of the greatest progressive politicians of the period, against the Austrian autocracy. His highly disciplined, pure and clear-cut personality had an enormous influence on his environment and his disciples. The two basic political trends which had been present together in him—the development of democratization and of the independence struggles of the county nobility—tended to separate his disciples from one another and even caused conflict among them. Eötvös and the Centralists came to oppose Kossuth's national policy in which the latter relied on the county nobility for support.

The leading personality of the process inaugurated by Károly Kisfaludy, of the organization of Hungarian romanticism, was MIHÁLY VÖRÖSMARTY (1800-1855). He was also the greatest creative artist of the whole of Hungarian romantic verse, lyrical poetry, epic writing and drama (including the translation of Shakespeare and also stage criticism).

Vörösmarty was of noble origin, one of the children of an impoverished father, an estate steward beset by cares. Already as an adolescent and later during his career as a tutor in the provinces and at Pest (where he also managed to obtain a university degree), but especially at the time of the dire need of his family resultant on his father's death, he developed common-sense and a calm approach, learning to subdue his temper and his

8                                                                                       113

flights of fancy. His experiences in the early twenties when a tutor on the large estate of the Perczel family in Tolna County, served both to nurture and to freeze his illusions. It was here that he joined the anti-Austrian movement of the county nobility. The hopeful prospects of political life which, with the temperament of the nobility's resistance, offered certainty of the achievement of national idependence, and a hopeless love for Etelka, daughter of the rich landowner, inspired him to write a tremendous national epic, unleashing his sensuous imagination. Proceeding in the footsteps of Virág and Berzsenyi, his historical tragedy *The Outlaws* (1823-28) already made him a significant poet, but *The Flight of Zalán*, a romantic national epic in hexameters, consisting of ten songs (publ. 1825), through satisfying the long-felt requirement for an epic about the conquest of the country, raised him among the great national poets. His theme of the country's conquest by the Hungarians—which had after a few fragmentary antecedents *(e.g.* Csokonai) been the subject of full works, though poetically limited, by Sándor Székely and Gergely Czuczor before Vörösmarty—concentrated public attention on the most effective feat of national heroism in such a way that it became, in a topical construction, a justification both of an independent state autonomy and also of the ancient property-rights of the nobility in the eyes of his contemporaries. Following in the mainstream of the earlier Hungarian epic traditions, and keeping to the models of the classical naive epic and of Ossian, this brilliantly coloured moving and heroically dramatic work is lyrically suggestive. This is due mainly to its love-story ; it is this that serves to amplify the elegiac feeling, which is incidentally present even at the depths of the otherwise heroic battle scenes crowded together with a certain lack of economy. The optimistic ring of his objective epic (the triumphant battles) is almost at odds with the elegiac recollections of the past, and with the morbid, idyllic love that runs separate from the warlike events. The basic web of the epic is torn by a dilemma of public and private life, there is a lyrical quality about this work in which Vörösmarty's extravagant imagination and the Hungarian mythology he created meet with the imagination of the people and the historical concept of the nobility.

114

the relative gone to distant parts. He adopted Kossuth's programme which advocated a unity of interests and cooperation between nobleman and serf; and even the feverish rhythm of his drinking songs expressed his belief and hope—though his heart was rent with doubts and his mind filled with rhapsodic thoughts —that the Hungarian people were unified in their readiness for constructive work. He propounded a patriotism with a new meaning and a new content—the homeland of "worker, serf and poor man" as well as that of "the glorious," even for Hungary's fastidious, foreign-hearted aristocratic ladies. And in his satires *(Fate and the Hungarian)*, he branded the effeminacy, degeneration and torpor of the nobility, in order to fortify the new bourgeois national characteristics. His greatest poems, however, were devoted to his inner philosophical struggle, to seeking the sense of man's existence. In *Thoughts in the Library* (1844), he posed the terrible conclusion ("While millions are born for misery, A few thousand would have bliss on earth") and the resultant passionate denial of the value of culture, with the teachings of the utopian socialists, and drew attention to the great tasks of the nation whose existence the struggle was to establish and to secure. With enormous power he combined brilliant and cruelly rough symbols with the images of reality and the phases of the poet's rebellious and despondent judgment. Another powerful though profoundly pessimistic poem *Men* (1846) served, with its startling tone, to express his horror at the bloody collision of class antagonisms, and at the contradictions of class society. It was also at about this period that his lyrical love poetry attained fulfilment in relation to his wife, Laura Csajághy. This was particularly so in *Dream*, with its cosmic counterpoint, where he laid the whole world of his imagination at her feet, and in *To a Dreamer* (1843), written in anxiously resigned tones, in which he cautioned his young wife against vain illusions.

In 1848-49 Vörösmarty, who had in his political articles also stood for the War of Independence and the revolution, and had welcomed the freedom of the press in a lovely poem, wrote but little. Although politically he did not share the plebeian revolutionary spirit of Petőfi, whom he had discovered and backed, he sided with the War of Independence to the end. He was forced

117

into hiding, then lived at Pest till the end of his life, in the deaf silence of oppression, beset by grave financial worries, his nerves shattered. Perturbed in spirit, he now wrote one of his great poems, *Preface* (1851), the vision of the ruthless war, which had drowned in blood his creative Magyardom. He put the crown on his entire *oeuvre* in his last and perhaps greatest lyrical poem, *The Old Gipsy* (1854). In the wild rhythm of his despair and surging doubts, casting himself as an old gipsy violinist who is about to die, he tells of his visions and hallucinations of disaster (disaster, indeed for all mankind), humanistic optimism breaking through his pain at the very end of the poem. This romantic vision of fear of the "curse of man's hatred of fellow man" and of the triumph of the tyrant is concluded by a passionate and confident reaffirmation of life, with the painful realization of eternal struggle and the hope that the tempest will once, ultimately, be stilled.

When the poet died in 1855, tens of thousands of people turned out for his funeral. This was the first mass demonstration at the time of the autocracy.

Gergely Czuczor and János Garai, two characteristic, romantic and highly influential poets of the Reform Age and the War of Independence, may be considered followers of Vörösmarty.

GERGELY CZUCZOR (1800-1866), a Benedictine schoolmaster and the son of serfs, came into grave conflict with his superiors in the Order on a number of occasions, owing to his progressive national views. Having to conform to the dominant nobiliary national opinions of the period, his gifts could not develop to the full. In a heroic hexameter poem which treated of an important and compact episode of the conquest of the country *(Battle of Augsburg*—1824), he forestalled Vörösmarty. His later heroic poems show the influence of Vörösmarty. In the mid-thirties he wrote highly effective national ballads *(Szondy, Hunyadi,* etc.*)* and folk songs, with the hidden aim of educating the people. They were important in the transformation of literary tastes, and many became a part of folklore. His genre pieces reflect considerable modernity *(Country Girl in Pest)*, and this is also a feature of the poems praising diligence and the middle-class virtues, and of the anti-feudal satires which express his liberal political views.

118

As an editor of the Academy's *Great Dictionary* (together with János Fogarasi), he was able to live more freely in the forties. An indication of his radical development was his very effective march *Alarm* (1848) written for the War of Independence, a poem for which he had to spend several years in prison during the period of despotism.

JÁNOS GARAI (1812-1853) was a characteristically middle-class poet who joined cause with the romanticism of the national reforms. For the Hungarian urban citizenry, he interpreted Vörösmarty's great subjects and passion in a style much like the German Biedermeier. He was outstanding as a newspaper editor, and his journalistic *feuilletons* and genre pieces were more original and livelier than his poetry. His name has been remembered for a ballad about Kont, the historic hero of nobiliary resistance, and particularly for a humorous narrative poem, *The Veteran* (1843), in which he formulated the vivid popular character of János Háry, the discharged soldier and inveterate liar. He remained a writer of poems on historical subjects in the Biedermeier mood to the end of his life, and his importance lay not only in his verse propaganda of the problems of the nobiliary reform movement, but also in the fact that in 1848 he supported in his poems the nation in arms on behalf of the bourgeoisie.

Vörösmarty led the literary life of the country together with Bajza and Toldy, from the thirties to the mid-forties. JÓZSEF BAJZA (1804-1858) was, next to Kölcsey and Gyulai, the greatest Hungarian critic. After his theoretical essay on the epigram (1828), he conducted polemics of national significance in defence of the civil liberties of literature. First, in the so-called encyclopaedia case (1830), in connection with the Hungarian encyclopaedia published by the bookseller Ottó Wigand, he gave an annihilating reply to GÁBOR DÖBRENTEI (1785-1851), an erudite, active organizer but unprincipled author of the period, and then to JÓZSEF DESSEWFFY (1771-1843), the old Kazinczyist aristocrat, who intervened on Döbrentei's behalf. Bajza enunciated the principle of equality in literature, and through his struggle for the establishment of a "writer's republic" where all writers were equal, dealt a blow of the greatest severity to feudal prejudices.

In another important dispute (over the ownership of the

119

*Aurora)* Bajza elucidated the writer's copyright, which the law did not defend at this stage, and achieved its recognition by public opinion at large. The problems raised in his controversies, the admirable purposefulness with which he organized the discussions by extending them to ever further participants, the deliberate mobilization of public opinion, his ardent democratic spirit, and his razor-sharp logic and irony in debate, show Bajza to have been one of the most attractive and militant characters of the period. The *Kritikai Lapok* (Critical Papers) which he edited (1831-1836) became the forum for great controversies. On the basis of his experiences as a theatre manager it was he who— beside Vörösmarty—established systematic and penetrating Hungarian stage criticism, fighting for the hegemony of French drama as against the slushy German romantic works. At the time of the Revolution he edited the daily *Kossuth Hírlapja* (Kossuth's Paper) and was thus the intermediary between the nation's leader and the masses. The rather average sentimental quality of his lyrical work was, up to the Revolution, only occasionally superseded by the flamboyant patriotic feeling which expressed the radical trend of the lesser nobility's progress (he wrote some fine poems on the Polish freedom struggle), but in 1848-49 he rose above the average in his confessions of revolutionary force and in the poems which convey the despair of defeat in moving terms. Like Vörösmarty he died with a diseased mind.

Bajza's close friend, FERENC TOLDY (Schedel) (1805-1875), born of a German family of burghers at Buda, became the "father of the historiography of Hungarian literature" and was the first to evaluate Vörösmarty's works critically (1827). Toldy also engaged in considerable critical activity up to the War of Independence, mainly in the *Figyelmező* (Observer) which he edited (1837-1840). In his anthology *Handbuch der ungarischen Poesie* (1828), he was the first to present the best of Hungarian literature to the foreign reader, with the first German-language critical survey of its development, written in the romantic spirit. After the War of Independence he devoted all his efforts to writing histories of literature and monographs and to editing texts. His increasingly elaborate histories of literature in the sixties were the first—after very meagre antecedents—to present a systematic and detailed history of the development of Hungarian literature, making use of the lessons of Gervinus and seeing the culmination of Hungarian literature in the work of Vörösmarty.

The most consistent and—next to Kölcsey—the theoretically best-grounded and most original Hungarian critic and aesthete was JÁNOS ERDÉLYI (1814-1868), of serf parentage, who as the editor of the critical organ of the Kisfaludy Society, the *Magyar Szépirodalmi Szemle* (Hungarian Literary Review), introduced a school of criticism based on strictly aesthetic considerations. Through his poetry and essays (on romanticism and on the folk trend) he prepared Petőfi's path. A characteristic feature of his critical work was his consistent application of the Hegelian dialectical method. Turning against Schiller's idealistic aesthetics, his typology in effect voiced the requirements of realism. Particularly important was his activity in collecting folk songs, the results of which were published in the three volumes of *Folksongs and Legends*, which he edited (1846-48).

The controversies over dramaturgy (over theatrical quality, with Bajza taking the side of French, and Henszlmann of German drama) indicate that the long cultural struggle for a permanent National Theatre had now been concluded and that the National Theatre, which was opened in 1837, had become the home of excellent actors (G. Egressy, Lendvay, Megyery, etc.) and of Hungarian dramatic culture. The demand of the period for realism was no longer satisfied by the basically nobiliary approach of K. Kisfaludy and his historical drama. Historical subjects only continued in the historical comedy, particularly in the recollections of the humorous, adventurous events connected with the popular national monarch Matthias Hunyadi. A far more direct reflection of Hungarian social realities was the political comedy, whose most outstanding exponent was IGNÁC NAGY (1810-1854), an excellent journalist and renowned satirical novelist. Ignác Nagy's most successful comedy, *County Elections* (1843), in which he ridiculed both the feudal election campaigns and the pseudo-democrats of the nobility, scored a great hit and founded a veritable school, influencing not only the world of drama, but even the narrative works of János Arany and József Eötvös. The development of the medium-weight social dramas and tragedies as a

121

literary form indicates the increasing sharpness of social and political struggles consequent upon the swift bourgeois transformation of Hungary's capital in the forties.

Apart from the up-to-date, democratically inspired pieces of Kölcsey's disciple KÁROLY OBERNYIK (1815-1855), special attention is also due to some of the tragedies of ZSIGMOND CZAKÓ (1820-1847), who committed suicide as a young man. He strove, by uniting the romantic "poetic image" with an analysis of destinies and characters, to achieve a striking effect on the stage. It was perhaps in *Leona* (1846), a piece with a pantheistic approach and psychological in its realism, valuable for its powerful, romantic social criticism, that he most effectively achieved this aim.

In the thirties and forties the novel came to the fore, in succession to the outdated heroic verse epics. Due to the peculiar development of Hungarian society it failed to become a representative literary form, but with its greatest exponent, Eötvös, it attained to the classical heights which were to appear in their full majesty in the revolutionary, popular and realistic narrative poetry of Petőfi and Arany.

A great impetus was given to the development of the Hungarian novel by a number of factors: the overall effect of the break-up of feudal relations in a commodity-producing nobiliary economy; the increasingly urgent problems of a bourgeois transformation and of the country's relations to Austria; the formation of a bourgeois-type urban intelligentsia as well as the adoption of juridicial and political experiences from abroad and the influence of foreign novels.

At a time when the tradition of Károly Kisfaludy's short stories was still alive, it was ANDRÁS FÁY (1786-1864) who published the first effective social novel of the Reform Age, *The House of Bélteky* in 1832, appeared on the scene contemporaneously with Károly Kisfaludy; in fact his comic story *The Strange Testament* in 1818 even cut ahead of the latter. His lively, folk-flavoured stories, with their liberal trend, and their mockery of the fashionable sentimentalism exercised considerable influence even on Széchenyi. This was particularly true of *His Tales*, published in 1820. His didactic novel, *The House of Bélteky* brought the broad circles of his readership closer to the

122

burning issues of the period. The literary activities of Fáy gave readers their first experience of an indigenous author who not only undertook excursions to the fields of the short story or the novel, but built up a continuously expanding and maturing list of works as a novelist. *The House of Bélteky* uses the conflict between a father and his son to reveal the antagonism between the conservative, older generation of nobles, and the younger ones who had broken with the old ways, in a manner closely interwoven with highly romantic motifs but not without considerable realism in the portraiture of the old Bélteky and his environment. The wide compass of his public activities made Fáy (who was incidentally the founder of the first Hungarian Savings Bank) one of the most significant reformers, Széchenyi's veritable lieutenant.

In *The Village Notary* by Eötvös, the classical work which marked the culmination of the development of the social novel aimed at furthering the cause of reform, it is easy to recognise the tendentious typology of Fáy's main novel, taken from county life, as being the fundamental pattern on which Eötvös constructed a world of complete and authentic human destinies. Beyond Eötvös, the anecdotal elements of Jókai's artistic novel-writing also permit the influence of Fáy's modest but pioneering art to be felt.

The Transylvanian aristocrat baron MIKLÓS JÓSIKA (1794-1865), in contrast to Fáy, introduced the romantic historical novel in the mid-thirties. This was at a time when the views held by the reform movement on history became important moral and political factors in the progress of the middle stratum of the nobility. European events (Napoleon, the Paris Revolution of 1830, etc.), and the increasing tension between Vienna and Hungary accelerated the modernization of the historical awareness of the middle stratum of the nobility, who were in any case receptive towards history. Jósika, following closely in the wake of Sir Walter Scott, applied his original gifts for narrative, colouring and description, to treating almost all the important phases of Hungarian history, from the age of the Hunyadis in the fifteenth century, to the *Kuruc* movements of the malcontents at the beginning of the eighteenth. The title of his first work was *Abafi* (1836), and it earned considerable praise from the critics and

123

obscured the significance of Fáy. In the framework of an evolutionary sketch of the moral improvement of the young nobleman Olivér Abafi, it takes the reader back to late sixteenth-century Transylvanian history. The characters and events arise mostly from the historical situation which is portrayed, and the novel does indeed have a historical atmosphere, though the author considered that his primary aim in writing novels should be a moral one. Like his master, Scott, he devoted great attention to the detailed precision of his descriptions; sometimes, in fact, they even obscure certain features of his accurate psychological portraits. He was never able to surpass his *Abafi* in later works. Other noteworthy historical novels he wrote were *The Czechs in Hungary* (1839) and *Ferenc Rákóczi II* (1848-1851). The first is an account of the survival of Hussite traditions and forces, and of the accession to the throne and the struggles fought by King Matthias, written without nationalist prejudice against the Czechs, in the framework of a romantic undertaking by a Hungarian knight to regain his honour. The second, an outline of the youth of the great national sovereign and champion of freedom, also draws a romantic picture of the popular participation in the *Kuruc* struggle for freedom and in its policy of fraternity between nationalities. In Jósika's later historical novels the traits of extreme romanticism and of adventure for its own sake came to predominate. His writing on social themes from life in Pest was characterized by the influence of Sue's French romanticism, with a plethora of extravagant events and horrors.

Jósika was one of the most prolific Hungarian narrators, but from the mid-forties the influence of his works waned considerably. By this time Eötvös had come to supersede him, and shortly afterwards Jókai's popularity far surpassed his. By the late forties, his works had grown insipid and outdated. His decline must also have been hastened by his emigration, for as one of the consistent advocates of the principles of the War of Independence he left the country, living at Leipzig, Brussels, and later Dresden to the end of his life. It was from there that he sent home his novels, under a pseudonym.

Beside the two trends of Fáy and Jósika, that of the social and of the historical novel, it is also worth noting the name of

JÓZSEF GAÁL (1811-1866). He was active in the thirties when he staged Gvadányi's *Notary* and wrote his wildly romantic novel *Ilona Szirmay* (1836), and his prose *Pictures of the Plains* through which he became Petőfi's immediate precursor in the discovery of the Plains.

A more important, increasingly isolated literary personality was PÉTER VAJDA (1808-1846), a democratic thinker and narrator, whose approach was derived from the natural sciences. His novels and stories were the most characteristic of the orientalistic trend of romanticism, for in them, as a deliberate piece of anachronism, he made his medieval heroes talk of the teachings of Kant and Rousseau, thus indulging in extreme irony over his own period in which all their teachings were still unfulfilled. His famous *Speeches on Morals*, delivered at the College of Szarvas from 1843, are among the most important documents of the progressive historical and scientific awakening of the age. Petőfi honoured him as a kindred spirit and called him "the most faithful child of nature" and the "hero of independence."

# POST-ROMANTICISM AND THE
# EVOLUTION OF REALISM
# (1844-1867)

Petőfi, who held Péter Vajda in such high esteem, represented the apex of nineteenth-century Hungarian literature and of the period of political awakening. Beside him, the works of his confidential friend and the recipient of his ideas, the great epic and lyric poet János Arany, and those of the novelist József Eötvös, signified the triumph of realism in Hungarian literature. This brilliant upsurge and rich efflorescence was essentially centred on the few years prior to the bourgeois revolution and national War of Independence of 1848-49. The aims of the bourgeois revolution were partly achieved through the emancipation of the serfs, but the national War of Independence failed, and its heroes died, emigrated or became silent in a profound crisis. However, during this considerably longer period which ensued after the initially triumphant War of Independence, the continuity of literature was not interrupted, despite the revival of the romantic trends which had been relegated to the background in the forties.

The transition to capitalism was completed by the victorious counter-revolution. The serfs were given hardly any land, the transition to wage labour was limited, the peasantry were robbed in numerous ways—the large estates continued to implement their interests without hindrance. "The capitalist transformation, which was confined to the interests of the big bourgeoisie, was most closely intertwined with the safeguarding of the political and economic interests of the monarchy and the feudal aristocracy," states Professor Aladár Mód, an outstanding scholar of the Hungarian independence movements. It was thus that the oppressive remnants of feudalism, those of absolutism and the oppression of the nationalities, were maintained.

The surrender at Világos was followed by the reign of terror of the foreign dictatorship, with a long series of executions. However, the Hapsburg dynasty did not succeed in its last attempt to weld its heterogeneous empire into a unified whole. Its internal economic and political instability also resulted in the failure of its great-power foreign policy (Solferino, 1859). The public acclamation of great national poets, the stubborn recollection of the memory of Petőfi, the vast mass demonstration of March 15, 1860 and that which followed it, the persecution and suicide of Széchenyi, the fifteen-year prison sentence of Táncsics—these were the threatening accompaniments to the events that led to the fall of the autocracy. A compromise between Hungary and Austria on the pre-1848 basis could not successfully be concluded—the landed nobility insisted on the bourgeois constitution of 1848, and in this even the conservative anti-revolutionary publicists (e.g. Zsigmond Kemény) agreed with them. The sovereign dissolved the Diet which demanded the restoration of 1848 in this spirit, and it was only in the mid-sixties that another attempt was made at a compromise. Finally the party of Ferenc Deák (1803-1876), a highly talented politician of outstanding moral qualities and intentions, brought about the Compromise of 1867, after the defeat suffered by the Austrian armies at Sadova.

The years from 1840 to the early 60's were those of the greatest period of Hungarian literature, which its historians later called the period of "national classicism"—a name to which exception may be taken on several ideological grounds, but which was not adopted without reason. During its first half Petőfi and beside him Arany and Eötvös developed Hungarian literary realism at a high artistic level, but the fifties also belong to the great period of Hungarian literature. Beside the popular realism then undergoing a process of transformation, the trend of national romanticism was still a dominant factor at this stage. By now it was the desire for conservation, to salvage and preserve, which was characteristic of both the cultural movements and of literature. Some writers taught that the nation should come to know itself and that illusions should be abandoned, and this view undoubtedly contained more than a hint of their disappointment in the revolution and even of their counter-revolutionary views. The revolutionary, popular realist tendencies thus diverged in the direction of considerable moral idealization. It was in this sense that romanticism and realistic writing were still intertwined with each other. At the same time Jókai's novels still propagated the great ideals of the War of Independence and the bourgeois development of 1848 to broad sections of the reading public.

The greatest lyrical poet of the fifties was János Arany. The two representative novelists of the period—with an intercommunion of romanticism and realism—were Zsigmond Kemény and Mór Jókai, who continued to live as each other's opponents. Pál Gyulai, who avoided intensive social conflicts and was the advocate and codifier of a realism that spoke in the name of moral ideals and with psychological faithfulness, was after Kölcsey and Bajza the century's last great Hungarian critic. The greatest dramatist of the period was Imre Madách, author of *The Tragedy of Man.*

In the forties, Hungarian publicistic writing and narrative prose turned with increasing interest to contemporary themes, while in fiction critical realism was maturing. The eventful political life of the times, the process of urban development and the literary journals all attracted the writers to topical matters and new, modern literary forms were evolved, journalism was modernized, the leading article and *feuilleton* established, genre pieces, humourous skits, feature novels, etc., came to be written. As a result of Kossuth's political agitation, the camp of nobiliary liberalism was expanded, and new, more progressive party groupings were established—that of the Centralists, and later the group of Revolutionary Democrats.

LAJOS KOSSUTH (1802-1894) was born at Monok in Zemplén County. He was the leading politician and most effective orator of the War of Independence. As a young lawyer, he first distinguished himself at the Diet of 1832-1836 and in 1837 was imprisoned for his hand-written political paper. On his release in 1840, he was already the most popular politician. The nobility of the Opposition were ardently enthusiastic for his paper, the *Pesti Hírlap* (Pest Journal), established in 1841, through which he introduced modern bourgeois publicistic writing in Hungary. By creating contact with the masses, he thus gave great impetus to the course of development which was to lead to the revolution. After the Diet of 1844 he abandoned the editorship of the *Pesti Hírlap* and entered on the course of social organization. His Protection Society movement strove for the establishment of independent industries and a domestic market—in sharp opposition to the interest of the large estates and of the Austrian manufacturing industries, which insisted on free trade.

The programme of the coordination of interests (which he developed partly in pursuance of Kölcsey), aiming at the elimination of the villein socages which were the main reason for the eternal friction between the nobility and the serfs, and so at the establishment of the national unity front which alone could win the country independence, thus became ever more concrete in the course of the forties. This coordination—or as he termed it, unification—of interests, which advocated the introduction of universal taxation and the compulsory manumission of serfs against compensation, went beyond the nobiliary limits of the reform movement.

The Protection Society actually played its historical part in preparing the way for the establishment of the Opposition Party. This party considered that its main task was to reinforce resistance in the counties and to achieve the fall of the government. The struggle with Széchenyi had now been finally fought, and Széchenyi had been left without supporters.

At the Diet of 1847-48 Kossuth gained a leading role. It was he who worked out the recommendation for the appointment of the first responsible cabinet. His real leading part began with the organization of the defence of the homeland and of the War of Independence. When Széchenyi, Eötvös and others—taking fright at the preparations for a military occupation—would have wished to enter on a path of reconciliation with the Vienna Government, Kossuth in one of his greatest speeches persuaded the National Assembly to vote for the establishment of an army of two hundred thousand men, and his personal agitation also resulted in the peasantry rallying to the banner. His campaign against the peace party in Debrecen in 1849 was a continuation of his struggle against the capitulators and appeasers. A nobleman, he was an adherent of the bourgeois revolution—he did not,

9

it is true, wish for the course of events to be determined by the masses of the people at Pest, but he knew and appreciated that the popular movement, together with all its more radical demands, was a powerful basis of his national endeavours as a fighter for freedom. He was not afraid to say to the faint-hearted or to the demagogues: "Do not be so afraid of anarchy that you should fear freedom itself!"

From the summer of 1848 he acted on his own in the Batthyány Government, in making financial, military and propaganda preparations for the country's defence, and when from September he undertook, with the support of the left wing, to head the Defence Committee, the actual power of government passed into his hands. Without him, without his superhuman work of organization and leadership, 1848-49 would not have become the heroic War of Independence, over which the best of contemporary mankind became so enthusiastic. Marx and Engels spoke of him in tones of admiration, in the *Neue Rheinische Zeitung* : "This is the first occasion in the course of the 1848 revolutionary movement, the first occasion since 1793, that a nation, surrounded by superior counter-revolutionary forces, has dared to pit revolutionary fervour against cowardly counter-revolutionary fury . . . This is the first occasion for a long time that we have come across a truly revolutionary character . . . who is for his nation a Danton and a Carnot in one person—Lajos Kossuth. The mass rising, the national manufacture of arms, paper money, making short shrift of all those who impede the revolutionary movement, the permanence of the revolution—in fact all the main features of the glorious year of 1793 may again be discovered in the Hungary which Kossuth has armed, organized and inspired."*

Although the revolution achieved the emancipation of the serfs, the War of Independence failed, for reasons of foreign policy and because of its rift with the nationalities. The most live and still effective part of Kossuth's heritage—the political principles he formulated in exile, in the late fifties—is a plan for a Danube Federation which not only contained a renunciation of Hungarian "hegemony," but also the idea of Hungarian-Slav-Rumanian co-

* Translated from the German: Marx—Engels Werke, Bd. VI. Dietz Verlag, Berlin, 1959. p. 165.

operation. The proof is there, in his concrete talks of 1858 with Cuza and Obrenovic.

Next to Széchenyi and Petőfi, Kossuth was the greatest representative of the Hungarian nation in the nineteenth century. He has become lodged in the memory of the people through the spell of his person, his words and his policies.

For a while the most consistent intellectual protagonists of the bourgeois transformation, the so-called Centralists, cooperated with Kossuth and the liberal nobiliary reform movement. Eötvös, László Szalay, Antal Csengery, Móric Lukács, Kemény jr. and Madách began their struggle in the mid-40's in the *Pesti Hírlap*, which Kossuth had abandoned, on behalf of the bourgeois democratic transformation of the country. Their chief aims were representation for the people, a responsible government and centralization. It was from this latter endeavour for the demolition of the county system, which backed Kossuth, that they derived their name. Although their consistently bourgeois theoretical, juridical and publicistic activities were superior to the liberalism of the middle stratum of the nobility represented by Kossuth, their loyalty to Vienna and their revulsion from revolution and from relying on the broad masses isolated them from the liberal progressives of the nobility. They, too, set out from Kölcsey's views but were not able to follow a Kossuth who, also on the basis of Kölcsey's teaching, relied on the "democratized county opposition" for support. As the most modern, travelled, highly educated and doctrinaire supporters of the cause of popular representation, of manufacturing industries and of the establishment of a bourgeois order, they even mooted the idea of socialist cooperatives to combat the pauperism that is a concomitant of capitalism. Their significance was to a certain extent preserved and their tradition vigorously pursued even after 1849, particularly in the thoughts of Kemény and in what were the more positive literary works of Madách.

Hungarian democratism in the forties exercised an important influence on the camp of liberalism, but it was not yet able to establish an independent party or become a national organization. Thus it was only at particular historical moments (in March and September 1848), that it could grow to become a leading force. At other times (essentially on the basis of the unification of interests) it remained a companion-in-arms to nobiliary national liberalism—to Kossuth and his followers. Petőfi's revolution in poetry and later, in 1846, the formation of the "Society of Ten," organized on a political basis, were signs of the advance of democratism. The "Ten" gathered round the periodical *Életképek* (Anecdotal Pictures). Its editor at this stage was that intelligent man of democratic sentiments Adolf Frankenburg— and beside their leader Petőfi, the group included Jókai, the great novelist of later days, the excellent poet Tompa, the narrator Albert Pálffy, who imitated French-style romanticism, and others. The advance of democratism was also marked by the approach of other important writers to this trend, in particular Mihály Táncsics, János Horárik and Pál Vasvári.

MIHÁLY TÁNCSICS (1799-1884), a widely travelled writer of serf extraction, had been to London and Paris, made friends with Cabot, and had studied socialist authors and the activities of the working men's associations. He was a man of restless spirit and it was in vain that the Austrian tyranny imprisoned him for his rebellious publicistic writing in the forties—he was freed from his captivity by the people of Pest on March 15, 1848. He was in favour of the complete emancipation of the peasantry, and the *Munkások Újsága* (Workers' Paper) which he edited was the most radical organ of the press in 1848. For this reason it was viewed with disfavour by the camp of the liberal nobles. Even though he was unable to harmonize his peasant revolutionary principles with the more universal national interest, his articles and leaflets after the defeat of the War of Independence maintained the idea of the revolution and propagated those of socialism and communism among the workers. At the close of his life he established contact with the incipient labour movement. His book *My Life* is a characteristic historical document of the progress of a plebeian who became a revolutionary.

JÁNOS HORÁRIK (1808-1864) was an ardent critic of feudalism and of the clergy. His work, *Johann Horáriks Kampf mit Hierarchie und Kirche in den Jahren 1841-45* was published at Leipzig in 1847. During the freedom-struggle he joined the Youth of March.

PÁL VASVÁRI (1826-1849) was Petőfi's meet companion in Jacobine republicanism. He published essays on the philosophy of history, which betray the influence of Hegel's dialectics, Michelet's romantic idealism and—as far as his ideal of the republican state in concerned—of French utopian socialism. In autumn 1848 he organized a group of *franc-tireurs* and fell in the Transylvanian campaign.

The Centralists were in agreement on several points with the ideas of these bourgeois Revolutionary Democrats. This is clear from their travel books which told of the experiences of their journeys in Western Europe, and from their pamphlets. An example of the former is *German, French and English Travel Notes* which appeared in Leipzig in 1846, by József Irinyi who served as a kind of connecting agent between the Centralists and the Revolutionary Democrats.

The democratic camp which appeared on the political field on March 15, 1848, was first organized in clubs and, together with the radical nobility, established the united organization of the left wing of March, the Equality Society.

The great consecutive waves of literary dispute which swept over one another, and the realistic trend in the development of narrative, poetry and drama, are the literary proofs of an increasingly revolutionary public life.

At the outset of the 40's the controversies over drama were at the centre of the struggle in literature. These were concerned with the primacy of stage qualities or of poesy and of the plot or the character. The appearance of Petőfi gave rise to the second wave of literary dispute. His choice of folk subjects, the folk tone and forms, led to a counter-attack by literary (and political) reaction. In about 1846 the third wave of the literary struggle got under way, now more overtly over the problems of poetry and political content, defending and attacking the right to create "tendentious poetry." Apart from Petőfi, Eötvös with his novel *The Village Notary* was now also a target for attack from all directions. The dispute had by this time developed on a national scale over the basic problems of the relations between literature and society, and the social function of literature, and it was to be precisely Eötvös, Petőfi and their companions—through their defence of tendentious poetry—who were also to become the first authors of critical realism. Their *ars poetica*, their attitude as writers, was now an overt testimony on behalf of a function of epic and lyrical poetry that points beyond its own confines, of a creative humanism that is not propagandistic, but based on the extant human, sensuous and social realities, of a conception that arises directly from the present tasks of mankind.

At the close of the 30's and in the early forties it had been Kölcsey, Vörösmarty and Bajza who imprinted their personalities on romantic lyricism concerned with public issues. The expansion of the sphere of experience available and the increased requirement for he tportraiture of real life now led further, to the fulfilment of lyrical realism with Petőfi.

In addition to the poets who have already been mentioned, two from Transylvania, JÁNOS KRIZA (1811-1875) and the highly talented MIHÁLY SZENTIVÁNI (1813-1842), who died young, developed the writing of folk-songs in a democratic spirit. By this time the lyrical situations arising from poverty and the social divisions among the people were also given natural expression. Szentiváni, with his intimate appreciation of the essence of the popular song as a literary form, and through his original and varied rhythms, was Petőfi's immediate predecessor. GYULA SÁROSY (1816-1861) in a series of poems *(Golden Trumpet)* recounted the events of the revolution in the fashion of a chronicle but full of revolutionary ardour. The poet, who belonged to Kossuth's closer entourage, suffered a prison term for his activities as a freedom fighter, but continued after his discharge to carry out agitation for the ideals of freedom through his lyrical poems, disseminated by readings and in manuscript. In consequence of his renewed persecution he died with a deranged mind.

An outstanding representative of lyrical poetry was MIHÁLY TOMPA (1817-1868), who with his folk-songs, versified folk-tales and legends had already become popular before 1848. He belonged to the intimate circle of the friends of Petőfi and Arany. In his poetry he was an enthusiastic, though by no means revolutionary, spokesman for the poor oppressed people and for an industrious life of labour. The most significant phase of his work was after the War of Independence (in which he had taken part), in the

134

period of autocracy. At first openly *(To the Stork ; On the Puszta)* and later allegorically he expressed his grief over the failure of the War of Independence. Some for the latently tense force of their emotion, others for their elegiac song-like qualities, these poems are still among the most valued items of Hungarian lyrical poetry.

The increasing realism of the social novel, derived from its topical character, from everyday life still developed in the framework of extremely romantic plots. This applies particularly to a novel, *Hungarian Secrets* (1844-45), written by the playwright Ignác Nagy after Sue's *The Mysteries of Paris,* which is rendered realistic by the very large number of details containing pictures of Hungarian life. Another novel inspired by Sue, *Homeland Mysteries* (1846-47) by LAJOS KUTHY (1813-1864) is more significant because of its descriptions of scenery, its broad social panorama and its satirical power. However, in its presentation of the actual social types of the period and of its historical "movement" it lags far behind Eötvös.

Special significance must be attributed in the democratization of literature and the evolution of realism to the birth in the early forties, beside bourgeois drama, of the folk play. A large part of the rich crop of plays by EDE SZIGLIGETI (1814-1878), who wrote over a hundred original pieces for the stage, dates from the period after 1849. However, his *The Deserter* (1843), *Two Pistols* (1844), and particularly *The Horseherd* (1847), presented at the time of the great upsurge in political life, served to ensure the triumph of the popular trend on the stage as well. In 1848 his patriotic, optimistic historical drama *The Captivity of Ferenc Rákóczi II* aroused enormous enthusiasm. It was in 1848-49 that he completed one of his finest plays, *Liliomfi,* a comedy about the lives of itinerant actors. The precursors of the folk play may be found in the peasant figures of the eighteenth-century school plays, in Csokonai's comedies with their folk subjects and grotesque tone, in Gaál's *Notary of Peleske,* as also in the influence of the Viennese *Volksstück.* In respect to its theme, approach and the nature of its characters and conflicts, however, it departed considerably from the Viennese *Volksstück,* and Szigligeti's best works already foreshadowed the possibilities of a folk drama. The folk plays of Szigligeti were, at least up to 1849, characterized by a democratic tendency and sharp criticism of the ruling class, accompanied by a fascinating presentation of the peasant people and the moral self-respect of those deprived of their all. At the same time the sentimental peasant figures and the folk-song insertions characteristic of the folk play also carried with them the danger of a shallow, melodramatic development. The fact that after the appearance of *The Village Notary* of Eötvös and the first showing of the *Horseherd*, literary reaction engaged in an uproar against tendentious poetry and the folk trend, regarding Eötvös, Szigligeti, Petőfi and Arany as belonging to one progressive camp, indicates the place of Szigligeti's democratic and critically realistic art.

The first, revolutionary phase of Hungarian critical realism was evolved in the works of these authors after the mid-40's, but without being able to attain to its full stature—the failure of the revolution and War of Independence prevented both the organic survival of the realist novel such as those of Eötvös, and also the deepening of the folk play to become a social folk drama. The essence of the new literary attitude in the works of Eötvös, Petőfi, the young Arany, and partly of Szigligeti and Tompa, was the importance of a world outlook, the subordination of literature to a lofty set of principles that are superior to aesthetic considerations.

Baron JÓZSEF EÖTVÖS (1813-1871) was born of a family of large estate-owners who were loyal to the Court. By the time he wrote his first great novel, *The Carthusian*, he had behind him the modern economic experiences of the large family estate undergoing capitalization, his studies in history and law completed in the mainstream of the patriotic movements of the 20's, the political lessons to be learnt from his circle of Centralist friends, and the copious information acquired in the course of his long journey in Western Europe. Even before he wrote his novel, all this was expressed in plays (the most successful being a comedy, *Long Live Equality*, 1840), in lyrical poetry, literary essays and publicistic writing. His was not a truly lyrical personality and his poems, with their sentimental tones, were rarely suffused with subjective power. An important work nevertheless, particularly for its elegiac expression of the universal and personal concept of the homeland, was his *Farewell*, written in 1836 before his departure on a journey abroad, and even more the later *I too Would Like it* (1846) and *Last Testament* (1848), with their powerful subjective acclamation of the social function of poetry, through which he defended Petőfi against reactionary attacks. His excellent essays on Victor Hugo and his publicistic works on prison reform, on pauperism in Ireland and on the emancipation of the Jews show him to have been the most comprehensive and versatile politician among the Centralists. It was in the course of this line of political development that he completed and published, in 1839-41, his great novel, *The Carthusian*, written in the first person singular and comprising the life story of a young French aristocrat who became a Carthusian because of his disappointments. This work was conceived in the same historial atmosphere as Balzac's *Illusion Perdues*, though not in order to escape Hungarian realities but to obtain an answer to the great problems that were then matters of lively concern in Hungarian politics, particularly among the Centralists. The bourgeois monarchy consequent on the July revolution was not a heartening prospect for Hungarian society—this is evident from this profound presentation of a new world that had given birth to selfishness, frivolity and irresponsible elbowing, and from the tragic conflicts into which Gusztáv, the hero of the novel, was driven by his disappointments in love and by his own moral deficiencies, the deficiencies of the period. An overcast and morbidly sentimental mood, similar to that of Musset's novel, pervades the book whose plot is slow to develop. Although the text is copiously interwoven with delicate reflections and contains some striking and grand scenes, it is not realistically elaborated. Its ponderous periods are also unsuited to epic narration.

It was after he had clarified his political principles (he sided with Kossuth against Széchenyi), and particularly in pursuit of his demand for a radical reform of the county system, that he wrote his great novel *The Village Notary* (1845), which is an apposite artistic illustration of his political views. In his detailed and suggestive description of the county environment and of the more or less distorted lives that sprang from it (with the exception

137

only of the young), Eötvös succeeded in formulating a comprehensive, artistic critique of Hungarian feudalism. The plot is laid
at the time and in the atmosphere of an election for county offices,
when the ambitious wife of the deputy-lieutenant Réthy attempts
to eliminate her husband's adversary in the contest for promo-
tion, the liberal-minded old notary Tengelyi, by having his patents
of nobility stolen and thus depriving him of his voice in public
affairs. The documents are rescued by Viola, a serf forced to lead
an outlaw's life through the despotism of the county authorities,
but the predatory, intriguing lawyer gets hold of them and Viola
is sentenced to death. Viola, who has been helped to escape, then
sacrifices his own life to save the incarcerated Tengelyi by hand-
ing him the documents. Tengelyi is no schematic character, and
it is only with mental revulsion that he can bring himself to
communicate with the outlaw, while his persecution gradually
deprives him of his balance. Viola, though his portrayal is
imbued with strong romantic traits, is a characteristic type of
the self-respecting serf, desirous of bettering himself and therefore
humiliated in his human dignity and forced to lead a life of
outlawry, without being a malefactor, like some of his companions. In this respect the environment and the psychological
portrait presented by Eötvös are authentic, too, particularly in
the picture of Viola's wife and of his friends leading their peasant
lives. Eötvös is, moreover, inexhaustible in the wealth of his
satire levelled at the county leaders. He presents a vast panorama,
reminiscent of Dickens, of power-hungry, corrupt, drunken and
dastardly characters.

It is true that the novel does, in a subordinate way, contain
romantic elements, especially through some of the threads of the
complex crime plot. Here too, there are reflexions, but the story
of the novel is tense and animated, a credit to the great gift of
Eötvös for composition.

The critics attacked the novel for its deliberate advocacy of
tendentious writing, but Eötvös reaffirmed his views in this
respect. It was thus that he made common cause with Petőfi,
about whose poetry, incidentally, he wrote one of his finest early
essays (1847).

In 1846 his appraisal of events in the course of the peasant rising in Galicia led to the birth of the idea of his other powerful novel *Hungary in 1514*. By conjuring up the memory of Dózsa and his peasant revolution, the novel served to warn Eötvös's contemporaries of the possible consequences of feudal oppression. Eötvös portrayed the peasant revolutionaries with modern middle-class sympathy and deep understanding—but not with revolutionary conviction. His realistic descriptive powers now reached their apogee, particularly in the precise analysis of the behaviour of the social classes and strata through their characteristic representatives, and in the large-scale mass scenes. Eötvös was masterly in his psychologically and historically crystal-clear descriptions of Dózsa's armies, of the actual historical forces and passions that appeared in religious garb, of the way in which the wavering heroes with their dual ties were forced to make their choice, of the dissension and murderous revenge of the politically conceptionless, anarchic nobility, of the character of Dózsa, and particularly of his lieutenant and ideologist, the priest Lőrinc. The closed and strict composition which unites the complex character portraits also makes this work the finest realistic novel of nineteenth-century Hungarian literature. The somewhat contradictory views of Eötvös—his understanding and at the same time his rejection of the peasant revolution—are reflected in the fact that he has shown not Dózsa but the priest Lőrincz to have been the main hero of the period, and even Lőrinc is, at the very end of the novel, made to turn against his revolutionary beliefs and to admit the error of his previous ways and suggests that he ought to have started by dispersing the spiritual darkness of the people...

Both novels, however, fail to pose the problem of national independence. This, and the foregoing considerations, will suffice to explain why Eötvös, though he was Minister of Education in the first responsible Hungarian government, avoided participation in the events that led to war with Austria—he could only imagine a reform within the framework of the empire as a whole— and fled to Vienna and then to Munich.

On his return he published a work on the theory of the state, *The Effect of the Dominant Ideas of the Nineteenth Century on the State* (1851-54), which though rich in thought, was of an essentially retrograde tendency. At about the same time he wrote

139

his last narrative works. From the sixties he played a new, important part in political life. Advocating dualism and a compromise, he returned to the laws of 1848, and as a liberal Minister of Education achieved considerable results—in the face of the clergy—in the establishment of progressive educational policies. After 1849 he was no longer able again to attain the pinnacles in his life's work which he had reached in the Reform Age.

SÁNDOR (Alexander) PETŐFI (1823-1849) was the greatest creative poetic genius of the Hungarian nation. His name signifies an immensely rich product of natural, life-like, popular literature and, in respect to his ideas, the fusion, at an uprecedentedly high poetic temperature, of national independence and revolutionary republicanism. He was born at Kiskőrös, to petty-bourgeois parents of Slovak descent (his father I. Petrovics was a butcher), and received his schooling in the Kiskunság district, then at Pest, Aszód and Selmec, his national consciousness becoming ever stronger in his strange environment. From the age of 15 he wrote poems, and his impoverished father, disapproving of the fact that his son, entranced with acting and literature, neglected his studies, would have nothing more to do with him. He now entered on a tremendously hard period of his life in which he more than once came to the brink of perishing. After working as an extra in a Pest theatre under a pseudonym, he wandered all over Transylvania and at Sopron joined the army (1839). He was discharged from the regiment on grounds of health in 1841. Periods at Sopron, Pápa and Pozsony were followed by some more acting in Southern Transdanubia, after which he returned to Pápa where he attended school for another year and struck up a friendship with Jókai. He then went off again and, staying with friends or joining an occasional troupe of itinerant actors, once more travelled all over the country from Debrecen to Pozsony. Here (in 1843) he earned a meagre livelihood by copying reports from the Diet.

His first published poem was *The Wine Drinker* (Athenaeum, 1842). In the poem *In my Homeland*, which he wrote a little later and to which he already signed the name of Petőfi, he gave an indication of great lyrical gifts, conjuring up the mood of his native place which he had revisited, and of the time he had recently spent

land. It is the yearning and hope of the people for a better future that is expressed in these adventures, characterized by scenes from real life (the village, the love of two young people, the inhuman farmer), the inventions of popular peasant-soldier exaggeration (the phantastic journey of the hussars, John the hero and the King of France) and familiar fairy-tale motifs (giants, witches, over the sea and far away, Fairyland), all appearing in the unity of the poet's imagination. Reactionary criticism hastened to attack the author for his "vulgar" approach.

During the months he spent with the *Pesti Divatlap* his circumstances became more settled. His loves and his journey in Northern Hungary inspired him to write cycles and a masterly travel diary. The latter showed that Petőfi was also a great and epoch-making artist of prose written in the spoken style. His love cycles tell of disappointment, of a desire for love rather than the feeling itself. They marked the beginning of his period of crisis which was to last till the spring of 1846.

The causes of this crisis lay equally in the attacks levelled against him, the financial ruin of his parents, his disappointments in love, and at the same time the rootlessness of the plebeian democratism then being formulated. He was tormented by his isolation and impotence—this also accounted for the bitterness of many of the poems in which he attacked feudal Hungary. In general terms he began to rise above the impersonality of the folksong and sought personal and weightier means for expressing his own self. It was now that he set out from the folk-song and the genre-picture on the path that was to lead him to the grand lyric poems. Disharmony, a Heinean pointing, Byronian and Shelleyan *Weltschmerz* characterize the poems that indicated the crisis *(Clouds*, 1846). They are pervaded by a sombre, romantic mood, and it is only in the poet's overwrought imagination that their experience appears so intensely personal, for their inspiration does not yet possess that quality. The naive lyricism of the song now gave way to deliberately purposeful, more complex, associative structures. Narrative poems, a historical drama and a wildly romantic novel *(The Hangman's Rope)* were the accompaniments to this crisis in outlook and sentiment.

It was in spring 1846 that Petőfi emerged from this crisis, his

143

recovery being marked by a great poem, *Letter to Antal Várady*. Here the pessimist assumes solidarity with pitiable, unhappy mankind and expresses his belief that the enslaved shall again become men. Now his poetry of moods attained its full purity. While the poetry of his great predecessors left much unsaid about the rich sentiments of their lives, Petőfi's inspiration came to be suffused with the instinct of continuous and full self-expression. His poetry of moods implied not only subjectivity but also objective reflections, such as those in his elegy *The Ruins of the Inn*, interwoven with a love of his native land and with the ideals of freedom, or his elegiac genre-pictures, replete with atmosphere, such as *The Good Old Publican* and *The Four-Ox Cart*. His longest lyrical poem, and one of the most enchanting, is the elegy *Fairy Dream*, reflecting a characteristic process of moods and recalling the memory of his first love.

By the second half of 1846, when political interest led him to travel to Szatmár County, his inspiration as a political poet, his vocation as a romantic poet-apostle, grew stronger. The split between nobiliary liberalism and plebeian democratism was hastened by the peasant rising in Galicia at the beginning of 1846. From this event Petőfi drew revolutionary conclusions and it was now that his poetic revolution broadened to become political. As one who felt high esteem for the great French Revolution, he once more made a study of the history of revolutions and increasingly turned towards the Jacobines. He organized the "Society of Ten," grouped from 1847 about the periodical *Életképek* (Anecdotal Pictures), edited by Jókai. Also in 1847 he struck up a friendship with János Arany, and this friendship led to the finest correspondence of poets in Hungarian literature. Petőfi was by now surrounded by friends and companions in arms. In September 1846 he made the acquaintance of Júlia Szendrey whom he married a year later. The lyricism of love now attained full maturity in his poetry, but in such a manner that the two main excitements of his soul, the political and the amorous, remained co-fraternal branches, intertwined with each other. Every instant inspired a lyrical mood in his poetry, returning a profuse echo of the fullness of life, and it was now that his lyrical works on the themes of politics and love became wholly personal. His instinct for folk-song was also reborn (a perfect example being *The Bush Trembles, for* . . .). But the overwhelming majority were poems of rich harmonic arrangement, in several movements (such as *'Twas a Poet's Dream* . . ., against which he now sets the wild flood of his passion—or *The Sad Autumn Wind Talks to the Trees* where the contradiction between a happy, singing love and a vision of thundering struggle is developed from stanza to stanza). There was the dithyramb of *What Shall I Call Thee* and *At the End of September*, written in 1847, where the fundamental feeling, developed in unparallelled richness, is the mortal foreboding of ill, blossoming upon the plant of honeymoon happiness.

Ultimately, however, all these trends converged into political lyricism. Politics were no passing stimulus to his lyrical writing; it was his yearning for the freedom of his own personality that became sublimated into the creation of an ideal—that of the plebeian revolutionary. This was to become his most personal form of lyrical expression, starting with his visionary poem of war written at the end of 1846, *One Thought Troubles me* . . . Here the desire for action, the rhythm of flamboyant passion, lyrical devotion and unselfishness of character are all present in a wonderful poem celebrating world freedom even at the price of death. What now followed, between 1847 and 1849, was a many-sided development of the revolutionary poet, the fighter for freedom, with a personal reaction to every turn of events. *The People* (1847) and *By Railway* (1847) are a few of the immense number of poems—soon to form a veritable revolutionary calendar of events—which were but a preparation for the great events of 1848. Indeed, *The Tisza* (1847), a tremendous descriptive poem of a landscape, surpassed the earlier masterpiece, *The Plain*, by the interweaving of the poet's personality with the vital rhythm of the scene, with the contrast of idyll and tempest, illusion and disillusionment (he describes how the apparently meek River Tisza floods the countryside with terrible force, from one day to the next). The sombreness of *The Plain in Winter* and the sensuous, intimate genre-picture, *Winter Evenings* also mark pinnacles of Hungarian lyrical writing.

Under the influence of the events in Vienna on March 15, 1848, the masses in Pest also stirred, with Petőfi and his companions at their head. It was for them that he wrote the *National Song*—the

10

Hungarian Marseillaise. A grand, menacing poem was his *The Ocean Has Arisen, the Ocean of the Peoples*. The temporary prevalence of the liberal trend, however, isolated Petőfi and his companions, and in August, when the armies of the Austrian General Jellačič already threatened the revolutionary capital, his pessimism erupted in *The Apostle*, a tremendous narrative poem with a modern plot and of romantic force. This depicts the radical republican and premature revolutionary in the form of Szilveszter, its hero, into whose fate he concentrates his own experiences and the lessons of the European revolutions. The events of September bore out the poet for the "ocean" of the people rose and drove out Jellačič who had endeavoured to restore tyranny.

The victories of autumn were followed by defeats, and then triumphs in the spring. In this historic atmosphere Petőfi's poetry was the sensitive conscience of the nation, fighting for its very life. He wrote genre-portraits like *The Old Standard-Bearer* about his father, a poem about the honour due to the common soldier, Jacobine poems of incitement against the kings, and magnificent, highly effective battle-songs.

The tense historical situation, the political and emotional saturation of these fateful weeks, served to charge the atmosphere of his works with a passion strained to bursting point, both in his war poetry and in the confessions of love expressing a foreboding of early death. He was a major, attached to the excellent Polish General Bem of the Transylvanian armies, and a fine soldier, though his revolutionary fervour led him frequently to clash with his bureaucratic Ministry. Petőfi fell on July 31, 1849, in Transylvania, at the age of 26, in a battle against the Tzarist cavalry, immediately before the defeat of the War of Independence.

He was the most consummate lyrical poet of the century's great democratic struggles, conducted throughout Europe in pursuit of national independence and revolutionary principles. His personal involvement and the breadth of his emotions establish him as one of the greatest lyricists of Hungary and of the world. With him—in the period when Baudelaire was striking out on new paths—the lyrical realism nurtured by the greatest ideals of the age, those of moral, national and universal freedom, achieved its culmination.

The inspiring and guiding influence of Petőfi was felt not only by all his contemporaries—even those opposed to him—but also by his greatest fellow-poet and confidential friend, his senior, JÁNOS ARANY (1817-1882). Arany, who was of peasant extraction, was after Vörösmarty and Petőfi the greatest Hungarian poet of the nineteenth century, the greatest master of objective lyrical poetry and of realistic narrative verse. His course of development was tragically cut asunder by the defeat of the War of Independence and Petőfi's death. A large part of his works was written between 1850 and 1880, amid inner conflicts and discord.

Born of a destitute family of the petty nobility who had sunk to the level of serfs, oversensitive, grave and of puritan morals, Arany was brought up in the environment of peasant culture. Kazinczy's "superior style" exercised hardly any influence on him; the patriarchal writers of the late eighteenth century and Csokonai, with their healthy naive realism, far more. He attended school at his native Szalonta and then at Debrecen. After a theatrical adventure he returned to his aged parents, the family, indeed the people, whom he had wished to leave in pursuit of his dreams of art. He entered the ranks of the small-town intelligentsia and became a notary. The widening of the horizon about this genius, who for moral reasons and timidity had confined himself to a narrow circle, was due in the first place to the brisk political life of the times.

It was for a competition set by the Kisfaludy Society in 1845, at a time when the county liberals and conservatives were engaged in the most heated quarrels, that he submitted his magnificent satirical narrative poem *The Lost Constitution*, in which he held them up to ridicule. This was a survey of the ruling class, in its public life, its meetings and electioneering, within the compass of a large-scale, jocular and ironic improvisation whose borrowed form—a parody of the heroic epic—was strained to bursting point by the immensely rich material of life, the realistic details and the mass of characteristic minor episodes that were crammed into it. At this stage, of course, all this was still confined within the loose framework of a pamphlet-like poetic narrative, with the human types lacking individuality and the various features being given their grotesque slant by calling the folk approach to the poet's aid.

This mixture, strange even from the point of view of style (for elements of folklore mingled with the tones of contemporary journalism and of political slogans), led nevertheless to excellent satire, for it reflected the intellectual and moral superiority of one outside the nobility, who was thus able, in his ambiguous tone of mocking praise, to toy with the petty, comic figures of the nobility.

It was in response to another competition set by the Kisfaludy Society that he submitted his first real masterpiece *Toldi* (1846), which not only won a prize but also indicated an important stage in the whole of Hungarian literary development. Arany, who had by now become an attentive reader of Petőfi, thus wrote the first classical work of popular realism.

This narrative poem is set in an historical frame, although actually concerned with the author's own times, with the long-awaited upsurge and folk-tale triumph of the peasant poor. It tells briefly how Toldi, a noble youth leading a peasant life in the fourteenth century, came to the court of King Louis the Great (1342-1382); through what adventures he passed and against what malevolence his resolution had to defend him while betraying and reinforcing his own peasant characteristics through the warmth, intimacy and frankness of his feelings. The author was influenced not only by Petőfi, but simultaneously by the folk tradition about this great hero of the Hungarians, and by his experience of the contemporary life of the people. It was this that led him to infuse into the character of Toldi a dramatic presentation of the spiritual and corporeal reality of the people's lives—always paying strict regard to the development and dramatic evolution of his hero's spirit and fate. With his folk vocabulary and idiom, his Hungarian-pattern stanzas, Arany achieved what had seemed impossible: the reproduction of the profundities of a psychological portrait through the use of simple means.

His *Toldi* earned the poet the friendship of Petőfi. And because this folk realism was also a faithful expression of the emergent plebeian movement, it bore fruit not only in the puny attacks of the magnates' papers, but also in deepening the friendship of Petőfi and Arany through the exchange of poetic letters and the establishment of personal contact between them. In establishing the dominance of the folk trend in written poetry, Petőfi prepared

meaning. An elegiac expression of this inner struggle is *In Autumn*, with its captivating qualities of atmosphere and music and its almost Parnassian objective perfection. The analogy with Ossian suggests the aching wounds he suffers on the personal, human, patriotic and moral level. In *Tamás Furkó* he criticised the noblemen who were in command during the war, as he did again in the narrative poem against a tragico-comic background entitled *The Gipsies of Nagyida*. He occasionally used striking allegories *(Rachel)* to castigate the despotic system or recall the passing spirit of Petőfi. Of the great poems glorifying the militant heroism of the resistance fighters, two magnificent ballads written in the mid-fifties deserve special mention as unsurpassably brilliant, suggestive works of dramatic and musical composition; these are *Szondi's Two Pages* and *Bards of Wales*. He returned, disheartened, to the warmth of his family circle, hardly able to conceal his suffering even in his elegiac and idyllic poems like *Family Circle* and *To my Son*.

The first song of his verse novel, *Crazy Steve*, completed in 1850, was, perhaps, the most characteristic of his modern poetic genius and of the way in which Arany, now that he had been left alone, sought the right path. He strove to continue the socially determined epic style of folk realism, and yet what he wrote was a poetry of aimlessly wasted force. This startling poetic fragment, recalling at first the hues of the Dutch realist painters, and then the atmospheric qualities of impressionism in its depiction of brilliant Hungarian landscapes, most vividly expressed his own crisis. After a few excellent essays and a magnificent series of ballads on historic themes, the crisis of the mid-sixties, when he moved up to Pest, soon to become General Secretary of the Hungarian Academy of Sciences, forced János Arany to cease writing. His tremendous narrative poem, *The Death of Buda*, completed in 1863, was an indication of the modernization of literature and in some respects fits into the series of verse novels then appearing.

This narrative poem was to have been the first part of a trilogy about the Hun conquest of Hungary. Here the poet introduced the intensive method of character portrayal of the modern novel in telling the story of the tragic conflict between

151

Buda and Attila, and of their military exploits and family lives. Everything, from the division of their power to the actual fratricide, is impelled by the motivation of psychological development, and in the course of the plot each event is linked to the next in chain-like succession of increasing dramatic tension. The morally imbued realism of Arany attained fulfilment in the delicate tints of the characters of Etele (Attila), of Buda and the latter's wife, and in the moral catastrophe which annihilated their dreams together with their power. This realism is closely akin—and artistically at all events of equivalent value—to that of Theodor Storm and of the C. F. Meyer who wrote *Jürg Jenatsch.*

Arany now stopped writing, and because of his doubts and of a world that offended the sensitive conscience of his declining age, he attended only to his official work at the Academy, with a pedantic diligence that consumed all inspiration. Twelve years had to pass before, at the close of his life, he again wrote poetry.

He then gave birth to a narrative poem *Toldi's Love,* an epic work forming the middle part of the Toldi trilogy, and concluding his career at the pinnacle of lyrical poetry. From the evidence of his great poem *Cosmopolitan Poetry* he may indeed have come to oppose those young urban poets who were breaking away from the popular-national verse, but he nevertheless pioneered the path of modern lyrical poetry in his last poems. These were collected in a little volume bearing the title *Autumn Bouquet* and are held to be one of the loveliest cycles in Hungarian literature. To his feelings of separation from society and to his self-effacement, he added in these poems a humorous approach to his own self, as if exchanging banter with someone who has become old and worn out. But beyond the half sincere, half playful irony about himself, true irony and true humour appeared, sometimes impish, sometimes caustic. This was the life and atmosphere noted by an old man, in a period where the glitter of society actually concealed its wounds. A placid renunciation of life and of reminiscence is expressed in the lyrical poetry of *Under the Oaks, The Old Waiter* and *The Old Complaint* in which the philosophical content is reduced to atmosphere. This, moreover, was the period of his late ballads, composed with an unsurpassable musical excellence of style and language, presenting dramatic pictures of the death and decay of village and town in an atmosphere of magic and superstition. *(Husking Maize; Red Rébék; Dedication of the Bridge.)*

It was amid the still progressive tendencies of the Hungarian social and political trends dominant up to the early sixties that the great life's work of Kemény and Jókai developed.

ZSIGMOND KEMÉNY (1814-1875) was in several respects akin to Arany, close to him in his moral realism and the mixture of objectiveness and idealism. Nevertheless there were considerable differences between them from the very first, because of Kemény's lack of confidence in the revolutionary people and, later, on account of his counter-revolutionary publicistic writings, as well as the moral preoccupation that frequently obscured the contours and structure of his novels and which in Arany's case never exerted an adverse effect on the plasticity of his writing.

Kemény was the scion of an illustrious but impoverished Transylvanian family, a progressive politician of the Reform Age in Transylvania, and later one of the most important members of the Centralist group, a rival of Eötvös and Szalay. Politically he was more radical than Széchenyi, but exercised considerable reserve in regard to democracy. He was opposed to Hapsburg reaction, but supported a liberal Austria relying on German imperial unity. This made him vacillate in his political attitude up to 1848. In 1848-49 he was ostensibly a supporter of Kossuth, but at the same time a stalwart member of the Peace Party seeking an armistice with Austria.

The deepest point in his career was in 1850-51, when his notorious pamphlets (the intention of these pamphlets was honourable, for the reason why he obsequiously kow-towed to the bloody-handed Haynau was to save the Hungarian nation, and he also recognized the rights of the nationalities) besmirched the revolution and the figure of Kossuth, propagating a Hungarian national character whose virtues according to him were to be surrender, passiveness and loyal submission to the monarchy. Overcoming the illusions expressed in these pamphlets, however, Kemény soon changed over to the more patriotic attitude of Deák, who advocated passive resistance. He now struggled for the legality of the legislation of 1848 and was one of the few people who demanded with complete unselfishness that a compromise be concluded on the basis of the Constitution of 1848. Although he regarded the subsistence of Austria as a European necessity (and was in this respect less far-sighted than Kossuth whom he mocked for being a dreamer), he sharply opposed the Austrian jurists who were preparing for the full annexation of Hungary.

His immense erudition, suppressed passion, historical and social prejudices, his tremendously contradictory thinking that never achieved harmony, were perfectly expressed in Kemény's work as an editor. The *Pesti Napló* (Pest Diary), which he edited from 1855 to 1869, was the best newspaper of the period. In his masterly historical essays, his portraits (of Széchenyi and Wesselényi), and above all in his novels, the same qualities are evident.

As a young man Kemény studied medicine in Vienna and armoured himself with the materialism of Feuerbach. Later, however, he turned to the Stoics and then to the principle of self-expression, of the free manifestation of the personality. It was on top of this that the considerable influence of German romanticism and the historical school came to be deposited. The lessons derived from various trends, each contradictory to the other, led him to adopt the unconditional and generally tragic creed of letting the individual's personality triumph. In both his over-all outlook and in the heroes of his novels he considered it more important to manifest individual personality than to adhere to reality. In his view life is lost where personality has to be abandoned. He was pessimistic because he held the individual's life in the midst of social reality to be tragic. This tragic, pessimistic, hopeless portrayal of man, impinging on romanticism, was the intimate exposure and annihilation of his own illusionless concept of life.

Kemény's novels are not particularly successful from the point of view of the traditional novel form. Their drawbacks are their ponderous, tortuous and artificial plots, their hesitant and anaemic dialogues, the poor arrangement of the scenes—yet where he had to describe a perfected situation, a state of mind or the correspondence of states of mind with mutual references and a reciprocally reinforcing role, he produced masterpieces. This was the case with his greatest works; in his *The Widow and her Daughter* (1855-57), where reference is made to a largely psychological basic situation, that of a seventeenth-century abduction in Transylvania, which is

the most popular figures of public life. The beginning of his period of decay was in 1875, the year when Kálmán Tisza came to power and Jókai agreed to become a Member of Parliament on behalf of the Liberal Party, whose grave errors he now seemed to have forgotten. He continued for decades to show ingratiating reverence for the dynasty. It was only in the nineties that he became somewhat disillusioned with the whole of his previous attitude. His humanity and his truly sincere liberalism nevertheless ensured respect for him even in this period of descent, when his name was becoming known and recognized abroad, when the publication in foreign languages of the works of Jókai—who numbered Vereshchagin among his friends and corresponded with Zola—was proceeding at a lively pace. The young generation of writers—those opposed to Pál Gyulai—preferred to seek the senescent master's hand, and several among the young declared that he was their teacher.

The great novels he wrote in the era of the Compromise of 1867 concluded with Austria were *The Baron's Sons* (1869), the most brilliant heroic poem in prose of the War of Independence, one of the most beautiful and most exciting Hungarian narrative works of the nineteenth century, and *Eppur si Muove* (1872), where he recalled the tremendous human, political and literary figures of the incipient Reform Age (Katona, K. Kisfaludy, Kazinczy), in the course of a novel-like plot sequence based on anecdotes. *Black Diamonds* (1870) was already concerned with the problems of national capitalism, having as its main hero a scholar and democrat of strong national consciousness who fought valiantly against the colonizing capital that had become allied with Austrian oppression. Problems related to capitalism continued to be the theme in Jókai's greatest novel, *The Man with the Golden Touch* (1872), which comes closest among all his works to portraying people in the manner of critical realism. He also wrote a few important novels after 1875, including *The Strange Story of Ráby Rab* (1879), which was the most courageous and artistic treatment of the struggles, so full of contradictions, of the Hungarian Enlightenment. In the richness of its realistic traits it is almost unique among Jókai's works. *The Yellow Rose* (1892) was the most mature work of Jókai's old age and his greatest artistic achievement next to *The Man with the Golden Touch*. It furnished clear proof of the author's disillusionment with squirearchal politics and of his warmhearted approach to the people. This novelette revealed the possibilities of a new, passion-charged, modern peasant romanticism.

Jókai, beside showing the great past, also imagined a great future for his nation, but he filled the period between the two with illusions. His illusory view of the present was, it is true, also a form of confidence in the great promises of the future (*e.g.* in national capitalism) but these illusions were mainly required by the middle stratum of the nobility in order that they might play their part in the political struggles of the sixties and seventies. Their delusions did not furnish them with strength, but merely served to veil the realities of life. For this reason Jókai was, as early as in his own period, subjected to powerful criticism on behalf of the realistic, illusion-free approach of Pál Gyulai and Jenő Péterfy.

His most valuable novels were nevertheless those recalling the memory of the Reform Age and the War of Independence, but the time at which he recalled this most stormy and eruptive period of the great social upsurge of the nation, was when the rising trajectory had suffered a break and the formerly real social forces had increasingly become nostalgic illusions and poetic reflections within a decaying patriotic nobility. The subjectivization of the objective forces of history prevented the full development of Jókai's great gifts in the direction of realism. The realistic traits continued to develop in a romantic framework, relegated to masterly episodes of observation, of the knowledge of life and of his plot—though Jókai knew Hungarian life and the people of the countryside far better than most of his compatriots. It was in this way that a peculiar form of expression, of critical vision became conspicuous in his writing—a form enveloping the facts in humour, presenting occasional flashes of the life-like phenomena of reality, but stopping short of its full development. This was the anecdote. His art attained its greatest fulfilment in his grandiose scenes, the "vast tableaux seeking the excuse of floods, battles, earthquakes, sieges, sudden thaws, famines or a rowdy carousal for what was at the same time a primordially pictorial description of reality," wrote István Sőtér, the novelist and literary historian, in his monograph about Jókai. Jókai perceived reality in pictures, very colourfully, with an extraordinarily vivid imagination. His romantic idealism, his exoticism, his great fantasy and narrative talent, his virtuosity in the development of plots still render him highly popular.

Grave criticism, applying the criteria of English and French realism, was levelled at Jókai by PÁL GYULAI (1826-1909), the greatest critic of the second half of the century, the codifier of so-called national classicism—particularly on the basis of the works of Petőfi, Arany and Kemény.

Gyulai came from Transylvania, where, during the movements of 1848, he acted as one of the leaders of the liberal youth. In 1862 he moved permanently to Pest from Transylvania, became vice-director of the Academy of Dramatic Art and its professor of dramaturgy, and from 1876 held the Chair of the History of Hungarian Literature. The literary forums—in the hands of the pro-compromise party in literature, the so-called literary Deák Party—functioned under his general direction, with Gyulai becoming (after Arany) the General Secretary of the Academy, the director of the Kisfaludy Society, one of the heads of the Franklin Society, which was the greatest publishing house, and editor-in-chief of the illustrious periodical of the Academy, the *Budapesti Szemle* (Budapest Review).

His work in the history of literature bore two facets. On the one hand he made the folk trend and realism the main criteria of value in literature, and demanded structural unity and clarity of form of the writers, setting Katona, Vörösmarty, Petőfi and Arany at the centre of Hungarian literature, but raging a sharp struggle against Petőfi's shameless, folksy epigons. On the other hand, however, he separated realism and revolutionism from each other, increasingly interpreting realism as a kind of unimaginative moderation, and formulating a conservative academism from the popular, revolutionary art of Petőfi and Arany, and particularly from that of Arany in his years of crisis. By the seventies this had become a fossilized impediment to progress. Gyulai did not in any case desire that profound character and psychological portrayal be coupled with an intensive depicting of society, and in this respect too, he sanctioned the moral realism of Kemény and of Arany's later period. During the last decades of his life he showed no understanding for the critical realism that emerged in Mikszáth's works, as indeed he was also incapable of comprehending the melancholy, pessimistic lyrical poetry of the cities.

His main ideal was folk and national poetry, and in this too Petőfi's folk-song poetry and the János Arany of the Toldi trilogy were his examples. Although he liked contemporary English and Russian realism, his anti-philosophic approach soon narrowed down his horizon. He still lives, however, in his magnificent analytical studies and monographs on Katona, Vörösmarty, Petőfi and Arany, as well as through a fine novelette, *The Last Master of an Old Manor* (1857), which he wrote about the disappearing middle nobility, and in which the critical realist line of development which could no longer assert itself after the failure of 1848, appeared with great literary virtues.

The attempt to form the most vehement opposition to Gyulai in the theoretical and critical fields was due to the highly gifted but short-lived KÁROLY ZILAHY (1838-1864) who joined János Vajda, the lone poet-genius neglected by Gyulai and his adherents, in struggling against dogmatism, on behalf of free criticism, for a new poetry and the right to passionate and imaginative writing.

The collapse of the traditional religious, idealistic view of the world and of the patriarchal moral conception, the incursion of the great scientific and philosophical theories which were to determine the future outline of the world, the break-through of the biological-positivist approach to man, appeared not only in the works of Kemény but also exercised a strong influence on IMRE MADÁCH (1823-1864) in his masterpiece *The Tragedy of Man* (1860), which, despite its romantic foundations, rose to the proximity of the new critical realism, going beyond the purely moral approach. Madách was a Centralist, studied philosophy and law, and after the War of Independence—in which he did not actively participate because of his illness—he was persecuted for his anti-Hapsburg attitude. This, and especially the collapse of his family life and the crisis of his views, together prompted him to write his great work. The fundamental conflicts of this play, which in its literary form is lyrical and dramatic, showing kinship with the *poème d'humanité*

IMRE MADÁCH (1823-1864)

(Vigny, Lamartine, Quinet, Hugo, etc.), were born of the romantic world outlook, with its contest of Good and Evil, of the "divine" and "diabolic" principles for mankind (the struggle of the Lord and Lucifer for Adam, the man), with, also, the cult of giant statures, formulated in the conflicts of "the great man" and the uncomprehending masses. In the historical scenes of the play Adam enters the lists on behalf of great ideals and these ideals always meet with the resistance of the period and the masses, driving Adam into repeated disappointments though he remains unchanged in spirit through all his historical metamorphoses. The eminent Hungarian Madách scholar, István Sőtér, has pointed out that the abstractness of the figure of Adam would indeed land the drama itself in an impasse if Eve were not there beside him, as a companion and as his antithesis in character. "While in the case of Adam it is the continuity of character which is striking, with Eve it is its ceaseless change that engages our attention. We see her as a slave girl (in Egypt), as a classical heroine (in Athens), then as a hetaera (in Rome), the inmate of a convent (in Byzantium) and a loose woman (in Prague), even appearing in two opposite countenances in the Paris scene. Eve's personality is fraught with contradictions and contrasts, while her relation to Adam is one of continual approach and estrangement. The relation of Adam and Eve is at once that of devoted love (in Egypt); of the heroic, august partnership of a lifetime (in Athens); of frivolity (in Rome); of asceticism (in Byzantium); of triviality (in Prague); but more often of inaccessibility (in Byzantium, Prague, Paris, London and the Phalanstery). Eve's role at Adam's side is extremely important from the dramatic point of view. She brings to Adam, who lives perhaps too much for his ideas and is on the verge of becoming divorced from the more everyday reality of life, a more intimate and warm message—the message of nature. Eve is the cause of Adam's fall, but she is also the means of his escape. The fruit of the forbidden tree and the world of motherhood that recall him from the precipice of suicide—these both belong to the character of Eve," István Sőtér writes.

The *Tragedy* voices the problems of the entire natural-material and historical world, with cosmic ambition. The problems concerned with nature are raised in the first three scenes, the historical ones in scenes four to fourteen; the succession being Egypt, Athens, Rome, Byzantium, the Prague of the Emperor Rudolph and of Kepler, the excursion to the revolutionary scene of the *Place de Grève* in Paris, the return to Prague after the dissolution of the great "dreams," London and the world of capitalism; the Phalanstery, which is simultaneously both the scene of the mortal finale of capitalism and the distorted, horrifying image of utopian socialist teachings, followed by Adam flying into space to escape, and—finally—the scene of his enforced return to a cooling Earth that will destroy all mankind, and of his eventual breakdown. It is in the last, fifteenth scene that the ultimate questions of the natural and material world return, with the establishment of the moral conclusions in which—according to the Lord's words: "Hark to Me, Man! Strive on, strive on, and trust!"—the inspiration of fideism may also be discovered.

The social ideas which Madách endeavoured to illustrate in the historical scenes are in each scene born and pass away in a manner fraught with conflict. In some, the conflicts of ideas, and parallel with them the psychological conflicts of Adam too, become socially typical—for instance in the scenes of Kepler's Prague and the capitalism of London, which are also the finest parts. By exposing the omnipresent, effective force of these conflicts, and particularly stressing the part played by society in the relations between society and the individual through the ages, Madách made a considerable contribution to the development of critical realism, and in this went beyond the purely moralistic realist approach.

Beside this great drama which earned the praise of János Arany, Madách is also noteworthy for his refined lyrical verse and his two other plays: *The Civilizer*, in which he derided both the lesser nobility who favoured passive resistance, and the hypocritical civilizing activities of the Bach period; and *Moses*, where "the great man" becomes a true hero through his ability to achieve unity with the people. The full development of the gifts of Madách was prevented by his early death. The course of development in drama did not continue along his path.

# THE AGE OF REALISM (1867-1900)

Hungarian literary realism developed in the period of decline after the Compromise with Austria.

The Compromise of 1867 recognized the constitutional, political and autonomous independence of Hungary and introduced a parliamentary system, while maintaining common Ministries for Foreign Affairs and War. Although the sharing of power between the Hungarian propertied classes and Viennese reaction at first suited the interests of the propertied classes, it led later to grave consequences for the economic and political development of the country. Capitalisation and the establishment of a trading and transport network were both accelerated and broadened in scope, but the intertwining of bank capital and the large estates, and at the same time the increased oppression of the toiling classes and the national minorities, considerably exacerbated class antagonisms and the question of national minorities. These problems became especially grave in the 1880's, when, under the government of Kálmán Tisza, all the harmful consequences of the Compromise came to be laid bare. This became a period of corruption, fraud and depravity in domestic politics, accompanied in foreign policy by the alliance with German imperialism. The Hungarian labour movement which started in the late sixties now began to grow stronger, a great part being played in this process by the activities of Leó Frankel, a famous Hungarian Minister of the Paris Commune, who came back to Hungary. Agrarian socialist movements were started and social unrest increased, but only the nineties were to witness the first display of the true strength of the labour movement.

The two, essentially misleading conclusions which led to the

Compromise, persisted for a long time among the best of the period's intelligentsia, including the most prominent writers. One of these was the illusion that the Hapsburg Empire was a European necessity. The other, even more decisive, idea—and one that actually seized upon a very real problem—was that even if an attempt to disrupt the Hapsburg Empire did succeed, the historic Hungary, whose multilingual nationalities had in 1848-49 already shown their desire to secede, would break up with it. The Hungarian ruling class was, however, unable to draw the proper conclusions from this realization, that is, to strive for agreement with the nationalities. And when the Hungarian landowning class was, as a result of the Compromise, given a free hand in the brutal oppression of the Slovaks and Rumanians, the Hungarian intelligentsia in this quandary lost its spirit of enterprise for the training of a courageous elite with a revolutionary outlook, and, itself also compromised, sought to rescue what could still be saved. Only the great names of Kossuth (who did not cease even from afar to comment on Hungarian events), of Táncsics and of Lajos Mocsáry, may be exempted from this decline in public thought.

The Hungarian writers took their first steps towards modern realism and the analytical style in the versified novel, first in the masterpieces of János Arany and then in the drama of Madách which have been discussed. These traditions were continued in the works of László Arany and of the playwrights, but it was especially in lyrical writing that the objective approach of "national classicism" disintegrated completely, giving way, beside the analytical realistic-naturalistic narrative, to the subjective approach of the lyrical expression of moods in the closing decade of the century. At the same time, however, while this trend was preparing the way for modern Hungarian poetry, official literature came increasingly to be dominated by the epigons of Arany and the followers of Pál Gyulai's conservative policies in literature. "National classicism" became devoid of all living, human expression, and the folk-national trend raised on a pedestal those poets who advocated contentment with a paltry, petty-bourgeois, sometimes idyllic life—the theatrical, ostentatious patriots (the *Kuruc* pretensions of Kálmán Thaly) and the bucolic simpletons (Pósa, Szabolcska), who rejected modern Budapest as a city of sin and national degeneration. This was why Hungarian literature in its rebirth—the *Nyugat* movement—had first to turn energetically against these poets.

János Arany's son, LÁSZLÓ ARANY (1844-1898), in his versified novel *The Hero of the Mirages* (1872) gave birth to a work arising from the new disillusionment. The background here was no longer the requirement of illusionless self-knowledge as advanced by Kemény and Arany, not a moral motivation, but a social disappointment—the realization in the seventies of the opportunism of the leading Hungarian class, the propertied nobility, of their retrograde character and cultural stagnation. László Arany was very talented, a popularizer of Lermontov, the author of masterly essays; but he soon stopped writing and was lost in administrative work. It was from his own youthful dreams and deceptions that he wove the character and tragi-comic story of Balázs Hübele, the main hero of his versified novel. The path of this hero leads through the gradual failure of his great dreams and great plans to his complete annihilation. The presentation of *The Hero of the Mirages* is consistently critical, rejecting a happy ending or a moral absolution, and by showing how an environment determined by social conditions assimilates the hero who sets out with different strivings, the immanent criticism of the story is levelled at that society.

The versified novel of László Arany was the finest among the numerous poetic narratives of the period (Gyulai and János Vajda also wrote some), which were incidentally strongly influenced by Károly Bérczy's magnificent translation of *Onegin* (1886).

In the post-1849 folk plays—and this also applies to Szigligeti's development—there was ever less evidence of a striving for the rendering of reality, and though there were experiments in the direction of realism (Szigligeti: *Foundling;* L. Abonyi: *The Outlaw's Kerchief,* etc.), the folk character of these plays—which had previously been one of the most important features of democratic realism—now became a curiosity, the folk concepts assumed a purely rural, agrarian colouring and became bearers of a stylized, pseudo-national, pseudo-folk character.

An approach to realism was made by GERGELY CSÍKY (1842-1891), who first wrote in the neo-romantic manner and later learned from French bourgeois drama. He exposed the conditions and morals of the decadent and domineering Hungarian squires and bourgeoisie of his time in his highly successful dramas, *The Proletarians* (1880) and *Fancy Poverty* (1881). Here, the character portrayal and conflicts are, however, not profound, while the characters are repetitive and not infrequently stereotyped. Csíky's concept of man and society was that of the average bourgeois and this did not permit his playwriting to attain fulfilment in the sense of critical realism.

The dissolution of the objective idealist approach of national classicism and of the folk-national school took place in the oppositional lyricism that turned against the epigons of Petőfi and Arany. Its greatest figure was János Vajda, other representative members being Gyula Reviczky and Jenő Komjáthy. It was in their lyrical writing and particularly in the realistic-naturalistic prose narrative of the turn of the century, both closely linked to the peasantry, that the great literary rebirth of the early twentieth century was rooted.

The greatest lyrical poet of the second half of the nineteenth century, thanks to the modernity of his approach, was JÁNOS VAJDA (1827-1897). A poet of plebeian origin, whose subsequent obstinacy and haughtiness were probably nurtured by his childhood experiences, he belonged to the circle of Petőfi. He took part in the War of Independence, with the failure of which he identified the fiasco of his own ascendancy and of his boundless ambitions. Adopting a course between that of the Jacobine Petőfi and of Kossuth, who represented the progressive nobility, the plebeian Vajda in his poetry of the fifties was akin to Arany. He opposed the political and social outlook of the autocracy, but his protest was more heated than that of Arany and suggested at the same time distance and isolation, to which he referred in a poem of his own. This was the period in which his hatred of the world expressed itself in his song-like, but philosophical nature-poems which asked the hopeless, melancholy question, "why be born? why live?" *(Lamentations*, 1854-1856).

His lyrical qualities and thoughtfulness found new soil in his love poetry: by the light of his love for an increasingly depraved prostitute, and in the sense of continuous failure, he came to recognize the injustice of social institutions. For years the beauty of Gina and his own rejected love were the sole subjects of his poetry; his was a sensuous, wild and desperate passion, not really love, but the contradictory emotional world of a pagan's hymn to beauty and the Christian's deliberate self-mortification, all of which he expressed in overwhelming pictures. In the second poem of the cycle entitled *Gina's Memory*, the torment of his love is expressed in the pictures of a forest fire, with the flame-ravaged wood as the image of his passion-scorched soul. His love poetry, with its ghostly, sepulchral overtones, diverged far from its beginnings (it had been Vörösmarty in particular whose influence had been added to Petőfi's) and the increasingly intense heat of the commonplaces of romanticism ever more faithfully reflected the suffering of this modern and harassed soul.

The 60's saw the advent of his most critical period. He apparently acquiesced in the compromise with Austria (according to the evidence of his pamphlets), but in actual fact it was his hatred of feudal Hungary and his insistent demand for bourgeois development that led him to this attitude, for he laboured under the delusion that he could expect a Hungary united with the Austrians to bring about the full achievement of the bourgeois world. This, too, was the beginning of his persecution, particularly by Gyulai, so that Vajda left Pest and took a post at the Chancellery in Vienna almost ceasing to write any lyrical works between 1862 and 1872. However, it was at this very period, from about 1867, that the opposition turned to him as to its leader and began to organize against the literary Deák Party and Gyulai's system of cliques, so that Vajda acquired enthusiastic young supporters at a time when both his political opponents and the official literary trend began their drive against him.

He became a great poet in the 70's. His realization of Hungary's drift to the imperialist side and of the darker aspects of capitalism lent him a more profound political insight, and it was now as part of his programme that he turned to poetry concerned thought and philosophy *(Infinity)*. With a tormenting desire for cognition, he kept returning to some of his permanent problems in the theory of knowledge (the principle of the conservation and the permanence of matter, the problems of existence and death), which are significant not for their originality, but because of their release of emotional feeling and the poetic, arresting and engaging pursuit to the ultimate end of his obsession. At the depth of this crisis—his torturing obsession with the conservation of matter— lay the latent crisis of a man searching for an escape, including a philosophical escape, from the conditions of post-1867 Hungary, and unable to find it. Even his greater political poems *(Jubilate,* a scourging of the avidity of Hungarian society for titles and ranks) were surpassed in beauty by his philosophical verse and by the love poems he wrote at the close of his life. Of the latter, his *Twenty Years Past* (1876) might be mentioned; it is a poem of intense subtle music and fine construction about the power of remembrance to reawaken a heart that no longer flames. Again in *After Thirty Years* (1892) his love is conveyed through the perfect sensory image of the quiescent nocturnal forest after a storm, suggesting the emotional atmosphere of relief, the awesome awareness of death and a heart that weeps despite its resignation. His tremendous philosophical poem *Summer Night* might almost be taken for a poetic paraphrase of Pascal's saying: *"Le silence éternel des espaces infinies m'effraie."* In the poems *In the Forest of Vál* and *Beneath the Trees of Bikol* he again expressed the almost obsessively oppressive ideas of the infinity and eternity of matter and the dizziness of space and time, but in a modern, song form of ephemeral delicacy.

Even more than Reviczky and Komjáthy, János Vajda was the representative figure of the lyricism and the lyrical rebirth of the second half of the nineteenth century, for his opposition to the social order of the whole of post-1867 Hungary simultaneously expressed the increasingly abstract human relations of the new urban life, and the apparently inescapable solitude, pregnant with modern, tormenting philosophical problems, which were a feature of capitalist society.

The characteristic features of the sad career of GYULA REVICZKY (1855-1889), leading to an early death in destitution, were his lack of a perspective in life, the unfavourable influence of the historical vacuum on the development of his character, and an involuntary, but later increasingly deliberate, decadence. He was an illegitimate child who—unable to sacrifice the appearance of gentle birth—assumed the name of the debauched father who ruined his life, and a consumptive who, for all his tribulations, could not escape from the philosophy of life embodied in "the world is but a mood." So he became far removed from the folk-national trend, but nevertheless stopped short of the school of symbolic lyricism. He was considerably influenced by Schopenhauer. In his song-like, city *chanson* poetry and the great poems in which he voiced his emotional suffering, he was the first to sing of love for prostitutes, the sincere love that is more valuable than the mendacious, perfidious morality of the bourgeoisie. Though the great Russian realists and his experiences of life also directed his attention to the true problems of the period, he reacted to these— including the lives of those crippled by capitalism—with intellectual cosmopolitanism and sentimental, decadent, pessimisticlyrics. However, in his poems of escape to the realm of dreams, of introversion of an almost disembodied world, he frequently rose to heights of revealing confessional sincerity. This new, extraordinarily suggestive lyrical hero, with his subjectivity and all-pervading sorrow, rendered Reviczky highly popular in his own period. He contributed considerably in preparing the way for Ady, the poetic giant of the twentieth century.

JENŐ KOMJÁTHY (1858-1895), Reviczky's friend, was a pessimistic poet but his inspiration was rebellious, with an urge to command and dominate. Under the liberating influence of Petőfi, Nietzsche and Spinoza, he made the individual's recklessness, the superman's immoderate will and self-assertion almost his form of existence. This devotee of the religion of the self adopted idea of the ego as his divinity, and thus marked the culmination of the genius-theory of Vajda and Reviczky. It was an inmost lyrical need that drove him to the discovery of this approach, at whose rock bottom lay contempt and the revolutionary castigation of the society extant at the close of the century, though this was only to be expressed in a few verses which came very close to voicing the class struggle and even betrayed an understanding for the labour movement. A characteristic lyrical attitude of the poet was his astonishment at himself and at the moment of "revelation" and enlightenment, followed by the magical metamorphosis of his person, flowing from one being to another. "The mysterious removal of his own self, his contemplation of his erstwhile latent state, waiting to erupt, followed without any transition or explanation by his present-day manifestation breaking forth with elemental force—this is one of his most portentous lyrical attitudes ... Ady's powerful symbolism suggests some inspiration derived from Komjáthy," as János Horváth, the eminent scholar of bourgeois literary history, who recently died, noted.

The great poetic and literary revolution of the beginning of the twentieth century which centred around Ady, reached back to this subjective lyricism, the poetry of Vajda, Reviczky and Komjáthy, as also to the analytical, critical realistic-naturalistic prose narrative that evolved from the eighties of the century.

Taking the literary periodical *A Hét* (The Week), edited by József Kiss and established in 1890, as the direct antecedent of the twentieth-century revival and the *Nyugat* movement, as indeed the membership of its set of authors shows it to be, the rejuvenation of narrative prose which began in the eighties is seen only to have reached fulfilment in the 1890's or even later, with the development and completion of the work of Elek Gozsdu, Ödön Iványi and Zsigmond Justh in the late eighties or early nineties.

The great "anecdotal" realist art of Jókai began to be developed into modern critical realism by ARNOLD VÉRTESI (1836-1911), in his most important novel, *His Honour Mr. Bert Gandy* (1886). The story is about the dizzy career of an insignificant little provincial journalist who has achieved prominence by means of an electioneering trick. Vértesi had written an enormous number of short stories by the seventies. As with several of his contemporaries, he, too, was influenced by the northern writers and the Russian realists; it was in this spirit that he became one of the early exposers of the squirearchal world and of corruption in public life.

LAJOS TOLNAI (1837-1902) was endowed with considerably greater talent than Vértesi, though his gifts became distorted and unable to find a form for their expression. Tolnai began his career as a poet, an epigon of Arany, and it was precisely in the year of the Compromise that he turned to narrative prose. In *The Gentlemen* (1872) he described the period of oppression through the fate of two peasant families, showing how the penurious alien officials exterminated the prosperous peasants with gentlemanly pretensions. Here already, Tolnai destroyed the illusions of passive resist-

170

ance. His greatest novels belonged to the eighties, including two in 1882: *Her Ladyship the Baroness* and *Noble Blood*. The former, in a graphic representation of the period that was broader than in *The Gentlemen*, showed the struggle of those who opposed the autocracy against the traitors. In the latter, and in his subsequent important novels, he portrayed the decline and moral depravity of the aristocracy and the landowners with powerful passion. In some of his works he presented the class divisions of the villages and their class struggle, particularly as manifested on the moral plane *(The Lords of the Village)*, as well as the hopeless fate of those county officials who stood for democratic ideals *(The Mayor)*. The novel which provided the broadest social vista was *The New County Lieutenant*, the story of a poor peasant's son who became the senior official of the county, and of the struggle for his principles and for the consistent execution of the laws, while one after another of the malpractices in the county is exposed.

Tolnai exercised sharp criticism of Hungarian society in the period of the Compromise, but his temper and moral prejudices prevented him from definitely establishing socially typical figures. In his characters it was frequently the moral aspect that was stressed, in accordance with his own smouldering acrimony. An arresting expression of his difficult nature at odds with all superior authority, quick-tempered and undisciplined, and also of his persecution, is to be found in his fine autobiographical novel *The Dark World*. His successors, and especially the greatest Hungarian realist, Zsigmond Móricz, came to like him for his courage as an author, for his frankness, and for overthrowing the principle of poetic justice required by Gyulai.

ELEK GOZSDU (1855-1919) was the first deliberately to break with the anecdotic approach of Jókai. In his short stories it was the Darwinian view of life that determined the fate of his characters, who eloquently revealed their socially determined status. They were the victims of social injustice. Gozsdu's pessimism was connected with Russian influences (Turgenev), which he was the first to accept in a fruitful fashion in his pithy stories.

ÖDÖN IVÁNYI (1859-1893), who died young, was more significant as a narrator and exercised a greater influence through his short stories, his satirical writing on the squires and the financial

171

avarice of capitalism and his works concerned with workers. His main novel, which appeared in 1888, was *The Bishop's Relatives*, whose principal hero was the newly appointed under-secretary and his kin. This swarm of squirearchs successively devour the more gifted and richer of their species who might have been worthy of a better fate. The novel gives a plastic rendering of life in the capital, of parliament, the new morals of the press, the evolving literary life and of the countryside, both on the episcopal estate and in the impoverished manors of the petty squires, all set in the framework of a dramatic plot which is comprehensively able to unite the panorama of contemporary society. The fact that Iványi, too, devoted attention to the European novel of his period and to the natural sciences is apparent from the often biologically deterministic presentation of his characters. As a journalist he smoothed the path of the militant bourgeois publicistic writing that was to culminate in the works of Ady.

ZSIGMOND JUSTH (1863-1894), who came from an illustrious family of the propertied nobility, was one of the most active members of the literary salons of Pest and Paris, a restless traveller in France, Italy, Egypt, Greece and India, and the initiator of peasant play-acting. In his vast cycle of novels *The Genesis of Excellence*, of which three volumes were completed, he aimed to present the Hungarian society of his epoch in a dialectical, and at the same time, under the influence of Zola, in a naturalistic manner. His principal work was *Fuimus*, with its striking self-criticism from inside the propertied class, and with the elevation of that peasantry—of the very poorest, the toiling peasants—from whom Justh expected the solution to lead out of the mire of the Compromise.

The brightest and most promising critical gifts of the period were those of JENŐ PÉTERFY (1850-1899), who was the last to appear beside Gyulai, and who committed suicide, thus ending a life early torn by inner conflict. He was the founder of modern Hungarian essay-writing and at the same time the advocate of a realism with a strong aesthetic emphasis. He was wryly critical of Jókai's illusionism. His finest essays were about Dante and the Greek classics.

It was at the end of the period—from the early 80's to the late

Buttler. Not all the wealth and influence of the fabulously rich Buttler had sufficed to have this "godless" bond dissolved and to enable him to win his true love. It was from this story that Mikszáth wrote his great novel in which both the structure and the characters expose and brand the desperate lust for power of the obsolete and decaying forces of society. This novel was an overt and unconcealed eruption of hatred in which Mikszáth depicted the feudal world—including its contemporary phase—as an enemy of human happiness. An even more comprehensive portrait of society was furnished in the novel *The Affair of Young Noszty with Mari Tóth* (1908). A haughty but declining and increasingly penurious family of the nobility stretched out their tentacles upon Mari Tóth, the daughter of a rich Hungarian bourgeois who had returned from America—this is the theme of the novel. Mikszáth excelled in his presentation of the Noszty family, of the County and of the public life of the country generally, directed from Pest. The whole of the nobiliary state machinery become Feri Noszty's game-beaters in his hunt for the dowry. Only that middle-class Hungarian, Mihály Tóth, successfully opposes this adventurer and he is the first plebeian hero to have been given a central place in the plot of a Mikszáth novel. This work brought a break with the traditional type of nobiliary family novel—it was the immediate precursor of the new content of Zsigmond Móricz's novels about the squire families. And though Mikszáth's work was not yet endowed with the dramatic tension to be found with Móricz, in his exacerbated conflicts and the broad panorama of the family he too presented a concentrated picture of the decaying world of the nobility. Mikszáth's last great novel, *The Black Town*, had a historical subject from the *Kuruc* period, being the story of the struggle of the town of Lőcse against the country's haughty, noble deputy-lieutenant, with a tragic end involving the annihilation of the deputy-lieutenant. Looking back from his own period Mikszáth saw in his seventeenth-century story only the disintegrating world of the nobility, a petty citizenry, in the process of degenerating into a bourgeoisie that suppressed all free and beautiful human happiness. These forces were engaged in a bitter struggle of sheer class selfishness. "The emphasis in his novel was not, however, placed on the class struggle but on the criticism of classes which

175

were unable to rise to the height of assuming responsibility for their country. It was not a class struggle that he depicted in the clash between Lőcse and County Szepes, but the prospectless self-ishness of classes," István Király writes. Recognizing and showing up in the historical novel the problems of his own age, he accused the nobility and the bourgeoisie of narrow-mindedness and re-proached both for having lost sight of the country's cause.

This work also marked the end of his life. The author, who had come close to great realism, became as valuable a precursor of Zsigmond Móricz, the great critical realist of the twentieth century, as a whole host of writers in the eighties and nineties had been, who, though they were further removed from the anecdotal trend and were anti-romantic, were of narrower vision and lesser gifts. The heritage of Mikszáth and of the minor writers like Gozsdu and Iványi was to be continued and would attain new classical heights in the tremendous *oeuvre* of Zsigmond Móricz.

# PART THREE

# THE TWENTIETH CENTURY

BY MIKLÓS SZABOLCSI

# THE BEGINNINGS
## OF MODERN LITERATURE (1890-1905)

As elsewhere in Europe, the end of the nineteenth century brought some momentous changes in Hungary. The political and social fabric resulting from the Compromise of 1867 had held water for some time, but was now rapidly falling out of date. New forces had arisen and were now straining to burst the seams of the Dual Monarchy of Austria-Hungary; capitalist development was gathering momentum in Hungary's national minority regions inhabited by Slovaks, Croats, Rumanians; manufacturing industry had sprung up and was now expanding on a large scale, and with it was growing up a Hungarian industrial working class; class division became sharply defined throughout the agricultural population; and an emergent and vigorous (though heterogeneous) Hungarian middle class of merchants, artisans, officials and intellectuals—composed of drop-away fragments of the Hungarian gentry and elements of German and Jewish descent—was becoming increasingly vociferous. The hectic growth which was turning Budapest into a big city was giving rise to fresh exigencies and demands; the influx of foreign ideas and trends of thought, and their absorption, became accelerated, producing an effervescent literary and cultural life. The popular-nationalist movement, by now fossilised into official academism, was still holding on to posts of command in literature and science; but a new Hungarian literature—though as yet in an embryonic stage and still fraught with contradictions—was already in the making.

At the outset, the new trends found an organ in the review *A Hét* (The Week), started in 1890 under the editorship of József Kiss, the poet. Uneven in content as the new periodical was as yet, it nevertheless managed to rally more than one writer who was searching for a way out of the stuffy atmosphere of conservatism that overhung the literary scene of the end of the century. Intellectually alert and lively in tone, and marked by an urbanism that mocked at rigid authority, *A Hét* strove, in essence, to create a modern—big-city—literature as opposed to the provincialism of the traditionalist school; it had, however, no radical, political programme.

Otherwise the dominant trends and schools of thought of the period were much the same as those which held sway in other countries of Europe at the time, namely, naturalism, calling for a more profound, unvarnished, ruthless representation of life; greater emphasis on psychological analysis; the physiological and biological outlook; "free-thinking"; anti-religious views; materialism. In philosophy, the influence of Schopenhauer and Nietzsche mingled with that of Comte, and many were acquainted with the writings of Spencer. In many respects the new literature was as yet a rather incongruous mixture of heterogeneous elements. Though *A Hét* did constitute some sort of a rallying point, the new movement of the moderns lacked a real pivot, and so, in the absence of such a centre, the modernist movement was but a mass of isolated, individual ambitions and divergent attempts, of experiments eagerly begun yet soon abandoned. By the early twentieth century, indeed, the energy generated by the urge to create something new had fizzled out.

The poetry of the period was characterized largely by a loosening of old forms and old manner and by a freshness, a lightness and urbanism of content. JÓZSEF KISS (1843-1921) was the first Hungarian man of letters to interpret Hungarian-Jewish themes at a high artistic standard, though still using the equipment of the popular-nationalist school. The son of a village publican, he built up a long record of service as teacher and white-collar worker in the country before attracting attention by his ballads with a Jewish theme. Following his literary success, he went to live in Budapest, where he strove to create a new-type, big-city poetry; he interpreted the moods and feelings of the city dweller, loosening up and reshaping old verse and mixing the characteristic Magyar metre with Western forms. About the turn of the century (in *Fires*, and later in the poem, *The Cruiser Potemkin*), he even voiced some revolutionary sympathies. Apart from that, Kiss moved in the world of Hungarian Liberalism—a circumstance that made him sound irrevocably dated when, after 1905, new and more radical trends made their appearance in Hungarian literature.

A more modern tone was struck by JENŐ HELTAI (1871-1957), the poet who initiated the light, satirical, humorous *chanson*-like poetry. Jenő Heltai was an interpreter of the peculiar temper of the Budapest citizen—a blend of sarcasm, a touch of sentimentality and a large dose of cynicism; the "Gallic" note of the metropolitan spirit ("Gallic" taken in the sense of the light "export Gallicism" of the end of the century) was first sounded by him, and he wrote numerous skits and lyrics for cabaret shows. He was certainly more important as a prose writer: his novels—witty, imaginative, full of surprise turns but without any deeper message—and hundreds of feuilletons show him as the exponent of the light-hearted short story hinging on a pointed joke. *The Silent Knight*, a neo-romantic comedy in verse, won much success in the 1930's and has retained its hold of the stage since.

During the preparatory period of modern Hungarian literature, more lasting work was produced by prose writers. SÁNDOR BRÓDY (1863-1924) declared himself to be a dedicated "naturalist." He attracted notice by a volume of short stories entitled *Poverty* in the 1880's and from that time onward published volumes of short stories, novels, dramas and newspaper articles each year. An uneven writer, he belonged to that class of authors in whom the urge to enjoy life, the social façade overshadowed the creative man. This strikingly handsome hedonist, who squandered his talent, was idolised by women and generally admired by turn-of-the-century Budapest. His *oeuvre*, too, is unequal: in his short stories, passion-filled and written in a style all his own but too often dashed off in a rough-and-ready manner, he captures themes of changing life, of love and poverty, of the merciless fate of the poor and of the Budapest world of finance, but is often checked by a certain conformism, social or artistic. In his plays *(The Nurse*, 1902, and *The Schoolmistress*, 1908), too, he broaches novel, social, topics with a certain sketchiness, but also with undeniable force and dynamism. He is at his best in those writings in which he cries out his lament over his ruined life and in which he expresses the profound lyricism of ripe manhood *(Cavalier of the Day and Rembrandt Sells his Corpse)*. Bródy was prolific as a writer of newspaper articles, critic and annalist—over many years he would bring out his *White Books* containing animated, colourful accounts of the events of the time and their protagonists. His lifework, though unfinished in character, exemplifies the incipient literature of the Hungarian middle class, and despite its contradictions, was one of the precursors of modern Hungarian literature.

Another harbinger of the rejuvenated literature was ZOLTÁN AMBRUS (1861-1932), a writer of a quite different stamp from Bródy. On a study-trip to Paris in his young manhood he embraced the achievements of end-of-the-century French literature, and this French prose—the analytical novel and the psychological play—remained his literary ideal throughout. A sense of proportion, restraint, and lucidity of style, an even, well-balanced composition and subdued narrative manner are the marks of his analytical writing. His portrayal of the life of the Budapest bourgeoisie, of the inner secrets of the *haute finance,* is delicately ironical. A theatrical expert of note, his ideals were those of the French dramatists and, in the field of criticism, of Sarcey. His personality provided a link with the new literature, whose aims he always treated with the sympathy and understanding of an elder brother.

Among the forerunners of modern literature we find a group of writers who—each speaking in an individual voice all his own— were representatives of critical realism, cultivating chiefly the psychoanalytical short story. The careers of nearly all of them were broken off soon as they died young, or lost interest, or their ambition spent itself. The most forceful and most distinct personality in the group was ZOLTÁN THURY (1870-1906). In his excellently constructed short stories he reproduces the world of the urban lower classes, and also of poverty-stricken peasants. He was one of the first writers to report, with a harsh pen, the unvarnished truth, the seething discontent, the social evils, that remained obscured behind the fireworks of Hungary's millenary celebrations. His style owes a good deal to Chekhov, but is sharper-cut and more wiry than its model. Also in his few plays *(e.g. Soldiers)*, which created a stir at the time, he explored the ills of contemporary Hungarian society. His poverty, his struggle to make ends meet, put him early into his grave; he did not live to see his initiative continued by the new generation of writers, including Endre Ady, who was a great admirer of Thury.

DÁNIEL PAPP's (1865-1900) literary career covers but a few years. This liberal newspaperman was a versatile and productive writer of *feuilletons*. The Bácska country (in South Hungary) is faithfully depicted in his writings, and the world of the man in the street, the bourgeois, the officer of the Austro-Hungarian Empire is represented with mild sarcasm. His works, which are imbued with an atmosphere of tragedy, are decidedly of an intellectual character and are an integral part of the reform endeavours of the end of the nineteenth century.

Another noted prose writer of the end of the nineteenth century was ISTVÁN PETELEI (1852-1910). His best works were written in the 1880's. He depicted the country middle class and village folks, concentrating on moral questions, particularly that of the emancipation of women, a burning issue by the end of the century. His writing is tinged with tragedy; its timbre and his muffled, at times languid, narrative are reminiscent of the Russian authors of the time.

Far from the hustle and bustle of the capital, in Szeged, the second largest city of Hungary at that period, lived and worked one of the most original (and still most widely read) narrative writers of the period, ISTVÁN TÖMÖRKÉNY (1866-1917), a country chemist turned journalist, then director of Szeged Museum, which post he retained until his death. At first, he cultivated the newspaper short story, a genre greatly in vogue at the end of the century; and he began by following in the footsteps of Bret Harte, but soon evolved an original style. In his short stories— revealing a touch of the folklorist, but nevertheless classically shaped and wrought with highly conscientious craftsmanship—he depicted the life and manners of the peasants and artisans of Szeged and its vicinity, a typically Hungarian area. Interest and sympathy for the poor, for the common people, careful observation of popular customs, and conscious realism hallmark his

writings. Though he was not consistently progressive in his views
—they were characterised by a conservative provincial liberalism
—his unquestioning respect for reality opened his eyes to the
growing impoverishment and to the plight of the peasantry; what
is more, it led him to represent in his most intense and dramatic
writings *(On Strike ; Hühü ; Workers)* the organised struggle of
labour and the solidarity of workers and peasants. A portrayer
of the world of "riverborne workers" and of the "hewers of wood
and drawers of water," Tömörkény still observed the life below
from without and above; yet his work stands out as one of the
highest peaks of realism, of sympathy for the common people, in
early twentieth-century literature. Even Tolstoy spoke highly of his
writings.

Another author who became known as a provincial writer
was GÉZA GÁRDONYI (1863-1922). The son of a village blacksmith,
he was a school-teacher for many years before entering journalism
in Budapest, to retire, eventually, as a celebrated author, into
seclusion in his cottage on a hill rising next to the old town of
Eger. Like Tömörkény, he attracted attention as an observer of
peasant life; after some peasant caricatures, he soon hit upon the
most congenial genre, the rural idyll, drawing idealised figures of
peasants with unsophisticated views and ways *(My Village, 1898)*.
He saw the peasants essentially through Rousseauian spectacles
and depicted the conflicts and little comedies of their private lives.
Written in his characteristic plain, clear-cut and concise style, his
stories made a strong impression upon his readers: the reading
public of the late nineteenth century preferred to see the Hungarian peasant life "unspoilt" and harmonious as Gárdonyi depicted it. In later years, Gárdonyi took to writing historical novels
and novels of manners. In his historical novels he sought an answer
to the question of how the impact of historic events affects the
withdrawn, passive individual *(The Invisible Man, 1902, whose
action takes place in the time of Attila of the Huns; and the
thirteenth-century story of The Captives of God, 1908)*. In his best,
and most widely read, historical novel—*Stars of Eger, 1901*—he
conjures up the sixteenth-century world of Hungarian fortresses
defying the advancing Turkish armies, doing this in a succession
of graphic, colourful scenes full of movement and pervaded by

his profound understanding of his fellow-man. His novels of manners are interesting variations on the central theme of love, the sweeping passion—that "fatal force" which issues from Woman and is the undoing of Man. Gárdonyi is the novelist *par excellence* of Unhappy Love, a misogynist and an abhorrer of marriage—a mentality engendered in him by a deep crisis in his own life. Gárdonyi was the product of a phase of transition: his view of the world, and the picture he paints of reality, reflect the concepts of Old Hungary, but his restlessness, his philosophy, his crisis tell the tale of an old system of values upset and a groping for something new.

The portrait gallery of this turn-of-the-century literature is wound up with the writer who for many years was the officially recognised leading writer of semi-feudal Hungary—FERENC HERCZEG (1863-1954). A "gentleman writer" he started by describing the life of revelries and love-affairs led by the gentry and nobility (mostly Hussar officers)—a devil-may-care life lived with some elegant nonchalance—and he described it with the facility and in the conversational tone of the well-informed insider. He made his name with these short stories; he fully satisfied the taste of his class and conformed to the light-minded, superficial style of living followed by the early twentieth-century Hungarian gentry. It is the position and problems—and, sometimes, inner conflicts— of this ruling class that we see reflected and solved in his (at one time widely read) historical novels and plays. Bitterly opposed to any new, progressive, literary trend, Herczeg lived to see, in the 20's and 30's, his own apotheosis as "author laureate" of Admiral Horthy's Hungary. The most durable pieces of his work are a number of short stories, written with a Maupassantian technique, in which he gives a realistic portrayal of his environment.

The last poets of note in the nationalist line were active during the first decade of the twentieth century. The poetry of GYULA VARGHA (1853-1929) flourished about 1900; his poems voice the fears of the Hungarian ruling classes in face of the looming threats to their rule. He wrote in a pessimistic tone and his lyrics added a new touch of colour to the spectrum of the nationalist school: his symbols, his exquisiteness and floating

185

melodiousness constituted, as it were, a bridge to *Nyugat*\* magazine. ANDOR KOZMA (1861-1933), whose facility of versification sometimes reaches peaks of virtuosity, and who spoke in the voice of the so-called conservative liberalism, was a popular poet in his time. MIHÁLY SZABOLCSKA (1862-1930) was the most diehard of all conservatives, an unsophisticated believer in the "idyll" of rural life and the "charm" of provincial tradition.

The literary "wave" of 1890 produced but initial and ambiguous results—a ferment was brought about in literature, a restless search for new ways; the rising Hungarian urban bourgeoisie found its voice; and fresh developments raised new problems. These trends were given both shape and an aim, and also a head, in the first decade of the new century, in the poetry of Endre Ady.

\* See page 190 for literary significance of *Nyugat*.

# THE RISE OF MODERN
# HUNGARIAN LITERATURE (1905-1914)

By the beginning of the twentieth century, the symptoms had multiplied of a deep-seated inner conflict going on behind the glittering façade of power of Austria-Hungary. At the same time, the conflict of imperialism in ascendancy all over the world called forth new trends in Hungarian political and intellectual life.

The continued development of big industry in Hungary was building up a head of steam that was bound, one day, to blow to pieces the extremely outdated, essentially feudal system of government. Unrest was brewing in the capital and throughout the countryside: the industrial working class, increased in both numbers and power, the radical sections of the rising intelligentsia, and the discontented agricultural labourers and poor peasants— all these elements were seething and organising. It was evident that a revolution was in the making—a bourgeois revolution that would be called upon to accomplish what the abortive Revolution of 1848-49 had failed to bring off; however, this new revolutionary upsurge subsided before it had actually begun. But this brewing of a bourgeois revolution, the strengthening of the labour movement and the Socialist Party, was accompanied by a cultural and literary revival of an extent that had not been seen since the Reform Age in the first half of the preceding century.

The conservative trend of literature continued in the popular-nationalist tradition; to rebel against it, to search for new forms, new sentiments and new ideas was to enter the battle for the new, modern, Hungarian literature and, what is more, for a new Hungary. The Academy, the Universities and the scientific bodies and literary societies were all controlled by the traditionalists, the only challenge to whose supremacy so far had come from some short-lived magazines, ephemeral attempts. However, the literary movement was favoured and supported by a variety of factors, such as the growing strength of trade unions, the continued spread of socialist views, the periodicals and circles started by the organising radical middle-class intellectuals—first of all the *XX. Század* (20th Century), a sociological review which devoted some space to literature; and then the movement of radical—and later socialist—students centred round the Galilei Circle.

The yearning for revival was not confined to the sphere of literature: new tendencies appeared in the arts as well. In painting, the new movement was marked by the Nagybánya School (Károly Ferenczy and circle), József Rippl-Rónai, who had close connections with the French *Nabis* during his studies in Paris, and Pál Szinyei-Merse, the initiator of impressionism in Hungary, a painter far in advance of his age. It was in these years that two young composers, Béla Bartók and Zoltán Kodály, reached a turning-point in their careers and began to explore the true Hungarian folk music which would supply them with the material from which they would create modern Hungarian music. The Thália Society, with an eye to a wide audience, made a new initiative in the theatre parallel with—and inspired by—Antoine and the *Freie Bühne*.

There was lively interest in the literary and philosophical trends of other countries—with Nietzsche's influence unabated, the philosophy of Spencer, Guyau and Bergson was discussed and analysed. Tolstoy and Dostoevsky, Baudelaire and Verlaine; then the French symbolist poets; the soft-toned lyrics of the German *fin de siècle* and, in particular, of Vienna, the poetry of Rilke, Dehmel and Hofmannsthal; the dramas of Ibsen and Hauptmann; Anatole France and the courageous naturalism of Zola, all exercised their influence and had a following. As in other countries of Europe, diverse trends made their impact felt simultaneously and, sometimes, produced conflicting influences: Tolstoy and Wilde, the idealist anarchists and Spencer, Lassalle and Bernstein all arrived at about the same time.

What the movement for literary revival aimed at was, above all, the creation of modern literature; it conceived the striving to catch up with the West, adopting (often in a random, haphazard way) all that seemed new and modern there. The literary product of this period breathes a *fin de siècle* atmosphere, shows the strong colours of naturalism, and suggests the technique of impressionism, the manner of the *art nouveau*, the enervation of the late symbolists—or even the freshness of the Parisian cabaret, the inventiveness of French comedy. Yet all this was not mere imitation—the foremost writers of Hungary were conscious of being heirs to a great literature and they grafted the new influences into the body of the Hungarian literary heritage. A lively, modern and truly national literature—that was the object which—whether they realised it or not—animated all. Ady's words, "the new songs of a new epoch," might serve as a motto for the movement as a whole.

For some time, the new literature still presented a rather motley, heterogeneous spectacle—mannerisms, imitation and passing vogues mingled in it with the truly new and significant. The struggle for the new literature was not without a contradictory element, in the same way as the struggle for bourgeois revolution was also fraught with contradiction. As the latter brought into alliance middle-class elements whose ambition was the achievement of a capitalist way of life in Hungary with others who stood for radical reforms and a consistent bourgeois democracy and with those who more or less consistently championed the cause of a socialist Hungary, so did the movement for literary revival unite people with all sorts of aims and ambitions who had one thing in common: that all of them were hostile to official literature. Some were motivated by no more than a search for new tones, new flavours, new sensations or new styles, conforming to the fashion of the *art nouveau* or of late nineteenth-century decadence. But there were those who realised that the revolution in letters did in fact conceal a social revolution and was part of the fight for a New Hungary. Some only fought for the consistent application of liberal views, for full freedom of writing; others strove for a ruthless exposure of reality. Often, these conflicting aspirations, this entanglement of diverse systems of thought would be apparent not only in the same review or within the same literary coterie, but also in the various stages of the careers of individual writers and critics.

The intellectual ferment in Hungary received a powerful stimulus in 1905 and the years that followed. The Russian Revolution of 1905 acted as an eye-opener and encouragement—between the years 1905 and 1908, agitation among the Hungarian industrial workers was at its height; it was in these years that the official government policies met with a crisis and cracks appeared in the edifice of the Dual Monarchy. The formerly brief and isolated attempts now began to assume a consolidated form.

After many short-lived attempts to bring out an authoritative literary magazine (*The Hungarian Genius, The Observer, Wednesday*), at last, early in 1908, was launched the review *Nyugat* (The West), which for over thirty years—until 1941—continued publication as one of the leading literary periodicals and, for the next ten years at least—until 1918—was to play a crucial part as the pivot and spearhead of the new literature, which it led to victory. It rallied and reared a generation of new writers: getting one's writing published in its columns meant a definite literary status. On the whole, *Nyugat* had only a negative programme: it tilted at everything and anything that was outdated, old-fashioned, and it gave space to every individual hue, tone and ambition. It advocated a revolution in literature and the arts; only one group of its contributors went further than that to embrace a programme of social transformation. It found its readers and source of financial basis in the Budapest middle class and it is to its everlasting credit that it gave space to the greatest geniuses —Endre Ady and Zsigmond Móricz.

Another centre of the struggle for the new literature was brought into being in Nagyvárad, Eastern Hungary. Here, local editors and writers contrived to compose an anthology, which was given the title *Holnap* (Tomorrow) and was brought out in 1908 and 1909; this anthology included every modern poet of note. The early volumes of *Nyugat* and those of *Holnap* as well as Endre Ady's volumes of poetry soon became the subject of heated and loud polemics, both literary and political. Not since the Reform Age in the last century had Hungary witnessed a literary controversy of such intensity and extent. The conservatives, infuriated, attacked the new trends, condemning them as unpatriotic, decadent and diseased, while their liberal adversaries

190

proper and Transylvania. He received a through-and-through Protestant education based on the Bible. On leaving secondary school, he went to Debrecen to study law, but soon took up journalism. It was in Debrecen that Ady's career as a poet began and he got his introduction into the world of the theatre—and night-life. A turning-point in his life came at the end of 1899, when he left Debrecen and went to live in Nagyvárad. In this bustling, vivacious and spirited city, whose intellectual, political and social life grew far beyond the proportions of a provincial town, the backward conditions of Hungary, the antiquated character and untenable situation of feudal Hungary came home to him in startling realisation; here he became, first a convinced liberal, then an ever more militant, consistent radical. From 1901 on, Ady rose as a notable representative of Hungarian political journalism who conducted a fierce and spirited battle against jingoism, clericalism and anti-Semitism, against obscurantism and ignorance. It became evident at this early stage in his career that his observant eye saw beyond the middle-class horizon and watched with sympathy the struggles of the working class; he showed understanding for socialist ideas. As a poet during his Nagyvárad years he still followed the beaten track of the light, cynical parlour poetry of the *fin de siècle*—his two early volumes show but faint traces of the poet-genius of later years.

In the summer of 1903—after many passing fancies—came a great experience: he fell in love with a beautiful, attractive woman, the wife of a Nagyvárad businessman, the Léda of his poems. Theirs was a great, sensuous, tormenting love and it gave birth to a great number of outstanding love-poems. Léda requited his love, and these relations, now harmonious, now wound-inflicting, lasted for many years. It was on her solicitation, and with her support, that Ady went to Paris, spending the whole of 1904, then again more than a year in 1906-07 in France. For him, Paris was a liberating and stimulating experience—there he saw the justification of what he had been trying to formulate at home. Those were the years when the French radicals started their anti-Church campaign and the counter-attacks of the Church got under way. The experience strengthened his anti-clericalism. Another experience that made a deep impression on him was his

realisation of the contradiction inherent in bourgeois democracy—
the rule of Mammon. This induced in him the belief that the progressive movement must not stop at bourgeois democracy, that
it was necessary to advance further than that. At times this
realisation would make him embrace Nietzschean principles and
plunge him into disillusion and despair; in other moments it
would dawn upon him that in Hungary, too, conditions called
for an advance to socialism. All this gained added momentum
from the internal situation of Hungary—the disintegration of the
Liberal Party, which had been in power for several decades, and
on top of all that came the Russian Revolution of 1905, which
gave the decisive impetus. Thus, when, on his return from his
first visit to Paris in 1905, Ady sat down by his desk in the editorial offices of *Budapesti Napló*, in Budapest (where from now on
he was to live and work), he was a man fortified by a rich experience, human as well as political.

About this time he began to publish his volumes of poetry—
poems which were entirely different from anything that Hungarian poetry had produced up to that time in both tone and message. His first volume of this type of verse—*New Poems*—was
brought out in 1906; this was followed by *Blood and Gold* (1907);
*In Elijah's Chariot* (1908); *I Would Love to Be Loved* (1909); *The
Verses of All Mysteries* (1910); *Fugitive Life* (1912); *Love of Our-
selves* (1913); and *Who Has Seen me?* (1914). In between, spread
over the whole period, there appeared volumes of short stories,
newspaper articles and speeches. Soon after the publication of
*New Poems*, Ady became the centre of literary and nationwide
interest. Controversies, one more passionate than the other, flared
up about him—his name became the countersign of all radical
aspirations and movements. He became the Great Divide on either
side of which the fronts took shape. Comic paper snipings, lam-
poons, and attacks by prime ministers alternated with tributes by
scholars. Opinions differed even within his own following. Though
his place among the greatest poets of Hungary has been firmly accepted, there are still disputes about his *oeuvre* and role.

What was the strikingly novel quality of the man and his
poetry? Ady's poetical world is a self-contained world, his language one that is all his own; the range of his themes is an extreme-

ly wide one. One group includes themes like the revolutionary heroes and movements of Hungarian national history; the backwardness of Hungary—the shocking visions of the "Hungarian Fallowland," of the "Hungarian Moorland"; the agony of the poet fighting the "Great Lord with the Boar's Head." Another group of themes: the thousand and one aspects of love, the unashamed presentation of his love for Leda; songs of all the warped complexities of love; and evocations of passing, sensual love-affairs. Another strand is constituted by poems evoking death, fleeting time, fear and solitude; verses that convey the restlessness, the strain and worries, of the modern big-city dweller, his seeking of refuge in God, or his personal quarrel with Him. Lastly, two entirely new themes of crucial importance: the proclamation of his historical mission, a drawing of his own personality, and—crowning his work—the verses of the poet stretching out his hand to the working class.

This is a self-contained world indeed, an entirely new world in Hungarian poetry! In his poems he speaks of himself and of the world around him with a candour, with an ingenuous exhibition of his soul, and with an ardour, that are quite unparalleled in Hungarian letters before him. His poetry grew out of the contradictions of contemporary Hungarian society—and those contradictions it mirrors—and while his poetry and intellectual system undoubtedly owe a good deal to French influences (Baudelaire, Verlaine), and his philosophical system to that of Nietzsche and others, it is absolutely original and unmistakably Hungarian. His basic experience was formed from the sorry plight of the Hungarian people, oppressed, prostrate, exhausted, and the blackguardism of the "well-born cads" who lorded it over them; the haughtiness, the arrogance of the aristocrats of birth and of finance. This was a country, he felt, where you must either be stifled to death or change the set-up boldly, implacably, and although, at times, weariness and disenchantment would overcome him, his revolutionary fervour, his determination to transform conditions, increased steadily. His poetry is charged with the restlessness and suffocating atmosphere of the age, and burns with its yearning for better things, with its feverish revolutionism.

If one were to revert to political terms, one might say that, in a Hungary encumbered with feudal survivals, Ady was championing the cause of a democratic, popular revolution. He felt he was living in a "country all set for an explosion" where "all things are clamouring for transformation, for renewal." He had a deep insight into the problems of being a Hungarian and he felt himself one with his race; he scolded it, castigated it, that he might rouse it from its torpor, stir it to action—he wanted to see his nation advance once again into the van of world progress.

His was a great role indeed, and he played that role with awareness. He had a strong poetic consciousness, a strong sense of vocation; he was one of the race of poet-apostles; and, for all the touches of the Nietzschean superman and Baudelairean Satanism that are evident in his poetic make-up, he was the poet champion of the cause of the people. He was a great individual, a personality integrating sensuality and retirement into quiet love, the lust for money and a hatred for "counts and the rich," and an overriding yearning for a real, full life.

For his individual experience and theme he created a highly individual poetic language and world.

Ady's poetical world is one great forest of symbols. But it is not one in the sense of the Baudelairean *correspondance* and is only too far removed from the French symbolists of the late nineteenth century like Albert Samain, who was in vogue in Hungary. He created a system of symbols, and through them he surveyed the world. These symbols (or, more precisely perhaps, metaphors) were taken from the world of Hungarian realities, of common notions. Under this system of symbols, money becomes the "God Baal," or "the Great Lord with the Boar's Head," Hungary appears as the "Hungarian Fallow," the "Moorland," "the Slough"; the workers are referred to as "the White Ones of the Future." He built for himself a novel prosody: the accent of his verse is determined by its meaning, but it is pierced by the beat of the Western metre and of old Hungarian verse. On the whole, Ady's poetry is at the same time modern and ancient; at the same time it is in the mainstream of the latest European intellectual trends and rooted in the time-honoured core of Magyar tradition. This perfect integration of progress and nationality is of great importance still. His poetical language, too, is new and full of surprise-turns teeming with words taken from the Hungarian linguistic heritage but at the same time endowed with metaphoric qualities. The richness of his store of adjectives, his verbal flow, and the multitude of his own coinages or revivals from the archaic vocabulary of the language combine into a fascinating idiom that is unlike anybody else's.

Following his *début* his poetry grew in power and gradually achieved fulness of development. As the number of his published volumes of poetry, short stories, and newspaper articles increased, so did he develop and grow in stature. After much painful hesitation, in 1912, he broke off his relations with Léda; by this time, he had become about the best-known personality in Hungary, the leading spirit of *Nyugat*. Now began his epic fight with Premier Count István Tisza, the leading representative of feudal Hungary. These were the years when Ady consciously and resolutely held out his hand to the radical students, represented by the Galilei Circle, and took sides with the working class, with socialism. Ady was no socialist revolutionary—he fought for a consistent, democratic bourgeois revolution, that was his ideal which he yearned and longed for. But he was well aware that, under the actual conditions existing in Hungary, with a newly formed and cowardly, spineless middle class, the working class was the only force capable of assuring the democratic freedoms even of capitalism. He saw further than his time, far into the future. He looked upon himself as the representative of the tired peasantry of Hungary—he was the "sad squireen grieving over the people's plight," and he appealed to the students in these words: "Up and along at full speed, O youthful host of Ardour!" And he formulated the address "O people of my blood, Hungarian Proletarians." In 1912 it seemed that the long-awaited revolution had come—on the Red Thursday, a mass demonstration swept through the streets of Budapest—but revolution died in the bud, and Hungary moved along towards the brink of war. In Ady's lyrics, his longing for death, the note of fleeing, a feeling of frustration and solitude became more frequent. However, behind the tones of frustration and world-weariness there is always a lurking note of hope; and his poetry seems to grow clearer, more simple, more refined. There began the cycle of his *Kuruc* verses: he

197

deliberately reached back, even in tone, to the Hungarian people's crushed independence struggle, in his desire to give expression to his virile grief over the downfall of the revolution and his fatherland.

When the First World War came, the poet, now an exhausted and sick man who had been badly tried by many frustrations, was about the only Hungarian writer to speak up unreservedly against the war. He was one of those European writers who held aloft the standard of pre-war ideals, of the good and noble fight for Progress—"a Man in the midst of Inhumanity" who protested against the war to the end, proclaiming it to be sheer senseless killing. His state of health grew steadily worse and it deteriorated so far that not even his marriage, in 1915, could save a life that had been badly undermined by disease. On the other hand, his poetry continued to increase in profundity, clarity and universality. Suddenly, in his later love-poems—the so-called Csinszka poems (addressed to his wife, to whom he had given that fancy name)—a new note was struck: here, the voice of a man in quest of the purity and beauty of Love, of happiness and refuge, was turned against the reign of Death and Inhumanity. He was looking for a companion who would be his comrade-in-arms in his battle of life. In his last poems—those of the volume, *In Death's Foreranks*, 1918, and of his posthumous volume, *The Last Ships*, 1923—we hear the voice of the poet, the lone giant, who suffers for the sake of mankind, which he loves passionately. This voice, increasingly simple and sombre, rings with the grim force of the Biblical prophets. It is the voice of a man yearning for peace and rest and at the same time of a poet ready to fight. Seriously ill, he yet lived to see the triumph of the long-awaited bourgeois revolution, which regarded him as the outstanding representative of the nation. When, in January 1919, he died, all Hungary mourned for him.

No sooner was Ady dead than the contention started for his heritage. The controversy about evaluating and interpreting his *oeuvre* which had sprung up during his life, and in which diverse tendencies joined issue, continued unabated after his death. Ady's work is of crucial significance for Hungarian letters as a whole: his work could not be directly continued, only imitated by countless epigons, but it has served as the great heritage on which many distinguished later poets have been groomed. By now, Ady's work has come to assume its rightful place in the great heritage of Hungarian revolutionary poetry; and it is felt that the whole seething world of the early twentieth century, the mental struggles —and, in general, the cast of mind—of Modern Man is mirrored in his great work.

## ZSIGMOND MÓRICZ (1879-1942)

The other outstanding figure in twentieth-century Hungarian literature and the other leading personality of the *Nyugat* movement besides Ady was ZSIGMOND MÓRICZ (1879-1942), whom many believe to have been the greatest prose writer Hungary has ever produced.

He was born in an out-of-the-way village in the Tisza river district. His father was of peasant stock and his mother a clergyman's daughter. His childhood—as he describes it in numerous short stories and in his brilliant autobiographical writing, *The Romance of my Life*—was spent amid the ups and downs of privation and financial recovery, of humiliation and happiness. His education was acquired in distinguished Hungarian Calvinist seats of learning, and here his intellectual interest was awakened and his literary vein discovered. On leaving secondary school, he became a divinity student, but he soon gave up the cloth for the bar, only to end up in journalism—a common-run newspaperman, an anonymous member on the staff of a Budapest daily, a low-salaried, conservative-minded square peg of a country bumpkin in the metropolitan round hole. It took a good deal of experience, fresh impressions, numerous trips through the countryside and contact established with the rising radical literature to make him find his own mode of expression and realise what he wanted to say. First he had to get rid of the taste, the ideological trappings of feudal Hungary before he could stand on his own feet. He had turned 30 when his first short story—*Seven Pennies*— was published in *Nyugat*, making him overnight a celebrated writer, one of the leading authors of the new literary movement.

His intellectual liberation was owed in a great measure to the poet, Ady, whose poetry—and, later, friendship—provided for him a stimulus and guidance to the end. In Ady, his stodgy, slow-moving temperament hailed the ardent, self-consuming genius, a kindred spirit who fought for the same ideals as himself.

From the publication of *Seven Pennies* until his death, Móricz's output was unbroken: he published novels, short stories, plays, newspaper articles, reportages, and essays, producing one of the most voluminous and most impressive *oeuvres* in Hungarian literature. In the initial phase (1908-1919) of his literary career he attracted notice primarily as a new portrayer of peasant life. The crowded world and stuffy atmosphere of *Pure Gold*, 1910, evokes the Hungarian village writhing in the stranglehold of the latifundium, a world from which the figure of the peasant hero, Dani Turi, stands out almost superhuman. Though it bears many traces of naturalism and of the *art nouveau* of the late nineteenth century, and for all its overemphasis on sex and larger-than-life portraiture, this novel is a significant work: it substitutes for the idyllic image of the peasant and of the Hungarian village as an oasis of harmony and peace the realistic picture of a Hungarian village full of talent but frustrated by obstructive circumstances. *Behind the Beyond*, 1911, calls up the stifling atmosphere, the mustiness and bleakness of life in Hungarian provincial towns in the early twentieth century, a *milieu* in which grotesque narrow-mindedness killed every aspiration to higher things. Apart from *Good Luck!* (1914) an unfinished novel on foundrymen's life, the most significant novel of this, initial, period is *The Torch*, 1917. The principal hero, a Calvinist minister, as he prepares to enter into a living in his native village, cherishes some very ambitious plans, intending to become the leader of his people. Confronted, however, with difficulties, with backwardness and selfishness, and worsted by his weakness and love of comfort, he ends up by accepting the actual conditions and conforming to the ways of the local gentry. Descriptions of good intentions that end in compromise, the character of the well-meaning-intellectual-who-fails, of the reluctant fence-sitter who cannot make up his mind which side he should join—the rulers or the ruled, crops up time and again in Móricz's later works. At the end of *The Torch*, shocked by the experience of a devastating fire, the

ZSIGMOND MÓRICZ (1879-1942)

clergyman utters the melancholy comment: "It hath been consummated; and nothing hath been resolved."

Already, in the course of these years his admirable short stories were appearing besides his novels. After some isolated attempts before him, Móricz succeeded in shaping the modern form of the Hungarian short story—a condensed, terse form, one that is tautly tragic and works up to a point, reminiscent of the Maupassantian short story. His good qualities include an ability to create an atmosphere with a few sentences, a terse presentation of his characters, and an extraordinary lifelikeness of dialogue—it is in the last quality that his rich experience of life shines at its best. In his short stories written in this period, too, he calls up memories of his childhood years, depicting the world of the Hungarian village and provincial town. Several classic stories *(e.g. Tragedy)* give a gripping picture of the peasant who rebels but goes under. In the second and third years of the world war, a new theme cropped up in his short stories: the tragic fate of the underdog, dehumanised, trained to kill, and unconsciously rebelling *(Poor Folks)*.

As an author of nationwide repute, who was the pride of *Nyugat* and the new literary movement, he was an enthusiastic supporter, first of the bourgeois revolution of 1918, then of the Hungarian Republic of Councils of 1919. In reportages, newspaper articles and in short stories he gave a true and authentic picture of the revolutionary peasantry of those months, described the great experience of the carving up of the large estates, the newly formed co-operative farms, and drew portraits of peasants turned leaders.

During the period of the "White Terror" following the downfall of the Hungarian Republic of Councils the great writer suffered persecution; for some time, his writings were not printed anywhere except in *Nyugat*. Dejection, depression and disillusionment overcame him in the early 1920'as: these were, for him, years of crisis and of search for a way out. This basic feeling—his search for a way out of his spiritual crisis, the search for a meaning in Hungarian history—lies at the root of his works written in the 1920's. His grippingly beautiful youth novel, *Be Faithful unto Death*—a story since then adapted to the stage and filmed—was written in 1920. In the hero—young Mishi Nyilas, a student of Debrecen Secondary School—he has portrayed himself, his own struggles in an inexplicable adult world, his yearning for innocence and love. Memories of his childhood, and his momentary alarm, lend a subjective lyrical touch to this novel as well as to its sequels—*Ferment of Wine* (1931) and *The Ball* (1936)—which conjure up the turbulent years of puberty.

In another group of his writings he delves into the past, painting a vast and vivid historical panel of the seventeenth-century Hungarian Principality of Transylvania (*Erdély*, a trilogy, 1922-1935), in which he contrasts two princes: one a fevered, inordinate man; the other a sober, level-headed man who favours slow but steady advance through compromise. A rich pageantry of diverse types of humanity and of landscapes passes in this work; and there comes up in it another motif characteristic of Móricz—that of man caught between the devil of a burdensome wife who represents Home and Family and the deep sea of a mistress who represents Beauty, Lightness of Spirit, and Sex—the very dilemma which harassed the author in his private life. (Those were the years which witnessed the grave crisis of his marriage.) *Erdély* has a rightful claim to a distinguished place among the great twentieth-century historical novels, such as Heinrich Mann's *Henry IV* or Alexei Tolstoy's *Peter the Great*.

A third group of his novels and short stories reaches back into the recent past; they give a portrayal of the life of the Hungarian gentry at the turn of the century—a picture of decay going on behind a glittering façade. *Until Daybreak* (1926) is the story of one night, the tragedy and undoing of the gentry. *Gentlemen on the Spree*, 1928, again, depicts the tragic failure of a man whose efforts to improve things are repeatedly foiled by a sleepy, inert environment until he loses all interest and sinks into lethargy. And finally —*The Relatives*, 1930-1932, takes us into a Hungarian provincial town writhing in the throes of the world economic crisis. This time the hero is a municipal attorney. He entertains some ideas of social reform, but—because of his relatives, some love-affairs and other things—he eventually becomes corrupted and is faced by the ultimate alternative of either howling with the pack or being torn to shreds.

Apart from these gloomier, weighty works, some lighter novels came from Móricz's pen in the twenties: *Butterfly*, 1925, is an idyll, a praise of pure love and lofty, humane sentiments, a hymn to the power of love; *Torrid Meadows* is a picture of society drawn with the paraphernalia of the standard "whodunit."

In the late 20's, Móricz took up other activities besides writing novels and short stories—he was making an attempt at closer participation in national politics and intellectual life. He made numerous walking tours of the country (*It's Good to Walk*, proclaims the title of a well-known reportage of his) and observed peasant life at close quarters. Notebook in hand, he would comb the countryside untiringly—any aspect of life and all classes and types of humanity interested him. In the general chauvinistic mood of the time, a witchhunt was started against him because of his ties with progressive movements in neighbouring Czechoslovakia. In 1931 he was publicly branded a traitor to his country and became the centre and subject of a nationwide dispute. He took over editorship of *Nyugat* for some time (1929-1933) and made an attempt to bring the review closer to everyday realities.

Like many others of his countrymen, Móricz became increasingly radical in his views under the impact of the economic crisis—from 1933 onward, he turned with growing interest to the life and problems of the poor peasantry. *A Happy Man*, 1932-35, is a peculiar experiment of much significance. Here, the story is of the unendurable humiliation and poverty that was the lot of the poor peasants at the time, of the hopeless struggle for life waged by industrious, hard-working people; and the narrative is told through the mouth of a poor peasant, in a succession of interviews with the author. The effect thus produced is one of extraordinary authenticity; a highly realistic impression is given. Móricz went far in breaking with the conventional form of the novel, too. *A Happy Man* is a strange mixture of epic and reportage, of factual sociography and confession. *The Outlaw*, 1937, is the portrait of a poor rebellious peasant: the leading character, unable to resign himself to privation, rebels single-handed against his fate. *The Romance of My Life*, 1939, is a factual, inner-view, autobiographical account and it also gives a searching analysis of the turn of the century.

The last years of his life were overclouded by expanding fascism, the approach, and eventually the outbreak, of the war. In his own way he was a militant anti-fascist, he would espouse every true cause, trying to resist Nazism by resorting to "intellectual defence." He became editor of the periodical *Kelet Népe* (The People of the East) and of books and anthologies. Handicapped by straitened circumstances and defying the political current of the time, he would tirelessly tour the countryside, gathering experience and giving advice, trying to improve the conditions of the peasants. He fathered a variety of schemes and plans; often naive but always inspired by genuine democratic principles, they were all meant to improve conditions for the people.

The great works of the last phase of his career point towards a new trend. *The Orphan* (1941)—perhaps his most essential and most flawless piece of writing—is the story of a little foundling presented from within. The child, who knows neither compromise nor acquiescence, pronounces the most authentic sentence on the society which has flouted its innocent humanism. Its theme the struggle between Good and Evil, between the natural and the unnatural, this novelette—divided into chapters that are called "Psalms"—is shot with an individual lyric pathos. His last great work—the two-volume novel *Sándor Rózsa*, 1940-1942, about a famous peasant outlaw—is a cross between the epic and the novel, between history and literature. Through the principal character, the events of 1848-49 are viewed "from below," from the angle of the serfs, and, though the historical picture presented is distorted here and there, the author makes his point clear and unmistakable: his advocacy of a peasant revolution "from below," the necessity of a settlement of social problems—voiced in the darkest years of fascist rule!—came as an eye-opener and a call to revolt.

In the meantime the flow of his brilliant short stories continued unbroken. Over the years, his short stories developed in two main directions: on the one hand, they acquired a quality of factual reportage, and, on the other, they were transformed into modern ballads in prose. To Móricz's great subjects—the peasant and the small town, the peasant and the gentry—they added a new one: the urban working class *(Chick*—Short stories).

It is next to impossible to survey all the genres Móricz cultivated in his multifarious literary activity—his plays and thrilling reportages, his profound essays and brief notes, his publicistic and book publishing work. Móricz's *oeuvre* is a vast world, and, beyond a doubt, Móricz has a place among the great twentieth-century prose writers, those who in these troubled decades have kept alive and further developed the realist tradition. His gamut comprises the classic-proportioned short story and the novelette, the novel of manners and the historical novel of epic proportions, and the few-line dialogues as well as the modern ballad in prose. It is through his eyes that the Hungarian reader and a whole generation of Hungarian writers have come to view the Hungarian peasant and middle class. His powerful vision, his character-drawing ability, his deep knowledge of life, as well as his loyalty and ardour, raise him far above his contemporaries as the greatest Hungarian prose writer.

Apart from, and behind, Ady and Móricz, *Nyugat* gathered an imposing body of gifted writers, who gave vigorous substance to the new literary movement. Among them, MARGIT KAFFKA (1880-1918) was Hungary's first woman writer of note, a friend and comrade-in-arms of Ady's.

Like several other members of the *Nyugat* movement, Kaffka was born into the impoverished nobility of the provinces. She acquired her education as a penurious student, and on graduating became, at first a teacher, then schoolmistress. She came to live in Budapest after spending many years in the country, practising her profession.

She made her début on the literary scene as a poetess; subsequently, she took to writing short stories. As her own voice and her own ideas asserted themselves, she cast off the trappings of the old style. She was intrigued by the problems which faced the Modern Woman—moral, social, human and vocational problems. Endowed with an uncommon sensitivity and a gift for drawing the emotive life of her characters, she evolved an individual impressionistic staccato style, a way of creating an atmosphere in her writings, and introduced a semblance of subjectivity into her description of objective processes; for instance, the decline of country gentlefolk and the succession of generations. *Colours and Years*, 1912, paints, through the life-story of a woman, a vast canvas on the disintegration of provincial nobility. The heroine, Magda Pórtelky, lives through the historical process in the course of her life, and relates with womanly subjectivity, nostalgia and lyricism the story of her marriages and her shattered life. Kaffka belongs to the line of great character portraitists rather than to that of the great novel constructors—hence her lyrical composition, her propensity to First Person Singular, and her sense of fine shades and nuances. Hers is an impressionistic idiom, peculiarly subjectivised, emotional and charged with tensions, attentive of details, and evocative. Her later novels and short stories witness a certain solidification of construction and a steadying down of the earlier flamboyance of her language; for instance: *The Ant-Hill*, 1917, a sketch of life in a convent; and the novelette *Two Summers*, 1916, a treatment of the life of women workers: the wife, fighting to retain her husband, battles against the other woman and war. Her war-time novel, *Stations*, 1917, is another major work: the motley life of writers' and real and bogus artists' coteries, and a profound analysis of the problems of a woman artist. During the war years Kaffka, like others of her fellow-writers, turned increasingly towards radical politics, becoming an ardent champion of bourgeois revolution. In November 1918 she was carried off by the influenza epidemic which swept across Europe. She was a gifted exponent of the modern, impressionist-subjectivist trend in the novel and in linguistic expression, and an analyst of the problems of Modern Woman.

Among the poets of the period ÁRPÁD TÓTH (1886-1928) stands out as one of the most likeable and most original of the *Nyugat* generation. He, too, came from the provinces, from Debrecen, where his youth had been overshadowed by griping cares and the maladjusted life of his father, a would-be sculptor. The gifted young man enrolled in Budapest University, where he studied for an arts degree. He took an active part in the intellectual movements that sprang up at the beginning of the century, but was soon compelled to break off his studies and take up work as a journalist on the staff of a provincial newspaper. He did not return to the capital until several years afterwards, and only published his first volume of poetry at a comparatively late date, in 1913. He stayed in journalism, in Budapest, and the drudgery of his profession went some way to undermine his health and hasten his untimely death from tuberculosis.

His first volume—*Morning Serenade*—is related in tone to the end-of-the-century decadents and the late French symbolists: it speaks in the voice of a tired, broken-down, melancholy man. His wistful sighs are those of a man longing to get away from this world and find refuge in other, imaginary, worlds; a reference to himself, however, as one of Ady's followers ("a timid apostle of my mighty Lord") points to a desire to win release of that mood. This diffident man with the delicate constitution was prompted to protest against the horrors of the world war. His pacifism gave wings to his poetry. With their dynamism, profundity of thought and lovely imagery, his great anti-war poems with their yearning for peace and tranquillity are the finest specimens of Hungarian lyric poetry and mark a change in Tóth's poetical tone. Following 1917, his pacifism changed into a longing for a new and better world: the plea for socialism became ever louder in his poetry, and thus it happened that this same poet who had started by striking a note of decadence and of weariness wrote the finest and boldest poems hailing the Hungarian Republic of Councils of 1919. *The New God*, a monumental dithyramb, was composed in April 1919: in it, the poet welcomes the Red God in compelling images and with fervour.

The victory of the counter-revolution may have halted the development of Tóth's radicalism, but the poet, soft-spoken and sick, did not break down. He turned his back on everyday struggles, but his loyalty was preserved. His poetry of the 1920's is marked by a clearer voice, manly lyricism, and self-confidence; these poems sound the voice of purified passion, and are overshadowed by approaching death. He remained in isolation as a silent protest against the counter-revolution. The profound humanity of his thought was brought out by a simplicity of form and clarity of structure.

Tóth was one of the foremost translators in this period of modern Hungarian literature. A gifted interpreter of late-nineteenth-century poetry (especially French), he was particularly intrigued by Baudelaire and Samain, Verlaine and Musset. Apart from them, he produced fine translations of great classic and romantic poems (Milton's *L'Allegro, Il penseroso*; Shelley's *Ode to the West Wind*). His Hungarian version of *Aucassin et Nicolette* is a masterpiece of high artistry and stylistic *bravura*. In those years around 1920, when the profound message of Hungarian letters found expression in the voice of translations, when translating the masterpieces of European literature was a means of preserving cherished values and one's human integrity, Tóth emerged as one of the great master translators into Hungarian.

The ill-fated GYULA JUHÁSZ (1883-1937) was a *Nyugat* poet who had at one time stood in the forefront of literary interest, but later slipped into the background. He was born in Szeged and was for most of his life compelled to live in the bitter solitude of backward provincial surroundings. Like Árpád Tóth, he enrolled in the Faculty of Arts at the University of Budapest, where he became a popular leader of the group of students who prepared the way for the modern trend of literature. Though he got off to a good start, he soon lost the initial momentum as he assumed mastership in one remote small town or the other, far from the stimulating company of friends and the effervescent intellectual life of the capital. There was a respite of three years; from 1908 till 1911 he lived in Nagyvárad, where he was drawn into the current of the *Holnap* (Tomorrow) movement. In 1911 he was again transferred to a little place, and this was to remain his condition until his death. The poet, of sickly constitution and always liable to neurasthenia, now became weary and lethargic. The 1918 revolution tore him out of his passivity; he embraced the ideals of the succeeding Communist regime and played a considerable part under it. For his role under the Hungarian Republic of Councils, he was deprived of his mastership in 1919. After this time he lived in Szeged in growing isolation from literary life, suffering from a neurosis that worsened steadily. In a fit of nerves, he took his own life.

Juhász's poetry falls into distinct periods. He started in the traditional line of Hungarian lyric poetry, in the *kuruc*-patriotic song; then, following his university years, became converted to Nietzsche's and Tolstoy's philosophy and followed the French impressionists. Landscapes, portraits, descriptions and moods condensed into sonnets are the most characteristic pieces of his lyric poetry, which has a strong pictorial quality, a keen sense of colour and many ties with the traditions of Hungarian history and literature. He carried in him the typical weariness and decadence of the early twentieth century, the then fashionable *art nouveau;* but, as disease played its part with Árpád Tóth, so, with him, loneliness and exile in the country lent authenticity to this attitude. His love-lyrics of hopeless desire—the deeply lyrical pieces of the "Anna-cycle" addressed to the distant woman, the unworthy actress-ideal—are masterpieces of Hungarian lyric poetry. A hankering after companionship and deep solidarity with mankind add warmth to his lines. The war and the socialist revolution represented a turning-point in his development: on the one hand, he deeply comprehended and felt the sufferings and loneliness endured by people; on the other, he took sides with the working class as the ascendant force of the future. The poems: *A Sonnet to Work* and *For the Façade of a Workers's Club* are fine examples of this sympathy. During the dark years of the counter-revolutionary regime his lyrics became gloomy; Hungary, brooding and downtrodden, weeps and sighs in his poems, and the dismal Hungarian landscapes are depicted in appealing pictures.

Juhász's lyric poetry does not excel with a variety of form: he is the master of one kind of style and one kind of tone. His language and imagery, apart from his pictorial experience and the Western European influence, derived a good deal from popular vocabulary and turn of speech. As most poets who had made their *début* through impressionism, he drew from an abundance of colours and epithets. Human integrity of a high order radiates from his work—it is an inspiring example of the humanist sympathy for socialism, of loyalty to an attitude once accepted, of a frame of mind that can rise above suffering and cares. His encouragement went a long way towards launching young Attila József on his career, and other poets of the 30's and 40's, too, have numerous bonds linking them with him.

The assessment—as well as the careers—of the other two *Nyugat* poets, Mihály Babits and Dezső Kosztolányi, is connected with the evaluation and validity of bourgeois humanism, with the problems of liberal principles and "pure aesthetics." Not even back in the 1910's had they been following the course set by Ady— these two poets represented a different trend in the *Nyugat* movement.

MIHÁLY BABITS (1883-1941) was a poet, translator, novelist

and essayist, the greatest figure in Hungarian letters during the
1930's and an outstanding bourgeois humanist.

His education and learning were rooted in the moderately conservative Hungarian intelligentsia of the turn of the century—a
stratum marked by a respect for classic culture and once-liberal
views that had taken on a conservative complexion. As a Budapest
student of philosophy, the young man was drawn into the animated intellectual life of the capital, and assimilated all those influences which this radical stratum of the middle class channelled
into Hungary's culture: he read and interpreted for Hungarian
readers Nietzsche and the poets of the late nineteenth century as
well as Bergson and the new English poets. Like Juhász, he began
as a schoolmaster in a country town in the most out-of-the-way
corner of Hungary. Some time afterwards, he moved up to the
capital, and lived and taught in a satellite town of Budapest until
the end of the war. After that time, he changed from mastership
to writing and editorship.

Babits started his career as a believer in art for art's sake,
a virtuoso in playing with various styles, a master of verse forms
displaying high artistry in his use of the language. An admirer
of the end-of-the-century poets, especially Swinburne, he was of
the type of the *poeta doctus*, with whom the polished forms serve
only to conceal his fevered inward disquietude, his tormented
solitude, the dilemma between thought and action. He is a thinking type of poet, one with a philosophical turn of mind, an outstanding representative of idealist philosophy, a past master in
bold and unusual verse constructions, and in the use of words. He
did not follow Ady's revolutionary fervour and desire for action.
In politics, too, he was rather on the conservative side—the popu-
lace scared and repulsed him. Nevertheless, the horrors of the world
war moved him to determined protest—the cry of pain that bursts
forth from his poem *Before Easter*, makes this verse a masterpiece
of Hungarian anti-war poetry.

After the revolution, his poetry, too, took a new course. Gone
were the stiff, set forms, the playful masquerades—weariness,
lethargy, and loss of direction are mirrored by his near-expression-
ist poems written in these years. The bookish idyll of the earlier
years had been lost, but it was now compensated for by closer

MIHÁLY BABITS (1883-1941)

ties with national life, by the protest of a staunch liberal intellectual at the sight of the new inhumanity. By the end of the 20's, Babits had established a new equilibrium: from his essays, novels and poems alike emerged the position of a man who, standing on the ground of nineteenth-century liberal humanism, now took up the defence of all that was positive in culture and literature, against challenges from both the Right and the Left. His stand was that of a new classicism, representing the aspiration towards a "Silver Age"—a rather precarious and unrealistic programme to put forward in an age so bedevilled by troubles. As the editor of the *Nyugat* and curator of the most important Hungarian literary prize, the Baumgarten foundation, he pursued from the early 30's a consistent literary policy, a liberal-conservative view of literature free of politics, an attitude characteristic of him, but one for which he was attacked from both Right and Left.

Babits changed his attitude and views in the last few years of his life. The spread of fascism and the approach and eventual advent of the Second World War drove him on to change his course. He sensed the approaching danger, and surveyed the pitfalls on the road he had travelled thus far; his dramatic search for a new way, his agony, his loyalty to higher ideas and his awareness of the need for taking a more militant stand are mirrored in poems like his *The Book of Jonah*, 1940, a self-avowal transposed into a Biblical setting. His fatal disease—cancer of the throat—caused him torment and physical suffering that inspired him to some extraordinarily forceful poems of classic purity in which he cast off all formal trappings.

Lyrics form but part of Babits's immense work. In his great novel, *Sons of Death*, 1927, he paints a canvas of the Hungarian intelligentsia of the late nineteenth century. This is a psychological, analytical novel, encumbered with some philological ponderousness, which views with scorn both conservatives and radicals. He made an attempt at a—slightly mystic—portrayal of the industrialising capital of Hungary of the 1910's *(House of Cards, 1923)*; wrote one novel about a split personality, based on Freudian teachings *(King Stork, 1916)*; and gave vent to his fears, to the loss of direction induced by those disjointed times, in a great utopian war-novel *(Flyer Elsa or Perfect Society, 1933)*. His novelettes

14*

and short stories, too, extend over a wide gamut, and his essays fill volumes. A man of great erudition, and equipped with a superior knowledge of Hungarian and European culture, he had a conservative humanist view of the world. His work as essayist and philologist culminated in *A History of European Literature*, 1934, a survey based on wide learning and full of personal experiences.

Art translation was an almost natural form of expression with this erudite poet, who had such strong ties with world literature. From the time when he became a novice to poetry till the last years of his life, he produced translations; we are indebted to him for the adequate interpretation of a number of masterpieces. Perhaps his greatest achievement in this direction is the Hungarian version—perfectly true to form and supported by penetrating studies—of the full *Divine Comedy*. Close rivals to this are Babits's very learned and appealing interpretations of several Greek tragedies, of Shakespeare's *Tempest*, Baudelaire's poems, and his rendering of medieval Latin poets, of Goethe and George Meredith.

Babits was one of the most versatile and most complex figures in Hungarian letters, an outstanding representative of twentieth-century bourgeois humanism, and one of the most distinguished links between Hungarian and European literature.

The most extensive and, in its influence, the strongest *oeuvre* —second to Babits's—on the opposite wing of *Nyugat* from Ady is that of DEZSŐ KOSZTOLÁNYI (1885-1936). It is difficult to decide in which branch of writing his performance is the most impressive: as lyricist, short-story writer or novelist, contributor of articles or essayist, journalist or translator.

Like Babits, he was born into the provincial intelligentsia, the son of a schoolmaster proud of his noble ancestry. Along with Babits and Gyula Juhász, he was a member of the literary society of Budapest University students, but in 1906 discontinued his studies and took up journalism, and later on lived by his income as a writer.

Unlike Babits and Juhász, Kosztolányi did not become a schoolmaster in the country—he struck roots in the life of Budapest as a fashionable publicist, the "King of Life." He was successful as a poet too. The child-cult of the early twentieth century is

212

mirrored in his *Laments of the Poor Little Child,* 1910; his poems—colourful, full of music and embodying a facility and high artistry of form—display all the requisites, brightness and riches of the *art nouveau.* With the superior skill of a virtuoso of form, he moulds the language as if it were a malleable material. He had no definite political views and, with a curious ethical indifference, was able to sympathise with any shade of opinion, from the Catholics to the Social Democrats. This peculiar artistic nihilism continued to be characteristic of him in later years: he hailed the revolution, but when it had been crushed, joined the staffs of reactionary newspapers with equal ease. Later on, he became a senior member of the staff of the liberal-conservative daily *Pesti Napló.*

His post-1920 lyrics point to the same crisis, the same simplification of form as is shown by Babits and other contemporaries. He advanced as far as free verse; and, in the 30's, as with Babits, physical suffering and humanist protest made his voice ring ever clearer and gave it a noble tone. His very playfulness and airiness now became a protest against totalitarian barbarism; a sense of moral responsibility began to enrich his world outlook, formerly restricted by a conscious rejection of moral attitudes and politics.

Kosztolányi was a sovereign artist of the Hungarian language, which he loved passionately. In his novels and especially in his short stories the best Hungarian linguistic heritage is alloyed with the polish and clarity of French; the pointed sentence-construction of the early twentieth century is combined with sensuously colourful images. His major novels: *Our Skylark,* 1919, is an exposure of the false pretences of small-town middle-class life. In *The Blood-Stained Poet,* 1922, the self-admiring, power-thirsting and self-destroying artist is portrayed in Nero's figure and the upright humanist in that of Britannicus. *The Golden Dragon,* 1924, is among the most typical stories of adolescence in the 20's: the helpless struggle of a kind-hearted, learned schoolmaster in the midst of bullying, rowdy students, under mean and paltry conditions. Undoubtedly his most important novel is *Wonder Maid,* 1926, the tragic story of a little servant girl, a masterly psychological analysis and incisive social sketch of "self-righteous Christian gentlefolks." His short stories—filling several volumes—are characterised by a sense of proportion, a mastery of the language and a flair for the quaint and the exotic—and, in the best, a delicate intellectual irony, playfulness, and penetrating knowledge of life. Kosztolányi was one of the most zealous adherents and propagators in Hungarian letters of the Freudian achievements. The *Kornél Esti* stories (1933) represent perhaps his best writing in the field of the short story; they stand out on account of the mature art and the masterly sense of proportion evident in his treatment of language and the experience it is used to depict. Their irony conveys his feelings of the fundamental senselessness and comedy of life.

His numerous essays and literary profiles—including some of the great figures in European literature—are representative specimens of impressionistic criticism: a few excellently-drawn lines and well-placed touches of colour—with an occasional casualness and superficiality—opposed Ady, now openly, now covertly, throughout his life; in 1929, he engaged in a great controversy about his poetry.

The body of contributors to *Nyugat* included many other prose writers of great original talent.

FRIGYES KARINTHY (1888-1938) achieved wide popularity as a humorous writer; yet, as a matter of fact, he was one of the most versatile, many-sided talents who ever published in *Nyugat*.

He was born into a family of Budapest intellectuals, and as he was the prototype of a city-dweller, the principal scenes of his life were the café, the editorial office and the street. The meaning and essence of his lifework was to criticise and re-assess the philosophy, social conditions, manners and morality of his time, in the terms of an outlook that was a blend of French rationalism, Freudism and the modern achievements of natural sciences. That objective was pursued in his curiously fragmented *oeuvre*.

His *The Way You Write*, 1912, is a collection of superb pastiches giving a complete satirical panorama of the literary world, Hungarian and international, of the age. An immense number of humoresques and skits—often intended only as pot-boilers, but nonetheless excellent specimens of their kind—in which his uncommon ability to discover the absurd and the preposterous in human behaviour is seen at full play, went a long way towards earning the label of humorist affixed to him. Using the caricature,

214

finely pointed intellectual irony and the nonsensical paradox as his tools, he knocks the bottom out of lies and fashionable false concepts. The same sort of philosophical thinking is apparent in his short stories, reflexions and novels. Karinthy entertained the ambition to write a comprehensive "New Encyclopedia," in which he hoped to fill calcified old formulas with new meaning, but, in the last analysis—because of the incoherence of his system—he produced only flashes of genius, compelling but partial achievements.

In *Permission, Sir!*, 1916, he provides a deeply perceptive and accomplished treatment of the crowded world of adolescence, the clash between unfolding intellect and the restraints of school, which is unsurpassed to this day.

His quest for the fantastic and the grotesque and his interest in actual and utopian scientific achievements are evident in his novels and plays. *Capillaria* (1922) and *Faremido* (1916) are further travels by Gulliver, in the Land of Gynaeocracy and the World of Machines, respectively; the experimental drama, *Tomorrow Morning*, 1918, formulates the human ideal based on modern achievements in natural science. His most durable prose work, *Journey around my Skull*, 1937, is the story of the brain operation he had undergone, an uncannily accurate account, a triumph of the inquisitive creative mind which has conquered ailment and fear.

Karinthy was greatly interested in the works of G. B. Shaw and H. G. Wells, and was an inspired translator of Stephen Leacock and A. A. Milne.

His short stories and poems, with their puritanical, near-prose-diction form, concentrate upon the crisis of the age, the disillusionment and hopes of an entire generation; of a generation which at the beginning of the century got off to an ambitious start and cherished plans of building up a new world, a society founded on reason, but with no other lifeline to grasp than the bourgeois *Weltanschauung* on which it had lost its grip, grew up disenchanted, painfully aware of the senselessness of the world and of the futility of its own ambitions, and distressed at the approach of a new war. Karinthy's work, for all its fragmented character, still has a stimulating influence on the present generation of writers.

215

GYULA KRÚDY (1878-1933) was a unique personality in Hungarian letters; his only point of contact with *Nyugat* was the similarity of the goals they both pursued—otherwise this great artist was a truly singular figure.

Born into the gentry, the impoverished provincial nobility, Krúdy suggested the country squire by his exterior; but his way of life was that of the struggling Budapest journalist and author, and his views brought him close to the radical bourgeoisie.

Next to the creations of Mór (Maurice) Jókai and Sándor Bródy, his is the most impressive *oeuvre*, though the almost impenetrable luxuriance of atmosphere in his works is so Hungarian that it is impossible to translate. His early novels and short stories show the influence of Mikszáth, Turgenev and Dickens; soon afterwards, in the 1910's, he evolved his individual style. This is a lyric style all his own, in which "atmosphere" overshadows plot and character-development and construction is dissolved in a web of reflexions and rambling digressions. We enter into a peculiar dream-world where Present and Past are blurred and blend together, and the characters lose their contours to dissolve into local colour. His novels written at the time are centred round an idle day-dreamer, a man wallowing in memories of the past, hankering for the unattainable, and setting out on precarious adventures. (The *Sindbad* novels and short stories, 1912; *The Scarlet Stage-Coach*, 1913.) His figures move in the dreary world of the contemporary gentry for whom life is one long bout of drinking and card-playing, with occasional amorous adventures to break the aimless monotony.

Though apparently feeling at home only in the tangled world of dreams, even Krúdy was susceptible to the influence of revolutions: he expressed his sympathy in a number of newspaper articles, reportages and pamphlets. He remained loyal to his stand even amidst the ravings of the White Terror; the world depicted in his works written after that time is more richly painted and more realistic; there appear as scenes of action the outlying— working- and lower-middle-class—districts of Budapest; and nobles and bourgeois are portrayed with colder irony *(Seven Owls, 1922)*. It is almost as though—in his own peculiar, stylised, transposed way—he were making a re-assessment of all that he had brought with him, all that was decadent and enervated, immoral and brutal in the Hungarian nobility. The finest piece of writing of his last period—*When I Was a Young Gentleman*, 1930—is the story of a single day spent in one and the same place, and it is, in a way, the *danse macabre* of a passing world. A peculiar atmosphere of half-dream, half-reality and an almost total absence of any plot make the novelettes and short stories of his last years unique pieces in Hungarian literature *(Life's a Dream*, 1930).

On account of both his style and technique, Krúdy has been compared with Proust, and some have attempted to discover ties between him and the surrealists. Actually, he owes nothing to either of these influences. He, too, dissolves prose into dream and lyricism, but his peculiar technique and method of construction appreciably serve to mirror a class and a world living a curious sham existence; his technique of merging past and present was a hankering, in an age that had become strange, after an idealised, imaginary Hungarian middle-class-that-never-was.

One of the significant poets in the *Nyugat* set was MILÁN FÜST (b. 1888), who is also important as a critic and novelist. For long a schoolmaster, he is now professor of aesthetics in the University of Budapest.

The masters who taught Füst were not writers of the late nineteenth century—his literary umbilical chord links him with the Bible, Tolstoy and Shakespeare. His philosophy and concept of the world as expressed in his writings have stayed essentially unchanged to this day. The poems with which he made his *début* have for a long time been taken for *vers libre*, although, in point of fact, they are liturgical texts, singular choruses, throbbing with a palpable inner rhythm and intoned in a powerful voice. They are the sighs or whispers of Loneliness, of Fear of Death—and, after 1919, horror and aversion at the sight of brutal barbarity, and later still, the experience of old age; all that is expressed against a peculiar mythological background created by him, in a never-has-been geographical or historical setting, in the pathetic-plaintive tone of the psalms or dirges.

Of his prose works, the novel *Advent* (1923) is a protest against the White Terror. *The Story of my Wife*, 1942, a visionary, psychological novel, proclaims the flowering of fundamental human values however stunting the circumstances. As an analyst Füst has a marked preference for the quaint, the warped, the psychologically unique, the peripheral; through such characters, he searches for the fundamental human virtues and expresses his longing for a purer (though abstract) world in short stories written in a style teeming with images and allusions.

His principal aesthetic work—*Vision and Impulse in the Arts*—furnishes a system based upon the great classic artists which is full of interesting observations and remarkable points of view; here the author speaks with the authoritative voice of one who knows all the tricks of the writer's "craft."

JENŐ J. TERSÁNSZKY (b. 1888) was the *enfant terrible*—both in his works and behaviour—of the *Nyugat* generation of authors. After a start as a prospective painter, he fought in the First World War, and has ever since lived a life that is half literary, half bohemian; his free and easy manners, his *Naturbursch* attitude, make him a characteristic figure.

He made his *début* with a war novel—*Goodbye, Darling*, 1917; he attracted attention by the outspokenness and informality and near-naturalism of his early novels and short stories. He is a prolific writer who has contributed to every genre and has written works varying in value.

His most important work is the so-called *Kakuk Marci* cycle. Marci Kakuk—a latter-day Hungarian descendant of Lazarillo de Tormes—is a poor vagabond, a cheerful out-at-the-elbow type who lives beyond the pale of society; through his many vicissitudes he has learnt to view society from below, and he does not rebel against his fate as his only concern in life is to keep living. In this submerged world of social outcasts—described by the author in several other works—there is nothing but chance friendships and rebellion against all social form. Not far removed from this anarchism himself, Tersánszky portrays his heroes with much gusto and compassion. In other books, though with a naturalism that borders on cynicism, he presents the upper classes "stripped to their skins," exposing their filthiness and showing the relativity of values. The moral of a celebrated short story of his—*The Harlot and the Virgin*—contends that the prostitute is pure, whereas the "respectable woman" is the one who is rotten to the core.

Tersánszky's art stands apart from all literary fashions and mannerisms characteristic of the writers of *Nyugat* ; he may seem careless and rough-hewn, whereas, in reality, he only uses the ancient, unstudied means of making his characters speak and act, omitting stylisation and transposition.

The current of the new literary revival at the beginning of the century brought to the surface a number of gifted and colourful writers. ERNŐ SZÉP (1884-1953), poet and prose writer, evolved a peculiarly simple, neo-primitive tone of voice not unlike some big-city Jammes.

DEZSŐ SZOMORY (1869-1944) was a colourfully individual artist, dramatist and prose writer. In his youth he lived for some time in France, and here he published his first book, written in French, under the *nom de plume* Jean Berge. He has created a peculiar musical idiom: verbal torrents and rioting colours surge —sometimes mannered, but always splendid—in his wide-horizoned historical plays and stylised short stories.

GÉZA CSÁTH (1887-1919) was a physician. He began his literary career with music criticism and continued it with short stories. Beneath the objective, level-headed tone of these writings is a peculiarly smouldering inner tension. Morphinism, the fateful vice that caused the author's early death, can be detected between the lines.

The poet OSZKÁR GELLÉRT (b. 1882) was one of the earliest contributors to *Nyugat*. He had contributed to periodicals known as forerunners of *Nyugat* ; and later, he was on the staff of the latter periodical for many years, along with Ernő Osvát and the poet Mihály Babits. He wrote markedly virile lyrics conveying the young married man's declarations of love with sensual passion. In later years his poetry, plain and gaunt, became more intellectual. After a long spell of silence, he spoke up again in an advanced age, after 1945. He is an enthusiastic believer in socialism: in his poems, having drawn the conclusions from his long career, he adheres to the new society.

LAJOS BÍRÓ (1880-1948) began his career as a radical journalist and Endre Ady's friend, in Nagyvárad. His feuilletons, short stories and novels are devoted to social and psychological questions and show him to be an imaginative and shrewd observer and critic of early twentieth-century society. As a journalist he boldly protested against the war, and played a significant role in the revolution of 1918-19. In later years, he lived abroad; his chief writings were well-constructed plays reminiscent of the Bernsteinian precept dramas *(Hotel Imperial)*. In the last few decades of his life—spent in London—he devoted himself solely to script-writing.

GYULA TÖRÖK (1888-1918) has left two important novels. *In the Dust* is the story of a talent that goes to pieces in the stifling atmosphere of the small town; *The Emerald Ring* is a delicately sympathetic account of the life of a decadent offspring of an ancient noble family. Török was the last in the line of writers (which included, among others, Mikszáth, Cholnoky and Krúdy) who picture "from within" the fall of the country gentlefolk as a class.

There were some symptoms of a Catholic religious literary revival at the beginning of the century, not unconnected with the trend of European development. The magazine *Élet* (Life) rallied modernist Catholic writers who strove to amalgamate the achievements of the new literature with Catholic religious feeling. The most prominent figure of the neo-Catholic literary movement has been SÁNDOR SÍK (1889-1963), a Piarist monk, for many years a university professor, now editor of the Catholic literary magazine *Vigilia*. Sík renewed Hungarian religious lyrics: he sings the faith of the highly strung modern man. He mirrors the individual's relationship with faith and between the two world wars he, too, expresses the social consciousness of modern Catholicism, in a search for a way out of the horrors and chaos of the age, and with a sympathy for the poor.

Early twentieth-century bourgeois literature had a branch which ran parallel with the *Nyugat* movement, but for reasons of literary standard or personal antagonisms, most representatives kept out or were left out of the *Nyugat* set. This coterie comprised feuilleton-writers, writers cultivating the entertainment genres, authors for the most part connected with the magazine *Hét*, and was responsible for a crop of plays and a few other works that found their way to other countries—chiefly Germany—to be, for many years to come,the sole representatives of the new Hungarian literature. (This circumstance has led some Hungarian literary scholars to refer to these plays by the term "export drama.")

FERENC MOLNÁR (1878-1952) was the most prominent, most gifted member of this group. Molnár grew up in a Budapest middle-class environment, entered journalism, and soon became one of the best-known and most sought-after play-wrights; his plays scored one success after the other in other countries, as well as in Hungary. His reputation continued to grow after the First World War and he stayed more and more abroad; at last, the sharpening pressure of fascism forced him to emigrate to the United States, where he lived until his death. Ferenc Molnár was a many-sided author: his short stories and light humorous sketches are the works of a sharp-eyed, very perceptive man capable of caustic satire who recognised and ruthlessly exposed the faults of the Budapest bourgeoisie and the decaying of Old Hungary. His short story *Coal Pilferers* is a sympathetic portrayal of the downtrodden and the poor. Even his best writing is stamped with some cynicism and, at the same time, a measure of—often spurious—sentimentalism. Several of his novels—*The Starving City*, 1900, and *Andor*, 1918—are products of this leaning and are shrewdly observed, coldly ironical treatments of the mental struggle of the average Budapest citizen. His most popular prose work is *The Paul Street Boys*, 1907, a novel for adolescents which, by its unstudied and objective treatment of its subject, poignantly captures all the beauty and torment of childhood.

Molnár's rise as a successful dramatist began with *Liliom— A Legend in Seven Scenes and a Prologue*, 1909, a piece that is half drama, half mystery play with the local colour typical of Budapest in those days. The play starts by presenting a slice of the contemporary Budapest underworld, the world of tramps and hooligans, and proceeds to perform a bold sleight-of-hand in conjuring up something that is a grotesque, slum-dweller's idea of heaven. In this play cynicism alternates with sentimentalism, mordant satire with tearfulness. *Liliom* (since then turned into the successful musical *Carousel)* opened a long succession of widely-acclaimed Molnár plays, the most effective among which were *The Devil* and

*Red Mill*. A brilliant knowledge of stagecraft and a skilful handling of tricks and effects are characteristic of these plays. The theme itself, as a rule, tends to be more commonplace: in *The Devil* it is the friction between a woman's social morality and her subconscious desires, while in the *Red Mill* it is the conflict between innocence and sensuality, naiveté and vice. Almost invariably, in Molnár's plays, brilliant technique gains the upper hand of theme, or of thought. The tendency of his plays is always tainted by the presence, however latent, of bourgeois compromise.

The career of MENYHÉRT LENGYEL (b. 1880) has been somewhat similar to Molnár's; he has scored successes with dramas treating social issues and presenting ardent passions, in which his brilliant stagecraft shines at its best. Béla Bartók's *The Miraculous Mandarin* is based on a work by Lengyel. His *Typhoon* (1909) has been a world-wide success. Lengyel has lived in America for several decades.

Simultaneously with the great *Nyugat* surge of radical bourgeois literature, and even before it, in the early years of the century, there had arisen a trend of specifically working-class literature fostered by writers who came either from the trade-union movement or the Social Democratic Party. Hungarian socialistic lyrics can be traced back to the 1870's; they were cultivated in the beginning by writers of bourgeois or noble antecedents "descending," as it were, to lower depths, until the appearance, years afterwards, of poets who came from the working class and were reared in the working-class movement.

The most notable among this class of writers is SÁNDOR CSIZMADIA (1871-1929). In the 1900's, he was, for all practical purposes, a kind of "poet laureate" of the Social Democratic Party, until his great controversy with Ady undermined his prestige, and the sulking poet was relegated to the background.

For the development of socialist writing and for establishing contact between Ady and the socialists, between the radical writers and labour, much credit is due to BÉLA RÉVÉSZ (1876-1944), who for many years was the literary editor on the staff of the Social Democratic daily *Népszava* (People's Voice). One of Ady's most intimate friends, he erected a monument to the great poet's memory in a fine *Ady Trilogy*. He is not insignificant as a creative writer either: his lyrical short stories about workers, poverty and destitution are ruthlessly outspoken and decidedly socialist-inclined. They are pervaded by a quite original lyric quality, and their author seems to employ—at a very early date—the expressionist method to convey the feelings of the masses, the collective psyche. Révész's later writings tend towards lyricism and mysticism, and his miniatures, as though divorced from their subjects, became more and more enigmatic.

Another important figure of the unfolding socialist literature of the 1910's was LAJOS BARTA (b. 1878). After his university years, he entered journalism in the provinces, then, in 1910, joined the staff of the Budapest radical daily *Világ* (World). Gradually, Barta drifted from bourgeois radicalism to socialism. A militant newspaper editor at the beginning of 1919, he played an important role under the Hungarian Republic of Councils. From 1919 to 1945, Barta lived in exile, working, editing newspapers and carrying on other propaganda activities in Vienna, Bratislava and Paris. After 1945, he returned to his native Hungary.

From the 1910's onwards he published in quick succession short stories whose characters are destitute farmhands, agricultural labourers fighting for their daily bread, downtrodden little men. The beautiful countryside of Southern Hungary as well as the poverty of its inhabitants, the splendour of bishoprics and the fight waged by socialist agitators are here depicted sensuously, with passion and artistic economy. His was a robust, individual talent. Beginning with the volume entitled *The Spread of the Gospel* (1917), socialist workers and agitators appear in his writings drawn at first rather abstractly, then in more and more vigorous lines.

He has achieved some note also as a dramatist: *Peasants* (1911), an attack upon the latifundia, *Madness of Spring* (1912), and, in particular, *Zsuzsi* (1916), and *Love* (1916), pointed the way—in theme, tone and technique—towards the Hungarian popular drama.

Among the socialist critics and theoreticians who were active in the 1910's, ERVIN SZABÓ (1877-1918) exercised by far the strongest influence. His fields of activity were numerous and his contribution was especially marked in the sphere of cultural policy. He very strongly influenced the young socialist writers, among them a group of young talents who joined the communists after 1917.

223

## HUNGARIAN LITERATURE IN AND AFTER THE FIRST WORLD WAR

As in every other country affected, the First World War was a severe test for men of culture in Hungary. After the first heady months of jingoist enthusiasm for the war, came a general disillusionment. Only the most conservative fringe of literature still kept grinding out war propaganda; there arose a powerful chorus of voices longing for peace and exposing the senselessness of war. Many middle-class writers associated with *Nyugat* protested against the war—Mihály Babits's poems *Fortissimo* and *Before Easter*, Frigyes Karinthy's courageous sketches and Árpád Tóth's poetical yearning for peace, harmony and purity testify to this feeling. Hungarians were acquainted with European pacifist literature: Barbusse's and Andreas Latzko's novels, Romain Rolland's staunch anti-war writings and news of the Zimmerwaldians' actions, were printed more and more frequently in the Hungarian press.

No writer was more clearly aware of the wantonness, senselessness and anti-progressive features of the war than the poet Endre Ady. In poem after poem, the sick poet insisted on the need to remain faithful to progressive ideas, to the objective of a democratic Hungary, for which the fight had been waged in preceding years ("our strife is against the Hungarian Inferno . . ."); he insisted that even in the midst of the holocaust one must retain one's human dignity, preserve the assets of human intellect, civilization and culture, and to prepare for the revolution that was bound to come, that could not be postponed.

Along with the protest at the war, the voices of social discontent reached a higher pitch as growing numbers of people recognized the necessity of basic changes once the war was over, the inevitability of a revolution. Socialist ideas were steadily gaining ground; this process was accelerated by the February Revolution of 1917 in Russia and the subsequent Great October Socialist Revolution, which came as an encouragement for the masses and set them an example. Tension was building up inside Hungary; the war became protracted, engulfing more and more countries; increasing poverty and starvation were causing widespread bitterness; a wave of workers' demonstrations and strikes swept across the belligerent nations. This process could not pass without having a significant effect upon the Left wing of bourgeois literature: the anti-war attack gathered momentum, the voices became more strident, and an increasing number of poems and short stories appeared clamouring for socialism.

The most forceful protest was made by the novelist Zsigmond Móricz: in a short story entitled *Poor Folks*, he not only depicted in glaring colours the dehumanisation caused by the war, but also had a front-line soldier point out that the separating line runs, not between Hungarian and Russian, but between officers and the ranks—oppressors and oppressed—whichever side they were fighting on.

Hungary, as a matter of fact, had only one "poet of war": GÉZA GYÓNI (1884-1917). In the beginning, this provincial journalist and civil servant was one of the conservative epigons; then, his later poems showed the influence of Ady. In the war he attracted attention by bold, exciting poems that breathed the front-line atmosphere; and indeed, the conservative side played these poems off against Ady *(On the Fields of Poland; Beside the Campfire,*—1914). However, when Przemysl Fortress fell to the Russians, Gyóni was taken prisoner, and in the POW camp mounted his own "Calvary." His voice acquired a deeper pitch and a ring that was more truthful and more rebellious. Formerly a favourite of the conservative *literati*, the poet now took the long step to becoming a man who showed understanding for the Russian socialist revolution *(Letters from Calvary*, 1916; *In Captivity*, 1919).

During the years of the First World War, new literary groups formed, new trends arose. Various attempts to develop "isms" had been made earlier, parallel with Italian futurism, to get away from traditional forms of style, but the representatives of these efforts coagulated into a group only in 1915, with the launching of the periodical *Tett* (Action). The organiser, and most prominent figure, of the new literary trend was Lajos Kassák.

LAJOS KASSÁK (b. 1887) is a self-taught poet. As a locksmith he roamed all over Europe, working in factories. After a period of heavily stylised romanticism, he found the tone of voice which was struck—almost at the same time—by the Italian futurists and the German expressionists. In flowing, rolling free verse, he sang of the new awareness of life, the crumbling of the old world, of

15

youth and of the workers who were building a new one—the desire, unshaped as yet, for something better than the existing state of things. At that time, Kassák was member of the Social Democratic Party, but he soon found that the scope it offered did not satisfy him. This was not only because of the opportunism of the SDP, but because of the writer's anarchical temperament and rebellious nature which balked at all forms of restraint. At the end of 1915, his magazine—*Tett*—was launched. The periodical had a decidedly pacifist approach, and from a violent anti-war protest it gradually shifted over to revolutionism: it sympathised with the Zimmerwaldians and recognized kinship with the Unanimists and expressionists. *Ma* (Today) was started in November 1916 as a direct continuation of *Tett;* the new magazine came out still more unequivocally against war and for an international revolution; at the same time, *Ma* turned against *Nyugat* and bourgeois literature as a whole and expressed its sympathy with the most extremist "isms," devoting space to masters—later celebrities—of expressionism, cubism, constructivism—all trends of abstract writing.

In the weeks that followed the bourgeois revolution of 1918, Kassák and his friends gave their support to the newly founded Communist Party. But differences of opinion multiplied; already at the end of 1917, shortly after the Great October Socialist Revolution in Russia, four writers (Mátyás György, Aladár Komját, József Lengyel and József Révai) had seceded from the *Ma* group; these writers were consistent advocates of a proletarian revolutionary literature, and, later on, became great names in Hungarian communist literature. Early in 1919 and under the subsequent Republic of Councils, Kassák drifted steadily farther away from the working-class movement. Kassák held the view that the political and economic construction of the new society was the task of the party, whereas the work of spiritual construction was a mission to be accomplished by a literature independent from all party commitments. He looked down upon the leaders of the revolution as well as the popular masses, and opposed the policies of the party.

After the fall of the Republic of Councils, Kassák, too, was forced into exile, and lived in Vienna until 1926. He went on publishing *Ma* and supported it by founding a publishing house

226

and launching a library series. With him, the shock caused by the downfall of the Republic of Councils turned into a profound and general disillusionment, and he began to preach the gospel of pure art, one which was above politics. In his artistic principle—parallel with European trends—he drifted all the way to the extremes of the 20's, finding contact with dadaism and abstract writing. Even after his return to Hungary Kassák was active as an organizer of literary activity, launching several short-lived periodicals until one—entitled *Munka* (Labour)—started in 1928, seemed to have come to stay. When all is said and done, however, the trend which Kassák represented ran out of the main stream of Hungarian literature; his position was that of the maverick, in literature as well as in politics; and he fiercely opposed both the social democrats and the underground Communist Party. Eventually, from the thirties onwards, he did settle down somewhat, but this process was not without resignation and withdrawal; his poetry now reflected the plainness of things, living and dead, moods of weariness and acquiescence, the drabness of life. However, he remains the most zealous Hungarian propagandist of abstract literature, an enemy of regular forms.

Kassák is significant not only as a poet and organizer of literary activity, but also as a prose writer. While his earlier writing mirrored the drab, dull and hopeless existence of small-town workers *(Angyalföld* and *Men out of Work)*, in his later novels he is concerned with problems of artists' lives. His most outstanding prose work is *Life of a Man* (1927-1935), a detailed and deeply candid autobiographical account of the early stage of his development and literary career, which, for all his precise matter-of-factness (or because of it), presents an enduring picture of an age.

In Hungary, the First World War came to an end in the democratic revolution of October 31, 1918. The dual monarchy of Austro-Hungary gave way to an independent Republic of Hungary, and government passed into the hands of the former opposition parties, with the strong participation of radicals and socialists. But bourgeois leadership proved unable to cope with the problems it was facing; it failed to meet the revolutionary demands of the masses, neither had it the power to resist the extravagant territorial claims of the Entente. On March 21, 1919, the united party of communists and socialists took over, and the Hungarian Republic of Councils was proclaimed. Faced with overwhelming odds, the Republic nevertheless carried through a number of vital reforms, successfully defended the national frontiers, and drew up ambitious schemes of cultural and educational reform.

The vast majority of Hungarian writers hailed the bourgeois revolution and also enthusiastically adhered to the dictatorship of the proletariat. In one of his finest poems *(The New God)*, the poet Árpád Tóth saluted the "Red God"; Zsigmond Móricz wrote penetrating and passionate reportages and short stories; the poet Mihály Babits assumed a chair in the University of Budapest, and Ernő Osvát became member of a directory in charge of literary activities. Authors and poets of varying shades of political opinion —bourgeois progressives, social democrats and members of a newly formed group of communist writers alike—did their share of literary activity. Some ambitious schemes were launched for raising the general standard of education, for extending the radius of theatrical and literary activity to the broad masses of the people, and for providing financial support for writers.

The Hungarian Republic of Councils was short lived, and finally succumbed to the pressure of external forces, on August 1, 1919. Still, those 133 days did not pass without leaving their mark upon Hungarian literature. The number of literary works written under the Republic is considerable. Even if the time was too short for the emergence of 'big' novels or dramas, those few months supplied for long years to come the theme of novels, short stories and memoires by authors deriving fresh strength from, or spilling their hatred in, memories of those weeks. In a way, the response to the Hungarian Republic of Councils has become a touch-stone —every trend and every group of writers took a stand for or against it; and the lessons that have been drawn from it have determined subsequent development. It was under the Republic of Councils that a nucleus of communist writers was formed (partly around the periodical *Internacionálé*, edited by Aladár Komját) which was consolidated in later years; but the roots of many other trends go back to that regime, too.

# BETWEEN TWO WORLD WARS (1919-1944)

## GENERAL SURVEY

A lost war, a crushed revolution, a fierce and brutal counter-revolutionary terror—this onerous legacy marked the beginning of the inter-war period in Hungary. From the autumn of 1919 the White Terror raged unbridled in the capital and the country; and at the beginning of 1920 a kingless kingdom of Hungary was established and became consolidated, a form of government under which the latifundium survived uncurbed and gave a strongly feudal character to the state, even though some capitalist development did take place. On the surface, this establishment was all glitter and brilliance; there was the sham romanticism of the *puszta* (the Hungarian plains) and quaint herdsmen driving stampeding herds—an image deliberately built up and touted by tourist admen; and there was a eucharistic congress. This glittering exterior concealed a downtrodden working class, an impoverished peasantry and a shilly-shallying intelligentsia. The Establishment was strongly conservative and Catholic; prejudices and privileges inherited from Austro-Hungary mingled with extreme chauvinistic, anti-Semitic and anti-social demagoguery. Sham parliamentarianism and a sham opposition were used as a smokescreen for a deeply undemocratic content.

No investigation of the intellectual spectrum of the period can ignore the factor of nationalism, which pervaded almost the whole of national life. One of its sources was in the diminished national territory resulting from the Peace Treaty of 1920. Chauvinistic propaganda, which glossed over internal social problems, pervaded nearly every social stratum and left its stamp on intellectual life, on literature and on every activity.

The inter-war era was opened by a period of political extrem-

229

ism when counter-revolutionary officers' detachments maintained a region of bloody terror. Gradual stabilisation—or, to use the term current at the time, consolidation—began about the middle of the 20's: dominant conservatism became tinged with liberal tendencies. After 1932 however—parallel with the world economic crisis and Hitler's accession to power—fascism also became increasingly overt and aggressive in Hungary; the rulers of the nation tied it definitively to the Axis Powers. Hungary became an ally of nazi Germany, and entered the Second World War; anti-Jewish legislation was introduced. The road led inevitably to catastrophe: the dark period of twenty-five years culminated, in 1944, in another reign of terror, a period of organized mass murder.

Throughout this difficult and contradiction-ridden period, Hungarian literature survived under conditions of considerable hardships. In considering every literary work and every writer, one has to make allowance for the immense pressure which weighed down upon them, the difficult conditions and threats—often of persecution by the police—under which the writers were constrained to work, and for the arduous struggle the progressive forces waged against the forces of clericalism and conservatism and in the face of an increasingly aggressive fascism. The official ideology of the period was conservative nationalism; yet the various trends of irrational thought—like the German *Geistesgeschichte* and Spengler and, to an ever greater extent, the newer offshoots of racial theory—found a following and unofficial support, too. In intellectual life the front-lines assumed a criss-cross pattern, so that often it was difficult to distinguish between what was progressive and what retarding, what was modern and what outdated. Yet even under such unfavourable conditions literature was capable of producing some remarkable achievements. The revolutionary ardour of the early twentieth century, the spirit of *Nyugat* and Ady was still alive though sometimes it assumed different forms; nor did the incentive provided by international working class and progressive humanist literature remain ineffective. Nevertheless, by far the greatest influence shaping the development of literature was exercised by the unresolved questions of Hungarian national life, the oppression and dire poverty of the lower classes and the revolutionary energies of the popular masses.

Several main trends can be distinguished clearly in the literature of the period. In the official top-flight, there was the conservative tradition; next came the liberal-radical literature of the progressive middle class, headed by *Nyugat* and several minor groups of liberal writers either following the lead of *Nyugat* or opposing it; then there was the movement of populist writers initiated in the early 30's; and, lastly, the revolutionary trend, which had two branches: writers living in Hungary, and those active in exile. By the mid-twenties, literature had begun to emerge from the torpor in which it had found itself during the years that followed the autumn of 1919. Around 1930, as all over Europe, the economic crisis and the approaching wave of revolution brought about a new literary upsurge, increased attention to social problems, and a consolidation of style. Although the nazi takeover in 1933 checked and distorted development, the momentum lasted until 1938. From that year on, the literary scene became once more fragmented and split into groupings hostile one to another. Only between 1941 and 1944 did the outlines of an anti-fascist literature begin to emerge.

This division of the literature of the period into political and ideological trends is no hindsight classification; vital issues of the day, clear-cut and sharply defined, erected ideological barriers separating the various groups and individual writers, bringing about groupings that were clearly recognized at the time.

## CONSERVATIVE LITERATURE

The official literature of Admiral Horthy's Hungary—government-subsidised, eulogised, showered with honours and benefits and exported—was conservative and epigon-ridden. It reached back deliberately to the nationalist school of the late nineteenth century; desirous of skipping *Nyugat* revolutionism, it defied Ady and aimed to continue the thread that had been dropped at the beginning of the twentieth century. In expression, it was characterized by pedestrian intelligibility and mawkishness. Of European literature, it recognized only the kindred trends (Henri Bordeaux and the German conservatives); and politically, it was violently anti-progressive, religious and nationalistic. This group controlled the

231

Academy, the official literary societies and a large section of the daily press and of scientific periodicals. The most wide-spread literary weekly—Ferenc Herczeg's *Új Idők* (New Times)—propagated their writings. To counter the influence of *Nyugat*, they started a literary magazine called *Napkelet* (Orient). The most noted writer of the conservative group, the "literary prince" of the regime, was Ferenc Herczeg, who soon petrified into a statue of himself. Next to him in the conservative hierarchy came Cecil Tormay (1876-1937), who—greatly influenced by Grazia Deledda and Thomas Mann's *Buddenbrooks*—emerged as a novelist-historian of the middle class and nobility, with a strong nationalist and religious flavour. Renée Erdős (1879-1956), after a start as a poetess, turned to writing novels and short stories. In her novels she elevated on a pedestal carnal love, but after her spectacular conversion she gave her writings a religious, Catholic complexion. Though displaying many original colours, her writings verge on the track most best-sellers follow. Miklós Surányi (1882-1936), in novels richly endowed with picturesque images and drama, painted historical panels of the Middle Ages, the Renaissance and the rococo age—doing so in a manner strongly reminiscent of Mereshkovsky, whose pupil he professed himself to be.

On the more social-minded wing of the conservative Parnassus, we find the poet László Mécs (b. 1895), a Catholic priest, who at one time enjoyed a measure of popularity in Hungary as well as abroad. His verse has a verbal richness and an abundance of images, but, in essence, resounds with hollow pathos and rhetoric. A certain "social vein" shows here and there; yet, in the last analysis, it is an extremely conservative outlook, the narrow world of the village parson, that emerges from among the teeming platitudes. József Nyírő (1889-1955) derived his themes from the life of the Hungarian peasants of Transylvania, but his unquestionable talent was before long vitiated by his straining for effect and cheaply-acquired popularity. He became the ruling classes' own "populist" writer, entered politics with pronouncedly Rightist views and maintained connexions with the nazis. After 1945, he left Hungary and settled in the West.

János Komáromi (1890-1937) was one of the group of conservative writers. With much genuine talent and with original colours, he depicted episodes of Hungarian national history, drawing a true picture of the outlawed poor soldiers of Prince Rákóczi's War of Independence in the early eigteenth century. In a widely-read novel—*Imperial and Royal Halcyon Days*—he draws with a satirical edge, reminiscent of Hašek, the tragicomic disruption of the armed forces of the Hapsburg empire. ZSOLT HARSÁNYI (1887-1943) was a widely-read author whose many-volume biographical novels *(Liszt, Galilei, Rubens, Munkácsy)* were all best-sellers pandering to the reading public's need for cheap sensation and intimate detail. Easily-won success carried this not untalented author, after a good start, on to the road of superficial treatment and artistic as well as human compromise.

One of the younger generation of conservative writers is LAJOS ZILAHY (b. 1891), an author much talked about in the last few decades. In his novels written in the 20's, the post-war social and moral problems of the Hungarian middle class are treated. (The most popular of these novels has been *Two Prisoners.)* Essentially, he viewed his class "from within," writing with a conservative-nationalist tinge. The success of his early novels attracted him increasingly towards the best-seller: the second-rate books he wrote in the 30's, with their colourful requisites, lead us into the world of Hungarian—and other European—aristocracy and plutocracy. In the 30's, Zilahy took part in almost every new movement, standing with one leg in the government circles and with the other among the young intellectuals who rebelled against the former, thus doing the double part of a loyal publicist of the Establishment and an "Angry Young Man" of the time. For some time after the war, he seemed to adapt himself to the changed life of new Hungary, but finally decided to emigrate. He now lives in the United States, writing most of his books in English.

The most outstanding literary scholar of the age, who continued, until his death, as the Grand Old Man of Hungarian historians of literature, was JÁNOS HORVÁTH (1878-1961), essentially a member of the conservative group. A graduate of the École Normale Supérieure and a pupil of Brunetière and Lanson, he attracted attention at an early date on account of his refined literary sense, wide erudition and a unity of research into detail and synthesis. He was the only critic on the conservative side who analysed and appreciated Ady and the *Nyugat* with understanding. In later years, he retired and devoted himself entirely to studies in literary history; his books on the poet Petőfi, on the populist trend in Hungarian literature and the early centuries of Hungarian literature, and his trail-blazing prosodic researches constitute the highest achievement of Hungarian bourgeois literary scholarship; his writings aim at a searching analysis of facts and at considering the reader as a participant in the literary process.

## THE *NYUGAT* GROUP

After Ady's death there came a change in the role played by *Nyugat*. The front-page of the magazine continued to bear the name of the former editor-in-chief Ignotus, although he now lived in exile. (He only returned to Hungary in 1948—to die.) The "acting" editor was—until his death—Ernő Osvát, but real guidance came, more and more, from Mihály Babits. The magazine lost a good deal of its militancy—and some of its liveliness, too, and, under the great pressure that was brought to bear on it, sought from time to time to make a compromise with the Establishment. Although it carefully preserved its high literary standard, it dodged the burning issues of the time and withdrew into its ivory tower. Babits expounded his programme of a non-political, "pure" art in an essay on Julien Benda's *Trahison des Clercs*. For some time after 1930, the second editorship was assumed by Zsigmond Móricz, who made an unsuccessful attempt to infuse more life into the magazine and give it a more topical slant. Until the autumn of 1941, when it ceased publication, *Nyugat* was a bulwark of high-standard bourgeois literature. At a time when fascism was on the march, the humanist attitude of *Nyugat* constituted in some measure a barrier, but it did not prove a sufficiently powerful weapon and although the magazine retained its high standard to the end (appearing between its covers was considered a mark of high distinction), yet it became fossilised and aristocratic in tenor; new initiatives were started without its cooperation, and even in the face of resistance from it.

Throughout the period under review, the bourgeois Left had no other literary centre that could be likened to *Nyugat*. There were several attempts by young writers and radical intellectuals to launch periodicals as a counterpart to *Nyugat* and to form cultural centres livelier and more full of "fight" than *Nyugat*, but none of these attempts was long-lived. *Pandora* was published in the 20's; it was followed by *A Toll* (The Pen), a periodical, which combined journalism and belles-lettres, and *Apollo*, a humanistic periodical. *Szép Szó* (Fair Word), a magazine rallying young Leftist writers, appeared in 1935 and was followed, some time later, by *Ezüstkor* (Silver Age). These represented unsuccessful attempts to counterbalance *Nyugat* by creating a Left-wing liberal or radical centre.

The literature of the bourgeois Left was, in the last analysis, never more than a conglomeration of small groups representing trends of thought such as liberalism, classic or reformed, petty-bourgeois radicalism, and ancient, Catholic or Protestant-complexioned bourgeois humanism; it remained a rather loose confederation held together by occasional alliances and individual ambitions. A real, internal unity was never achieved. It is beyond dispute that, even during this period, the literature of the bourgeois Left acted as a channel through which many assets of European culture were transmitted to Hungary; it sensitively registered every new phenomenon, and fostered and conserved all values. Yet—whether unwittingly or not—to the end it remained isolated from the real issues that concerned the Hungarian people.

In and around *Nyugat* grew up the "second" and "third" generations of *Nyugat* writers whose literary career was begun in the 20's and 30's, respectively. These writers had not taken part in the struggles against the old feudal order; they made their *début* after the First World War and the abortive revolutions, in an atmosphere of dejection, by the experience that values had become relative. An atmosphere of crisis and shock, despair and hopelessness marked their careers. Some threw themselves into anarchical revolt; others, anxious to shirk the issues which the age posed to them, chose to withdraw into "art for art's sake." These were no smooth, straight-lined careers: trial and error marked them, and sudden diversions. The careers of some of these writers were brought to an abrupt end by German rifles in 1944; others awoke to a new life following the liberation of the country, while others again persisted in their former views even afterwards.

LŐRINC SZABÓ (1900-1957) was one of the most significant and most contradictory poets of the post-Ady "second" generation. The son of an engine-driver in the provinces, he attracted attention at an early age by his exceptional gifts, his poetical sensitivity. When, after the revolutions, he attended the University, he was a mature poet with a strikingly keen sense of style. In 1919 he co-operated with Mihály Babits and Árpád Tóth in producing a translation of the full Baudelaire. Even before his first volume of poetry was published he had attracted notice by a number of brilliant translations (Omar Khayyam, Coleridge, Shakespeare's *Sonnets*). His early volumes—*Earth, Woods, God* (1922); *Caliban* (1923); *Light, Light, Light* (1925) and *Satan's Masterpieces* (1926) —resound with a mad, anarchical revolt against capitalism, the existing order of things, a subversive urge to reject and destroy everything—voiced in staccato outbursts and tirades often tinged and influenced by expressionism. These verses are alive and red-hot with an extremely intensified sensuality and the experiences of a bustling metropolis. A settling down came in the 30's: the poet concluded a "separate peace": *You and the World* (1932); *Separate Peace* (1935). His revolt gave way to total disenchantment; he lost his faith in reason, culture, and human values: everything turns out to be relative, existence is aimless, only the forms of matter are important. His individual revolutionism gave way to chilled isolationism, self-centred individualism. His poetry turned into the painful-aggressive confessions of the Ego, isolated under the conditions of capitalism. These processes, this mental agony and search for problems, are conveyed by a passionately intellectual poetry; comprehensive thought constructions and lyric snapshots alternate with self-created myths. Lőrinc Szabó's poetry reflects modern city life with all its flavours, the feverish, tormented, and harsh, broken voice of the lonely and searching man. (Szabó had always a peculiar liking for the amassing of *enjambments* and was a master of broken and uneven verse structure.)

It was this individualism that, from the mid-1930's on,

brought Szabó closer to the Right: in several statements and articles, he gave voice to his sympathy with German nazism; on the plane of individualism and aloofness, of contempt for his fellow-men, he found contact with the ideology of fascism *(Struggle for Holiday*, 1938; *Collected Poems*, 1940). The years of the Second World War shook him deeply; his illness and the passion of a new love provided other novel experiences. Following the liberation of the country in 1945, he felt the need for a reappraisal of his life and career—this determination gave birth to one of his finest poems—*Cricket Song*, 1947-1957—which he continued to expand and polish until his death. In point of fact, this is an autobiographical cycle of little lyric masterpieces; a description of his childhood, youth, and development into a poet, and flashes of scenes from his later years; a polished compound of the Proustian techniques of reminiscence, profound self-analysis, cosmic and philosophical perspectives and of intimate lyricism. Another product of his later years is the cycle *The Twenty-sixth Year* (1956), a poetic monument to a great love, to a beloved mistress who died.

As a translator Szabó was a worthy successor to the great *Nyugat* generation of poets; he even surpassed his predecessors in intellectual power, accuracy, and for sheer volume of translation work. He is responsible for the best Hungarian versions of Shakespeare and Goethe, Villon and Kleist. A collection of minor translations, published in a bulky volume under the title *Eternal Friends*, comprises a very broad spectrum of world poetry, from the Chinese poets to nineteenth-century European classicism and from Jammes and George to the twentieth-century English poets.

The course followed by JÓZSEF FODOR (b. 1898), the other leading poet of the "second generation," has led him to different achievements from Szabó's. The poetical career of Fodor, who had seen military service during the world war, also began in the early 20's. He started as a follower of Ady, without, however, being an epigon; his sense of mission, his ardent espousal of great ideals were the signs of kinship between him and the great model. His early volumes—*Panting Forests* (1927); *Write it upon Leaves* (1931); and *Epilogue* (1935)—are marked by an impassioned, ode-like tone. Striking a solemn note, he extols mankind's great humanistic ideals and grapples with the great questions of life, on a philosophical level. The poetry he wrote about this time is sheer burning passion, almost formless. In his later volumes—*Out of Harmony* (1940) and *Years of Revelations* (1957)—his voice acquired depth and fullness. He remained faithful to his ideals and preserved his loyalty to his Leftist friends in the most difficult years. In these years, his lyrics struck a tragic note. After 1945, he hailed the liberation and the rising new life of Hungary with ardour *(In the Scales,* 1945, *Man and the Voice,* 1947; and *Happy Revolt,* 1949). He expanded conventional verse-forms of the ode, the elegy and the rhapsody in the direction of great "symphonic" poems. Besides the solemn and the sublime, he was susceptible also to lighter, more cheerful moods in his descriptive poetry, poems describing flowers and gardens or evoking the moods of seasons *(The Years of Revelations,* 1947).

In the years after 1948, Fodor, the former bourgeois humanist, became converted to socialism and he remained a staunch socialist during and after the 1956 counter-revolutionary rising. In his latest volumes his philosophical mind and dynamism, combined with a socialist theme, have produced an original, modern off-shoot of Hungarian socialist lyric poetry.

Another kind of attitude, a different type of poetry, is that of LÁSZLÓ FENYŐ (1902-1945), who died an early victim of nazism. He started in the "isms," but very soon he found his true keynote: dejection, sadness, a feeling of loneliness. Fenyő was an urban poet, a café-dweller (one of his volumes is entitled: *A Café in Autumn).* His life was one of frustration: he suffered the whole pressure of the time, unemployment, poverty and loneliness. His lyrics are the confessions of a sad suffering man in quest of beauty, peace and tranquillity. His protest against his time is not revolt, not appeal to the new forces, but sadness and complaint. He never got beyond a certain petty-bourgeois rebellion. His poems convey an impression of unceasing rain and permanent November. His dejected poetry and tragic death are an indictment of the oppressive age in which he lived.

The second generation of *Nyugat* gave many other significant poets, exponents of many refined varieties of bourgeois poetry. LAJOS ÁPRILY (b. 1887), who for many years was principal of a Calvinist secondary school for girls in Budapest, writes highly accomplished, sensitive poetry. The hills of his native Transylvania, the beauty of brooks and forests appeal strongly to him; reticent, decent and polished, his poetry runs in the best of tradition. In recent years, Áprily has turned out some excellent translations; he is responsible for the best Hungarian version of Pushkin's *Onegin*. The poetry of JENŐ DSIDA (1907-1938)—springing from a fear of death, mysterious fears, superstitious tremblings, and strongly reminiscent of Trakl and A. Wildgans—began, towards the end of his short life, to acquire the colours of reality; a Villonesque kind of fraternisation with God and Death appeared in his poetry. Expressing ethereal moments and moods, his language is uniquely subtle and flexible.

In his early volumes GYÖRGY SÁRKÖZI (1899-1945) made his *début* as a poet of the neo-Catholic lyric poetry made fashionable by Claudel; in the early 20's he was regarded as one of the infant prodigies of the new generation of lyricists then beginning to rise. Later on he joined the movement of the populist writers, becoming one of its organizers and editor of the movement's magazine and library series. After a silence of one and a half decades, in the middle of the 30's his lyrics found a new voice, one of a harsher timbre, but still reflecting a world of abstract ideals. It is an interesting but tragic fact about György Sárközi that although he was of Jewish descent, he became a neo-Catholic writer and one of the organisers of a rather nationalistic literary and political movement—only to be killed by the Hungarian nazis.

JÓZSEF BERDA (b. 1902) is a unique figure, almost an *enfant terrible*, of Hungarian literary life. His is a modern "highwayman" poetry—free verse of original rhythm; he praises the simple joys of life: eating, drinking and love-making. He is at once lewd and innocent, jauntily defiant and candidly wide-eyed in his admiration for real beauty.

The *Nyugat* generation which made its appearance around 1920 has made a smaller contribution to prose writing than its predecessors. There was, however, one ambition which animated this generation, their desire to pass beyond the world Móricz had created, to assimilate new emotions and new themes, to mirror the emotions and problems of the urban middle class and at the same time assimilate the new achievements of the bourgeois literature of Western Europe, to learn from Proust and Thomas Mann, and later on, from Giraudoux, Joyce and Huxley. Under the specific conditions of Hungary, this trend did not prove sufficiently fertile, but remained experimental and isolated. Its leading exponent was Sándor Márai.

SÁNDOR MÁRAI (b. 1900), the son of a well-to-do middle-class family of Kassa*, consciously strove to become a writer of the Hungarian bourgeoisie of Western learning. Like many of his fellow-writers, Márai, in his youth, wrote reportages in support of the Hungarian Republic of Councils of 1919. After the fall of the Republic, he plunged into the colourful world of the Weimar republic and Paris of the 20's. He started as a poet, but when, after his wanderings abroad, he returned to Budapest, he was primarily a prose writer. He has two great themes: revolt and flight, the shedding of conventions. (*Aliens* and *Baby or the First Love*). Perhaps his most successful work on this theme is *The Mutineers*, 1930, a teenager novel like Cocteau's *Enfants terribles* or Gide's *Faux-monnayeurs*, depicting the world of adolescents who cling to the rules of boyhood until the world crumbles all around them. The other group of his novels is centred round the life of the middle class, its past and present place in the social set-up. The most valuable work in this line in *Confessions of a Bourgeois*, 1934, a candid evocation of his family and youth and a brilliant sketch of the vanishing world of the Hungarian provincial middle class and of the disjointed Europe of the post-war years. *The Jealous Ones*, 1937, describes the death of the patrician middle-class way of life (patrician taken in the sense of Thomas Mann's *Budden-brooks*)—a fictitious way of life in Hungary. He varied his themes in a number of novels—some well-written, other less so—published in the latter half of the 30's. More and more, he was leaning towards reflexions, presentation of moods, and maxims; his settled outlook was moderately conservative. Márai's art as a novelist—contrary to the Hungarian antecedents—followed in the footsteps of the twentieth-century West European—primarily French—novel; his ideal is the symbolical-suggestive presentation, the technique of association, the preponderance of intellectual reflexions. His indi-

* Today Košice, Czechoslovakia

vidual style, however, was soon reduced to sheer routine and mannerism; the countless variations of his basic experience and the constant repetition of his themes and thoughts become trying. After 1945 Márai lived in Hungary for some time, but later on he emigrated and has been living in Western Europe and the United States. In his recent work he still appears inconfident of socialist development and gives voice to the homesickness and misery felt by the exile.

Márai's novels have been translated into several languages, as have those of FERENC KÖRMENDI (b. 1900), who wrote best-sellers for intelligentsia: *A Budapest Adventure; A Happy Generation; Departure 7.15; Via Bodenbach*, etc.

Of course, there were between the two wars quite a few writers who were not closely associated with *Nyugat*, yet who in their mode of life, outlook and writing represented one or other trend of progressive bourgeois literature.

ALADÁR KUNCZ (1886-1931), a highly gifted professor and aesthete, has won his place in the history of Hungarian literature by a single remarkable work. A contemporary of the "great" *Nyugat* generation, and a scholar, he started as a schoolmaster; he was a Francophile and a lover of French literature. The outbreak of the First World War found him on a study-trip in Paris; as the citizen of an enemy country he was interned at Noirmoutier. After five years in internment he returned to Hungary. The book he wrote about those five years—*The Black Monastery*, 1931—is one of the most coherent and concise books of reminiscences in Hungarian literature, both a diary and novel, with a perfect milieu and psychological depth. It is the dramatic history of the inner development of a man, showing the way illusions are cast off and sentiments deepen, and how a superficial Francomania gives way to a profound understanding of the French people. It is also a startling memento and indictment of naked force, tyranny and imprisonment, coming as it did right on the eve of the period of extermination camps.

The conventional trend of Hungarian prose writing between the two wars was loosened with mild irony by FERENC MÓRA (1879-1934). He was a journalist and, later, museum director in Szeged. He continued in the *conte* and anecdote tradition of Hungarian prose-writing, but his social-mindedness and thorough

16

knowledge of the life of poor peasants made him a destroyer of illusions about the lower classes. Himself the son of desperately poor peasants of the Great Plain, he had known dire poverty in his childhood and youth; the peculiar attitude of the poor peasant— his wily ambiguity when confronted with the gentry—appears in his work, elevated to a literary standard. The largest part of Móra's *oeuvre* comprises sketches, short stories and tales. Even before the First World War, he had attracted notice with several very well written books for the young. During the Horthy era, his political views became better defined, as could be seen in his minor and major works alike: *Daughter of Four Fathers*, 1923; *Resurrection of Hannibal*, 1924—an ironical panorama of the early stage of the reactionary Horthy era through the ordeal of a frustrated little schoolmaster; *Song of the Wheatfields*, 1927, one of the leading anti-war novels in Hungarian literature, which shows how war affects life in the hinterland—a lyrical portrayal of the life of the poor. *The Gold Coffin*, 1932, is a vast historical panel depicting the struggle between the heathen world and Christianity in the last days of the Roman Empire. Yet, Móra was greatest in short stories and short novels. His work presents a unique blend of European learning and the Hungarian peasant's voice.

Another good writer of short stories and novelettes with an original voice is SÁNDOR HUNYADY (1893-1942). On the surface he seems like a short-story writer reminiscent of Maugham, with strong colours and a hedonistic attitude. In reality, he was a writer with a knowledge of life who well understood the great problems too. His most frequent theme was the contact and clash between the members of diverse classes. He was equally familiar with the ways of the aristocracy, the gentry and the upper middle class. His natural easy-going manner and Bohemian mode of life prevented him from probing deeper into political aspects and aspiring to higher artistic achievements, but his remarkable gifts enabled him to make a not insignificant contribution to Hungarian prose-writing. Perhaps his most enduring work is *Family Album*, 1934, a sensuous reproduction of the literary and theatrical world of the early twentieth century.

Farther down the literary spectrum and always in opposition to the *Nyugat* movement, we find a group of liberal petty-bourgeois writers headed by the gifted BÉLA ZSOLT (1898-1949), journalist and writer who ruthlessly exposed the Jewish petty bourgeoisie of Budapest, whom he also served by his pen as journalist. The most valuable part of his belletristic work comprises a large number of novels and plays which present with the vivisectionist's keenness and gossipy maliciousness the precarious world of shop-keepers and small capitalists.

ANDOR NÉMETH (1891-1953), a fastidious critic, essayist and novelist whose principal influence was owed to his profound understanding, represented a slightly different trend of bourgeois literature. He lived in Vienna in the 20's, and in Paris during the Second World War. He counted among his friends many well-known writers, Hungarian and other, including, for some time, the poet Attila József (about whom he wrote a very fine book). From his historical novels and novels of manners there emerges an author with restraint and a sense of proportion. In the work of ALADÁR KOMLÓS (b. 1892) we find bourgeois-radical criticism at its best. After a start as poet, he became a perceptive critic of the young generation of Hungarian poets; his series of essays (New Hungarian Lyric Poetry, 1928; Writers and Principles, 1937) excel by the writer's level-headed judgement and reasonable views. After the last war, he greatly expanded his activity as a historian of literature (his books discuss the lyrics of the latter half of the nineteenth century and the turn of the century).

MARCELL BENEDEK (b. 1885) has rendered signal services as an interpreter of the assets of world literature. He has edited several library series and written summaries and encyclopaedias of modern Hungarian literature; he is a writer with refined taste and a consistent adherent of progressive views. The bulk of his translation work has been done from French, and he is an ardent propagator in Hungary of French literature. His correspondence with Romain Rolland is an important literary record of our time.

The "third generation" made its appearance in the 30's, in association with Nyugat and other contemporary—more or less short-lived—magazines (Apollo, Ezüstkor). This generation began its rise under difficult conditions: the growing pressure of fascism and an increasingly dehumanised world bore down upon its members. They arrived equipped with a considerable learning in world literature and a high responsiveness to foreign cultures; the age of "isms" and the playfulness of the 1930's having passed, they soberly oriented themselves towards a new kind of realism. They had to work their way up with much effort since the leading posts of literature were occupied by still-living great men, members of the second generation. Nearly all stepped aside to get away from the pressure of the age: they were strongly influenced by the "decline of the West" mood, a sense of crisis; they susceptibly responded to Spengler and Berdyaev, Ortega and Hendrik de Man, assimilated Huxley's and Giraudoux's works, and were influenced by Freud and Jung, by the classicism of the Altheim-Kerényi stamp and by Frazer and Frobenius. Translations are an almost natural form of expression with each member of this generation— by means of translations and essays, they tried to introduce into Hungarian culture and learning the assets of bourgeois literature. Their ways branched off in many directions: some withdrew into splendid isolation, others sought refuge in irrationalism, while others again tried to find contact with the labouring classes. Many an eminent member of the generation was murdered by nazism; their artistic career, hardly beyond the early, formative stages, was broken off by the war. The most gifted survivors—after periods of varying length—have come so far in their development as to approve of socialism.

A characteristic poet-member of this generation is SÁNDOR WEÖRES (b. 1913). He was a boy when he first attracted public notice by his poems; he impressed everyone by his superb mastery of form, in almost every style. A man of wide, universal erudition, he translated everything and everybody from ancient Indian texts to T. S. Eliot. He soon evolved his own message and individual voice: his basic experiences were disgust with the world, the desire to escape from life, the total senselessness of life and society. From these tormenting problems he escaped into nihilism, trying to find consolation in irrationalist philosophies and pseudo-Oriental myths. The fundamental position both of his poetry and of his life has remained unchanged—the war, the subsequent liberation of the country and the years that have elapsed since have but confirmed his aloofness and escapism, his sense of total senselessness, the spectacle of broken-up and fractured reality which holds him spellbound. He is, in essence, a twentieth-century successor of the German magic romantic poets; if one were to try to find a comparison in present-day western lyric poetry, his attitude to life most resembles Reverdy's. In the course of his poetical development Weöres has reached the stage of the utter lack of sense, of collocations that make no sense whatever, of reliance on mere sound effects. He is at the same time a brilliant versifier and a great master of form; he has created an almost entirely new rhythmic pattern and held up bright and undreamt-of possibilities inherent in Hungarian verse.

Another typical example of the attitude of this group is provided by ISTVÁN VAS (b. 1910). At the beginning of his career he stood near to the working-class movement; from the mid-1930's onward, the attitude of the Leftist, rationalist and socialist-sympathiser bourgeois became dominant in his make-up; he was painfully and most keenly aware of the inhumanity of nazism and protested against the barbarity from the standpoint of pure reason. Vas's poetry belongs characteristically to the neo-classic trends; he reveals himself in well-built, speculative poems heated by an inner passion, poems in which all the achievements of preceding periods are utilised. The themes that have engaged his attention since 1945 are the new human behaviour, the problems facing and the place occupied in the new society by the progressive though non-communist intellectual, the role played in the new order by reason and culture. In some of his recent poems he has given appealing landscape descriptions, penetrating psychological drawing, the lyrics of a man who has arrived on the threshold of old age. Vas is an eminent translator, an interpreter mainly of English poets and of plays. His outstanding achievements are Hungarian versions of Shakespeare, Schiller, the English baroque poets, of T. S. Eliot and Apollinaire.

ZOLTÁN JÉKELY (b. 1913) is another poet-member of the "third generation." He is a poet of romantic-mystic dream-pictures moods and reveries, whose poetry is pervaded by unrelieved melancholy, a longing for death, by irony and self-mockery.

The prose-writer members of the "third generation" had just begun to unfold their talent before the war. EMIL GRANDPIERRE KOLOZSVÁRI (b. 1907) looks upon the French analytical novel as

245

his ideal. He describes the lives of members of the middle class, of clerks and officials, analysing queer, distorted characters in terms of psychological formulas. An irony that is always present behind his objectivity, strong sexuality and interest in the instincts characterize his works. *The Great Man* (1936) and *The Loves of Dr. Csibráky* (1935) depict the conflicts between intellect and instincts. His autobiography *Yesterday* (1942) describes the writer's childhood and through it gives a picture of Hungarian middle-class life. After the liberation he attempted a comprehensive social novel, *On the Balance* (1950). Other writings also show an interest in the recent past. Writing about its sexual aberrations, he suggests the internal decay of a stratum of society. His observations of the present show a certain bourgeois scepticism. ENDRE ILLÉS (b. 1902) describes in his short stories the barren and self-deceiving life of some Budapest upper middle-class families, viewed with cold, ruthless precision. In his recent writings he portrays members of the former ruling classes—and especially their short-lived resurrection and failure in 1956—viewed from a socialist angle, while preserving the fine technical qualities of his earlier writing (*The Sharpers*, 1958). Endre Illés is an excellent essayist: he has written some highly penetrating essays on most great twentieth-century artists. An eminent translator, his outstanding achievement is the interpretation of Stendhal, whom he closely resembles in literary temper. Prior to 1945, ISTVÁN SŐTÉR (b. 1913) wrote novels and short stories in which he depicted the total disruption of bourgeois ways of life, the inevitable deliquescence of the middle class on the eve of, and its total atomisation during the war. A graduate of the École Normale Supérieure, Sőtér, inspired by the latest achievements of the French novel, describes this process with the aid of a mystic-surrealist technique. In his works— *Walking in the Clouds*, 1939; *Church Robbers*, 1941; *Ghost*, 1943—an iconoclastic revolt is in the making which will assail many a cherished belief of the past, such as cold intellectualism and foolish playfulness. His works written after 1945—*The Fall*, 1947 and *Falling Bridges*, 1948—do indeed describe the final failure, debasement and falling apart of this bourgeoisie. His latest stories depict the life of the old and new intelligentsia *Garden of Eden*, 1960). In recent years, Sőtér has devoted his energies to the history of literature, writing extensive monographs on the great names in nineteenth-century Hungarian literature, combining the philologist's thoroughness with belletristic style and with a firmly-based Marxist method of analysis; in his essays, he treats outstanding novels of world literature, from Dostoevsky to Camus and from Thomas Mann to Simone de Beauvoir.

GÁBOR THURZÓ (b. 1912) started his career as a member of the neo-Catholic group, describing the world of upper-middle-class homes. His hatred for fascism, the horrors of the war, and the reappearance of the old world in October 1956 have brought him closer to the views of socialism. His polished writing, brilliant short-story technique and irony make him a significant author. GYÖRGY RÓNAY (b. 1913) is a discerning translator of modern French poets, novelist and erudite essayist, a member of the neo-Catholic group. ANDRÁS HEVESI (1902-1940) exposed in his two novels the profound crisis and split which cut through the bourgeois intelligentsia. He was killed on active service in the French army.

High-level scholarship was characteristic of members of the "third generation," a quality that earned for them the epithet, applied by contemporary critics, of "generation of essayists." Several critics and essayists unfolded their work in the face of constant opposition from official literary scholarship. ANTAL SZERB (1901-1945) is significant also as fiction writer; he is a master of intellectual prose, and author of colourfully ironic historical panels and profiles. *The Pendragon Legend*, an ironic and yet emotional novel which expresses the nostalgia of many young writers of the period, is set in Wales. The novel *Traveller and Moonlight*, 1937, is a most important document regarding the opinions and literary orientation of the author's generation. *Weekdays and Wonders*, 1936, is a comprehensive survey of modern English and French fiction. As he was debarred from holding university posts because of his Jewish parentage and radical views, he was compelled to rely on his own energy and resources in writing his *History of Hungarian Literature*, 1934, the most remarkable bourgeois progressive work of its kind, which was diametrically opposed to the prevalent official view of literature. As a matter of fact, this work shows the influence of bourgeois sociology, of Spengler's cycle-theory, yet the author's love of literature, keen sense and observant eye break through the self-imposed framework. Another great achievement was his *History of World Literature*, 1941, a systematic work, yet full of the individual observations of a widely-read, enthusiastic man of letters of a quite original style. Antal Szerb made a special study of English literature and wrote several brilliant essays on the subject. He was murdered by the nazis early in 1945.

GÁBOR HALÁSZ (1901-1945) was another important and sensitive critic. A highly cultured librarian, he started his career with the *Napkelet*. When he joined the *Nyugat* circle, he first represented a neo-conservative trend, a Chestertonian attitude. The English Victorians and the Hungarian late nineteenth century were his ideals. His essays, which he wrote in a dry and precise style, are pregnant with ideas. Later, in the mid-1930's, he turned to a more social-minded approach and in his critical writings took a stand for the new realism proclaiming that the "isms" were outdated. Halász, too, died a victim of fascism.

Another member of this essayist generation is LÁSZLÓ Cs. SZABÓ (b. 1905). Originally, Szabó was an historian of economics, but switched over to writing short stories and finely pointed, learned essays in which he worked towards a synthesis of Hungarian nationalism and European supra-nationalism. In the forties, he acquired a strongly nationalistic complexion, and left Hungary after 1945; he now lives in London.

The careers of many outstanding present-day literary scholars and critics began in the circle of *Nyugat*'s "third generation." ALBERT GYERGYAI (b. 1893) is a polished writer, an original essayist, a learned student of French literature, who is responsible for translations of Proust, Flaubert and others and author of book on the *Modern French Novel*. Albert Gyergyai is now professor of French literature in the University of Budapest. LÁSZLÓ BÓKA (b. 1910) is a poet, novelist and literary scholar. After a start as philologist, he joined various radical, liberal groups of writers as a witty and learned essayist. His studies in literary history are marked by a high poetic sensitivity, a keen analytical mind, observant eye, and easy-flowing and flexible style. He is professor of Modern Hungarian Literature at the University of Budapest. The distinctive qualities of his novels on events of the recent

history are skilful treatment and sure craftsmanship. GÁBOR
TOLNAI (b. 1910) is a professor at the University of Budapest.
His major writings are essays dealing with old Hungarian literature, the literature of Spain, and the literature of the inter-war
years and critical essays discussing present-day problems.

## THE POPULIST WRITERS' MOVEMENT

The group of writers whom it is customary to call populist (rural
or peasant writers) is a complex political and literary grouping
with a profile all its own. An intellectual "third force" movement
which looked to the peasantry as its mainstay, the movement of
populist writers had few, if any, counterparts in other countries.

Though the movement of populist writers started after 1930,
its antedecedents go back, as a matter of fact, to the 20's, the years
that followed the crushed revolution. Those were the years when
the work of Dezső Szabó, the predecessor and master of the populist writers and one of the most characteristic authors of counter-
revolutionary Hungary, was at its height, and when József Erdélyi,
the first populist poet, began his career.

DEZSŐ SZABÓ (1879-1945) was the son of a Protestant official
of Kolozsvár.* An eminent student, he graduated from the Eötvös
Kollégium of Budapest, the Hungarian École Normale Supérieure;
he aimed to become a philologist, and conceived a devoted admiration for French literature. (Already at that time, he was greatly
susceptible to the influence of Barrès, conveyed to him by Jérome
Tharaud, then teaching in Budapest.) After spending a year in
Paris, he returned to Hungary to assume an assistant mastership
in the provinces in 1906. From then on, like Mihály Babits and
Gyula Juhász, he was transferred from one provincial town to the
other and led the life of a provincial schoolmaster.

But this young man was bursting with tremendous energies,
an almost morbid self-esteem, and a sense of mission as pronounced
as Ady's. From a clerical anti-Semite he turned into an extremist
radical; after philology and politics, his interest turned to litera-

*Today Cluj, Rumania

249

ture, and he joined the editorial staff of *Nyugat*. In his essays he discusses the past and present of Hungarian literature, and the rebel poets of French literature—Rimbaud, Laforgue and Corbière; his aesthetic concepts were evolved under the influence of Comte and Guyau, while his taste was shaped by Hugoesque romanticism, and his style, even at this early date, was close to romantic expressionism. In his bold political writings, he put his finger on the most burning issues of his time. The philosophical foundation of these writings was a unique combination of Nietzscheanism and positivism, and they were marked by extreme anti-rationalism, anti-democratic views, and a yearning for "the new Middle Ages" and a "new Unity." He was against capitalism, but his views meant a step back in the anti-capitalist struggle. Eventually, racialism came to dominate his thought, the idolisation of the "Hungarian race," the extremist cult of the Hungarian peasant as the vehicle of the vital national force. Essentially, he became the exponent of a social stratum of petty-bourgeois intellectuals who were becoming increasingly reactionary. He hailed the revolutions of 1918-19, only to turn against them before long—the one-time progressive had now turned an anti-revolutionary extremist and anti-Semite agitator. His most impressive novel— *The Village That Was Swept Away*, 1919—was published in the days of the revolution. This is a three-volume saga, written in an expressionist free-flowing, torrential style; in it, through the mythically magnified figures of a few heroes, he depicts the diminution of the Hungarian race, extols the primitive soundness of the Hungarian village, and the depraving, enervating influence of the Town, against a full panorama of Hungarian life before the war. This is a distorted panorama: he has a wrong approach to the problems of the Hungarian scene—everything is viewed as a symptom of the wrestling between the Hungarian and the Jewish races; every problem is simplified into a struggle between the peasantry and foreign capital. The impact of *The Village That Was Swept Away* in the first years of the counter-revolutionary regime was tremendous: its pathos and expressionist-romantic style, its readily acceptable anti-Semitism and racialism, the reunion in the vital force of the Hungarian race of lord and peasant, and its social criticism—all that chimed in with the hazy

250

discontent and increasingly reactionary temper of the post-1919 youth and petty bourgeoisie. Thus it happened that the former contributor to *Nyugat*, the learned schoolmaster who had been groomed on French culture, came to be one of the ideological leaders of Hungarian fascism. During the early years of the counter-revolutionary regime, Dezső Szabó became a popular leader, yet hardly had a few years passed when he found that Jewish had been succeeded by German rule. He now turned the edge of his racial theory against the "Swabians," pouring his venom upon the influence of the German sham-culture that hamstrung the Hungarian intelligentsia. This new element is expressed in his articles and new novels—*Thou Shalt Kill*, 1921; *Marvellous Life*, 1921; *Help!* 1925—with their verbal torrents, dimly-drawn characters and hardly a trace of a plot. He became more and more isolated—a lone wolf; his quaint, unsociable nature, his self-worship and mercilessly scornful criticism that was at the same time right and wrong alienated the literary world from him. From 1934 almost until his death, he published his own articles and booklets. With the advance of German nazism his life took a strangely tragic turn: he assailed racial theory from a racial standpoint, and, when lashing the Hungarian nazis, he found himself up against his own disciples.

Dezső Szabó's contradiction-ridden career exercised great influence upon the succeeding generation of writers who grew up under the counter-revolutionary regime; his erudition, dynamism and social criticism, and his love of life and courage exercised a beneficial influence. All the more harmful were his basically irrational philosophy, his racialism, peasant cult, and obscure, romantic-expressionist style.

In the early 1920's, the years in which *Nyugat*'s refined artistry of form and the "isms" were gaining ground, a new note was struck in Hungarian lyric poetry by JÓZSEF ERDÉLYI (b. 1896). Half Hungarian, half Rumanian by birth, and a white-collar worker, Erdélyi saw military service throughout the First World War. His poems began to appear in periodicals from 1920 onward. His early volumes—*Violet-Leaf*, 1922; and *At World's End*, 1924—reveal a plain, clear voice, facile versification and clear-cut imagery reminiscent of folk-songs and Petőfi, and a cosmic vision, the way of seeing the things of the world and of nature in a simple, primitive unity that is reminiscent of popular ballads. Erdélyi's early verse burns with a revolutionary passion which finds expression sometimes in hot anger, and other times in a more covert way. It is an outcry against the lot of the downtrodden poor peasantry of Hungary, a rebellious cursing of the lords, and also a hope for a better future. It is the voice of the peasantry who felt they had been deceived in the early years of the counter-revolutionary regime. Erdélyi was an anarchist peasant revolutionary, not a socialist one—that was why his revolutionary fervour became misdirected into various poses. In the 20's, he made walking tours of Hungary and printed his own volumes of poetry; his poetical consciousness and constructive power could not keep pace with his imagination. A few fine poetic achievements came from him in the 30's—*The Last Golden Eagle*, 1928; *Winter Rhapsody*, 1934; *The White Tower*, 1938—then he began to decline. His discontent and rebellion, too, became displaced in the direction of the Right: he caused a stir by Jew-baiting verses and joined several parties of the extreme Right. After 1945, he was brought to trial as a war criminal; and, for some time after serving his sentence, he brought out some poems, repenting and condemning his earlier actions as fallacious and sinful—*Coming Back*, 1954. He has since been a participant in literary life in Hungary, showing flashes of his former power in a few poems, often inspired by the momentous transformation that has taken place in the life of the Hungarian peasantry.

In point of fact, Erdélyi was only one of the forerunners of the populist movement of Hungarian writers; the movement proper unfolded only after 1930. Its rise was due to a number of causes: the fall of the Hungarian Republic of Councils; the demagogic peasant-policy of the counter-revolution; the fragmentation of the forces of the Left; and—this factor is not negligible, either—the influence of various crisis theories and irrationalist trends of thought which were widely diffused throughout Europe.

The economic crisis of 1929-31 deepened the social evils of Hungary. The search by young Hungarians for new paths gave rise to a legion of societies and movements. With the revolutionary wave of 1930 over, and Hitler's accession to power in 1933, it seemed to many that solutions to the above problems would not come from the working-class movement. These circumstances gave rise to an outlook and concept which may well be described by the epithet "third force" and which was upheld by a political movement with an impressive literary record. The chief characteristic of this movement was the strongly nationalist conception of a "special Hungarian road," the insistence on a "third position" between the clashing extremes of imperialism and socialism. This complex movement rendered signal services in directing public attention, in the Horthy era, to the social problems of rural Hungary—primarily the untenability of the system of latifundia—doing so in political writings, sociological studies as well as fiction, and in propagating its comparatively democratic concepts with much vigour and courage. But no matter how fine and well-meant the designs of the individual members of the movement might be, they were always thwarted by the nationalist character of the movement, the contamination of their thinking by racial theory.

The progress of the populist movement of writers is divided into several stages. It was after a preparatory stage—essentially in 1932—that the participants joined together to form a movement. That year saw the launching of László Németh's periodical, *Tanú* (The Witness) and in 1934 was started the leading magazine of the first stage—*Válasz* (Answer). In this first stage, the chief theoretician of the movement was László Németh, with his peculiar concept of "socialism without Marxism"—a "quality brand" of socialism drawing heavily, at this period, on Ortega y Gasset, Hendrik de Man and the German *Tat* circle. In 1935 the populist writers even blindly accepted—for some time—the social demagoguery of the Gömbös government; before long, however, they saw the absurdity of a compromise of this kind. The heyday of the populist writers'movement came after 1935: that was the stage at which the democratic and anti-fascist tendencies grew stronger within the movement. These were the years when members of the movement wrote their major works—fiction as well as sociological monographs exposing conditions in Hungary; *Válasz* now emerged almost as a rival of *Nyugat*. The formation on March 15, 1937, of the March Front as the supreme organization governing the movement; its demonstrative public actions against fascism and its advocacy of a democratic transformation in Hungary; declaration of its readiness to co-operate with the working-class movement, that is, to participate in a United Front of all Left parties and forces—those were some outstanding events of these few years.

However, external pressure from the fascist state power as well as internal strife soon disrupted the group. After 1938 the greater part of the members of the movement ceased to be active, a good many drifted to the political Right—a few even to the extreme Right—while a minority persisted in their leftist views and joined the anti-fascist resistance, participating in the activities of the Independence Front. In this period, the political programme and watchword of the populist writers, vulgarised and oversimplified, was incorporated in the government programme; official publishing firms (Bolyai Publishers) and periodicals *(Magyar Élet, Hungarian Life)* blended nazi mottos with populist goals. During the Second World War—that great historical test—a good many members of the movement professed middle-of-the-road views, which meant, in practice, an attitude of wait and see.

The populist writers' movement was joined by many writers with varying degrees of talent who represented varying shades of political opinion, writers who joined the movement either for the duration of a phase in their development or to stay in it to the end. There was hardly any question of a literary quality common to them all, of a community of style, only an interest in rural themes and a tendency towards realism.

GYULA ILLYÉS (b. 1902), one of the leading figures of modern Hungarian literature, also joined the movement of the populist writers. He was born in a manor in Western Hungary, descended from cotters and shepherds. His parents had gone to great sacrificies to give an education for their son. Under the Hungarian Republic of Councils of 1919, Illyés broke off his studies to join the Hungarian Red Army. After the fall of the Republic, he emigrated to Paris, where he came into contact with the working-class movement, with the Hungarian communist exiles; here, too, he formed ties of friendship with many young French writers, including Tzara, Aragon, Eluard, Breton and others. His literary career, too, dates back to those years of exile; he made a start with free verse and surrealist and expressionist experiments.

254

In 1925 Illyés returned to Hungary and earned his living as a white-collar worker. In the beginning he joined some Leftist bourgeois-radical circles and also had some contact with the underground Communist Party. Later, he became one of the most highly-thought-of young contributors to *Nyugat*, a protégé of Babits's. In his first two volumes—*Heavy Earth*, 1928, and *Second Harvest*, 1930—he laments over the plight of poor villagers in sweeping, rhythmical free verse. With each passing year, his tone of voice became more strident and ringing: the epic poem *Three Old Men*, 1931; the poem *Youth*, 1932; the epic poem *I Speak of Heroes*, 1935; and *Under Soaring Skies*, 1935, a collection of his recent verse are so many milestones of the revolutionary period of his lyric poetry. In the Hungarian literature of the inter-war period, Illyés created realist lyrics marked by transparent verse construction of Gallic lucidity, an almost inevitably epic flavour, a thorough knowledge and skilful evocation of everyday life, a free-and-easy manner and the cadence of informal speech, and a harmony of rustic impulses and of European civilisation.

In the mid-1930's, Illyés joined the populist writers' movement; essentially, he stood throughout at the centre—in a political as well as ideological sense—of the group, while as regards his literary connections and stylistic concepts, he was a liaison, as it were, between *Nyugat* and the populists. His major works were written at the radical phase of the populist writers' movement: soaring new lyrics *Order among the Ruins*, 1938, a travel diary *Russia*, 1934—and two remarkable prose works: *People of the Puszta*, 1936; and *Petőfi*, 1936. As regards its genre, *People of the Puszta* is a sociological study, but superior literary craftsmanship, a latent irony and the broad perspective of vision have developed the facts of his inquiry into a major work. Autobiographical elements and historical analysis, descriptive passages and thrilling episodes are here woven into a coherent fabric, bearing intelligence about a sunken world known only by the few—the toiling population, downtrodden yet full of human feelings and aspiring to higher things, of the almost sub-civilisation world of manorial estates. *Petőfi* is one of the finest books ever written on the great Hungarian poet—at once an essay and biography, analysis of his work and personal impressions, an assessment with unmistakable political tendency of the stature of the poet-revolutionary, and an appraisal of his significance. Illyés reveals a superb mastery of Hungarian prose; his polished, crystal-clear style, sensuous imagery and restrained and mild irony make him a master of the Latin school of Hungarian prose.

The change of front by the populist writers' movement and the breakthrough of nazism left their trace on Illyés's career as well. His poetry after 1938 is more wearied, more dejected, breathing the atmosphere of lost battle *In a Separate World*, 1939. The pressure of the times is noticeable also in his essays and novels; he continued to profess himself a representative and mouthpiece of the poor peasantry, yet as his views came to be influenced by nationalist ideas, his attention was attracted more and more towards the problem of the national character of Hungary *(Hungarians*, 1938). In an essay called *Jackboot on the Table*, 1941, he is seen trying to put a new edge on the village-versus-town conflict almost reminding one of Giono's mystic-romantic anti-capitalism. In two novels—*Early Spring*, 1941, and *Like the Cranes*, 1942—he again returns to the theme of his childhood, but the earlier keenness appears somewhat dimmed, the colours a little faded here. These books contain a gently ironical criticism of his one-time youthful ardour. This criticism is developed further in *Huns in Paris*, 1944, a brilliantly-written witty sketch of the years he spent in Paris and also an unmistakable account of why he had lost his faith in the working-class movement.

In 1941, after Babits's death, Illyés started the periodical *Magyar Csillag* (The Hungarian Star), intended to be the successor of *Nyugat* and also as an organ that would join the populist writers' movement together and gather all the assets of Hungarian literature.

The liberation of Hungary in 1945 and the ensuing land reform were hailed by Illyés: in numerous reportages and poems he saluted the national reconstruction efforts and the Hungarian peasant as he entered upon a new life of freedom: *Facing It*, 1946; *Collected Poems* Vols. I—III, 1947. Besides writing he engaged in important public activities, organising an Institute for Popular Culture and again launching the periodical *Válasz*. A peculiar dichotomy became increasingly apparent in both his works and views, and this dichotomy became more glaring than ever after 1949: on the one hand he hailed many of the achievements of people's democracy as a victory for his own ideals; on the other, he found it impossible, because of the mistakes of the personality cult, to identify himself completely with the dictatorship of the proletariat. The same dichotomy breaks surface in his works, too: in some of his poems, he expresses sympathy with the achievements of people's democracy, whereas in others he evinces weariness and dejection, voices his reservations, and appears concerned about Hungary's lot (*Hand-clasps*, 1956). After 1949, he wrote a number of successful dramas and screenplays: *The Example of Ozora*, 1952, is a dramatic treatment of an episode of the War of Independence of 1848-49, purporting to show that national aspirations and class interests were intertwined in that independence struggle; the scenario *Two Men*, 1950, besides portraying the poet Petőfi and General Bem, is a brilliant, tension-charged sketch of those gloomy yet glorious days of 1849. This unity is seen broken in Illyés' later works—the play *Torch Light*, 1953, already suggests doubt as to the necessity of revolutionary struggle and the drama *György Dózsa*, 1954, a clash between the fight for national independence and the social struggle.

After 1955 Illyés, like other writers, was tormented by profound crises, but in recent years his art shows a new rise. Two contradictory thoughts—and feelings—run through his works. In the new series of his tragedies (*The Favourite, The Eccentric*) he portrays conflicts between a fine personality and the meanness of the times in which that personality lives. Some of his poems show him to be haunted by the fear of old age and death. In other poems and also in some of his notes and diary entries (*New Poems*, 1961; *Notes from Rácegres*, 1960; *Lunch in the Castle*, 1962) he is captivated by the changes and the development, the transformation of the Hungarian village and he sings of work that has meaning, and life that has a purpose.

The other eminent figure of the populist writers' movement, one whose life and career abounds in contradictions, is LÁSZLÓ NÉMETH (b. 1901). At once philosopher and man of letters, his successive fiction works constantly correct and criticise his own intellectual system.

17

The son of a secondary-school teacher, he took a degree in medicine, but eventually acquired hardly any practice at all—after a few years as medical officer of schools, he gave up medicine for literature, which he has since cultivated, apart from a brief interruption. His literary career began in the late 20's, in conservative literary coteries. Here he created a stir by his essays and a big family saga. For some time after that, he belonged to the *Nyugat* set, with which, however, he soon parted company—in 1932 he started a journal *(Tanú,* The Witness) written and edited all by himself, and, in subsequent years, emerged as the most powerful theoretician, critic, and politician of the populist writers' movement.

Németh's intellectual world in the 30's and 40's was pivoted round a theory of civilisation founded upon an irrationalist philosophy akin to the theories of Spengler and Ortega y Gasset; his social programme was based on a "quality socialism," "socialism minus Marxism," on the basis of which he advocated the transformation of Hungary into a free association of small commodity producers. Even in his approach to the history of Hungarian literature he applied a peculiar yardstick, classifying writings as either "deep-rootedly Hungarian" or "diluted Hungarian," depending on whether he found in them certain typical Hungarian national characteristics. In the late 30's, elements of a "Third Way," of "retreat to the island" became pronounced in his intellectual world, which was reflected in the actual political field by his advocacy of a passive attitude of withdrawal.

Németh has expounded his ideas and views in a succession of magazine contributions, essays and books, which owe their attractiveness to his wide erudition, a style rich in imagery and ideas, to a fountain of startling formulations, and an all-pervading subjective ardour. Apposite remarks, shrewd observations that have lost none of their validity, alternate in these writings with erroneous judgements and concepts that are fundamentally wrong and naive, but all are set forth with intellectual poignancy and a sense of mission. His major theoretical studies have been collected in six volumes: *Preparation,* I-II; *The Revolution of Quality,* I-II; *In Minority,* I-II—all 1941. Also of note is *The Mission of the Intelligentsia,* 1943.

Németh's belletristic work has followed several courses. First, he has published autobiographies and autobiographical fragments. These are full of interesting facts and ruthlessly candid and at the same time prejudiced in their presentation (*Man and Role*, 1934; *The School in Medve Street*, 1943; *Proxy for Myself*, 1943). In these works he criticizes rather than illustrates his own theories. His novels present a panorama of contemporary society, mainly of the intelligentsia and middle class, using the techniques of the Western European great realist novel and employing thoughtful psychological analysis. Nearly every one of his novels is autobiographical and dynamic in its presentation of character development (*Vehicles in September*, 1937; *Fair Down Town*, 1939; *The Other Master*, 1941; *At Home on Wednesday*, 1940). In his more "objective" novels, Németh comes to grips with the great questions of his time and his intellectual world: *Mourning*, 1935, brings to the surface the tangled mass of village morals, their trammels akin to the world of Greek tragedies, in *Guilt*, 1936, he appears engrossed in the problem of social conscience, and suggests the absolute impossibility of an understanding between intelligentsia and peasantry. His most monumental and most successful novels appeared after 1945: *Repulsion*, 1947; is an inquiry into the problem of family and public morals, presented in the form of the confessions of a frigid wife—this masterpiece of a novel is a triumph of austere composition and psychological analysis at its most perfect. *Eszter Égető*, 1956, is Németh's biggest family saga: in narrating the story of three generations of a middle-class family in a Hungarian provincial town, the author paints a vast canvas of the Hungarian history of recent decades, and provides a ruthlessly sharp criticism of his own progress and work.

Similarly, his dramatic work is an illustration, as well as criticism, of his philosophical system. In his historical plays (*Galilei; Huss; Joseph II; Pope Gregory VII; Széchenyi*, etc.), Németh investigates the relationship between great personalities on the one hand, and history-shaping forces on the other. His plays of manners contain criticism of his own progress: the central figure of each is an intellectual embodying the ideas of one phase or another of his intellectual development (*Cherry Patch* and *A Stroke of Lightning*) and almost invariably this intellectual hero ends up in failure: his undoing is caused either by an impracticable utopia he cherishes, or by distressing affairs or by the "monstrosity" of his own personality.

Like most writers of his generation—and to an even greater degree—Németh has been a teacher, cultural politician and natural scientist as well. And, of course, translator: his interpretation of Shakespeare and a great number of works translated from the Czech and Russian (among them Jirásek and Tolstoy) bespeak a strict discipline and wide learning. A transformation, which has long been ripening in Németh's intellectual world and his world outlook, has been gathering momentum of late, under the effect of socialist achievements. Returning from a trip to the Soviet Union in the autumn of 1959, he finally stated his firm belief that the future belonged to socialism, which would bring the right solutions to both human and national problems. In *Evenings in Sajkód* (1961) and *The Journey* (1962) he traces the path and interprets the problems of the intelligentsia who want to bring out the humanistic qualities of socialism.

The populist writers' movement attracted other interesting personalities, too. PÁL GULYÁS (1899-1944) lived all his life in Debrecen, where he was a secondary-school teacher. A man of an all-round learning and a polyglot with a strong leaning for philology, Gulyás bore a passionate love for the *Kalevala* and ancient civilisations in general. His poetry is especially closed, a product of a meeting of the Hungarian provinces and ancient cultures; it contains nostalgia engendered by seclusion in the country, and the desire to identify oneself with the great cultures. He has a predilection for mystic gloom, complex transpositions and a multitude of allusions. His poetry is charged with general humanism and a philosophy that is quite close to the intellectual world of populist writers.

ISTVÁN SINKA (b. 1887) was born into the poorest and most downtrodden stratum of the peasantry, and cultivated the most mystic and most formal version of poetry in the populist spectrum. His favourite genre was the peasant ballad—tiny pieces of drama full of mysterious eerie forces that draw a pall of murk and mist over rural poverty. Sinka presents a curious blend of real poetical gift and dilettantism, of fascinating images and theatricalism. At one time, racialist aestheticism held him up as a model and spur for Hungarian poets. In the 40's, Sinka belonged to the extreme Right wing of the populist writers' movement.

From a populist inception, FERENC JANKOVICH's (b. 1907) career later took a different turn. He prepared to enter the teaching profession, and concerned himself intensively with music, spending one year in Paris. In his captivating poems he evokes the scenes and humanity of the undulating Transdanubian countryside. In him, too, we see Western European civilisation alloyed with a message about the Hungarian peasantry; his polished and harmonious lines are animated by passion and dynamism. He has tried his hand at several genres: minor epics, folk plays, and drama in verse. After the war, Jankovich's poetry took a new lease of life: as his lyrics unfolded more and more, he gave expression to aspects of the transformation that was taking place in Hungary, to the dynamism of creative labour. His development has brought him closer and closer to socialism—he identified himself with socialism, at first emotionally, then more and more consciously. His new lyrics are characterised by a far-seeing world outlook, dynamism and passion, a polished and yet original idiom, and confidence in people.

The most typical representative of the poor-peasant wing of the populist writers' movement, and at once its most prolific fiction writer and publicist, has been PÉTER VERES (b. 1897). Born in Hajdú County, one of the bleakest parts of the Great Plain, he lived from early youth a life full of hardships such as was the lot of the toilers of the land, doing odd jobs as swineherd, cowman, navvy, sharecropper, and surfaceman. At 16, he joined the Social Democratic Union of navvies and assiduously taught himself, soaking himself in the best of the political literature and fiction of the labour movement of those years. Under the Hungarian Republic of Councils of 1919, Veres was a revolutionary village executive, a position which landed him in jail for a term of more than a year, when the Republic was overthrown. After his release and return to his village, and right until the liberation in 1945 of Hungary, he lived the life of a poor peasant, under constant supervision and harassed by the gendarmerie.

Veres's beginnings as a writer were associated with the labour movement; his early writings appeared in the social democratic daily and a bourgeois radical review; subsequently, he joined the populist writers' movement, whose Left wing he represented for a long time. He produced some take-the-lid-off writings, half socio-graphical, half autobiographical—*The Peasantry of the Great Plain*, 1936; *Giving Account*, 1937; *Outskirts of the Village*, 1940; and *Village Chronicle*,1941—were among the first writings in Hungarian literature to reveal the arduous life, the hard struggle for a penurious existence, that was the lot of farm labourers, cowmen, and herdsmen on the Great Plain.

Veres has written a large number of newspaper and magazine articles, essays, and books: this self-taught peasant turned writer and thinker has been grappling with some of the thorniest issues of Hungarian history, politics and development *(Socialism-Nationalism*, 1939; *What Is One Worth if he Is a Hungarian?* 1940; *Populism and Socialism*, 1942; *Out of the Years of Crisis*, 1944). His thinking and methods were rooted in Marxism; but from 1939 on, nationalist influence appeared in the work of a hitherto consistently Leftist writer—and especially racial theory intruded on his writing.

For several years after the war, Veres was active in politics; he was the national chairman of the National Peasant Party, had a part in the land reform, and held, successively, ministerial portfolios. Only after 1949 did he return to fiction—to enter upon what turned out to be one of the most prolific and most successful periods of his literary career. In *Test*, 1950, a volume of short stories, he was about the first in Hungarian literature to draw portraits of the new men of the Hungarian village as it entered upon the collective way of life; *Surfaceman*, 1951, one of his most even writings, is, as a matter of fact, an autobiographical piece, a penetrating, sensuous narrative of human labour; the pieces of the volume *Apple Orchard*, 1954, investigate the new morality and the problems of peasants who move up to the city. To the accuracy of description and abundance of detail which were known as hall-marks of Veres's were now added such characteristics as more varied plot, and a more vivid, more graphic portrayal of human types. The ambitious trilogy *Three Generations*, 1950-1957, is a fresh attempt at writing an autobiographical novel.

Another leading fiction writer of the populist Left was PÁL SZABÓ (b. 1893). Where Veres's *forte* lay in meticulous detail, Szabó's was in the colourful narrative and a lyric quality that pervades all of his work. Like Veres, Szabó too was born in a village in Eastern Hungary; as a serviceman he fought throughout the First World War. He deliberately broke out of the status of a poor farmer, rising to that of village bricklayer—an occupation that certainly enabled him to see more and live a more eventful life, thus widening his horizon. His first work *People*, written in 1929, but only published in 1931, was hailed enthusiastically by Zsigmond Móricz. ("The Hungarian countryside has sent us a new great writer.") From then on, Szabó published a novel almost every year. His accumulated life-experience, extremely rich and exciting, took a long time to free itself from literary influences, primarily that of Dezső Szabó, but by and by he managed to clear his voice and shed irrelevant flourishes. The themes of his novels cover the lives of smallholder peasants writhing in the stranglehold of the latifundium and the life of village intelligentsia, all painted in vivid colours, thrilling detail, and an underlying lyrical note, and shot with passion and eroticism. The outstanding work of his early period is the trilogy *The Wedding—The Cradle—The Christening*, 1941-42, a grandiose portrait of the poor peasant in his gruelling struggle for land. (From this trilogy, after the war, he wrote the novel *An Inch of Soil* which applied the material for the script of a highly acclaimed film of the same title.)

After the war, Szabó, like Veres, was member of the National Peasant Party, and was active in the political arena (he is now national Deputy Chairman of the Patriotic People's Front). In his *The Mills of God*, 1949, he was the first Hungarian writer to depict the liberation of the Hungarian countryside, giving a portrayal full of zest and action. *New Land*, 1953, was the first attempt to paint on a broad canvas the process which was transforming a Hungarian village into a cooperative community. All these works, as well as a large number of short stories, novelettes and screenplays have as their strong points a lyrically coloured narrative, a stirring plot, a sense of humour, and pleasing local colour. His recent autobiographical cycle *(Restless Life*, 1955-58) presents a lyrical and eventful panorama.

263

ÁRON TAMÁSI (b. 1897) stands quite apart amongst Hungarian fiction writers. Born in a Transylvanian village, into a family of poor farmers, he lived, after completing his education, for two years (1923-25) in the United States. It was after his return that he took up writing: his first volume of short stories—*Soul Slide*—appeared in 1925.

Tamási's writings have an atmosphere all their own; he has a unique style, and employs an unusual technique of portrayal. His is a fundamentally romantic, stylised art, his short stories and plays in particular contain many elements of folklore, a large dose of ballad-like obscurity, of allusions, and, sometimes, mysticism. His writing is an amalgam of folk-tale and folk ballad, Christian mythology and myths of his own making—conveyed through an artistry of style more perfected and mature with each passing year. His range of themes has, as a matter of fact, been and still remains unchanged: the life of the Hungarians of Transylvania, their day-to-day struggle for life, against nature, death, and the gentry. Tamási, better than any other author, evokes the world of Magyars living in the wild, mountain-locked country of Transylvania. His men and women are, despite their arduous way of life, cheerful people who appreciate beauty and goodness, and are courageous and independent.

Outstanding in his voluminous work are his short stories; *The Titled Ones*, 1931, a novel with a social-critical edge; and the so-called *Abel Trilogy*, 1932-34, which is the story of a cheerful, wide-awake and honest Hungarian lad from Eastern Transylvania, his adventures in his village and the woods, in town, and, lastly, in America; a representation of social injustice, which is here held up to unequivocal ridicule.

Tamási's literary progress has not been unproblematic—from romantic beginnings, it proceeded towards a clearer and more realist art, only to veer back, from the mid-30's on, towards mysticism. Apart from a sound critical attitude towards society, his outlook has been coloured by some fallacious ideas, an idealism that advocates only moral revival, views that put national above social considerations, and, at times, even by a touch of racial mysticism. Nor is the standard of his work universally even: often has success lured him into a routine imitation of his own idiosyncratic style. His penmanship is at its best perhaps in his short stories. At the beginning of his career, he attracted attention by a great revolutionary short story—*Ordinary Resurrection*—which was followed by many more short stories with lyrical undertones and full of sensuous, colourful descriptions.

The years since the last war have made their influence felt on Tamási's work: he has written two books of outstanding value. One is *A Review of Our Country*, 1953, which is a sketch of the period preceding the War of Independence of 1848, through portrayal of life in a college in Transylvania. The other is *Cradle and Owl*, 1949, an autobiographical novel. In this—as well as in a third book, *Szirom and the Others*, 1960—his good qualities of old are shining untarnished, and he is seen progressing towards a purer realism, one which is unfettered by mysticism.

JÁNOS KODOLÁNYI (b. 1899) is a populist author whose literary and intellectual make-up, approaching gloomy and ruthlessly sober naturalism, is almost vertically opposed to Tamási's. Kodolányi came from the passion-ridden, latifundium-strangled, decadent Ormánság district. Born into the middle class, he soon broke with his family, and joined the Leftist political movements, being for some time regarded as a Communist Party author. His basic experience has been the crack-up of the old bourgeois and peasant world, aberrations and break-downs under the influence of Mammon, the predominance of passions and emotionalism, the whole complex, and often dismal, life and inner conflict of the peasantry. That is the world he depicts, a shrewd observer using strong words coloured by disappointment, bitterness and hatred, but nevertheless impelled in his early writings by an intention to improve things *(Pretty Zsuzska*, 1924; *Prison*, 1925; *Chasms*, 1927; *Wildfire*, 1929; and *Darkness*, 1933). In the years after 1932 Kodolányi, like some other authors, did not remain immune from the contagion of the era: he left the working-class movement, drifting more and more towards nationalism and ending up as one of the representatives of the populist Right. He fell prey to anti-Semitism and muddled mythical theories; his change of direction brought him into violent conflict with his former comrades-in-arms—hatred and wounded pride made him violently hostile to the forces of the Left. A new chapter was opened also in his literary work—he now processed his old stock of experiences anew, this time imbued with racialism and anti-Semitism. He sought escape from reality into history—at first he would make excursions into medieval Hungary, then going further back in time into the world of the Assyrian epics about the deluge. The revival of a mythical ancient pagan tradition distorts his work. Kodolányi persisted in his Rightist views even after 1945, and it was only after prolonged silence, in 1957, that he went once more into print, with rewritten versions of his former novels and an intention to describe the changed life of the countryside.

SÁNDOR TATAY (b. 1910) is a narrator for whom the plot has retained its importance. After some earlier works which bear the imprint of populist ideology, he recently came out with screen plays and short stories that show a new approach, and also with a sweeping social novel *The Simeon House*, which describes the fall of a family of the gentry, against a wide historical background. In his novel *The White Coach* (1959) and in recent reportage he takes a definite stand on the side of socialist development. *Guns and Doves* (1960) is a fine example of the novel for young people.

One of the most striking literary profiles in the Hungarian literature of the inter-war years was that of KÁROLY PAP (1900-1944), an author dealing and struggling mostly with Jewish problems who, while not a member of the populist writers' movement proper, nevertheless moved in the same sphere of ideas. He was the son of a rabbi, and though he broke off his ties with his family an early age, questions of Jewish life and religion remained the most absorbing interests for him throughout his life. While still a secondary-school student, he volunteered for national service in the First World War; the revolutionary upheaval at the end of the war found him in the Hungarian Red Army, though, as a matter of fact, he was a romantic anarchist rather than a true revolutionary. When he made his *début* in the mid-20's, he had an all but fully evolved literary programme—to give expression in Hungarian literature to Jewry as a separate racial entity with a cultural and spiritual background of its own, and to do so with an earnestness and severity reminiscent of the prophets of the Bible. It was not the life of Jewry as a social group that he depicted; he was out to create a new ethic, a new attitude. Throughout his life he wrestled with a novel treatment of the Jesus theme *(Michael, 1929;*

*Thou Hast Delivered Me from Death*, 1932; *The Eighth Station*, 1933), trying to create the figure of a child who defies the high and mighty, and introduces a new morality among men. His auto-biographical writing *(Azarel*, 1937) is a psychological treatment of rare depth of his childhood and adolescence, of the stuffy atmosphere of the milieu he grew up in. His short stories have an original atmosphere, being fraught with tragic events and irreconcilable antagonisms.

## SOCIALIST WRITING AFTER 1919
### In Emigration

The downfall of the Hungarian Republic of Councils of 1919 dealt a heavy blow at all practitioners of progressive and revolutionary literature. The ensuing savage White Terror did not only stamp out any possibility of non-conformist literary expression—it subjected to police persecution all those writers who had espoused the cause of the Hungarian Republic of Councils, or even only of the bourgeois democratic revolution that had preceded it. The body of socialist writers that had formed in 1919 now became dispersed —some of its members went into exile, others were intimidated into silence. After 1919, the activity of the writers consistently of the Left proceeded under new conditions following a fresh course. On the one hand, the emigré writers formed groups in a number of cities (first in Vienna, then in Berlin, Paris, Bratislava and, mainly, Moscow); on the other, a revolutionary literature emerged inside Hungary itself, in the teeth of tremendous difficulties and defying thousands of obstacles, objective as well as ideological. These two wings of Hungarian revolutionary writing were wide apart only in space; they were one in their goals and ideals.

These writers, more than any of their colleagues, maintained the true unbroken continuity of 1910—the dynamism and striving for better things that characterised the aspirations of Ady and his contemporaries. An unflagging revolutionary spirit and a profound analysis and exposure of conditions inside Hungary; true inter-nationalism and humanism of the highest order characterised these writings ideologically. From the artistic point of view, the

267

revolutionary writers did in the beginning cultivate diverse trends, but, in the 30's, the diverse trends met in a confluence which yielded Hungarian socialist realist literature. A good many writers only adhered to the revolutionary movement during one period of their career; others—the foremost authors among them—kept faith to the end.

This type of literature had quite a peculiar form of existence, and peculiar was the progress of each individual writer that cultivated it. At times, they had at their disposal the facilities offered by established periodicals and publishing firms; at others, their only possibility to appear in print was in leaflets; at other times again, the only medium left to them would be living speech (there are a few works which have had to be recorded from memory). The writers themselves were, in part, party activists, professional revolutionaries, whose literary activity would be interrupted by prison terms and persecutions. All the same, this revolutionary literature produced works of considerable value, and it was the fertile soil from which grew the poetry of the most significant poet of inter-war Hungary—Attila József, a poet ranking with Petőfi and Ady.

Hungarian revolutionary literature was linked with the other literary trends by a hundred and one bonds. Itself a tributary of the mainstream of Hungarian literature, it had an influence upon the other writers and was itself enriched by them. At the same time, it was part of the European revolutionary literary spectrum that came into existence in the 20's; what is more, for this very reason it formed the most European segment of Hungarian literature; it had ties with the progressive literature of Germany and France, was closely linked with Czechoslovak and Rumanian literature and thrived in close unity with the vigorously developing literature of the Soviet Union.

It was not communist writers alone who made up the body of revolutionary literature: they constituted the hard core, but among the constituent elements are counted writers who had but a passing encounter with this trend, and also writers whose allegiance bound them to other parties or political groups of the working-class movement, and who represent slightly divergent trends.

The first workshop—or arsenal—of post-1919 revolutionary

literature was in Vienna. This is where the leading (and for some time communist-controlled) emigré daily, *Bécsi Magyar Újság* (The Vienna Hungarian Journal) was published; a number of periodicals were founded: *Akasztott ember* (Hanged Man), an offshoot of Kassák's *Ma;* then *Ék* (The Wedge), and *Egység* (Unity), two magazines that pursued a more consistently revolutionary policy. This was a period of fermenting ideas: disappointment at the defeat of the revolution often drew forth voices of black despair and anarchy from the poets, while others hoped for a second coming of the Republic of Councils. Most writers found themselves under the influence of one of the many "isms" that were in their heyday just then: constructivism, cubism, and not long after, surrealism; the poems written at the time show responses to the works of the then ascendant Becher, Weinert, Ivan Goll and Cendrars; and translators were rendering Blok and Mayakovsky. It seemed as if the revolutionary times demanded the discarding of all existing forms, and called for the establishment of a staccato form, one broken down to the point of unintelligibility. At this time, the "proletarian revolution" wing had not yet wholly cut its umbilical cord with *Proletkult.* That seething, turbulent period saw the rise of a few creative writers who were to remain loyal soldiers of revolution through the stormy years that followed.

A considerable role was played by ALADÁR KOMJÁT (1891-1937), one of the leading revolutionary poets. As a youth he joined various progressive students' movements, and, in later years, as a white-collar worker in an industrial company, he soon established contact with Left-wing socialists. After writing some poems conceived in a dejected mood, he joined the activist school, contributing to Kassák's review poems of dissolved form, lines sharply broken by the use of interjections and abounding in outbursts of passion, poems evocative of a divided world. In 1917, he was in the group which seceded from *Ma,* and was one of the founders of the periodical *Kilencszáztizenhét* (Nineteen Seventeen); at the end of 1918 he started a periodical entitled *Internacionálé,* a review rallying a group of young writers who supported the Communist Party of Hungary. Having played an active role under the communist Republic of 1919, Komját was forced into exile after the Republic's defeat. At first he worked in Italy, then, in 1921-22, in Vienna (where he started editing *Egység*—Unity). From 1922 on, he lived in Berlin, where he worked on the staff of *Inprekorr*, a communist international publication, and was very active in the *Bund proletarisch-revolutionärer Schriftsteller* (Union of Writers for Proletarian Revolution). He continued to work in Germany until the nazi takeover when he emigrated again first to Switzerland, then to France. He died in France, suddenly, amidst hectic activity.

Komját's life was that of the tireless organiser, of an international revolutionary: he went from one country to the other, editing papers and magazines and making propaganda. He was editor, orator, poet, translator and essayist in one. His poetry, once it had got over the period of *Sturm und Drang* prior to 1919, steadily became clearer and more mature; his dynamic verse-construction became happily married to forceful simplicity and informality. The poetry of his later years, while still retaining a few activist survivals (a preference for irregular forms, exclamations, near-prose diction), reflected his unequivocal position and was hot with revolutionary passion and a singular pathos—the homesickness of the exile, and his confidence in his nation, together with a compelling evocation of the conditions of the Hungarian working class and peasantry, downtrodden and exploited. Komját had a knack for summing up whole eras and suggesting all the flavours and the rawness of life by a few apposite epithets and in a few lines.

Komját was a poet, not only of the Hungarian, but also of international, revolution: he sang about Chinese workers as well as of the Hamburg rebels, and we are indebted to him for the finest march-song of Republican Spain. Two volumes of poetry— *We Want All!*, Moscow 1931, and *Landslide*, Paris 1937—testify to the growing richness of his lyrics, which can strike the tone of true and much-tormented love and sing of the beauty of the landscape, too. In his essays on literature, Komját waged a two-front battle: On the one hand, he condemned literary aloofness, the tendency to "get away from it all"; on the other, he combated the sectarian, pseudo-revolutionary and myopic contempt for literary standard and form.

ANDOR GÁBOR (1884-1953) was converted to communism while living in exile in Vienna. He first went into print at the age of 18.

Before long, this highly cultured man with a strongly rationalistic and satirical bent emerged as a prolific and middle-class author able to earn a good living with his pen; a journalist and playwright, writer of chansons and sketches, the translator responsible for a masterly Hungarian version of Mistral's *Mireille*. He became best known, however, for his caustically witty criticism of the petty bourgeois way of life of a certain stratum of Budapest citizens. His often cynical censure was made from an essentially bourgeois, radical-nihilist angle, his tone of voice only acquired a new edge during the war—when he succumbed to an all-pervading pessimism, and his condemnation of war profiteers, the irresponsible and the happy-go-lucky, was gaining in asperity. He took an active part in the 1918 bourgeois democratic revolution and under the subsequent Hungarian Republic of Councils of 1919. In January 1920, he fled to Vienna, and here, where disappointment and disenchantment led some of his contemporaries and fellow-writers to make the about-face to anti-revolutionism, Gábor was won over to communism.

During his years in Vienna his poetry attained fulness of development. His poems owed nothing to the "isms" but have a note reminiscent of the old Arany, and so they convey his homesickness, his indignation at human meanness, and his disgust at, and hatred for, the White Terror. They are poems written with brilliant technique, and full of surprise turns and trenchant satire (*My Country*, 1920; *Cataclysm*, 1922; *For It's Shameful to Live and Not to Shout*, 1923). A new phase began also in his translation work: European proletarian poetry gained an interpreter in him. But by far the most important product of his Vienna years was his journalistic work, extensive in volume and extensively published, in Vienna as well as in Czechoslovakia, in Berlin as well as in New York. Within a short period, he had five collections of newspaper articles published (*This Is my Message*, 1920; *Faces of the Dead*, 1921; *And Here Comes Oszkár Jászi*, 1922; *Bank Street*, 1923; and *Epilogue*, 1924). This was publicistic work of a range and face never before known in Hungarian literature. It employed all means of persuasion, from the political pamphlet to the satire. Its targets were the White Terror; the traitors, the renegades; and human folly and wickedness.

271

In 1925 Gábor left Vienna and went first to Berlin, then to Paris, ending up, after 1933, in Moscow. He contributed to the work of the *Bund proletarisch-revolutionärer Schriftsteller*, and for some time was assistant editor of *Linkskurve*. He wrote a large number of essays, polemic articles, and short stories in German. In Moscow, he soon found himself joining other emigré writers in cultivating Hungarian literature, although his close ties with German literature were never broken off. He was made editor of *Új Hang* (New Voice), a popular-front-oriented literary magazine of Hungarian communist writers, when it was founded in 1938, and he wrote articles, essays, short stories, and commentaries, appearing as a militant literary commentator and theoretician. During the years of the Second World War, his lyric poetry received a fresh stimulus: his dynamic patriotic and anti-nazi poems were printed in leaflets distributed among the soldiers at the front and broadcast over the radio.

After 1945 Gábor, like his fellow-writers in exile, returned to Hungary and contributed to the literary activity of his native country. He was editor of a satirical weekly until his death.

Like Gábor, Béla Balázs (1884-1949) was converted to communism after he had made a name as a bourgeois writer. He was one of the eminent members of the first *Nyugat* generation, schoolmaster and aesthete. His *The Aesthetics of Death*, 1907, was a typical highbrow product of the irrationalist, decadent aesthetics of the time. Of all Hungarian poets he was the most radical in carrying through one of the great turns of twentieth-century lyric poetry: brushing aside the outside world, he turned inward, in order to probe the world of the spirit in a number of singular poetical short stories, original tales, and dramas. Bartók's *Prince Bluebeard's Castle* was written to his libretto. In his poems *(The Wanderer Sings*, 1910), in mystery play (1916) and dialogues, he appears as a representative of esoteric symbolism carried *ad extremum;* his peculiar world is composed of motifs of Hungarian folk-tales and European literature.

There formed around Balázs in the 1910's a little coterie of admirers and followers (one of his most fervent admirers was György Lukács, then a fledgling writer). It was the world war that dislodged this sensitive, introvert author from his groove:

he volunteered for the army, originally with the intention of gaining fresh artistic experience, but soon the true aspect of war was brought home to him with dramatic force, and he turned socialist. He was one of the first to join the newly founded Communist Party of Hungary. Under the Hungarian Republic of Councils he was put in charge of theatres, and so was compelled to go into exile after the fall of the Republic.

At first he lived in Vienna, then, until 1931, in Berlin. His attention was attracted to film aesthetics and he wrote novels. His novel *Unmögliche Menschen*, 1922-1930, is an attempt at a showdown with the ideals of his youth, at a portrayal of the world of artists and other intellectuals living "far from the madding crowd." He became a socialist critic and theoretician of the screen; *The Visible Man* and *The Spirit of the Screen* are fundamental works of socialist cinema aesthetics and have had an influence on many an outstanding artist and film director.

In 1931 Balázs transferred his residence to the Soviet Union, where he continued to work in the cinematographic field, and also contributed to *Új Hang* and took part in the activities of the Hungarian emigré writers. He published scripts, essays, and short stories. The volume *Man's Song*, marking a turning-point in his lyric poetry, had been published in 1923, in Vienna; since then, he had written no poetry until the Second World War. Already the poetry of his Vienna years reflected his new ideological and political insight: he now turned his gaze towards the earth, anxious to harken to the lament of suffering humanity. When, fifteen years later, he once more took up poetry, he spoke with the voice of the political poet—singing in the service of a great cause: the socialist future of mankind.

After the Second World War, Balázs returned to his native Hungary. Here, he continued his work as a cinema aesthete, and published an autobiographical novel of great evocative power— *Dreaming Youth*, 1946—and tales.

SÁNDOR BARTA (1897-1938), too, played an important part in exile in Vienna. He made his *début* during the war, as one of the extremist members of the group of writers rallied behind Kassák's *Ma*. In exile in Vienna, he broke with Kassák, the latter's apolitical art and programme having lost their appeal to him

18                                                                            273

and was attracted to militant and equally extremist "isms," cultivating a trend approaching dadaism (Yes, 1920; Honoured Mortuary, 1921; A Tale of the Student with a Trumpet-Hand, 1922). In their amorphous unity of poetry and prose, of lyrics and epics, his poems of this period express the post-revolutionary turbulent world, the changed attitude towards life, the "everything's relative" outlook. In 1924, he joined the Communist Party; from 1925 onwards, he lived in the Soviet Union. He wrote several novels, short stories and tragicomedies in quick succession, striking an increasingly realistic note but retaining from his earlier period his predilection for the grotesque, the exaggerated, the satirical. A Miraculous Story, 1925, about the fantastic travels of a bourgeois newspaperman in the land of incipient Fascism and, subsequently, in the Land of the Soviets, is a bold mixture of utopia and vision, satire and reportage; Circus Capitalismus, 1926, depicts the world of capitalism with a technique that reminds one of expressionist dramas. His novels and short stories evoke his experience in Austria, in counter-revolutionary Hungary, and with capitalist realities: The Last Day-Dreamer, 1928; Panic in the City, 1930; 350,000, 1931; No Mercy, 1933. Gold Diggers, 1937, is already the work of an author who has settled down, and presents a picture of the "roaring" Nineteen Hundreds through life in a Budapest tenement house. Sándor Barta died a victim of Stalinism.

A Hungarian emigré centre was formed in the late 20's also in Berlin, with the participation primarily of Béla Balázs, Andor Gábor, György Lukács and Aladár Komját. Berlin publishers would bring out works written by Hungarian authors, Hungarian writers took part in the work of the Union of German Revolutionary Writers, and worked on the staff of its magazine, Linkskurve.

GYULA HÁY (b. 1900) made his name as a playwright in the Hungarian emigré centre in Germany. Though he started to write in Hungary, his first play, the powerful historical tragedy entitled God, Emperor, Peasant, attracted notice in the Weimar Republic of 1932. Among his plays dealing with the tragic atmosphere and conflicts of counter-revolutionary Hungary, Tisza Nook and The Turkey Shepherd are the most outstanding. After some years spent in emigration in the Soviet Union, Háy returned to Hungary in 1945. His play *The Bridge of Life*, written in this country since his homecoming, was significant. In the period directly preceding and during the counter-revolution of 1956 Gyula Háy became a representative of revisionist views.

For some time, Paris was also a centre of the Hungarian emigrés, although it never became a literary centre of the calibre of Vienna or Moscow. Many Hungarian writers went to Paris, either in exile or of their own accord, for stays of varying length, and, especially in the 20's, a minor centre of Hungarian progressive writing was active there. Such rallying points were the Hungarian-language daily *Párizsi Magyar Munkás* (The Paris Hungarian Worker), the publishing firm *Le Monde* (inspired—and supported—by Barbusse's *Le Monde)*, and, later on, the periodical *Üzenet* (Message).

Of the Hungarian writers who were active in Paris, the most outstanding was GYÖRGY BÖLÖNI (1882-1959). A sensitive literary and art critic prior to the First World War, he was one of the most zealous propagators of modern French painting and a militant supporter of modern trends in Hungarian art. One of the closest friends of Endre Ady's, he was a co-fighter of the poet, and, during his Paris years, his guide. In 1919 Bölöni was active under the Hungarian Republic of Councils; he worked assiduously in the press and diplomacy. In exile he joined the group around Mihály Károlyi. Bölöni was one of the founders and executives of the *Le Monde* library series of progressive Soviet and Western European literature, which used to be smuggled into Hungary. It was in exile that he wrote his major work on *The Real Ady*, a well-documented, vivid portrait of the progressive poet, an ally of the working class. After his return to Hungary, Bölöni was active in politics for some time and later became one of the leading personalities on the literary scene. Following the counter-revolutionary rising of 1956, he took the lion's share in reorganising the literary field; much of the credit for the achievements attained is due to his authority and staidness. Until his death, he was Chairman of the State Literary Fund and editor-in-chief of the leading literary weekly.

His wife (1882-1951) also was a writer of note: using the

*nom de plume* SÁNDOR KÉMERI, she authored *Anatole France Walks* and *Visage de Bourdelle,* which appeared in French and English versions. Her *The Book of Sufferings,* prefaced by Barbusse, a dramatic prison diary about her personal experiences after the fall of the revolution, attracted much attention.

The real centre of Hungarian revolutionary emigré literature was in the Soviet Union. From the early 20's on, Hungarian writers lived in large numbers in the Soviet Union.

The Hungarian communist emigré writers were first organised in 1925—in that year the Federation of Hungarian Revolutionary Writers and Artists was formed, then, in 1926, the Hungarian section of RAPP (Revolutionary Association of Proletarian Writers). In 1926 the *Hammer and Sickle Yearbook* was brought out in Vienna; in 1929, *Hammer and Sickle* started publication, each issue carrying a bulky literary supplement. The Hungarian writers carried on considerable activity in the midst of their compatriots as well as in Soviet literary life; several of them held leading posts in such international literary organisations as the International Federation of Revolutionary Writers and on the staff of *Internationale Literatur ;* Béla Illés, Antal Hidas and others were active in this work. Hungarian literary works had a wide diffusion throughout the Soviet Union: the Hungarian revolutionary authors were assured of a large and steadily increasing readership. Ever since their establishment, the Hungarian writers' organisations followed the policy and programme of RAPP, sharing both the good points (revolutionary verve, attention to workaday problems, high ideological standards) and the weaknesses (a certain amount of sectarian intolerance, distrust of non-communists, blurred concept of realism) of that organisation. Prolonged debates were held before a "literary platform" was reached in 1932 for the clarification of problems—theoretical as well as practical—confronting socialist literature.

The dissolution of RAPP (1932) and the formation of a homogeneous Soviet Writers' Union (1934) ushered in a new phase in the development of Hungarian emigré literature in the Soviet Union. This reorganisation coincided with the arrival in the Soviet Union of several writers who had been working in Germany until then and were now refugees from nazism. The establishment of the Writers' Union, and the Popular Front policies of the international communist movement, altered to a certain extent the tasks that faced the Hungarian writers. The need to influence literary life inside Hungary, cooperation with allied social forces, establishment of an anti-fascist United Front, were now made the principal tasks of the hour. *Új Hang* (New Voice), one of the most remarkable Hungarian literary reviews in those years, started publication in 1938; until 1941, when it ceased publication, this review forged a spirit of unity among all emigré writers, watched and reported on the Hungarian literary scene, carried on high-level ideological work, and laid the foundations upon which the literature of New Hungary was built after 1945.

At the same time the political and ideological mistakes and narrow-mindedness of the personality cult prevented the development of genuine socialist literature.

Of the emigré writers in the Soviet Union, BÉLA ILLÉS (b. 1895) was one of the most prolific and most popular. In his childhood years Illés lived in Carpatho-Ukraine, then North-eastern Hungary, a region charged with nationality conflicts. His literary *début* was made in 1916, in *Nyugat ;* in the last years of the world war, he saw military service under arduous conditions. In 1918 Illés was on the Revolutionary Council of Soldiers, and was active in the cultural field under the Hungarian Republic of Councils. He too went into exile in Vienna—from here, the newly organising Communist Party sent him to Carpatho-Ukraine, then annexed to Czechoslovakia, where he carried on editorial work and was a party activist.

From 1923 Illés lived in the Soviet Union, where he played an active part in emigré literary life as well as in Soviet literary activities and in the international organisations of revolutionary writers. As general secretary of RAPP, he was one of the most active and many-sided workers of revolutionary literature, Hungarian as well as international, and counted among his friends Gorky and Nexö, Sholokhov and Romain Rolland, Becher and Barbusse. When the Second World War came, Illés volunteered for the army in spite of his age, and fought through the war, beginning as a private and finishing as a major. He took part in the liberation of Budapest. His activities after the war were manifold: he began as editor of *Új Szó* (New Word), the Hungarian-language daily of the Soviet Armed Forces in Hungary; years afterwards he became editor-in-chief of the literary weekly *Irodalmi Újság* (Literary Gazette). He is still a leading figure on the Hungarian literary scene.

This colourful life, in the course of which Illés worked for the cause of the working-class movement in very many different places and under most diverse conditions, has yielded the raw material of his fictional works. It is to this very wealth of experience and knowledge, combined with a firmly established world outlook and the free-flowing narrative of the born raconteur, that his works owe their magic and convincing power. For the tools of his craft Illés has adopted a good deal from the great traditions of Hungarian fiction, from the Hungarian narrative style as fashioned by Kálmán Mikszáth, but Illés is more modern, more thrilled and thrilling, more impassioned than his predecessor: his novels throb with the excitement of newspaper reportage, with the influence of the screen.

His experience in the First World War received a treatment in *Skipetars* (1941), a novelette whose story is laid in the Albanian theatre-of-war. The hectic days, the glory and the fall of the Hungarian Republic of Councils of 1919 are depicted in his most outstanding novel, *The Tisza Ablaze*, 1929. Another major work is *Carpathian Rhapsody*, 1939-1941: a vast panel of Carpatho-Ukraine, pictured between the pre-war years and 1923, the motley world of Ukrainian, Hungarian, German and Jewish workers, peasants and lords, a seething world from which emerge the new-type heroes: workers and peasants turned socialist—then communist—militants and leaders of the people.

Illés has written several novels about the Second World War—*I Sing of Arms and Men*, 1949; *The Battle of the Comedy Theatre*, 1950—but the most significant of them is the three-volume *They've Come into Their Own*, 1952-54.

Illés is excellent also as a writer of short stories: his strong points—his gift for spinning yarns, his sense of drama, and his colourful, full-blooded narrative—show off still better in the condensed form of the short story. The stir and bustle of exile

278

in Vienna, the years spent in the Soviet Union, his war-time experience, and that of New Hungary, supply the themes of his short stories, *Thirty-Six Years*, 1956. In his writings preceding the 1956 counter-revolutionary rising, he sounded a warning against the approaching danger *(Válaszúton*—Cross-Roads, 1957).

Next to Béla Illés, ANTAL HIDAS (b. 1899) played an important role in Soviet literary life. His early poems *(In the Land of Counter-revolution*, 1925) were published in Vienna, and were circulated in Hungary either anonymously or under a pseudonym. These poems were imbued with a spirit of militancy and revolutionary fervour, and were a summons to join the battle; many of them were written for choral speaking, others enjoyed a popularity almost as wide as though they had been folk-songs. In these poems, as well as in later volumes *The Trial Goes on*, Moscow 1930; and *A Shout from the Colonies*, Moscow 1933, Hidas shows himself to be the most typical exponent in Hungarian literature of the militant and dynamic, direct revolutionary lyric poetry of the 1930's. For many years, Hidas functioned as secretary of the International Federation of Revolutionary Writers and Assistant Editor of *Internationale Literatur*. In recent years, he has been busying himself with acquainting Soviet readers with Hungarian literature: he has been responsible for Russian translations of Petőfi and other classic poets, has himself edited an anthology of Hungarian poetry and has been the moving spirit behind numerous subsequent editions. His lyric themes have been refreshed through the infusion of new colours, such as the voice of the homesick communist exile, then that of the repatriates after many years, and the man who looks back wistfully upon his vanished youth *(My Aunt's Garden*, 1958). He has authored some novels of note: *Mr. Ficzek*, which has run into several Russian editions, is the first volume of a projected trilogy, whose second volume is *Martin and his Friends*, 1959, a vivid (in places ironical and wrathful) portrayal of the world of workers and lower middle-class people in pre-war Budapest.

MÁTÉ ZALKA (1898-1937) was a particularly fascinating personality. His was a militant life full of adventures and battles. Born in a small town, Zalka was in his teens when he followed the example of the poet Petőfi by joining a troupe of players.

279

He fought on many battle-fronts of the war, with a commission, then was a P.O.W. in Russia, where he eventually became a legendary Red commander in the interventionist wars, one of the heroes of the operation in the Crimea against Wrangel. He was not a man given to peaceful meditation: the wars of intervention over, he was soon found fighting in the Turkish army under Kemal, as one of the organisers of the latter's cavalry. He was killed in the Spanish Civil War, as the legendary General Lukács of the International Brigades.

This hard-living revolutionary fighter was at once a fastidious writer with an abiding love of the Hungarian language and literature. His abundant experience and knowledge of life he has fashioned into novels and short stories. *Doberdo* is a comprehensive representation of how an army officer at first full of enthusiasm for the war becomes an anti-war agitator, eventually to join the international revolutionary organisations. In his numerous short stories (some of which were first published in Russian), episodes of the First World War and the Russian Civil War come to life, written up with polished craftsmanship, in racy Hungarian; a warm-hearted humanism, tender feelings for humble folk, and radiant optimism are the hallmarks of these pieces of Zalka's writing.

The ardous life of the professional revolutionist fell to the share of FRIGYES KARIKÁS (1892-1938) also. As in Zalka's case, the path of this youth, born of a poor family, led him via First World War and Russian P.O.W. camps to membership of the Bolshevik Party. Karikás played an outstanding role in the battles fought in defence of the Hungarian Republic of Councils, as the political commissar attached to the famed 39th Brigade. Years in exile, work for the party in Paris, underground activity inside Hungary, then imprisonment mark stages of his life. And in the meantime, all the while, he studied, improved his mind, and was busy writing. For him, writing constituted only part of a man's full activities: even so—in his casual way—he created works of lasting value. The event of 1919, the revolutionary upsurge of Hungarian peasants and workers, live in his novelettes and short stories as vividly as in the works of few other contemporary authors. He strikes one as the prototype of the communist peasant writer: he had a profound, first-hand knowledge of the Hungarian peasantry, he writes a delectable dialect, but builds no peasant myth—his peasants are drawn true to reality, with their arduous struggle, their weaknesses and confidence in the revolution. Karikás died a victim of the personality cult.

SÁNDOR GERGELY (b. 1896) began his literary career in counter-revolutionary Hungary and brought it to fulness in Moscow. He returned from the First World War blinded and only after many years did he regain his sight. At an early age, he joined the underground, and became one of the first, and much-read, authors of the incipient Hungarian communist movement of the 20's. In his works written at the time, Gergely depicts counter-revolutionary Hungary in forceful, sometimes naturalist, colours and with burning passion and bitterness, often creating symbols (*The Desert*, 1922; *Peace*, 1924; *On the Margins of Latifundia*, 1926; *Death-Watch Beetle*, 1929; and *Slave Market*, 1930). From 1931 to 1945 Gergely lived in the Soviet Union. Outstanding among his works written at the time are: *The Drums Roll*, 1934, a sketch of the Hungarian village; and the *Dózsa trilogy* (consisting of *Manor Court*, *The Big Camp*, and *The Fiery Throne*, 1936-39), an authentic panel about the Hungarian peasant revolt of 1514; and the play *Knights and Heroes*, 1938, which is a homogeneous and effective sketch of a communist party activist in inter-war Hungary and of brutal oppression in those years.

Since his return to Hungary, Gergely has been an active figure on the literary scene. He is engaged in writing an autobiographical novel, a kind of summing up of his progress to date; the first volume of this projected work, *The Thorny Path*, 1955, offers a ruthlessly truthful, crowded picture of the post-war years.

EMIL MADARÁSZ (1884-1962) was a well-known social democratic poet prior to the First World War; between 1922 and 1946 he became known in the Soviet Union through poetry of peasant simplicity and through narrative poems, a genre peculiar to him. *Csihajda* (1937) is an epic poem about a Red sailor of 1919; the subject of other narrative poems by Madarász are underground party work, construction in the Soviet Union, and the suppression of the 1956 counter-revolution in Hungary.

SAROLTA LÁNYI (b. 1891) started out as a subtle lyricist in the *Nyugat* circle, but moved to the Soviet Union in the 1920's together with her husband Ernő Czóbel, a historian of Marxism. After 1945 she returned to Hungary. In her lyrics the wife, and later mother, speaks in a soft and yet powerful voice. She wrote polished and reserved, yet forceful poems about the great events of socialism and the crises affecting the life of individuals.

JÓZSEF LENGYEL (b. 1896) began his career as an expressionist poet, and developed into an author of short stories and novels of clear construction, written in an informal style. His major work is *Visegrádi Street,* 1929, a series of portraits, reportages and "snapshots" of the event leading up to and of the days of the Republic of Councils of 1919, as seen by an ordinary observer of strong human feelings. In his novels written after his return to Hungary, Lengyel has drawn a crowded picture of Budapest during the First World War and the days of the revolutions *(The Vicissitudes of Ferenc Prenn,* 1958). His most recent writings *(The Spell,* 1961), narratives written in a composed tone with suppressed irony, recount the tragic and uplifting events of a hard life, of internment during the years of the personality cult in the U.S.S.R.

This survey of Hungarian revolutionary literature would not be complete without a glimpse at Hungarian progressive literature that has evolved in Hungary's neighbour countries. Following 1919, and especially after 1923, numerous writers forced into exile settled down in the bourgeois democratic Czechoslovakia, while others went to live in Rumania, which still seemed relatively liberal at that time. Emigré writers and local Hungarian authors joined efforts to bring into being literary centres and found revolutionary-inclined periodicals—always in close connection with the vernacular literature, forming a segment of it, as it were, and in constant struggle against conservative, reactionary trends in literature. In Czechoslovakia, such centres sprang up in Prague, Bratislava and Košice. A notable part in these activities was played by reviews published by Lajos Barta, especially *Az Út* (The Road), 1931-36, and Zoltán Fábry's high-standard and wide-horizoned magazine whose revolutionary spirit drew freely on German Leftist writings and had close ties with progressive writers in Hungary. ZOLTÁN FÁBRY (b. 1897) is an outstanding essayist of revolutionary literature in Czechoslovakia. The ascendance of nazism made him a militant defender of culture and humanism. His volume of essays entitled *Command of Our Times*, 1934, and his recently published "summing-up" books (*The Truth of Thought*, 1955; *The Truth of Peace*, 1956; and *Bridges and Ditches*, 1958) show him up as an enthusiastic essayist rich in ideas whose interests are as varied as human civilisation and culture—a literary publicist in the most exalted sense of the word.

In inter-war Rumania, too, there was opportunity for a Hungarian-language revolutionary literature to develop. After several attempts and a number of short-lived periodicals, *Korunk* (Our Time), 1926-1940, a magazine published at Cluj, emerged as one of the leading organs of Hungarian revolutionary writing. Started as a bourgeois radical review, it became increasingly revolutionary in tone from 1929 onwards, and for some time ruled the scene as the leading periodical publication of Hungarian Left writing, a meeting-point of socialist and communist writers. *Korunk* reviewed and popularized Soviet literature as well as trends in Western European writing; it gave space to many authors to whom conditions in Hungary denied freedom of expression, and was sharply critical of Hungarian literature as a whole. Particular credit goes to it for having been instrumental, by means of translations and criticism, in acquainting Hungarian and Rumanian readers with each other's literature. The editor of *Korunk* was GÁBOR GAÁL (1893-1949). Himself an emigré, having settled in Cluj after some periods of exile in Vienna and Berlin, Gaál showed infinite patience and tact in guiding budding authors. His voluminous correspondence is important source-material for Hungarian literary historians. His essays reveal a highly erudite, wide-horizoned man of letters with high ideological and literary standards, an eminent critic, well-grounded in Marxist ideology.

A populous group of youthful revolutionary authors and poets was formed in Rumania, most of them are still active today as Hungarian-writing contributors to the literary scene in the Rumanian People's Republic.

## In Hungary

For long after the bloody days of the White Terror in 1919, revolutionary writing was banished from Hungary—its most eminent practitioners had been driven into exile, and conditions prevailing in the country were not favourable to attempts on these lines. Yet from 1923 on, several radical-tinged periodicals were started, and literary circles and groups formed, often on the platform of half-boiled programmes and concepts and presenting a mixture of true literature and dilettantism. The actual context of life in Hungary in the old days explains the frequent appearance of political thought as a composite of radical bourgeois non-conformism, early-twentieth-century social democracy, and proletarian revolutionism; in the arts, the most diverse "isms" appeared blended with classic realism and naturalism. In the early days, the strong influence of Kassák and his *Ma* circle made itself felt, and for some time it appeared that the breaking up of conventional styles was itself tantamount to revolutionary art. The general pattern became still more checkered with the return, in 1925-26, of some of the exiles from Vienna. A few short-lived, constructivist and cubist periodicals enlivened the literary scene.

Meanwhile the underground Communist Party was reorganized; and with this, it became possible for a revolutionary literary centre to crystallise. In 1927 the magazine *100%* was started. A periodical of political, literary and general cultural interest, *100%* became the centre of a far-flung cultural movement. About this time in Hungary, there emerged a wide-spread network of workers' enlightenment associations, choral speaking and art societies, which became the vehicle and creator of revolutionary literature and culture. *100%* played an important role providing guidance for these movements; its activity in the field of criticism was largely responsible for the clarification of concepts and ideas. As so many other cultural offshoots of the working-class movement, *100%* bore vestiges of RAPP-ism, of sectarianism, a concept of literature as merely a tool of propaganda. In its fiction section *100%* gave space, besides Soviet and Western European literature, to the writings of members of a generation of revolutionary writers just then taking off: one finds on its pages names like Sándor Gergely, János Kodolányi and Zoltán Fábry. The magazine was edited by ALADÁR TAMÁS (b. 1899), one of the most active representatives of contemporary working-class literature. Tamás's important activities as magazine editor and an influence on the literary scene were broken off owing to police persecution: in the 1930's, he emigrated and went to live in Mexico, where he edited a Hungarian-language daily. Since 1945, when he returned to Hungary, Tamás has been an important figure in Hungarian literary life. He has treated his vast storehouse of experience in a number of novels and short stories.

LÁSZLÓ GEREBLYÉS (b. 1904), too, made his début in *100%*. He has written enthusiastic poetry of revolutionary ardour and some remarkable literary reportages and sociographical essays on working-class life. The Second World War found Gereblyés in France, where he took part in the French resistance. He has been an active participant of literary life in Hungary since 1945.

*100%* was eventually banned; its heritage passed to a couple of short-lived periodicals *(Forrás*—Wellspring; and *Front)*. Yet —as a result also of the work done by *100%*—a core of Hungarian revolutionary writers had been formed in these years. A revolutionary upsurge was apparent throughout Europe, and in Hungary, too, cracks appeared all over the edifice of post-war "consolidation." Revolutionary writing at the time counted among its practitioners names like Gyula Illyés, János Kodolányi, Sándor Gergely, Lajos Nagy and Attila József—writers whose later careers would follow so very divergent courses. The whole of Hungarian literature was then permeated by the spirit of social revolt and waiting for revolution. The subsequent growth of fascism scattered this body of writers in its formative period, but revolutionary Left-wing unity re-emerged a few years afterwards.

These were the years of the Popular Front policy when there seemed to be some hope of an ultimate victory by the forces of democracy. The Popular Front in France, and the Civil War in Spain did not fail to make their effects felt in Hungary; the policy of the underground Communist Party too, was directed towards promoting a joining of democratic forces. This was the period which saw the radicalisation of the populist writers' movement and a drift towards the Left of several bourgeois writers. *Gondolat*

285

(Thought), a communist-controlled periodical which represented the highest standard in revolutionary journalism, edited by György Vértes, was launched in these years and remained in existence from 1935 to 1938. It rallied militant progressives, and gave space to the eminent poets and novelists of the period; its helpful, principled criticism exercised great influence on every trend in Hungarian literature. *Gondolat* absorbed all the values which had been produced by the revolutionary Hungarian writing of the twenties. It made a clean break with the somewhat strident and slogan-like poetry and tone of earlier years; the writing it published was more profound and more sophisticated, combining all that was good in the living progressive heritage in Hungarian letters with a firm ideological stand.

## ATTILA JÓZSEF (1905-1937)

The 30's saw the maturing and rise to greatness of the outstanding working-class poet and creative spirit of inter-war Hungary— Attila József, who joined Sándor Petőfi and Endre Ady on the highest summits of Hungarian poetry.

ATTILA JÓZSEF was born in Budapest. His father, a worker in a soap factory, emigrated when József was three years old, leaving his mother the back-breaking task of fending for her little family by taking in washing. During the ever more difficult years of the First World War, József's family sank into dire poverty; his mother was attacked by uterine cancer, and wasted away rapidly. A childhood full of hardships and privations was succeeded by an adolescence no less arduous. After his mother's death, József was enrolled, with his brother-in-law's support, in a secondary school in a small town, and, on leaving school, he matriculated at Szeged University.

His career as a poet had begun while he was attending secondary school. At 17 he went into print with his first volume of poetry, *Beggar of Beauty*, 1922; and the second (characteristically entitled *It's Not me Shouting : It's the Earth Rumbling)* appeared in 1924, when he was a student. There followed one year in Vienna, and one in Paris—a period of penniless student life during which

ATTILA JÓZSEF (1905-1937)

the young man got his introduction into literature and politics, and became acquainted with many people. In 1927 he returned to Budapest and put in one more year at Budapest University. Hereafter he was to be a freelance writer who tried to eke out a living by writing poetry. Still in his formative period when trying to find his voice, he published his third volume: *Fatherless and Motherless*, 1929.

At the time of the great economic crisis and revolutionary wave of 1930, József joined the underground Communist Party and from then on, although some years later his ties with the party were severed, he preserved his loyalty to the working class and Marxism to the end. These years brought the great turning-point in his poetry *(Chop at the Roots*, 1930), and it attained fulness of development in 1931-33, when, beset by personal cares and troubles and struggling against the growing pressure of nazism in Hungary, he wrote his great intellectual poems, those which represent a turning-point in the course of Hungarian poetry as a whole and are believed to have added a new touch of colour to the spectrum of European lyrics *(Night in the Slums*, 1931; *Bear's Dance*, 1934; *How it Hurts*, 1936). The last years of his life were blighted by steadily worsening psychosis, yet even through the last excruciating months, his poetry continued to soar high and plumb hitherto unprobed depths. On December 3, 1937, at a small Lake Balaton resort, József took his own life by hurling himself in front of a speeding train.

At the beginning of his career, the young poet followed, not the traditionalist-conservative epigon line of Hungarian lyric poetry, but *Nyugat's* modern trends. He was still back in his old secondary school when he absorbed new influences; the impact of expressionism—both direct and indirect—was the greatest of all. These influences had a fertilising effect on the young József's poetry—in content as well as form. At one phase of his poetic development—mainly during his year in Vienna—he wrote rolling, flowing free verse as he tried to absorb the sight of a world robbed of all sense in an age of fractured reality, and to understand the roaring development of technology, while he attempted to sketch rough portraits of the Man of the Years to Come. However, not even when his expressionism was at its highest did he

287

become entirely incomprehensible: his fundamental respect for reality prevented him from drifting to extremes; his keen sense of form, too, effectively guarded him against such excesses.

In Paris, his poetry was enriched by fresh poetical experience. He proved susceptible above all to the influence of Villon and Apollinaire, two great masters of poetry much referred to at the time. He assimilated a good deal from these trends, but, in so doing, also managed to strip much of their influence on him, transcending such influence and merging it in his own poetical conception. The free-association technique had come to stay in his poetry, in the form of bold associations, striking metaphors, and images that open up great depths. He employed a daring manner of construction, a highly concentrated composition technique and he learned to master the type of "cuttings" reminiscent of expressionism; his blending of colours owes a great deal to the "isms." Also, he mastered *l'Humour Noir*, and was introduced into the poetry of the stylized grotesque. Entire cycles by the young poet *(Medals)* represent a staid variant of surrealism, lunacy brought under control, reality rigidified and turned grotesque, set forth in ever weightier and ever more regular form. The stylised picture condensed in song form, the flash of fairy-tale cut from reality, and the sardonic-ironical distorted portrait of surrounding humanity (primarily, of course, of the contemporary middle class), became permanent features of his poetry even in later years.

Though having learned from the "isms," he conquered them and rose above them. The impact of the "isms" was always effectively counterbalanced in him by a protective cushion of ancient folk-poetry influence. During the 20's, Hungarian poetry and music were affected by the rediscovery and elevation to the plane of polished art of the folk-song and of folk-poetry. The works of Béla Bartók and Zoltán Kodály, and their activity in folk-song collecting, did not fail to exercise a strong influence upon literature: the crystal-clear imagery and characteristic symbols, the rebellious or sorrowful spirit of the ancient folk-song, Hungarian and East European, crop up in the so-called new populist poetry of the period. József, from the outset one of the most enthusiastic admirers of Bartók, also tried his hand at collecting folk music and made use of its inspiration extensively in his poetry. Moreover, he too, like Bartók, went beyond evincing sheer ethnographic interest; not remaining within the narrow bounds of nationality, he elevated this influence on to a universal plane, making it a constituent part of philosophical poetry of the highest order.

There was one more trend whose influence came into play during József's formative years—the "proletarian" poetry of European communist movements, mainly of Germany under the Weimar Republic. That, too, he assimilated and made use of in a number of high-powered poems, improving and raising its equipage to the highest possible degree in poetical force as well as in revolutionary message, only to abandon this trend, too, in the course of his poetical development. For all these influences were only stones and bricks which József used for building up the edifice of his entirely original poetry, which were to raise Hungarian working-class verse to new heights after 1932.

The themes of Attila József's mature lyric poetry are highly varied. The poems conceived at the time of the volume *Chop at the Roots* were written in a mood of impatient expectation of an eagerly desired coming revolution: in some of them, nature—both living and dead—is charged with suspense; in other poems the poet is preparing himself for the coming struggle, while in another group of poems he strikes a direct political note, addressing the masses. *Night in the Slums* was only the first of his great meditative poems in which he surveys the condition and ponders on the historic mission of the working class and considers the whole process of world-wide progress. In those years, also, were written the poems brooding on various evils afflicting Hungarian life and society, and the Hungarian countryside. Besides his passionate interest in wider issues, his personal sorrows and passion were given expression—ardent life, sudden sadness, and memories of childhood years are all voiced in his poems. He reached the depths of desperation in the years 1935-36, when his mental suffering, his neurotic depression (and often obsessions) were expressed in a number of poems. In the summer of 1936 there followed a new soaring rise: a succession of great poems depict Europe drifting into war, the darkening horizon, and his anxiety for the future of his native Hungary writhing in the stranglehold of German nazism; he proclaims far and wide his belief in the power of his poetry and his confidence in the strength of humanity and in a better future for mankind.

All that has been said, is, of course, no more than a cursory survey of the themes treated by the great lyricist. Now, in an equally cursory survey: what are the characteristics of József's lyrics? Their most salient characteristics are a profound knowledge of conditions and a fundamental realism. Absolute loyalty and devotion to realities; an awareness of the most distinguishing traits of landscape and humanity, of groups of people; the permanent urge to season his imagination with reality, even if that reality is frustrating and disillusioning. Attila József, for instance, discarded certain features fairly common in working-class lyrics, the superficial and stylised representation of working-class types. He speaks in the voice of a poet who, even in the lyrical representation of his own class, had the capacity of discerning the contradictions as well as distress and predicament, and the greatness of mind never to varnish human conditions. It is this quality that renders his historical optimism, his confidence in the historical mission of the working class, so convincing.

But he does not leave it at that. He takes the bits and fragments of reality and fits them into a single system of reasonable thought, builds them into a single intellectual conception. Reality and a speculative quality; minute details and broad conceptions; the unity of accurate observation and the ability to see reality in full; and a harmony underlying it all—those are the makings of his unique greatness. He is a typical and yet original intellectual poet; "Order," "Reason" and "Knowledge" are his favoured words and by these key-words he means that harmony of a higher order under which man, released from class oppression, economic and social (and having put things to rights about his instincts and spiritual life), will find his place. With him, this fundamental intellectual approach is built on Marxism—the Marxist concept of the world and of society pervades his poetry. With him this means that he looks at the world through the eyes of the working class; that individual and universal, personal and public find an integration in every line; that his joys and sorrows, that his loneliness and release all reflect those of a whole class and beyond that—of an entire people. That is why Attila József deserves to be called a socialist realist poet.

His devotion to pure reason is an instrument to restrain the poet's seething emotions. It also served, of course, as a shield against nazi barbarity.

He adopted as the motto of one of his volumes a stanza from a Hungarian folk-song:

> *He who would do his piping well*
> *Must descend the very depths of hell*
> *Only there can he hope to tell*
> *What to do to blow the pipe well.*

Attila József had gone through hell—the inferno of destitution, solitude, of isolation. He was compelled to compile in his mind a list of the missed joys of childhood. From this inferno, there arose an image of his poor beloved mother and—so often and with such compelling force—a tormenting, terrifying vision of his childhood. And, even as a grown man, he had to descend to hell—the inferno of his mind, down deeper and deeper abysses of his aggravating sickness, his worsening schizophrenia. Besides the inferno of his individual troubles and sufferings, he had to endure that of his nation and his class. After 1932, in an age of steadily darkening horizon and growing barbarism, to the accompaniment of creaking boots marching towards the abyss of war, he had to probe the hell of the downtrodden peasantry and humiliated working class, the struggling intelligentsia and impoverished lower middle class, of Hungary—of his entire, beloved nation. It is a most amazing experience to watch him go down and rise again, and awake to a realisation of his sickness (and thereby conquer it); to admire his ability to explain the debasement of people and to face and throw light on his most tormenting trouble. The yearning for the revolution, the evocation of a more humane, a more just social system, confidence and perspective are never absent from his lyric poems.

He is not always brooding and pensive: playfulness, mockery and irony, a fondness for the grotesque and play as a part of human life are always present in his poetry. A Mozartian fulness, a rope-walking above the dark abyss, endows many of his poems with a poignant, dramatic quality.

All these elements are brought out by means of an extremely keen artistic instinct for condensing and fashioning. His mature lyrics—whether it is his great speculative poems or his "Freudian folk-songs" that one considers—are examples of poetic experience pressed into severe form. For Attila József there was a strict connection between the structure of poetry and that of the world. And since he regarded the structure of the world as fundamentally rational he preferred his own verse rational. He wanted to see the solution of the problems of reality in poetry and looked upon poetry as "a superfluous thing that is absolutely necessary." Accordingly, in his compositions every word is put into its place with the precision of a surveying engineer. In his last few years, József frequently had recourse to the most classic forms, such as the sonnet or the distich. The throbbing of rhythm was for him a basic experience; he had a highly susceptible musical ear—many of his poems carry suggestions of remembered tunes. His poems present an endless array of verse-forms, strophic structures and airs, as though he were aware of the intellectual power and disciplinary force, the anti-irrationality, of regular forms. A good deal of his imagery is drawn from the life of the toilers, the workers and the peasants. It is a measure of his great intellectual power that, twenty years after his death, a wealth of condensed lines, formulated in something approaching proverb-like finality, had found its way not only into the Hungarian poetical idiom, but also into colloquial speech.

Chronologically his *oeuvre* fits into the atmosphere of the *deuxième avant-guerre*, the 30's—the period when, following the hectic, turbulent 20's, and the succeeding period of playfulness (often irresponsible)—dark shadows were beginning to loom up, and the voices of poets and novelists were taking on a serious note. It was in those years that József's poetry unfolded itself and attained fulness of development, to evoke the intricacy of the time. Like several other members of his generation, József was one of those poets who had the ability to evoke the great complexity and contradictions of this age.

Attila József's *oeuvre* is part of the mainstream of European socialist poetry: he is one of those writers whose lives and works have been shaped and enriched by the great philosophical trend of our times—Marxism. He is one of those writers who, having adopted and accepted this intellectual system of international validity, have adapted it in their works to their national cultural heritage, filled it with the problems of their time and of their nations, and enriched it with their individual colours.

This trend represented also a new phase of development in the poetry of the working-class movement of the 20's: in this poetry, the Big City, in all its complexity and greatness, had by now ceased to be looked upon as a romantic chaos regarded with shocked surprise—it had been accepted and was now taken for granted as the existing reality, whose beauty, meaning and importance could be mirrored in lyric poetry. Similarly, the working class had by now ceased to be represented as a conglomeration of stylized mythical figures and was now depicted as a new class—represented "from within"—with a specific attitude towards life and a specific way of life. In these terms, József's progress shows some common traits with the development of Soviet poetry—or, for that matter, with that of Aragon, Neruda and C. Pavese, poets whose works are a measure of the fermenting and enriching impact of the working-class movement, its uplifting and releasing effect, even in the field of the arts. In Hungarian literature, József represents the pinnacle of working-class poetry; but he is more than that—in the name of his class, he has a message for his entire nation: he is one of the great assets of Hungarian literature.

Although József has established no school, his influence can be felt distinctly on nearly every one of his contemporaries. Progressive and revolutionary poets who began their career at later dates carry traces of his influence. Between 1938 and 1944, conditions in Hungary went from bad to worse: the political leaders of Hungary brought about a tie-up with the Axis powers, and Hungary entered the war as a member of the nazi-fascist alliance; Hungarians died on the battlefields for a wrong cause, while the home front was being increasingly nazified, with all progressive people ruthlessly persecuted and anti-Jewish legislation enacted. The growing fascisation of the war years led to a bloody reign of terror by the extreme Right in 1944, and to ultimate disaster.

The voices of poets who had preserved their loyalty to humane ideals were heard even during that most gloomy period. The younger and older liberal writers of *Nyugat*'s bourgeois group, writers at the Centre and Left of the populist movement, and a few lone hands refused to defer to nazism; other individual writers or groups of writers wrote actively anti-fascist lyrics—often clandestinely or expressed allegorically. During this period, poetry's voice was the strongest, and so there came into being a peculiar Hungarian anti-fascist lyric poetry which voiced protest against the era, and by preserving the values of the past added its own bricks to the edifice of a better future.

The most prominent member of this group was the lyricist MIKLÓS RADNÓTI (1909-1944). In 1930 the budding poet enrolled in Szeged University where he took up Hungarian and French literature. Here, he became a leader of the "Szeged Young Men" —a group of students who engaged in "village exploration," that is, studied rural conditions and wrote sociological studies on village-life. Although Radnóti was an erudite, highly gifted poet and translator with a schoolmaster's diploma, he was refused employment everywhere on account of his Jewish extraction, and was compelled to do odd jobs and translations for a living. From 1941 he was called up several times to do service spells in forced labour camps, and finally, in 1944, was sent to one of the most horrible extermination camps, in Bor, Yugoslavia. When the Germans evacuated Yugoslavia, the inmates of the forced labour camps were marched on long death-marches to Germany. Tragically it was already in Hungary, in the beloved native land for which he yearned so much that the exhausted poet was shot dead by an SS man. When his body was exhumed, his last poems, written on the threshold of death, were found in his greatcoat pocket.

A spirit of rebellious jauntiness is dominant in his early volumes *(Pagan Greeting,* 1930; *Song of Modern Shepherds,* 1931; and *Rising Wind,* 1933). In these poems the feeling of frustration is expressed in crabbed exclamations, expressionist imagery, in

MIKLÓS RADNÓTI (1909-1944)

fractured forms: they evidently owe a good deal to contemporary French lyricists—Cendrars and the surrealists. Yet already in some of the poems of *Rising Wind,* the poet's voice gains in richness and clarity—the development proceeds in several directions simultaneously: the poet's message is here more unequivocal, more revolutionary, matched by an ever bolder use of the elements of reality and a growing tendency for more polished, more classical forms. The volumes published between 1935 and 1939 *(New Moon,* 1935; *Keep on Walking You Doomed,* 1936; and *Steep Road,* 1938) are further milestones along the same road; the poet yearns for optimism, idyll, peace and harmony, for quiet pleasures, and longs to live in a land of culture and classicism. However, the darkening horizon—the "prelude to the war"—mars the idyll, and suggests thoughts of gloom and doom. Awareness of death is a motif that runs through Radnóti's poetry: even amidst the most radiant harmony, in the most serene and peaceful regions, he has a nagging presentiment that he is going to perish miserably. In his, as in József's poetry, the unity of landscape, nature and man is of significance. There are poems openly proclaiming his political creed evoking the Spanish Civil War; then, side by side with them, intimately warm declarations of love to Fanny, his wife—love-poems charged with intense feeling.

Radnóti's voice soared highest in the last few years of his life, in the years of humiliation and persecution, of horror and extreme peril. In eight *Eclogues* (the last of which was written behind the barbed-wire fences of Lager Heidemann, in Bor, Yugoslavia), he expresses in dialogue, through the rigorous discipline of the classical verse-form, and by using all the delicate shades of meaning and bold imagery of twentieth-century poetry, his perturbation at the ever more savage horror of the era, and, for all that, his confidence in an idyllic peace that would come—perhaps when he was dead. In these dreadful throes, love became a truly great, releasing sentiment, the last refuge; now the real meaning became apparent of words like Fatherland (on the lips of the poet who was being driven into death by his country, in the name of patriotism) or People (pronounced with confidence in the people, dehumanised and herded into destructiveness and yet depositories of cultural assets). As a marvellous example of

295

poetical self-discipline and human resistance, Radnóti kept writing poems until the last moment: he evoked the world of concentration camps with a rare degree of perceptivity, describing each station of his calvary with more and more perfected versification, in an ever more condensed and mature poetry.

Radnóti is a sensitive, polished, and erudite poet who—like many other members of his generation—progressed towards a novel classicism. He also excelled as an essayist, carrying on in the great tradition of the *Nyugat* generation. Also, he is responsible for translations of La Fontaine, Nerval, Apollinaire, Cocteau, Shelley and many other poets *(In the Wake of Orpheus, 1943)*. Translation in the Hungary of the early 40's was a kind of self-defence in the face of the barbarity of the era, a means of preserving human values.

ERNŐ SALAMON (1912-1943) wrote lyrics more rugged, harsher and more charged with strain and worries. His childhood years of much hardship were spent in Rumania; and the needy student soon found contact with the movement of Rumanian and Hungarian workers and became an activist of the underground Communist Party. He was a reporter, newspaper distributor and worker; participant of revolutionary writer's movements, a member of the *Korunk* group. When the northern part of Transylvania was annexed by Hungary, the Hungarian authorities persecuted him: first he was sent to an internment camp, then to the eastern front as member of a forced labour service unit. Seriously ill, Salamon was shot dead in the Ukraine by an Italian fascist soldier. Salamon's lyrics are harsher, more charged with nervousness, and more militant, than Radnóti's; more rustic than the latter's, they breathe the keen, invigorating air of the high snow-capped mountains of his native region. His was a basically passionate, emotional nature, a man tormented by and protesting against his hard lot, dire poverty, and the hideousness of the times *(Wonderful Destiny, 1937; On the Threshold of the Poor, 1938; To a Poor Man's Son, 1945)*. The scenes of peasant, working-class life often receive in his poems a treatment which strike the note of stylized popular ballads and folks-songs.

LÁSZLÓ LUKÁCS (1906-1944) was another writer whose poetry grew to significance against the background of the Hungarian working-class movement of the 30's and 40's. Office worker and journalist, he was an underground Communist Party activist during the 30's, and served several prison terms. His short life was ended in the forced labour camp at Bor. In his life, he published a single volume (*The Repressed Soul*, 1941), but his poems constitute one of the most typical poetical *oeuvres* of the era. Lukács turned a communist poet from a bourgeois humanist and a *Nyugat* enthusiast; he applies a highly polished poetic technique to his treatment of new themes with new meaning and significance, mirroring the inner world, the aspirations and worries, of the communist intellectual.

Born the son of poor peasants, IMRE NAGY (1896-1942) became a poet and, to the end, experienced the hard lot of his class. He never allowed himself to be beguiled by populist romanticism; in depicting peasant life, abject and penurious, his protest is unequivocally that of the rebel; he longs for beauty and human values. Restrained, economical and plain in tone, yet full of beauty, his lyrics mirror a man of integrity who remained detached from the heart of literary life.

ANTAL FORGÁCS (1910-1944), a poet who fell into the hands of the Gestapo in France, was considered a follower of Attila József. In his poems he strikes a pessimistic note, and they mirror the confusion and despair prevalent in that grim period. Yet they are filled with profoundly human content. In the poems he wrote in France, he speaks with the voice of calm wisdom of the fighter who has grown into mature manhood. His reaction to the storm of war and the horrors of nazi occupation found expression in mature poems in which the resigned note conveys the poet's confidence in a better future.

The poetical and private career of ZOLTÁN ZELK (b. 1906) presents a more complex pattern. In his beginnings, he was an expressionist, a member of Kassák's *Munka* (Labour) circle. His tone of voice changed about the middle of the 30's, becoming clearer and more sedate. Between the two wars, he lived under very straitened circumstances, and did several years in a forced labour unit. His well-turned poems written at the time are sonorous with an underlying melancholy. In 1945 Zelk, who up to that date had not taken an active part in the working-class movement, joined the Communist Party; his poetry now received an impetus, and his poems became fired with partisan dynamism, an enthusiasm for new institutions, a fervent belief in the Communist Party's goals and ideals. For several years, his poetry was one of the leading voices in the emerging new lyrics of Hungary. From 1953 on, the troubles that cropped up in public life as well as in the field of literature did not fail to influence Zelk's attitude, which, together with his poetry, placed him in the opposition and he succumbed to the pessimism which had been so typical of his earlier years. In the poems he was written since, he has been trying to survey the road he has travelled, and to recognise and assess the errors of judgement he had made. He writes in a very moving manner about the tragic death of his wife and the gap she left.

Peculiar forms of anti-fascist protest are found in the poetry of BÉLA PÁSZTOR (1907-1943). Stylized, image-cluttered poems are dominant in *Samplers of Poison*, 1939, and the posthumous volume *Marionettes and Corpses*, 1948; scenes of fairy tales, grotesque images and horror reflect the wickedness and preposterousness of a disjointed world. His hatred for the oppressors, his fears, and his desires for a better world are expressed in transposed forms.

The progressive radical and revolutionary prose writers of the 30's and 40's formed no homogeneous group; the specific conditions of Hungary did not permit the formation of groups. Not even in ideology and world outlook was this body of writers homogeneous; there were amongst them fighters of the underground communist movement, socialist, and others who had but short-lived contact with the working-class movement. What was common to them all was a determined resistance to fascism and a resolute Leftism in their search for solutions.

LAJOS NAGY (1883-1954) was the foremost representative of progressive prose writers in inter-war Hungary whose sympathies brought them close to the working-class movement. Essentially, he was a member of the *Nyugat* generation—his literary *début*, too, was made on the pages of *Nyugat*. But actually his ties with the *Nyugat* circle were rather loose. He was born in a hamlet in the Danube-Tisza interstream area, an illegitimate child, whose lot was dire poverty and humiliation from his early youth. As a university student he earned the money for his upkeep as a private tutor (his experience of several months of private tutorship with a family

ism. For all the periodic contradictions and scepticism of his literary career, Lajos Nagy is an outstanding representative of Hungarian socialist writing.

At the beginning of his literary career, JÓZSEF DARVAS (b. 1912) belonged to the younger generation of populist writers, in whose movement he represented the Left wing; before long, he was converted to communism. Born into a family of poor farm-hands, in the southern part of the Great Plain, he grew up to become a teacher. Even his earliest novels are marked by a sharply social outlook, ruthless exposure of real conditions, militancy, and clear-cut construction. He is one of those writers who most consistently advocated (and demonstrated in their writings) the inevitability of the revolutionary struggle. This attitude is evident in his novels about the struggles of the poor peasants (*Black Bread*, 1934; *From Twelfth Night to New Year's Eve*, 1935) and in those about the uprooted small-town intelligentsia (*The Station*, 1936). The year 1936 saw a great leap in his literary course: his description of the township of Orosháza (*Hungary's Biggest Village*, 1936) is one of the best, the most thoroughgoing, sociological studies written in Hungary. In 1938 Darvas wrote an historical novel—*The Turk Beater*—in which he not only presents a strikingly new approach to the relationship between the individual person and the mass movements, but also produces, at a time when nazi Germany's sinister expansionist policy was beginning to be translated to practice, an example of a successful resistance to threatening invasion. *History of a Peasant Family* (1940) traces the history of the author's family back to the seventeenth century, in the process giving an answer to problems facing the Hungarian peasantry as a whole. One of Darvas's frequently treated themes is the relationship between the low-born intellectual (mostly a village teacher) and the peasants: the clash in the mind of the same person of the two worlds—of the peasant and of the educated middle-class man. This is the theme of the two novels *Overnight* (1939) and *He Started out in September* (1939) and of his best play *The Abyss* (1941). In politics, he remained consistent throughout: he repudiated the fascist poison in all its appearances, declared himself a Marxist, looking to the working class for a solution of the problems facing the peasantry.

301

*A City on Quagmire* (1945), half diary, half novel, is the story of the siege of Budapest and at the same time an inexorable exposure of all the crimes and lies of the counter-revolutionary era. For several years following the liberation of Hungary, Darvas devoted his energies to politics, held successive ministerial portfolios, and as minister of culture was one of the men responsible for Hungary's cultural policy. In 1955, while retaining his public functions, he once more turned his attention to writing; since then, he has written several successful screenplays, and is responsible for the most dramatic literary treatment of the counter-revolutionary rising of 1956; his play *Sooty Sky*, 1959, is centred around the inner conflict of a writer under the impact of conflicting influences in the difficult days of the 1956 counter-revolutionary rising.

His novel *Dizzy Rain* (1963) is the self-examination of an entire generation; the horrors of fascism, the mistakes of the personality cult, and the events of 1956 are flashed up in a feverish plot.

ANDOR ENDRE GELLÉRI (1908-1945) was one of the most original talents among Leftist prose writers. A member of the tragic-fated generation, he had a life full of hardships. Living through long spells of unemployment gave him a first-hand experience of the life of manual workers. His life was ended in a German concentration camp. His *oeuvre* thus remained tragically unfinished—a single, not very successful, novel *(The Laundry Works*, 1932) is evidence of an ambition for longer fiction. He left a bulky volume of short stories, which—in their themes as well as their atmosphere—reveal an entirely new world, the life of poor people in Óbuda, one of the districts of Budapest, the world of people living on the periphery of life—"the superfluous" jobless workers, apprentices, hard-working dyers and transport workers. This is a waxworks where the portraits depict the underdog, the bossed-over subordinate, the quiet malcontents, the senselessly defiant, the self-destructive. This is a world apart, with an atmosphere all its own, governed by laws of its own, and having its own customs. This world comes to life in Gelléri's admirable atmosphere-creating penmanship: each one of his short stories has an autobiographical flavour about it, and is pervaded with an original lyric quality. These stories are shards—broken pieces of a fragmented, atomised reality having their own particular way of refracting light, presenting a peculiar mixture of the real and the fantastic, of naturalism and myth, charged with passions and outbursts, ethereal airiness and the smell of human sweat, a heavy dose of sex, and twisted impulses. The constant mingling of reality and its opposite, and a ballad-like milieu mark his work.

The inner lines of Belléri's development can be drawn: the fantastic—an escapism into a fairy world—is the characteristic trait of his first volume *(Thirsty Apprentices*, 1933). Later on in *Moon Street* (1934) and *The Harbour* (1935) his voice became better defined and more revolutionary, though still anarchic. After the revolutionary upheaval had abated, he acquired a more gentle, more compassionate, tone, while the ironical note became stronger, and firmer his belief in a better future *(Lightning and Evening Fire*, 1940).

A significant and militant communist prose writer of the period was ISTVÁN NAGY (b. 1904), a Hungarian of Rumania. A worker turned writer, he established contact with the working-class movement while a young man and for several decades has been a member of the Communist Party. His writings have been published ever since 1932, and nearly every one of them treats some burning issue, and is marked by a profound knowledge of life, especially the life of workers. *There's No Stopping* (1933) is a sketch of peasants who leave the village for the town and become workers; the *Olteanu Grandchildren* (1934-1943) is a saga about a Rumanian family; *The Precincts* (1938) is true sociographic study on working-class life. Nagy played an important part in the literary disputes in the 1940's: his ties with the populist writers enabled him to uphold a consistent Marxist point of view in their circle. Since 1945 Nagy has been a leading figure in the Rumanian People's Republic, in both the political and literary fields. The main themes of his writings since 1945 have been socialist construction, the transformation of the village, the emergence of workers of a new type, and memories of the past *(One of Thirty Years; At the Highest Degree of Temperature; Our Daughters).*

One of the most original authors in Hungarian revolutionary writing, SÁNDOR RIDEG (b. 1903), was also a worker when he took up writing. At first, he was a labourer working on an isolated farm, from where he had to flee after the downfall of the Hungarian Republic of Councils of 1919. He was a farm labourer and factory worker, tramp and newspaper editor. He has been an active participant in the working-class movement since 1926, and has served a prison term for his activity. He took up writing late in life—his first novel *The Track Watchman's House*, appeared in 1943; it was followed by short stories *(In a Gentlemen's Country*, 1945) and two novels that are partly autobiographies, partly adventure stories *(Ordeal by Fire*, 1949; and *Samson*, 1951). Rideg is interested in the raw, strong colours of life, almost to the point of violence, and has a predilection for grotesque, farcical situations and for points sharpened in the extreme. He likes to spice his story with the atmoshpere of folk-tales and with anecdotes. His life experience treated in his writings is the poor man's lot, the farm-hand's life, the struggle of the oppressed against their betters. In *Samson* he has created a half-mythical, half-folk-tale hero whom he has invested with his own traits. Some of his short stories are veritable modern folk-tales *(The Hussar with a Mirror-Heart*, 1950); in others his hyperbolical literary temperament, his leaning towards caricature and high colouring are preponderant.

TIBOR DÉRY (b. 1894) has trodden an offbeat track of progressive literature which from time to time has joined up with the road of the working-class movement. Coming from a well-to-do family, the young man made his *début* with some short stories in the pages of *Nyugat* soon after the First World War. In the 1920's he lived in Austria, writing expressionist poetry. In 1926, he returned to Hungary and here he has lived with longer interruptions, at times establishing ties with the working-class movement, at other times opposing it. In the 20's, he wrote a long novel, *The Unfinished Sentence*, a full portrayal of some intellectual circles and the working-class movement of those years, treated with the aid of the stylistic achievements of the modern psychological novel and the literature of the "Weimar era." Of his writings since the war, *Underworld Games* (1946) is a record of the siege of Budapest, and the two volumes of *The Answer* (1950-52) is another attempt at a portroyal of the working-class movement, and also the ruling classes, of the 1930's. Tibor Déry played an important part with his passionate criticism of the personality cult (his short story *Love*).

Although he professed himself a socialist, his criticism dug at the very foundations of socialism and so paved the way for the counter-revolution of 1956, and afterwards acted to retard consolidation. In his most recent volume of short stories (*Love,* 1963) he portrays reality with mature art and serenity and even attempts to take stock of his own role and responsibility.

KÁLMÁN SÁNDOR (1903-1963) started as a bourgeois radical in the 1930's, but the course of his progress has been different from Déry's. In his pre-war short stories (he began writing in 1930), he depicted the dreary, pedestrian lives of petty-bourgeois intellectuals in Budapest. After the war, his penmanship became more mature—mordant satire became coupled with an almost scientific thoroughness and devotion to detail in his writing. *The Pillory* (1951) presents a shocking picture of the early days of the Hungarian counter-revolution of 1919; *The Day of Wrath* (1952), one of the most successful Hungarian plays ever written, is about the suspense-charged days of the Hungarian Republic of Councils of 1919; while *No Man's City* (1955) brings to life the dramatic moments of the liberation of Hungary in 1945.

Chronologically the last group of anti-fascist, revolutionary writers was that of the so-called Worker-Writers (active between 1942 and 1944): it was formed by young writers either of working-class stock or newly become workers who were active either in the Social Democratic Party's Left wing or in the underground Communist Party. They published anthologies, and were determined to create a sharply anti-fascist literature that would mirror the everyday realities. Besides the young writers, István Nagy, Sándor Rideg and József Darvas were active in this group.

The most outstanding member of the group was LÁSZLÓ BENJAMIN (b. 1915). His early verse, written in the mid-30's, shows the influence of Attila József and other contemporaries. Before long, however, Benjámin evolved his own individual poetry—few other poets have conveyed with such convincing force oppression, frustration and hopelessness; he also gave voice to his belonging to the working class. His preoccupation with moral issues, an incessant—and at times convulsive—heart-searching, became apparent at this early period. This self-control and self-analysis, this moralising tendency, stamp the poems written during his first post-war period *(Type-Founders Triumphant*, 1946; and *After the Creation*, 1948); the road he covered progressing from solitude to community, from meditation to action, from doubts to certainty, is marked by well-turned, energetic poems with a latent passion. During the years that followed, Benjámin identified himself with the new order with the sincerity and enthusiasm of a poet who has found his feet *(To Live for Ever*, 1949; and *By Fire and Blade*, 1951). His intellectual lyrics, which are ardent without being loud, open up broad vistas and form an outstanding part of Hungarian socialist poetry. The impact of the errors made in political leadership, the vagaries of the political course, brought the moralist, the sceptic and the heart-searcher in him to the surface once more after 1953. His fundamental loyalty to his ideals lived in a painfully antagonistic coexistence in his mind with his doubts and misgivings and disappointment—a conflict that has often sent him into cramped seclusion *(To Live for Ever*, 1956). His new volume *The Fifth Season* (1962) is the confession of a poet struggling with doubts but finding his way to the community of men.

This account of revolutionary writing would not be complete without an account of communist criticism and literary scholarship. A highly philosophic and stimulating criticism exercised a strong influence throughout the period, providing guidance, transmitting cultural assets, and clarifying issues.

The foremost communist critic was JÓZSEF RÉVAI (1898-1959), one of the leaders of the Communist Party, as well as its outstanding theoretician and foremost publicist. Literary criticism and literary history claimed only part of his many-sided activities: he was eminent as a politician and journalist and, above all, as historian. His activity as an historian cannot be separated from his literary activity. When, in *Marx and the Hungarian Revolution* (1932), he put forward a brilliant analysis of the Hungarian War of Independence of 1848-49, at the same time he also threw light on the poet Petőfi's place in Hungarian literature; when he explains in his papers on Kossuth and the War of Independence the fundamental problems of Hungary's historical development or clarifies some problems of agricultural development and the populist writers' movement in *Marxism and Populism* (1937) he also investigates questions bearing on Hungarian literary history. The long line of his essays on strictly literary themes was opened by a paper (published in 1938) on *Ferenc Kölcsey*—the most penetrating analysis ever written of the literature of the era of Enlightenment and the Reform Age in Hungary. His book on *Ady* was the first comprehensive work assessing Ady within the context of his time, defining the poet's philosophy and world outlook and throwing light on the evolution of his poetical media. His essays on Petőfi and Attila József, and his analysis of the novelist Móricz, reveal a profound thinker, erudite scholar and brilliant stylist.

Although his work, on the whole, has been devoted to philosophy, aesthetics and world literature, GYÖRGY LUKÁCS (b. 1883), too, has several times turned his attention to questions of Hungarian literature—mainly during two periods of his work: at the start of his career and from 1945 to 1950. His writings analysing the *Nyugat* circle and Mihály Babits, as well as *Szép Szó* in *Responsibility of Literati* (Moscow, 1944) are of significance.

György Lukács's influence of Hungarian writing and literary criticism has been great. Students of his works have admired his brilliant application of Marxist analysis, his vast knowledge of his subject, and his disarming dialectics. In the years from 1945 to 1949 his work was an important contribution helping to find a sound orientation for Hungarian literature: his fight against irrationalism and the decadent schools, his criticism of the populist writers' movement and his analysis of bourgeois radicals greatly promoted the emergence of socialist writing. However, Lukács's aesthetic views contained some very questionable elements. As early as the years 1935-36, Lukács had shown an inclination to discover—and try to preserve—an umbilical connection between socialist realism on the one hand, and, on the other, the great critical realists and the twentieth-century bourgeois humanists, to the almost absolute exclusion of all other schools. He was right in repudiating the extremism of decadence and, at the same time, the distortions and vulgarizations of the *Proletkult*. Yet his approach was one-sided; for, in examining the works of the early twentieth century, he applied too severe a yardstick, viewing them exclusively from the standpoint of broad-horizoned critical realism. In consequence, he rejected much that was of value. Similarly, Lukács has formed too summary a judgment of the various offshoots of the

*Avantgarde* (including such writers as Brecht); and he has rejected several—perhaps not yet fully developed or over-simplified—products of the socialist writing of the 1920's and the 30's. His views on partisanship in literature and on socialist realism were also highly controversial. In 1949-50—in what has come to be referred to as "the Lukács Controversy"—Professor Lukács came under heavy fire; this controversy, however—although some peculiarities of Lukács's aesthetics and philosophical system were correctly exposed—led, on the whole, to vulgarization and schematism. Since those years Lukács has ceased to be active in literary criticism and in proposing a literary policy; nevertheless his influence can still be felt, both through his pupils and through his opponents. His comprehensive *Aesthetics* summarizes his most recent thinking.

The most distinguished of the critics who worked in Hungary throughout his literary career, was GYÖRGY BÁLINT (1906-1943). Like so many other members of his generation—among them writers—he ended his life in a labour service camp on the eastern front. He has written a vast number of literary articles, reportages, newspaper comments and columns and short stories which show the hand of an erudite, refined writer, critic and wit whose political views brought him all the way from bourgeois radicalism to socialism. His only big work—a travel diary on Spain—was banned by the censor. The volumes in which his collected newspaper articles and comments, short stories and sketches were published *(A Captive of Time,* 1935; *Ice-Floes, Books and Beggars,* 1937; and *A Farewell to Reason,* 1940) constitute but a fraction of his lifework. A gloomy message expressed in a sparklingly witty style, and an awareness of the intellectual who is undauntedly holding his ground in the face of persecution and who, having soaked himself in European culture and civilisation, has keen insight, mark his writings.

# AFTER THE SECOND WORLD WAR

In a state of disintegration, with the ranks of writers decimated by nazism, and still reeling under the impact of recent horrible experiences, Hungarian literature scrambled to its feet and began to live again in the early months of 1945. The way was now clear for all democratic trends and ambitions; only openly fascist writers were denied any opportunity of expression. The literary scene as a whole was marked by a coexistence of diverse trends—progressive and conservative, one pandering to petty-bourgeois mass tastes and one that shut itself up hermetically in an ivory tower, socialist and anti-socialist trends were thriving side by side. The populist writers' group rallied around the magazine *Válasz* (Answer); anti-conventional, modernistic, abstract trends found expression on the pages of the *Kortárs* (The Contemporary) magazine, under Kassák's wings; while neo-Catholic writers grouped themselves in the *Vigilia* circle. The review *Magyarok* (Hungarians) represented the progressive bourgeois writers, that is, the "second" and "third" generations of *Nyugat*. Even the writers of the youngest generation (who looked upon Babits as their poet-ideal) founded a magazine of their own entitled *Újhold* (New Moon).

Given this motley crowd of trends and ideas, the Communist Party's literary policy-makers and critics worked to rally all progressive forces, to strengthen the democratic trends, and, in the field of aesthetics, battled against the anti-realist, decadent schools. *Fórum*, a consistently Leftist magazine which followed the tradition of the old-time people's front policy and which rallied the most outstanding forces of intellectual life, was started as early as 1946. It was followed at the end of 1947 by *Csillag* (Star), which published writings by authors of the older as well as of the youngest generation, and which steadily rose to the status of a leading literary review.

In 1948—the year in which the retrograde forces were pushed back in Hungarian politics and socialist construction in Hungary became the question of the day—a new departure was made in national cultural policy, thus also in the field of literature. On the ideological plane, the way was opened for the new development in the so-called Lukács controversy in 1949-50; in the organisational field, the breaking of new ground was marked by the foundation of the unified Hungarian Writers'Association, of the review *Csillag* and the literary weekly *Irodalmi Újság*, and, later on, of *Új Hang* (New Voice), a monthly magazine of young writers (all three organs published under the aegis of the Writers' Association), and by the dissolution and discontinuance of various literary groups and reviews that represented diverse trends of political opinion.

The period between 1949 and 1953 was one of lively activity in Hungarian literary life. Beyond question, the reading public expanded extraordinarily in these years, and editions were correspondingly enlarged; public reaction to literary works grew in force; life at the Writers' Association was full of ferment and activity, with discussions and conferences arranged frequently. A substantial number of writers (some quickly, other more slowly) came to accept and adopt the goals of socialist literature—a homogeneous body of writers was beginning to emerge. Hungarian readers came to know the outstanding works of Soviet literature, from which they had been shut off earlier. Even such a short period saw the creation of new works, and new departures made; new writers—and even new generations of writers—made their appearance on the scene.

Writers of the older generation published works that were either an impassioned depiction of the past seen from the communist standpoint, or pictured the current process of the socialist transformation of Hungary: *Conquest*—by Béla Illés; *Pillory*—by Kálmán Sándor; *New Land*—by Pál Szabó; *Ordeal*—by Péter Veres. The impact of socialist transformation is clearly felt in the works even of writers who otherwise, on one issue or other, drew the line at socialism (Gyula Illyés, László Németh and Áron Tamási).

The pathos, the heroism and dynamism of the era, its wide

310

vistas and its everyday life were best captured by the lyricists. A new role in Hungarian socialist poetry was beginning to be heard, represented by the intellectual and soaring poetry of László Benjámin, and by the poetry of LAJOS KÓNYA (b. 1914), PÉTER KUCZKA (b. 1923), GYÖRGY SOMLYÓ (b. 1920) and others.

In the wake of these poets there arose a generation of new, gifted lyric poets who introduced a new colour into Hungarian lyrics. One of them was ISTVÁN SIMON (b. 1926), whose poetry is woven of such diverse strands as the Hungarian popular heritage, Illyés' epic realism and the modern European lyric tradition. After first conveying the warm tones of Transdanubian rural life, he gave expression to the feelings of a young man from the country who turned city dweller. His course of progress has brought Simon to a wider intellectual summing up, to wider perspectives; his attitude has always been marked by an unenraptured optimism— the poise of a young man who have grown up under the new system.

FERENC JUHÁSZ (b. 1928) first attracted attention by his epic poems *(My Father,* 1950; *The Sántha Family,* 1951). He has revived this genre—long neglected by Hungarian poets—and modernised it, making it fit for conveying contemporary ideas. In later years, his poetical progress tended towards ever bolder experimentation: his vigorous talent for evoking images, his great suggestive capacity, torrents of associations, and rich vocabulary and mastery of form make him stand out from the ranks of his contemporaries. In recent years, his lyrics have become less balanced and assumed a somewhat apocalyptic quality, mirroring a troubled, suffering frame of mind. Now he is turning more and more towards great visions, the grand world-view of the micro- and the macrocosm.

The poems of LÁSZLÓ NAGY (b. 1925) have the appeal of great force, an informal mode of expression, a strong talent for condensing and stylising, and a unique sense of rhythm. He evokes the inner world of the young peasant who has turned intellectual.

There survived also a non-political lyric poetry, more transposed, more indirect, even in the works of poets belonging to this generation; yet even in the work of these poets, there are indications, if not of a socialist world outlook, of an approach to social issues, problems raised by the new social and political order. JÁNOS PILINSZKY (b. 1921) and ÁGNES NEMES NAGY (b. 1922) re-appeared

311

in print after 1953. The former is close to the neo-Catholic school, writes suggestive, forceful and terse poetry which express his humanist views and his horror of war. The latter writes strongly intellectual and condensed verse which is full of sentiments moving between intellect and passion, and which captures the phenomena of a changing world.

A generation of young prose writers and playwrights grew up by the side of older dramatists; and even those writers formerly lingering in the background and slow to unfold their talent received fresh impetus in these years. LAJOS MESTERHÁZI (b. 1916) attracted attention with short stories that give a forceful treatment of the dramatic conflicts of the new life; PAULA ORAVECZ (b. 1903) made her mark with works about abandoned children, evoking the child's inner world. BORIS PALOTAI (b. 1907) is the authoress of sensitively-written short stories in which she boldly exposes both social and individual problems, and ZSUZSA THURY (b. 1903) writes novels for young people. Prose writers of the younger generation tried to tackle the complex problems of the present time. In a number of strong-coloured short stories and a powerful drama, *Baptism of Fire*, ERNŐ URBÁN (b. 1918) depicted conflicts generated in the process of the socialist transformation of the countryside. IMRE SARKADI (1921-1961) drew character portraits of the socialist village in short stories condensed with the Móriczian method of dramatic point. His career united all the achievements and all the stumbling blocks in the literary life of the last few decades. His works depict progress and at the same time the problems tormenting the individual. In his short stories and literary reportages FERENC KARINTHY (b. 1921) renders brilliantly ironical pictures of life in Budapest, of the new types of humanity currently in the making, and of problems that need solution. In a number of short stories and a novel *(Man and Wife)* ISTVÁN ÖRKÉNY (b. 1912) gave a portrayal of factory life, of workers and intellectuals in these years. In writings which have an atmosphere all their own, IVÁN MÁNDY (b. 1918) sketches—somewhat in the style of Gelléri—the nightmarish existence of types of humanity living on the periphery of big-city life.

Following in the footsteps of great predecessors, literary criticism and scholarship took a new lease on life. A new body of critics has come forward, not only in debates and day-to-day activity, but with more extensive works, monographs and volumes of essays. Critical editions of earlier contributions to Hungarian literature were now undertaken on an unprecedented scale.

As always during the periods of greatness and prolificity of Hungarian literature, translating activity was flourishing and some fine achievements were produced. Lőrinc Szabó and István Vas continued in the tradition of the best *Nyugat* translators. The work of ENDRE GÁSPÁR (1897-1955) introduced a fresh colour; he was a most facile Hungarian interpreter of the poetry, prose and plays of several nations, and it is to his special credit that he was the first to produce artistic translations of the Spanish progressive poets. The translating and editing work of an essayist and literary historian with a pen, LÁSZLÓ KARDOS (b. 1898) made an important pioneering contribution towards the translating of Soviet poetry by Hungarian poets. After the efforts of such Hungarian emigré poets as János Mácza, Andor Gábor, Sarolta Lányi and Antal Hidas, he continued their work by producing fine Hungarian interpretations of Soviet poetry and by editing a Hungarian anthology of Soviet poetry. GYÖRGY RADÓ (b. 1912) has also done significant work in translating and popularising Soviet poetry, both Russian authors and writers from the national minorities. GÉZA KÉPES (b. 1909), the Hungarian interpreter of Arabic, Persian and Finnish poets, attracts attention with his wide knowledge of languages and with his masterful reproduction of original forms. What is practically a new school of Hungarian translators has been founded by GÁBOR DEVECSERI (b. 1917). An excellent poet in his own right, he contributed beautiful translations of Greek classics, including the full Homer, which follow very closely the original both in meaning and in form. There is also a whole group of younger translators (Imre Makai, László Lator and György Rába), and Hungarian literature has in recent years produced such fine achievements of teamwork as the entire Hungarian Homer, Horace, Dante, Racine, Molière, Shakespeare and Rimbaud as well as Hungarian renderings of a long line of contemporary poetry. Since 1945 new complete translations have been made of the foremost poets and prose writers in the English language, including Chaucer and Blake, Walt Whitman and Carl Sandburg, T. S. Eliot and Yeats.

Encouraging as the growth of critical activity may have been, it was not immune from contradictions and errors in cultural policy in which the recently established unity in the literary scene did not prove solid enough. From 1949 onward, the errors which characterized the era of the personality cult became increasingly apparent. Many ills which had once plagued Hungarian society had by now been abolished; the demands for reform and progress that the writers had voiced for several decades back had been fulfilled. Nevertheless, the development of socialism was hindered by the errors committed by a dogmatic sectarian leadership. After a few years of dynamic development several deplorable facts began to stand out. It became apparent that the general standard of living had ceased to rise; the pace of industrialization was overstrained; and that excesses, unlawful acts were being committed in urban as well as rural areas. A peculiar duality was discernible in the official literary policy of the period and in the officially supported principles of aesthetics. The creation of a democratic literature of a new type, of socialist realism in the arts, was put forward as the goal towards which writers and artists were exhorted to direct creative efforts; at the same time, however, patient persuasion and constructive debate were supplanted by excessive authoritarianism and an intransigent, slating criticism as the means of official "encouragement" and "guidance." The meaning of socialist realism was interpreted in those years in a doctrinaire, narrow-minded, and inflexible manner, the style of the literature it produced was marked by critical realism, and its content by a tendency to varnish the unpalatable truth, which was in contradiction to official statements and declarations. Schematism, naive rhapsodizing reared its head in socialist writing.

These problems—which, after 1953, became even more sharpened in political life—the contradiction between reality and professed aims, between the admittedly correct and soul-stirring ideals and their distorted application in actual practice, elicited anxiety, doubts and dismay in the minds of many writers. The resulting crisis of conscience is reflected in a number of literary works created during the 1953-56 period. But, as in the political arena, so on the literary scene, there seemed to be no way out; the finest minds found themselves trapped between the devil of attachment to rigid dogmatism and political sectarianism, and the deep sea of complete disenchantment with socialism. To many it seemed that the developments since the war had vindicated the pre-1945 bourgeois, and even nationalist, views.

When, during the months preceding the upheaval in the autumn of 1956, Hungary's problems of internal politics became sharpened still further, the Writers' Association, like other bodies, was turned into a platform of political debate. The difference became less and less marked between the passion of upright communists and socialists seeking to correct errors and to cleanse socialism of the disgrace with which those past errors had loaded it, on the one hand, and the intention of forces that were aiming at a restoration of the *ancien régime* on the other. This painful dilemma drove, in October 1956, several writers to the side that strove to undo all socialist achievements. Many people failed to recognize the real forces behind the slogans of the counter-revolution. Hungarian writers—with the exception of a few who by leaving the country gave final evidence of their disbelief in the socialist way—after going through a period of severe conflict recognized the lesson of history and have committed themselves to the socialist construction of the present, which has freed itself of earlier mistakes and distortions. This—often painful and difficult—process is reflected in a number of exciting works.

The reorganisation of literary life was begun soon after the counter-revolutionary rising. The hectic events and the divergent influences that were at work caused much confusion; a good many writers did not know what to do in the midst of the turmoil. Much credit goes, therefore, to the group who took the initiative for reactivising literary life, who with all their weight took the side of the worker-peasant government and socialism. This group included, besides old-time communist writers, sympathisers of the bourgeois Left, some members of the "second generation" and writers and critics of the youngest generation. Increasing consolidation in the literary scene was marked by the reappearance of the literary periodical press—the weekly *Élet és Irodalom* (Life and Literature), and the monthlies *Kortárs* (Contemporary) and *Nagyvilág* (Wide World), as well as a number of provincial literary reviews. Reorganised, the Writers'

315

resumed its functions in the autumn of 1959 and once again became the centre of lively activity.

New works have been created since 1957, and new writers appeared on the literary scene—Hungarian socialist literature has taken a new lease on life; as the present work is being completed all Hungarian writers are engaged in creative work and appearing in print. Some remarkable symptoms of recent development are the publication of novels, plays and short stories treating of present-day themes or of the counter-revolutionary rising of 1956 *(Sooty Sky* by József Darvas; *Rolling Sea* by Géza Molnár; and *Before the Storm* by András Berkesi); a decided shift to socialism by a number of bourgeois writers of the older generation (Endre Illés, József Fodor, Ferenc Jankovich and Gábor Thurzó, who had hitherto passed as a neo-Catholic author); and the unfolding of new talents (among them, in the field of prose, LÁSZLÓ ERDŐS, GÉZA MOLNÁR and MAGDA SZABÓ). A highly gifted generation of young poets has grown up (GÁBOR GARAI, MIHÁLY VÁCI, IMRE GYÖRE, GYÖRGY HÁRS, JÁNOS CSANÁDY and LAJOS MARÓTI) who have demonstrated, through their individual volumes and their anthologies, their striving to express a socialist message through modern media, and to mirror the Nuclear Age Man's attitude to life in all its complexity. Youthful prose writers with individual voices in whom the spirit of experiment runs high (FERENC SÁNTHA, ISTVÁN SZABÓ, LÁSZLÓ TÓTH, GYÖRGY MOLDOVA, ENDRE FEJES, LAJOS GALAMBOS, ENDRE GERELYES and KÁROLY SZAKONYI) approach problems of present-day life. Besides writers with more or less close communist allegiance, members of non-socialist schools too, are publishing new books. Debates that are regaining their former liveliness, as well as revived criticism and literary scholarship, indicate a renewed growth and healthy ferment in new Hungarian letters.

That, however, is something which demands the attention of the critic, rather than that of the literary historian.

# APPENDIX

# BIBLIOGRAPHICAL ANNOTATIONS

COMPILED BY GYÖRGY SZABÓ

The bibliography and repertory of the works requisite to a more thorough knowledge and study of the history of Hungarian literature is contained—till about 1940—in the second volume of the bibliographical handbook by Pál Gulyás. (Gulyás, P.: *A bibliográfia kézikönyve*. Bevezetés a könyvészetbe. Vols. 1-2. Budapest, Országos Széchényi Könyvtár, 1941-1942. 584, 400 p.) The more recent publications on special subjects—since 1946— have been recorded in two current compilations of the Hungarian National Library. The *Magyar Nemzeti Bibliográfia*. *Bibliographia Hungarica* is a monthly catalogue following the universal system of decimal classification (U.D.C. system) which is a list of all works published in Hungary (including those dealing with the history of literature). The more important articles which have appeared in Hungarian periodicals (again in the order of international classification based upon the Dewey system) are listed in the *Magyar Folyóiratok Repertóriuma*. *Repertorium Periodicorum Hungaricorum*, also a monthly publication. (The National Széchényi Library, Budapest is responsible for both publications.) In addition, other, separate, Hungarian literary bibliographies were published between 1945 and 1955, thus the crop of histories of literature and *belles-lettres* which appeared during this decade may be easily surveyed. *( A magyar irodalom bibliográfiája, 1945-1949*. Edited by Sándor Kozocsa. Budapest, Közoktatásügyi Kiadó, 1950. 232 p. — *A magyar irodalom bibliográfiája, 1950*. Edited by Sándor Kozocsa. Budapest, Közoktatásügyi Kiadó, 1951. 80 p. — *A magyar irodalom bibliográfiája, 1951-1952*. Edited by Sándor Kozocsa. Budapest, Művelt Nép, 1954. 179 p. — *A magyar irodalom bibliográfiája, 1953*. Edited by Sándor Kozocsa. Budapest,

Művelt Nép, 1954. 207 p. — *A magyar irodalom bibliográfiája, 1954.* Edited by Sándor Kozocsa. Budapest, Művelt Nép, 1956. 231 p. — *A magyar irodalom bibliográfiája, 1955.* Edited by Sándor Kozocsa. Budapest, Gondolat, 1959. 333 p.)

On the basis of the above data the list of both the bibliographies relating to Hungarian literature, to its history and of individual works on special subjects can be compiled. Outstanding works dealing with certain periods and authors, especially those summing up the most recent scientific achievements, will, however, be mentioned separately. All major text editions are listed.

Of the *general histories of literature* we mention—in the first place—the compendium edited by László Bóka and Pál Pándi, a treatment of Hungarian literature from its earliest beginnings to Sándor Petőfi. (Bóka, L. and Pándi, P.: *A magyar irodalom története 1849-ig.* Edited by — —. Budapest, Bibliotheca, 1957. 492 p. With bibliography and chronological table.) The bibliography contained in this popular compendium (pp. 459-468) serves as a more detailed guide than the present work. The history of Hungarian literature by Antal Szerb—first published in 1934—deals with Magyar literature from its earliest beginnings to the first generation of the authors of the *Nyugat,* to the first quarter of the twentieth century. The most recent edition contains an introductory analysis by István Sőtér. (Szerb, A.: *Magyar irodalomtörténet.* Budapest, Magvető, 1958. 538 p.) The comprehensive history of literature by Jenő Pintér—the system and material of which was outdated already at the time of publication—is in use solely because of its data and extensive bibliographies. (Pintér, J.: *Magyar Irodalomtörténet.* Vols. 1-8. Budapest, Stephaneum, 1930-1941.) The literary "picture-book" by Dezső Keresztury introduces Hungarian literature in pictures from its earliest beginnings to the mid-forties of the twentieth century. (Keresztury, D.: *A magyar irodalom képeskönyve.* Budapest, Magvető, 1956. 343 p.)

Some studies are very helpful in presenting the whole of Hungarian literature. The book entitled *The Problems of Realism in Hungarian Literature* contains the minutes of the debates at the History of Literature Congress held in the beginning of November 1955. (*A realizmus kérdései a magyar irodalomban. Az Irodalomtörténeti Kongresszus vitái. November 1-3, 1955.* Edited by Tibor Klaniczay. Budapest, Akadémiai Kiadó, 1956. 517 p. [The problems of realism and ancient Hungarian literature: pp. 15-154. The problems of critical realism in Hungarian literature: pp. 155-334. The development of socialist realism in Hungarian literature: pp. 335-502.])—The volume of essays by János Horváth is noteworthy, in the first place, in respect of the nineteenth century, but several of his essays deal with other periods as well. (Horváth, J.: *Tanulmányok.* Budapest, Akadémiai Kiadó, 1956. 638 p.) — The selected literary essays by József Révai are primarily Marxist analyses of several problems of the nineteenth and twentieth century. (Révai, J.: *Válogatott irodalmi tanulmányok.* Budapest, Kossuth, 1960. 447 p. [On Kölcsey, Petőfi, Madách, Ady, Móricz and Attila József. Bibliographical notes: pp. 405-445.])—A two-volume collection by József Turóczi-Trostler also deals with several periods of Hungarian literature. (Turóczi-Trostler, J.: *Magyar irodalom—világirodalom.* Vols. 1-2. Budapest, Akadémiai Kiadó, 1961.)

The most important works about individual periods of the history of literature are listed in the alphabetical order of the names of the authors, separately for each period.

## EARLY HUNGARIAN LITERATURE

### MIDDLE AGES

Györffy, Gy.: *Krónikáink és a magyar őstörténet.* Budapest, Néptudományi Intézet, 1948. 189 p. [The Chronicles and Hungarian Prehistory. A summary in French: pp. 181-189.]

Horváth, J.: *A magyar irodalmi műveltség kezdetei.* Budapest, Magyar Szemle Társaság, 1931. 311 p. [On the development of Hungarian literature and its first periods up to the disastrous Battle of Mohács (1526).]

Horváth, J. jr.: *Árpád-kori latin nyelvű irodalmunk stílusproblémái.* Budapest, Akadémiai Kiadó, 1954. 400 p. [A systematization based upon the study of the style of Latin texts written in the Arpadian age—under the reign of the House of Árpád.]

Kardos, T.: *Középkori kultúra, középkori költészet. A magyar irodalom keletkezése.* Budapest, Magyar Történelmi Társulat, 1941. 290 p. [A study of Hungarian culture and poetry in the Middle Ages.]

Király, Gy.: *A magyar ősköltészet.* Budapest, Ethika, 1921. 134 pp. [A study of ancient Hungarian poetry—seventh to tenth centuries. Bibliography: pp. 115-128.]

Mezey, L.: *Irodalmi anyanyelviségünk kezdetei az Árpád-kor végén.* Budapest, Akadémiai Kiadó, 1955. 133 p. [A study of the first writings in Hungarian.]


RENAISSANCE


Balázs, J.: *Sylvester János és kora.* Budapest, Tankönyvkiadó, 1958. 473 p. [The biography of Sylvester, a panorama of his age. Bibliography: pp. 379-391. A summary in German: pp. 439-457.]

Eckhardt, S.: *Balassi Bálint.* Budapest, Franklin, 1941. 224 p. [The life and poetry of Balassi.]

Eckhardt, S.: *Új fejezetek Balassi Bálint viharos életéből.* Budapest, Akadémiai Kiadó, 1957. 104 p. 5 plates. (Irodalomtörténeti Füzetek, 10.) [The results of recent research dealing with the biography of Balassi.]

Eckhardt, S.: *Az ismeretlen Balassi Bálint.* Budapest, Magyar Szemle Társaság, 1943. 313 p. [The most comprehensive biography of Balassi, including several previously unpublished documents.]

Fitz, J.: *A magyar nyomdászat, könyvkiadás és könyvkereskedés története.* Budapest, Akadémiai Kiadó, 1959. 258 p. [The history of printing, publishing and the book trade in Hungary before the disastrous Battle of Mohács (1472-1526). Bibliography: pp. 42-52.]

Horváth, J.: *Az irodalmi műveltség megoszlása. Magyar humanizmus.* Budapest, Magyar Szemle Társaság, 1935. 307 p. [On the Hungarian humanist authors.]

Horváth, J.: *A reformáció jegyében. A Mohács utáni félszázad magyar irodalomtörténete.* Budapest, Akadémiai Kiadó, 1953.

544 p. [A study of the half century following the Battle of Mohács (from about 1520 to 1570) with particular regard to the Reformation.]

Kardos, T.: *A magyarországi humanizmus kora.* Budapest, Akadémiai Kiadó, 1955. 462 p. [On humanism in Hungary, up to 1526.]

Nemeskürty, I.: *Bornemisza Péter. Az ember és az író.* Budapest, Akadémiai Kiadó, 1959. 558 p. [A portrait of Bornemisza, the man and the writer.]

Tolnai, G.: *Régi magyar főurak. Életforma és műveltség az újkorban.* Budapest, Magyar Történelmi Társulat, 1939. 176 p. 8 plates. [On the significant literary aspects of Hungarian aristocratic culture from the sixteenth to the eighteenth century.]

Turóczi-Trostler, J.: *A magyar nyelv felfedezése. Két tanulmány az európai s a magyar humanizmus kapcsolatairól.* Budapest, Ranschburg, 1933. 98 p. [Two essays on the connections between European and Hungarian humanism.]

## BAROQUE

Bán, I.: *Apáczai Csere János.* Budapest, Akadémiai Kiadó, 1958. 606 p. 9 plates. (Irodalomtörténeti Könyvtár, 2.) [An examination of Apáczai's lifework. A summary in French: pp. 563-585.]

Esze, T.: *Magyar költészet Bocskaytól Rákócziig.* (An anthology. Introduction by — —. Edited by Tamás Esze, József Kiss, Tibor Klaniczay. Budapest, Szépirodalmi Kiadó, 1953. 512 p. [A thorough study of Hungarian poetry in the period of the insurrection led by Ferenc Rákóczi at the turn of the seventeenth century.]

Gálos, R.: *Mikes Kelemen.* Budapest, Művelt Nép, 1954. 139 p. 1 plate (Nagy Magyar Írók). [The life and *oeuvre* of Mikes.]

Horányi, M.: *The Magnificence of Eszterháza.* Budapest, Akadémiai Kiadó, 1962. 169 p. [The theatres of the Court in Hungary in the eighteenth and early nineteenth century. Published in English.]

Klaniczay, T.: *Reneszánsz és barokk.* Budapest, Szépirodalmi Kiadó, 1961. 595. p. [Collection of essays on several important

personalities and problems of the Hungarian Renaissance
and baroque.]

Klaniczay, T.: *Zrínyi Miklós*. Budapest, Akadémiai Kiadó, 1954.
548 p. [A comprehensive review of Zrínyi's life and work,
with the historical and literary background of his age.]

Sík, S.: *Pázmány (Péter), az ember és az író*. Budapest, Szent
István Társulat, 1939. 449 p. [About Pázmány.]

Sík, S.: *Zrínyi Miklós*. Budapest, Franklin, 1940. 177 p. 1 plate.
(Magyar Írók.) [Zrínyi and his work.]

Tolnai, G.: *Végzetes esztendők. Tanulmányok és jellemrajzok*.
Budapest, Anonymus, 1945. 130 p. (Anonymus Könyvtár, 2.)
[About the Transylvanian diarists of the seventeenth and
eighteenth centuries.]


MODERN HUNGARIAN LITERATURE

THE ENLIGHTENMENT AND THE REFORM ERA

Dienes, A.: *Petőfi a szabadságharcban*. Budapest, Akadémiai
Kiadó, 1958. 643 p. 84 plates. (Irodalomtörténeti Könyvtár,
3.) [The role played by Petőfi in the revolution and in the
War of Independence of 1848-49. A summary in French:
pp. 609-625.]

Fenyő, I.: *Kisfaludy Sándor*. Budapest, Akadémiai Kiadó, 1961.
440 p. [About Sándor Kisfaludy.]

Gálos, R.: *Bessenyei György életrajza*. Budapest, Közoktatásügyi
Kiadóvállalat, 1951. 425 p. [A biography of Bessenyei and
an analysis of his works.]

Gálos, R.: *Kármán József*. Budapest, Művelt Nép, 1954. 193 p.
[A biography of Kármán and an analysis of his *oeuvre*.]

György, L.: *A magyar regény előzményei*. Budapest, Magyar
Tudományos Akadémia, 1941. 540 p. [About the development of Hungarian prose from 1770 to 1840.]

Hatvany, L.: *Így élt Petőfi*. Vols. 1-5. Budapest, Akadémiai Kiadó,
1955-57. [The life of Petőfi is traced on the basis of reminiscences by contemporaries and of recently found records.]

Horváth, J.: *Kisfaludy Károly és íróbarátai*. Budapest, Művelt
Nép, 1955. 182 p. (Irodalomtörténeti Tanulmányok, 1.) [On

the life of Károly Kisfaludy and the relations among Hungarian authors of the Reform Era.]

Horváth, J.: *Berzsenyi és íróbarátai.* Budapest, Akadémiai Kiadó, 1960. 293 p. [An introduction to Berzsenyi's life, poetry and prose, his relations to Kölcsey and Kazinczy and a presentation of the circle of his author-friends.]

Horváth, J.: *Petőfi Sándor.* Budapest, Pallas, 1922. 597 p. [A comprehensive review of Petőfi's *oeuvre.*]

Horváth, J.: *A magyar irodalmi népiesség Faluditól Petőfiig.* Budapest, Magyar Tudományos Akadémia, 1927. 390 p. [The role of folklore in Hungarian literature from Faludi to Petőfi.]

Julow, V.: *Fazekas Mihály.* Budapest, Művelt Nép, 1955. 222 p. [A biography of Fazekas and an analysis of his works. Bibliography: pp. 208-220.]

Osváth, B.: *Szigligeti Ede.* Budapest, Művelt Nép, 1955. 168 p. [An analysis of Szigligeti's works with special regard to the Hungarian theatre of the age. Bibliography: pp. 161-167.]

Sőtér, I.: *Eötvös József.* Budapest, Akadémiai Kiadó, 1953. 418 p. [A comprehensive review of the life and works of Eötvös.]

Sőtér, I.: *Romantika és realizmus.* Budapest, Szépirodalmi Kiadó, 1954. 611 p. [A collection of essays on the main literary problems of the nineteenth century.]

Szauder, J.: *Bessenyei.* Budapest, Művelt Nép, 1953. 155 p. [About the works of Bessenyei and their significance.]

Szauder, J.: *Kazinczy Ferenc válogatott művei.* (Selected, prefaced and prepared for the press by — —.) Vols. 1-2. Budapest, Szépirodalmi Kiadó, 1960. (Magyar Klasszikusok.) [A detailed treatise on Kazinczy's lifework.]

Szauder, J.: *Kölcsey.* Budapest, Művelt Nép, 1955. 263 p. [Kölcsey's works are viewed against a biographic background.]

Szinnyei, F.: *Novella- és regényirodalmunk a szabadságharcig.* Vols. 1-2. Budapest, Magyar Tudományos Akadémia, 1925-26. [A history of the Hungarian short story and novel from the end of the eighteenth century to 1849. Bibliography: Vol. 2, pp. 315-351.]

Tóth, D.: *Vörösmarty Mihály.* Budapest, Akadémiai Kiadó, 1957. 631 p. (Irodalomtörténeti Könyvtár, 1.) [A biography of

Vörösmarty with an analysis of his works and his era. A summary in German: pp. 599-614.]

Vargha, B.: *Berzsenyi Dániel.* Budapest, Gondolat, 1959. 289 p. [The *oeuvre* of Berzsenyi with a biography. Bibliography: pp. 271-273.]

Waldapfel, J.: *Katona József.* Budapest, Franklin, n. d. 200 p. [A survey of the *oeuvre* of Katona.]

Waldapfel, J.: *A magyar irodalom a felvilágosodás korában.* Budapest, Akadémiai Kiadó, 1954. 336 pp. (2nd enlarged edition: *ibid.* 1957. 313 p.) [Hungarian literature from the end of the eighteenth century with special regard to Bessenyei. Bibliography: pp. 325-334.]

Waldapfel, J.: *Ötven év Buda és Pest irodalmi életéből. 1780-1830.* Budapest, Magyar Tudományos Akadémia, 1935. 368 p. [Literary life and writers from 1780 to 1830 in the twin cities that were to become the Hungarian capital.]

Weber, A.: *A magyar regény kezdetei.* Budapest, Akadémiai Kiadó, 1959. 237 p. [Earliest beginnings of the Hungarian novel from 1818 to 1830. A summary in German: pp. 227-231.]


1849-1890


Barta, J.: *Arany János.* Budapest, Művelt Nép, 1953. 190 p. [An appreciation of the works of Arany.]

Barta, J.: *Madách Imre.* Budapest, Franklin, 1942. 187 p. [An analysis of Madách's lifework.]

Bóka, L.: *Vajda János.* Budapest, Franklin, n. d. 158 p. [An analysis of Vajda's poetry.]

Király, I.: *Mikszáth Kálmán.* Budapest, Művelt Nép, 1952. 269 p. [An analysis of Mikszáth's *oeuvre* against a biographical background.]

Komlós, A.: *Irodalmi ellenzéki mozgalmak a XIX. század második felében.* Budapest, Akadémiai Kiadó, 1956. 115 p. (Irodalomtörténeti Füzetek, 7.) [An analysis of various literary groups, circles and periods from 1860 to the end of the century.]

Komlós, A.: *A magyar költészet Petőfitől Adyig.* Budapest, Gondolat, 1959. 522 p. [Three periods in the history of Hungarian

poetry are presented through literary portraits: 1850-1867,
1867-1880, 1880-1896. Bibliography: pp. 495-508.]

Komlós, A.: *Vajda János.* Budapest, Akadémiai Kiadó, 1954.
363 p. [A presentation of Vajda's lifework against a biographical background. Bibliography: pp. 337-354.]

Rónay, Gy.: *Petőfi és Ady között.* Budapest, Magvető, 1958. 249 p.
[The development of Hungarian literature from 1849 to 1899.
Bibliography: pp. 245-247.]

Somogyi, S.: *Arany László.* Budapest, Művelt Nép, 1956. 143 p.
(Irodalomtörténeti Tanulmányok, 7.) [A biography of László
Arany and an analysis of his works.]

Sőtér, I.: *Jókai Mór.* Budapest, Franklin, n. d. 173 p. [The characteristic features of Jókai's lifework.]

Szinnyei, F.: *Novella- és regényirodalmunk a Bach-korszakban.*
Vols. 1-2. Budapest, Magyar Tudományos Akadémia, 1939-
1941. [The history of the Hungarian short story and novel
from 1849 to 1859. Bibliography: Vol. 2, pp. 661-716.]

Voinovich, G.: *Arany János életrajza.* Vols. 1-3. Budapest,
Magyar Tudományos Akadémia, 1929-1938. [A detailed
biography of János Arany.]


## RECENT HUNGARIAN LITERATURE

(From 1890 to our days)

Bóka, L.: *Ady Endre élete és művei. Ady Endre pályakezdése.*
Budapest, Akadémiai Kiadó, 1955. 319 p. [A biography of
Ady from 1877 to 1905 and an analysis of his first works.]

Bóka, L.: *Tegnaptól máig. Válogatott tanulmányok, esszék, cikkek.*
Budapest, Szépirodalmi Kiadó, 1958. 580 p. [Studies, essays
and articles, dealing, in the first place, with the problems of
modern Hungarian literature.]

Bölöni, Gy.: *Az igazi Ady.* Budapest, Magvető, 1955. 359 p.
[A biography of Ady based on personal contact, with documents.]

Czine, M.: *Móricz Zsigmond útja a forradalmakig.* Budapest,
Magvető, 1960. 611 p. [A biography of Móricz, an analysis
of his works and several problems of contemporary Hun-

garian literature from the turn of the century to the end of 1919.]

Földessy, Gy.: *Ady minden titkai*. Budapest, Akadémiai Kiadó, 1949. 318 p. [A commentary on Ady's poems.]

Hatvany, L.: *Ady*. Vols. 1-2. Budapest, Szépirodalmi Kiadó, 1959. [Essays on Ady.]

József, F.: „*Rohanunk a forradalomba...*" *A modern magyar irodalom útja 1914-1919*. Budapest, Bibliotheca, 1957. 264 p. [The attitude of Hungarian literature during the First World War and the revolutions of 1918-19. Bibliography: pp. 239-262.]

Kardos, L.: *Tóth Árpád*. Budapest, Akadémiai Kiadó, 1955. 455 p. [A biography of Tóth and a detailed analysis of his works.]

Kardos, P.: *Nagy Lajos élete és művei*. Budapest, Bibliotheca, 1958. 416 p. 1 plate. (Nagy Magyar Írók.) [The biography of Lajos Nagy, with an analysis of his works. Bibliography: pp. 398-409.]

Lukács, Gy.: *Írástudók felelőssége*. Budapest, Szikra, 1945. 144 p. [A collection of essays published between 1939 and 1941 on several important representatives (Ady, Babits) and problems ("Szép szó", populist literature) of twentieth-century Hungarian literature.]

Nagy, P.: *Móricz Zsigmond*. Budapest, Művelt Nép, 1953. 416 p. [A biography of Móricz and an analysis of his works. Bibliography: pp. 411-413.]

Nagy, P.: *Új csapáson. Regényirodalmunk a szocialista realizmus útján*. Budapest, Magvető, 1956. 150 p. [Problems of Hungarian prose from 1948 to 1954.]

„A népi írókról. Az MSZMP Központi Bizottsága mellett működő kulturális elméleti munkaközösség állásfoglalása." *Társadalmi Szemle*, 1958. No. 6. pp. 38-69. [The only article in a periodical listed in this bibliography contains the views of the Cultural and Theoretical Research Team working attached to the Central Committee of the Hungarian Socialist Workers' Party in respect of the "populist" authors and analyses in detail the ideology of "populist" literature, summing up at the same time the history of the "populist" writers' movement.]

Schöpflin, A.: *Ady Endre.* 2nd edition. Budapest, Nyugat, 1945. 188 p. [The presentation of Ady's *oeuvre.*]

Schöpflin, A.: *A magyar irodalom története a XX. században.* Budapest, Nyugat-Grill, 1937. 311 p. [Hungarian literature from the end of the nineteenth century to the leading writers in the period following the First World War.]

Szabolcsi, M.: *Költészet és korszerűség.* Budapest, Magvető, 1959. 266 p. [Essays on Attila József (pp. 52-94: "Attila József, Gyula Derkovics, Béla Bartók"), on several poets of the twentieth century and on the problems of research into contemporary literature and Hungarian proletarian literature.]

Tolnai, G.: *Évek — századok. (Tanulmányok, cikkek, bírálatok.)* Budapest, Magvető, 1958. 319 p. [Essays and articles about Hungarian poets of the twentieth century (Ady, Gyula Juhász, Attila József, Radnóti), polemical essays and contemporary criticism. Including several papers on early Hungarian literature.]

Várkonyi, N.: *Az újabb magyar irodalom. 1880-1940.* Budapest, Szukits, 1942. 579 p. [Portraits to the history of Hungarian literature from 1880 to 1940. In use primarily on account of its biographical and bibliographical data.]

In conclusion we call the attention of those interested in twentieth-century Hungarian literature to a collection of articles from the periodical *Nyugat* as a very important source of understanding of the literature of the first part of the century.

*Nyugat-repertórium.* Edited by Ferenc Galambos. Budapest, Akadémiai Kiadó, 1959. 571 p. [In addition to the periodical *Nyugat* (1908-1940), a complete repertory of its predecessors: *Magyar Géniusz* (1902-1903), *Figyelő* (1905), *Szerda* (1906) and of its successor, *Magyar Csillag* (1941-1944) with a combined index (compiled by Lajos Pók).]

*

Of the *text editions,* some comprehensive collections should be mentioned. The volumes of the *Magyar Irodalmi Szöveggyűjtemény* may serve as university handbooks.

To early Hungarian literature:

Barta, J. and Klaniczay, T.: *Magyar irodalmi szöveggyűjtemény*,
Vol. 1. *Szöveggyűjtemény a régi magyar irodalomból*. Parts 1-2.
Edited by — — . Budapest, Tankönyvkiadó, 1951-52.
1273 p. 38 plates.

To the literature of the Enlightenment and Reform Era:

Waldapfel, J.: *Magyar irodalmi szöveggyűjtemény*. Vol. 2.: *Szöveggyűjtemény a felvilágosodás és a reformkorszak irodalmából*.
Part 1. Edited by — — . Budapest, Tankönyvkiadó, 1953.
847 p. 20 plates.

Szauder, J.—Tóth, D.—Waldapfel, J.: *Magyar irodalmi szöveggyűjtemény*. Vol. 2. *Szöveggyűjtemény a reformkorszak irodalmából*. Part 2. Edited by — — . Budapest, Tankönyvkiadó,
1955. 1527 p. 24 plates.

A collection of texts from the second part of the nineteenth
century:

Bóka, L.—Nagy, M.—Németh, G. B.: *Magyar irodalmi szöveggyűjtemény*. Vol. 3. *Szöveggyűjtemény a XIX. század második
felének irodalmából*. Part 2. Edited by — — . Budapest,
Tankönyvkiadó, 1961. 1078 p.

A popular collection of Hungarian *poetry* is the anthology
*Hét évszázad magyar versei* (Hungarian poetry of seven
centuries):

*Hét évszázad magyar versei. (Antológia.)* Edited by Tibor Klaniczay, Aladár Komlós, etc. Vols. 1-4. Budapest, Szépirodalmi
Kiadó, 1954.

Another selection of the best Hungarian poems—up to 1940—
is collected in the *Magyar versek könyve* (The book of Hungarian poetry) and *Magyar próza könyve* (The book of
Hungarian prose) in the field of prose:

*Magyar versek könyve*. Edited, prefaced and annotated by János
Horváth. 2nd enlarged edition. Budapest, Magyar Szemle
Társaság, 1942. 784 p.

*Magyar próza könyve.* Edited by Gyula Bisztray and Dezső Kerecsényi. Vols. 1-2. Budapest, Magyar Szemle Társaság, 1942-1943.

The largest number of comprehensive text editions relating to particular periods refer to early Hungarian literature.

Text editions in Latin:
*Scriptores rerum Hungaricarum tempore ducum regumque stirpis Arpadianae gestarum. Edendo operi praefuit* [Imre] Emericus Szentpéteri. Socii operis erant J[oseph] Balogh, E[mma] Bartoniek, etc. Budapestini, Magyar Tudományos Akadémia, 1937.
And another series:
*Bibliotheca scriptorum medii recentisque aevorum.* Redigit [László] Ladislaus Juhász. Budapest—Bologna, 1931.
The facsimile editions of codices are to be found in the serial edition Codices Hungarici: *Jókai-kódex.* Preface by Dezső Pais. Budapest, Kir. M. Pázmány Péter Tudomány-egyetem Magyarságtudományi Intézete—Stockholmi Magyar Intézet, 1942. XV. p. 81 plates. (Codices Hungarici, 1.) *Apor-kódex.* Prefaced and edited by Dénes Szabó. Kolozsvár, Erdélyi Tudományos Intézet, 1942. XX. 228 p. (Codices Hungarici, 2.) *Guary-kódex.* Prefaced and edited by Dénes Szabó. Budapest, Magyar Tudományos Akadémia, 1944. XXI. 134 p. (Codices Hungarici, 3.) *Példák könyve 1510. Hasonmás és kritikai szövegkiadás.* Annotated, analysed and edited by András Bognár, Ferenc Levárdy. Budapest, Akadémiai Kiadó, 1960. 304 p. (Codices Hungarici, 4.) *Birk-kódex. 1474. Az emlék hasonmása, betűhív olvasata és latin megfelelője.* Prefaced and edited by István Pusztai. Budapest, Akadémiai Kiadó, 1960. 81 p. (Codices Hungarici, 5.)

Early Hungarian texts are to be found also in the following series:
*Nyelvemléktár. Régi magyar kódexek és nyomtatványok.* Published by the Linguistic Committee of the Hungarian Academy of Sciences. Edited by József Budenz, Gábor Szarvas and

Áron Szilády. Vols. 1-15. Budapest, Magyar Tudományos Akadémia, 1874-1908.

*Régi Magyar Könyvtár.* Edited by Gusztáv Heinrich and Elemér Császár. Vols. 1-41. Budapest, Franklin, 1897-1937.

*Régi magyar költők tára.* Published and edited on behalf of the Hungarian Academy of Sciences by Áron Szilády and Lajos Dézsi, Ferenc Badics. Vols. 1-12. Budapest, Magyar Tudományos Akadémia, 1877-1937.

The first volume of *Régi magyar költők tára* (Anthology of ancient Hungarian poets) was also published in a revised edition: *Régi magyar költők tára.* 2nd fully revised edition. Vol. 1. Edited by Cyrill Horváth. Budapest, Magyar Tudományos Akadémia, 1921. 532 p.

The publication of this series was recently resumed:

*Régi magyar költők tára. XVII. század. Új sorozat.* Edited by Tibor Klaniczay, Béla Stoll and Gyula Bisztray. Vol. 1. Budapest, Akadémiai Kiadó, 1959. 658 p.

*The Bibliotheca Hungarica Antiqua* is a letter-perfect fac-simile edition. Its three volumes hitherto published contain János Sylvester's translation of the *New Testament,* Tinódi Lantos Sebestyén's *Chronicle* and István Székely's *Chronicle.*

(János Sylvester:) Vy Testamentu Mag'ar n'elwen, mell'et az Goeroeg, és Diak nelwboel vyonnan fordytank . . . (Translated by — —.) Újsziget, 1541. (Fac-simile edition. Edited and annotated by Béla Varjas.) Budapest, Akadémiai Kiadó, 1960. Leaves (4), 207, (1), 158 (14), 1 appendix: 46 p. (Bibliotheca Hungarica Antiqua, 1.) (Sebestyén Tinódi) Chronica Tinódi Sebestien szoerzese: Elsoe reszebe Janos Kiral halalatul fogua ez esztendeig . . . Mas reszebe kueloemb idoekbe es orszagokba loet dolgoc Istoriac vannac. Colosvarba. 1554 esztendoebe . . . (Fac-simile edition.) (Prepared for the press by Béla Varjas. Commentary by László Bóta.) Budapest, Akadémiai Kiadó, 1959. (160) leaves, 1 appendix: 29 pp. (Bibliotheca Hungarica Antiqua, 2.) (István Székely) Szekel Estvan: *Chronica ez világnac yeles dolgairol.* Craccoba Niomtatot — — — 1559. (Fac-simile edition.) (Prepared for the press and commented by Rabán

Gerézdi.) Budapest, Akadémiai Kiadó, 1960. Leaves (4), 237, 1 appendix: 46 pp. (Bibliotheca Hungarica Antiqua, 3.)

The texts of ancient Hungarian dramas are made available in two editions:

*Régi magyar drámai emlékek.* Vols. 1-2. Edited by Tibor Kardos, prepared for the press by Tibor Kardos and Tekla Dömötör. Co-editor: Gyula Szilvás. Budapest, Akadémiai Kiadó, 1960.

*Régi magyar vígjátékok.* Prepared for the press and introduced by Tekla Dömötör. Budapest, Szépirodalmi Kiadó, 1954. 398 p. (Magyar Klasszikusok.)

Individual volumes of two currently published series also contain early Hungarian literary material.

The *Magyar Könyvtár* (Hungarian Library) is a popularizing series offered to the general public. (Edited by Imre Csanádi. Budapest, Magvető, 1955.) In this series appeared:

*Magyar széphistóriák.* Prepared for the press and annotated by Béla Stoll. Budapest, Magvető, 1955. 181 p. 4 plates [Hungarian romances.]

*Virágénekek és mulatónóták. XVII—XVIII. század.* Edited and annotated by Béla Stoll. Budapest, Magvető, 1956. 243 p. [Love-songs and songs of entertainment of the seventeenth and the eighteenth centuries.]

*Magyar költők. XVII. század.* Compiled by Ferenc Jenei. Budapest, Magvető, 1956. 389 p. 11 plates. [A general anthology of the poets of the seventeenth century.]

*Középkori magyar írások.* Compilation and postscript by László Mezey. Budapest, Magvető, 1957. 433 p. [Hungarian documents from the Middle Ages. Bibliography: pp. 413-414.]

The series of "Magyar Klasszikusok" (edited by László Bóka, István Király, etc. Budapest, Szépirodalmi Kiadó, 1951) publishes the texts of the Hungarian standard authors, some volumes of which will be mentioned later.

The texts of recent Hungarian literature are available—in general—in editions of the works of each pictlaruar author. The collection of the complete belletristic and critical material of the 1918-19 revolutions (the first and third volumes have already appeared) deserves particular attention.

*„Mindenki újakra készül..."* *Az 1918—1919-es forradalmak irodalma.* Vols. 1 and 3. Edited and annotated by Farkas József. Budapest, Akadémiai Kiadó, 1959-1960. (Irodalom — Szocializmus.)


## STANDARD TEXT EDITIONS
## OF THE WORKS OF INDIVIDUAL AUTHORS

The works of the following outstanding Hungarian writers and poets (arranged under author) are available in reliable standard editions:

ADY, E.

*Ady Endre Összes prózai művei.* Edited by Gyula Földessy. Vol. 1-2. Budapest, Akadémiai Kiadó, 1955. [Collected prose works. Vol. 1. 1897-1901. — Vol. 2. Newspaper articles, essays between 1901 and 1902.]
*Ady Endre Összes versei.* Prepared for the press by Gyula Földessy. Vols. 1-2. Budapest, Szépirodalmi Kiadó, 1955. [Collected verses.]

APÁCZAI CSERE, J.

*Apáczai Csere János : Magyar enciklopédia.* Prepared for the press by Imre Bán. Budapest, Szépirodalmi Kiadó, 1959. 441 p. [An edition of Apáczai's *Hungarian Encyclopaedia.*]
*Apáczai Csere János Művei. Magyar Enciklopédia. I. Logika.* Edited by György Lázár, József Molnár and Lajos Orosz. Budapest, Akadémiai Kiadó, 1959. 159 p.

ARANY, J.

*Arany János Összes művei.* Prepared for the press by Géza Voinovich. Vols. 1-6. Budapest, Akadémiai Kiadó, 1951-1952. [Complete works.]

BABITS, M.

*Babits Mihály Válogatott művei.* Selection and preface by Dezső Keresztury, prepared for the press by Tamás Ungvári, an-

notated by György Belia. Vols. 1-2. Budapest, Szépirodalmi
Kiadó, 1959. (Magyar Klasszikusok.) [Selected works.]

BAJZA, J.

*Bajza József Válogatott művei.* Prepared for the press by Imre
Kordé. Selected, prefaced and annotated by Dezső Tóth.
Budapest, Szépirodalmi Kiadó, 1959. 526 p. 1 plate (Magyar
Klasszikusok.) [Selected works.]

BALASSI, B.

*Balassi Bálint Összes művei.* Compiled by Sándor Eckhardt.
Vols. 1-2. Budapest, Akadémiai Kiadó, 1951-1955. [Collected
works.]

Misianik, J.—Eckhardt, S.—Klaniczay, T.: *Balassi Bálint szép
magyar komédiája. A Fanchali Jóv-kódex magyar és szlovák
versei.* Budapest, Akadémiai Kiadó, 1959. 207 p. 4 plates.
(Irodalomtörténeti Füzetek, 25.) [A publication of Balassi's
recently discovered work.]

BATSÁNYI, J.

*Batsányi János Összes művei.* Prepared for the press and annotated
by Dezső Keresztury and Andor Tarnai. Vols. 1-2. Budapest,
Akadémiai Kiadó, 1953-1960. [Collected works.]

BERZSENYI, D.

*Berzsenyi Dániel Összes művei.* (Edited by Oszkár Merényi.)
Budapest, Szépirodalmi Kiadó, 1956. 925 p. [Collected
works.]

BESSENYEI, GY.

*Bessenyei György Válogatott művei.* Prepared for the press and
prefaced by József Szauder. Budapest, Szépirodalmi Kiadó,
1953. 465 p. (Magyar Klasszikusok.) [Selected works.]

BETHLEN, M.

*Bethlen Miklós Önéletírása.* Prefaced by Gábor Tolnai, prepared
for the press and annotated by Éva V. Windisch. Vols. 1-2.
Budapest, Szépirodalmi Kiadó, 1955. (Magyar Századok.)

BORNEMISZA, P.

*Bornemisza Péter : Ördögi kísértetek.* Annotated by Sándor Eckhardt. Budapest, Akadémiai Kiadó, 1955. 239 p. [A critical edition of Bornemisza's *Infernal Ghosts.*]
*Bornemisza Péter : Válogatott írások. 1553-1584.* Compiled and annotated by István Nemeskürty. Budapest, Magvető, 1955. 327 p. (Magyar Könyvtár.) [Selected works.]

BRÓDY, S.

*Bródy Sándor : A sas Pesten. Válogatott írások.* Prepared for the press by József Szauder. Preface by Aurél Kárpáti. Budapest, Szépirodalmi Kiadó, 1954. 516 p. [Selected works.]
*Bródy Sándor : Húsevők. Novellák.* Selected and annotated by András Bródy. Preface by Mihály Czine. Vols. 1-2. Budapest, Magvető, 1960. [Selected short stories.]

CSOKONAI VITÉZ, M.

*Csokonai Vitéz Mihály Összes versei.* Prepared for the press by Balázs Vargha. Vols. 1-2. Budapest, Szépirodalmi Kiadó, 1956-1957. [Collected verses.]

ERDÉLYI, J.

*Erdélyi János : Válogatott esztétikai tanulmányok.* Compiled, prefaced and annotated by Ágnes Heller. Budapest, Művelt Nép, 1953. 127 p. (Filozófiai Kiskönyvtár, 2.) [Selected critical essays.]
*Erdélyi János levelezése. I.* Prepared for the press and annotated by Ilona I. Erdélyi. Budapest, Akadémiai Kiadó, 1960. 520 p. (A Magyar Irodalomtörténetírás Forrásai. Fontes ad Historiam Literariam Hungariae Spectantes, 2. [First part of Erdélyi's correspondence.]

FAZEKAS, M.

*Fazekas Mihály összes művei.* Prepared for the press, by Viktor Julow and László Kéry. Vols. 1-2. Budapest, Akadémiai Kiadó, 1955. [Complete works.]

GYULAI, P.

*Gyulai Pál levelezése 1843-1867-ig.* Prepared for the press and annotated by Sándor Somogyi. Budapest, Akadémiai Kiadó, 1961. 723 p. 4 plates. (A Magyar Irodalomtörténetírás Forrásai. Fontes ad Historiam Literariam Hungariae Spectantes, 4.) [Gyulai's letters between 1843 and 1867.]

HELTAI, G.

*Heltai Gáspár : Válogatott írások.* Compiled and annotated by István Nemeskürty. Budapest, Magvető, 1957. 275 p. 1 plate. (Magyar Könyvtár.) [Selected works.]

HERMÁNYI-DIENES, J.

*Hermányi-Dienes József : Nagyenyedi Demokritus.* Prepared for the press and the postscript written by Tibor Klaniczay. Budapest, Magvető, 1960. 161 p. (Magyar Könyvtár.)

JANUS PANNONIUS

*Jani Pannonii Poemata.* Quae uspiam reperiri potuerunt omnia. Ed. Samuel Teleki. Tom. 1-2. Trajecti ad Rhenum, 1784. [The most complete Latin edition up to now.]

*Janus Pannonius Válogatott versei.* Preface and annotation by Rabán Gerézdi. Prepared for the press by Rabán Gerézdi and László Kálnoki. Budapest, Szépirodalmi Kiadó, 1953. 195 p. [Hungarian translation of Janus Pannonius's selected poems.]

JÓKAI, M.

*Jókai Mór Válogatott művei.* Budapest, Szépirodalmi Kiadó, 1954. [Jókai's selected works are published in a continuous series.]

JÓZSEF, A.

*József Attila Összes művei.* Prepared for the press by József Waldapfel and Miklós Szabolcsi. Vols. 1-3. Budapest, Akadémiai Kiadó, 1952-1958. [The first two volumes: collected poems; third volume: essays, articles.]

JUHÁSZ, GY.

*Juhász Gyula Összes versei.* Prepared for the press by Mihály Ilia and László Péter. Budapest, Szépirodalmi Kiadó, 1959. 1239 p.

KATONA, J.

*Katona József Összes művei.* Prepared for the press and annotated by Andor Solt. Vols. 1-2. Budapest, Szépirodalmi Kiadó, 1959. [Collected works.]

KAZINCZY, F.

*Kazinczy Ferenc levelezése.* Edited by János Váczy and István Harsányi (the 22nd volume). Budapest, Magyar Tudományos Akadémia, 1890-1927. Vols. 1-22. (Kazinczy Ferenc összes művei. 3. osztály. Levelezés.) [Correspondence.]

*Kazinczy Ferenc levelezése.* 23. köt. *(1927 óta előkerült és kötetbe nem foglalt levelek gyűjteménye.)* Edited by Jenő Berlász, Margit Busa, Klára Cs. Gárdonyi, Géza Fülöp. Budapest, Akadémiai Kiadó, 1960. 594 p. (Kazinczy Ferenc összes művei. Levelezés 23. köt. 2. pótkötet.) [A supplementary volume of Kazinczy's Correspondence.]

KISS, J.

*Kiss József, Reviczky Gyula, Komjáthy Jenő Válogatott művei.* Prefaced and prepared for the press by Aladár Komlós. Budapest, Szépirodalmi Kiadó, 1955. 620 p. (Magyar Klasszikusok.) [The selected works of József Kiss, Reviczky and Komjáthy.]

KOMJÁT, A.

*Komját Aladár Összegyűjtött művei.* Preface by Irén Komját. Edited, prepared for the press and annotated by Éva Hegedüs. Translation of the texts from foreign language by György Gábor. Budapest, Szépirodalmi Kiadó, 1957. 496 p. [Complete works. Bibliography: pp. 471-492.]

KOSZTOLÁNYI, D.

*Kosztolányi Dezső Válogatott versei.* Prefaced, selected and prepared for the press by István Vas. 2nd edition. Budapest, Szépirodalmi Kiadó, 1956. 383 p. 1 plate. [Selected poems.]

KÖLCSEY, F.

*Kölcsey Ferenc Összes művei.* Edited, prepared for the press and annotated by Mrs. József Szauder, József Szauder. Vols. 1-3. Budapest, Szépirodalmi Kiadó, 1960. (Magyar Parnasszus, 1.) [Collected works.]

KRÚDY, GY.

*Krúdy Gyula : Válogatott novellák.* Prepared for the press and prefaced by Ede Szabó. Budapest, Szépirodalmi Kiadó, 1957. 549 p. 1 plate. (Magyar Klasszikusok.) [Selected short stories.]

MADÁCH, I.

*Madách Imre Válogatott művei.* Prefaced, prepared for the press and annotated by István Sőtér. Budapest, Szépirodalmi Kiadó, 1958. 647 p. (Magyar Klasszikusok.) [Selected works.]

MIKES, K.

*Mikes Kelemen : Törökországi levelek.* Preface and annotation by János Barta. Prepared for the press by Gyula Bisztray. Budapest, Szépirodalmi Kiadó, 1958. 387 p. [An edition of *Letters from Turkey.*]

MIKSZÁTH, K.

*Mikszáth Kálmán Összes művei.* Edited by Gyula Bisztray and István Király. Budapest, Akadémiai Kiadó, 1956. [Mikszáth's collected works are published in a continuous series.]

MISZTÓTFALUSI KIS, MIKLÓS

*Misztótfalusi Kis Miklós : Maga személyének életének és különös cselekedeteinek mentsége.* Preface by Tibor Klaniczay. Prepared for the press by Imre Bán. Budapest, Szépirodalmi Kiadó, 1952. 170 p.

MÓRICZ, ZS.

*Móricz Zsigmond Összegyűjtött művei.* Budapest, Szépirodalmi Kiadó, 1952. [Móricz's collected works are published in a continuous series.]

*Móricz Zsigmond hagyatékából.* (Prefaced, prepared for the press and annotated by Pál Réz.) Budapest, Akadémiai Kiadó, 1960. 485 p. (Új Magyar Múzeum, 4.) [Unpublished posthumous works.]

PÁZMÁNY, P.

*Pázmány Péter Válogatott írásai.* Compiled by György Rónay. Budapest, Magvető, 1956. 321 p. (Magyar Könyvtár.) [Selected works.]

PETŐFI, S.

*Petőfi Sándor Összes művei.* Vols. 1-6. Budapest, Akadémiai Kiadó, 1951-1956. [Complete works.]

*Petőfi Sándor Összes művei.* Vols. 1-3. Prefaced, edited and prepared for the press by Pál Pándi. Budapest, Szépirodalmi Kiadó, 1955. (Magyar Klasszikusok.) [Complete works.]

RADNÓTI, M.

*Radnóti Miklós : Versek és műfordítások.* Prefaced and prepared for the press by Sándor Koczkás. Budapest, Szépirodalmi Kiadó, 1954. 498 p. [Collected poems and literary translations.]

RÁKÓCZI, F. II.

(Brenner, Antal): Histoire des revolutions de Hongrie ... avec les mémories du prince François Rákóczi sur la guerre de Hongrie depuis 1703 jusqu'à sa fin, et ceux de comte Betlen Niklos (Miklós Bethlen) sur les affaires de Transilvanie. Tom. 1-2. La Haye, Nesulme, 1739. [Original French edition of Rákóczi's memoirs.]

*Rákóczi Ferenc II. Emlékiratai.* (Mémoires sur la guerre de Hongrie depuis 1703 jusqu'à sa fin.) With some fragments of Saint-Simon's (Louis de Rouvray, duc de) memoirs. Annotated by Kálmán Thaly. Translated by István Vas. Prefaced by

Zsigmond Pál Pach. Budapest, Szépirodalmi Kiadó, 1951. 243 p. [Rákóczi's memoirs in Hungarian.]

*Rákóczi Ferenc II. Válogatott levelei.* Edited and introduced by Béla Köpeczi. Budapest, Bibliotheca, 1958. 367 p. 13 plates, 1 map. (Aurora, 10.) [Selected letters.]

RIMAY, J.

*Rimay János Összes művei.* Compiled and prefaced by Sándor Eckhardt. Budapest, Akadémiai Kiadó, 1955. 469 p. [Collected works.]

SÁROSI, GY.

*Sárosi Gyula kisebb költeményei, prózai munkái és levelezése.* Preface and annotation by Gyula Bisztray. Budapest, Akadémiai Kiadó, 1954. 644 p. (Magyar Irodalmi Tár.) [Sárosi's lesser poems, prose and letters.]

TINÓDI LANTOS, S.

*Tinódi Lantos Sebestyén Válogatott munkái.* Compiled and annotated by László Bóta. Budapest, Magvető, 1956. 259 p. 5 plates. (Magyar Könyvtár.) [Selected works.]

VAJDA, J.

*Vajda János Válogatott művei.* Prepared for the press and prefaced by Aladár Komlós. Budapest, Szépirodalmi Kiadó, 1951. 344 p. (Magyar Klasszikusok. ) [Selected works.]

VÖRÖSMARTY, M.

*Vörösmarty Mihály Összes drámai művei.* Prepared for the press by Károly Horváth and Dezső Tóth. Vols. 1-2. Budapest, Szépirodalmi Kiadó, 1955. [Collected dramatic works.]

*Vörösmarty Mihály Összes művei.* Edited by Károly Horváth and Dezső Tóth. Prepared for the press by Károly Horváth. Vols. 1-2. Budapest, Akadémiai Kiadó, 1960. [Collected works. Lesser poems up to 1826 (1st vol.); 1827-1839 (2nd vol.).]

ZRÍNYI, M.

*Zrínyi Miklós Összes művei.* Prepared for the press by Tibor Klaniczay and Csaba Csapodi. Vols. 1-2. Budapest, Szépirodalmi Kiadó, 1958. [Complete works.]

*

In conclusion the periodicals of Hungarian literary scholarship should be mentioned, for they are the best source for the findings of recent research. Most of them contain English, French, German, or Russian extracts of the more important studies. The *Acta Litteraria (Academiae Scientiarum Hungaricae)* is a multilingual periodical of the literary history published by the Hungarian Academy of Sciences since 1957, edited by József Turóczi-Trostler. *A Magyar Tudományos Akadémia Nyelv- és Irodalomtudományi Osztályának Közleményei* contain the publications of the Hungarian Academy of Sciences, Department for Languages and Literary Science. *Irodalomtörténet* (History of Literature) appears as a publication of the Hungarian Society for the History of Literature, while *Irodalomtörténeti Közlemények* (Publications on the History of Literature) is published by the Institute for the History of Literature of the Hungarian Academy of Sciences. The *Világirodalmi Figyelő* (Observer of World Literature), also a critical and documentary periodical, is another publication of the Institute for the History of Literature, and the *Filológiai Közlöny* (Philological Journal) dealing with the philological problems of foreign literature is also published by the Academy. These periodicals occasionally include shorter bibliographical compilations and extracts.

Budapest, April 1961.

*

Subsequent to the closing of these Bibliographical Annotations, a number of publications have appeared which deserve mention.

In the series of *bibliographies* Sándor Kozocsa has published a volume reviewing Hungarian literary production in the years 1956-1957. *(A magyar irodalom bibliográfiája, 1956-1957.* Budapest, Gondolat, 1961. 717 p.) [Bibliography of Hungarian literature.] Among *general histories of literature* the work of Tibor Klaniczay, József Szauder, and Miklós Szabolcsi *(Kis magyar irodalomtörténet.* Budapest, Gondolat, 1961. 493 p.) [A concise history of Hungarian literature], the original of the present Corvina publication, and the volume edited jointly by István Király, Pál Pándi, and István Sőtér dealing with the period between 1849 and 1905 *(A magyar irodalom története. 2. rész. 1849-1905.* Budapest, Gondolat, 1963. 492 p.) [History of Hungarian literature, Part 2. 1849-1905] should be mentioned. Of the volumes of *essays and studies* that of László Bóka *(Arcképvázlatok és tanulmányok.* Budapest, Akadémiai Kiadó, 1962. 542 p.) [Character sketches and essays]; a compilation dealing with the general problems of Hungarian stylistics *(Stilisztikai tanulmányok.* Budapest, Gondolat, 1961. 452 p.) [Studies in stylistics], and two important volumes in the field of comparative theory of literature, the first being the proceedings of the symposium held in Budapest in 1962, the second investigating Hungarian-Russian relations in literature *(La littérature comparée en Europe orientale.* Conférence de Budapest, 26-29 octobre 1962. Budapest, Akadémiai Kiadó, 1963. 534 p.; *Tanulmányok a magyar—orosz irodalmi kapcsolatok köréből.* Edited by G. Gábor Kemény. Budapest, Akadémiai Kiadó, 1961. 3 vols.) [Comparative theory of literature in Eastern Europe; Studies in Hungaro-Russian literary relations] deserve mention.

In addition to the various serial publications the following papers or collections of essays cover certain periods in Hungarian literary history:

The collection of Tibor Klaniczay of early Hungarian literature *(Reneszánsz és barokk.* Budapest, Szépirodalmi Kiadó, 1961. 595 p.) [Renaissance and Baroque], the amended and enlarged edition of József Waldapfel's collection of the Age of Enlightenment *(Magyar irodalom a felvilágosodás korában.* 3rd revised and enlarged edition. Budapest, Akadémiai Kiadó, 1963. 349 p.) [Hungarian literature in the Age of Enlightenment], and the work of József Szauder on Romanticism *(A romantika útján.* Budapest, Szépirodalmi Kiadó, 1961. 486 p. 7 plates) [On the path of Romanticism]. The book of Géza Bodolay on literary societies of students *(Irodalmi diáktársaságok.* Budapest, Akadémiai Kiadó,

1963. 809 p.) [Literary societies of students], the enlarged volume of Gyula Illyés on Petőfi *(Petőfi Sándor.* Budapest, Szépirodalmi Kiadó, 1963. 681 p. 1 plate) [Sándor Petőfi], the paper of Pál Pándi on the beginnings of Petőfi's career *(Petőfi. A költő útja 1844 végéig.* Budapest, Szépirodalmi Kiadó, 1961. 589 p.) [Petőfi. The poet's path till the end of 1844], and the paper of István Rejtő on Zoltán Thury *(Thury Zoltán.* Budapest, Szépirodalmi Kiadó, 1963. 419 p.) [Zoltán Thury] deal with the history of modern Hungarian literature, its personalities and problems. Traits and authors of Hungarian literature are discussed in the new and enlarged edition of Péter Nagy's monograph on Móricz *(Móricz Zsigmond.* 2nd revised edition. Budapest, Szépirodalmi Kiadó, 1962. 518 p. 1 plate) [Zsigmond Móricz], in Rezső Szalatnai's book on a period of the life of Gyula Juhász *(Juhász Gyula hatszáz napja.* Budapest, Magvető, 1962. 278 p. 4 plates) [The six hundred days of Gyula Juhász], Károly Szalay's biography of Frigyes Karinthy *(Karinthy Frigyes.* Budapest, Szépirodalmi Kiadó, 1961. 395 p. 9 plates) [Frigyes Karinthy], the document volume of Imre Paku on Gyula Juhász *(Juhász Gyula.* Budapest, Magvető, 1962. 733 p. 36 plates) [Gyula Juhász], and the bibliography, and collection of documents relating to Antal Szerb *(Szerb Antal.* Budapest, Fővárosi Szabó Ervin Könyvtár, 1961. 28, XXXIII p.) [Antal Szerb], the study of Magda K. Nagy on the periodical *Válasz (A Válasz.* Budapest, Szépirodalmi Kiadó, 1963. 379 p. 8 plates) [The *Válasz* (Answer)], the study of Pál Pándi on certain problems of literature between the two world wars *(Elsüllyedt az irodalom?* Budapest, Szépirodalmi Kiadó, 1963. 209 p.) [Has literature gone down?], the volume of essays by József Waldapfel *(Szocialista kultúra és irodalmi örökség. Tanulmányok, glosszák, kritikák.* Budapest, Akadémiai Kiadó, 1961. 385 p.) [Socialist culture and literary heritage. Studies, commentaries, criticisms], further the collection of criticisms on modern Hungarian prose compiled by Dezső Tóth *(Életünk — regényeink.* Budapest, Szépirodalmi Kiadó, 1963. 229 p.) [Our life—our novels].

The following volumes have been published in the various *series on literary history:*

*Irodalomtörténeti Könyvtár* (Akadémiai Kiadó, Budapest) [Library of literary history]: István Fenyő: *Kisfaludy Sándor*

(1961. 446 p. 5 plates) [Sándor Kisfaludy], Rabán Gerézdi: *A magyar világi líra kezdetei* (1962. 327 p. 2 plates) [Beginnings of Hungarian secular lyrical poetry], Kálmán Vargha: *Móricz Zsigmond és az irodalom* (1962. 402 p.) [Zsigmond Móricz and literature], Pál Pándi—Dezső Tóth (editors): *Tanulmányok Petőfiről* (1962. 509 p.) [Studies on Petőfi], Kálmán Kovács: *Fejezetek a magyar kritika történetéből. Gyulai Pál irodalmi elveinek kialakulása. 1850-1860.* (1963. 303 p.) [Chapters on the history of literary criticism in Hungary. Shaping of the literary principles of Pál Gyulai], and Miklós Szabolcsi: *Fiatal életek indulója. József Attila pályakezdése* (1963. 634 p. 18 plates) [First steps in literary careers. The beginnings of the career of Attila József].

*Irodalomtörténeti Füzetek* (Akadémiai Kiadó, Budapest) [Booklets on literary history]: István Csukás: *Ady Endre a szlovák irodalomban* (1961. 197 p. 3 plates) [Endre Ady in Slovak literature], Oszkár Merényi: *Ismeretlen és kiadatlan Kölcsey dokumentumok* (1961. 198 p. 2 plates) [Unknown and unpublished documents on Kölcsey], Ferenc Kiss: *A beérkezés küszöbén. Babits, Juhász és Kosztolányi ifjúkori barátsága* (1962. 153 p.) [On the threshold of making a name. Early friendship of Babits, Juhász and Kosztolányi], László Zrinszky: *A Magyar Tanácsköztársaság emléke költészetünkben 1919-1945.* (1962. 147 p.) [The memory of the Hungarian Republic of Councils in our poetry. 1919-1945], József Varga: *Ady útja az „Új versek" felé* (1963. 92 p.) [Ady's path to the "New Poems"], Géza Lengyel: *Magyar újságmágnások* (1963. 193 p.) [Hungarian press magnates], Imre Baranyi: *A fiatal Madách gondolatvilága. Madách és az Athenaeum* (1963. 149 p.) [The thinking of the young Madách. Madách and the Athenaeum].

*Új Magyar Múzeum* (Akadémiai Kiadó, Budapest) [New Hungarian museum]: *Emlékezések Ady Endréről* (Edited by Miklós Kovalovszky) (1961. 659 p. 16 plates, one map) [Reminiscences of Endre Ady], *Ambrus Zoltán levelezése* (Edited by Zoltán Fallenbüchl) (1963. 527 p. 5 plates) [The Correspondence of Zoltán Ambrus], *Móricz Zsigmond levelei. I-II.* (Edited by Dóra E. Csanak) (1963, two volumes) [The letters of Zsigmond Móricz, I-II].

*Bibliotheca Hungarica Antiqua* (Akadémiai Kiadó, Budapest):

*Ozorai Imre vitairata* (De Christo, et eius Ecclesia. Item de Anti-christo eiusque Ecclesia. Printed in Cracow by Jerome Vietor. 1535.) [Fac-simile edition. Edited by Béla Varjas. Introduction by István Nemeskürthy] (1961. 125 letters, one appendix: 30 p.) [Polemical treatise of Imre Ozorai], Gáspár Heltai: *Cancionale, az az*, Historias Enekes Koenyw ... a Magyari Királyokról és egyéb szép loet dolgokról ... Heltai Gaspar Colosvárot 1574) [Fac-simile edition, edited and introduced by Béla Varjas] (1962. 232 letters, one appendix: 31 p.) [Cancionale, that is book of hymns in rhyme ... of Hungarian kings and other fair past things ... by Gáspár Heltai at Kolozsvár, 1574].

*A Magyar Irodalomtörténetírás Forrásai. Fontes ad Historiam Literarium Hungariae Spectantes* (Akadémiai Kiadó, Budapest) [The sources of Hungarian literary history], Gyulai Pál: *Bírála-tok. Cikkek. Tanulmányok.* (Edited and provided with annotations by Gyula Bisztray and Aladár Komlós) (1961. 685 p. 1 plate.) [Criticism. Articles. Studies].

Of the collections of *literary texts* Parts 1 and 2 of Volume 3 of *Magyar Irodalmi Szöveggyűjtemény* [Collections of Hungarian literary texts], covering the literature of the Age of Revolution and the War of Independence as well as the second half of the 19th century, also Part 1 of Volume 4 covering the period of *Nyugat* (The West) and Ady, have been published by Tankönyv-kiadó, Budapest (1961-1963). In the *Régi Magyar Költők Tára* [Collection of early Hungarian poets] Volumes 2 and 3 covering the 17th century, edited by Tibor Klaniczay and Béla Stoll, have been published by Akadémiai Kiadó, Budapest, in 1961 and 1962. Also a bibliography has been compiled by Béla Stoll for the study of early Hungarian literature *(A magyar kéziratos énekeskönyvek és versgyűjtemények bibliográfiája 1565-1840.)* (Budapest, Akadémiai Kiadó, 1963. 537 p.) [Bibliography of Hungarian hymnals and collection of poems in MMS. 1565-1840].

In the series of *text editions* of individual authors the critical edition of the collected works of Mór Jókai is being published (Volume 1: 1962) by Akadémiai Kiadó; and an edition of the novels and short stories of Zsigmond Móricz by Magyar Helikon Kiadó (editors Mihály Czine, Péter Nagy, Kálmán Vargha). The collected works of Kálmán Mikszáth are being published by

Akadémiai Kiadó in a continuous series (edited by Gyula Bisztray and István Király). The critical editions of the collected works of János Arany (1963: Vol. 12. Editor: Dezső Keresztury. Budapest, Akadémiai Kiadó), of the collected works of János Batsányi (edited by Dezső Keresztury, Andor Tarnai. Budapest, Akadémiai Kiadó, 1962: Volume 3), and of the collected works of Mihály Vörösmarty started at an earlier date (Akadémiai Kiadó) have been continued.

In the series *Magyar Klasszikusok* [Hungarian Classics] (Szépirodalmi Kiadó, Budapest) the collected poems of Endre Ady (1962, two volumes), the selected works of Dániel Berzsenyi (1961, 536 p. 1 plate), the selected works of János Erdélyi (1961, 619 p. 1 plate), the selected works of Frigyes Karinthy (1962, 770 p.), the selected works of Aladár Komját (1962, 386 p. 1 plate), the selected works of Jenő Péterfy (1962. 672 p. 1 plate), the selected works of Miklós Radnóti (1962. 659 p. 1 plate), and the selected works of Mihály Tompa (1961. 719 p. 1 plate) have appeared. In the series of *Helikon Klasszikusok* [Helikon Classics] the collection of poems and translations of Attila József have been published (Budapest, Magyar Helikon, 1963, 973 p.). Not included in the series the collection of Ady's short stories (Budapest, Szépirodalmi Kiadó, 1961, 1406 p. 20 plates), the selected poems of József Kiss (Budapest, Szépirodalmi Kiadó, 1961, 297 p. 1 plate), the collected poems of Dezső Kosztolányi (Budapest, Szépirodalmi Kiadó, 1962, two volumes), and the collected works of Gyula Juhász have come out, the latter in a critical edition. (The collected works of Gyula Juhász. Editor: László Péter, prepared for the press by Mihály Ilia and László Péter. Budapest, Akadémiai Kiadó, 1962, three volumes.)

Publication of the collection of documents „*Mindenki újakra készül* . . ." [All prepare for new things . . . ] on the literature of the revolutionary period 1918-1919 has been continued. Volume 2 (edited by József Farkas) deals with political writings and literary life of the bourgeois revolution (Budapest, Akadémiai Kiadó, 1962, 790 p.). Under the title *Irodalom—Szocializmus* [Literature—Socialism] a new series has been launched treating the history of socialist literature in Hungary. The first volume of the new series is a collection of studies and essays relating to the subject-matter of the series *(Tanulmányok a magyar szocialista irodalom történetéből)* [Studies from the history of Hungarian socialist literature], (edited by Miklós Szabolcsi and László Illés. Budapest, Akadémiai Kiadó, 1962, 676 p.).

Finally it should be noted that the periodical *Irodalomtörténet* (Literary History) has been merged into *Irodalomtörténeti Közlemények* (Publications on Literary History), a periodical appearing at more frequent intervals. The Institute of Literary History of the Hungarian Academy of Sciences, the Hungarian Society of Literary History, and the Hungarian Writers' Association, in joint editorship, started a new periodical entitled *Kritika* (Criticism) in September 1963.

Budapest, 1st November, 1963.

# SELECTED TRANSLATIONS
## FROM HUNGARIAN LITERATURE

### COMPILED BY TIBOR DEMETER

### ANTHOLOGIES

1. *Magyar Poetry*—Selections from Hungarian Poets
   Translated by William N. Loew.
   New York, 1908. Amerikai Magyar Népszava. 349 p.

2. *Modern Magyar Lyrics*—Selected Gems from Alex. Petőfi and other Modern
   Hungarian Poets
   Translated by William N. Loew.
   Budapest, 1926. Wodianer F. 107 p.

3. *The Magyar Muse*—An Anthology of Hungarian Poetry
   Edited and translated by Watson Kirkconnell.
   Winnipeg, 1933. Kanadai Magyar Újság Press. 222 + 3 p.

4. *Hungaria*—Translated by Lawrence Wolfe
   London, 1936. Ivor Nicholson and Watson.

5. *Hungarian Anthology*
   Edited by Paul Tábori.
   London, 1943. John Bale & Staples Ltd. 147 p.

6. *A Little Treasury of Hungarian Verse*
   Washington, 1947. American-Hungarian Federation.

7. *Fifth Little Book*
   Hungarian Folktales and Illustrations by George Buday.
   London, 1949. Printed for the Artist and his Friends. 24 p.

8. *Hungarian Poetry*
   Selected and edited by Egon F. Kunz.
   Sydney, 1955. Pannonia Publ. 158 p.

9. *Hungarian Short Stories, 19th and 20th Centuries.*
   Budapest, 1962. Corvina Press. 392 p.

10. *The Plough and the Pen*—Writings from Hungary 1930-1956.
    Edited by I. Duczynska and K. Polanyi. London, 1963. P. Owen.

# AUTHORS

\* The numbers refer to the anthologies.

GVADÁNYI József
—3.

GYÖNGYÖSI István
—8.

GYÓNI Géza
—3, 6.

GYULAI Pál
—1, 2, 8.

HARSÁNYI Zsolt
—*Hungarian Rhapsody*. Translated by Lynton Hudson. Sydney, 195?. Pannonia Publ. 520 p.

HELTAI Jenő
—4, 9.
—"The Silent Knight." Translated by Humber Wolfe. Budapest, 1937. *Hungarian Quarterly* III. p. 721.

HUNYADI Sándor
—4, 9.

ILLÉS Béla
—*Carpathian Rhapsody*. Translated by G. B. Gárdos. Budapest, 1963. Corvina Press. 268+290 p.

ILLYÉS Gyula
—10.

JÓKAI Mór
—9.
—*The Man with the Golden Touch*. Translated from the Hungarian by Mrs. H. Kennard. Revised by Elizabeth West. Budapest, 1963. Corvina Press. 410 p.
—*Black Diamonds*. Translated by Fr. A. Gerard. London, 1925. Jarrold & Sons. 452 p.

JÓZSEF Attila
—10.
—"*Voices. A Quarterly of Poetry*." 1947. (Cleveland) p. 55—62.
—*The New Hungarian Quarterly*. 1961. No. 2. "*A Portrait of Attila József the Poet*."

JUHÁSZ Ferenc
—10.

JUHÁSZ Gyula
—2, 3, 8.

KACZÉR Illés
—*The Siege (I). Fear not, my Servant Jacob (II). The Yellow House*. Translated by Lawrence Wolfe. New York, 1953. The Dial Press. 594 p.

KAFFKA Margit
—9.

KARINTHY Frigyes
—9.
—*Soliloquies in the Bath*. Translated by Lawrence Wolfe. London-Edinburgh, 1937. W. Hodge & Co.

KASSÁK Lajos
—4.

KAZINCZY Ferenc
—3, 6, 8.

KISS József
—1, 2, 3, 8.

KISFALUDY Károly
—1, 3, 6, 8.

KISFALUDY Sándor
—1, 3, 8.

KODOLÁNYI János
—4.

KÖLCSEY Ferenc
—1, 3, 6, 8.

KOMÁROMI János
—4.

KOMJÁTHY Jenő
—3.

KÖRMENDI Ferenc
—*The Forsaken (Years of Eclipse)*. Translated by Lawrence Wolfe. New York, 1952. Popular Library. 381 p.

KORMOS István
—*The Two Magic Oxen*. Translator unknown. London, 1961. Baucroft Publ. 16 p.

KOSZTOLÁNYI Dezső
—3, 8, 9.
—*Nero*. Translated from the Hungarian by Adam de Hegedüs. London, 1947. Staples Press Ltd. 288 p.
—*Wonder Maid*. Translated by Adam de Hegedüs. London, 1947. Staples Press Ltd. 211 p.

KRÚDY Gyula
—9.

KUCZKA Péter
—10.

KUNCZ Aladár
—*Black Monastery*. Translated by Ralph Murray. London, 1934. Chatto & Windus. 409 p.

LUKÁCS György
—*The Historical Novel*. London, 1962. Merlin Press.
—*The Meaning of Contemporary Realism*. London, 1962. Merlin Press.

MADÁCH Imre
—*The Tragedy of Man*. Translated by J. C. W. Horne. Budapest, 1963. Corvina Press. 200 p.

MIKSZÁTH Kálmán
—9.

—*St. Peter's Umbrella.* Translated from the Hungarian by B. W. Workswick. Revised by István Fekete. Budapest, 1962. Corvina Press. 190 p.

MOLNÁR Ferenc
—9.
—*No Greater Glory.* Translated by Louis Rittenberg. New York, 1927. Grossel & Dunlap. 292 p.
—*Captain Magnificent.* Translated by Barrows Mussey. London, 1946. Cassel and Company Ltd. 160 p.
— *Farewell my Heart.* Translator unknown. New York, 1945. Simon & Schuster Inc.
— *Stories for Two.* Translator unknown. New York, 1950. Horizon Press. 351 p.
—*Romantic Comedies.* Eight Plays. Translated by Sydney Howard. New York, 1952. Macy Masius. 331 p.

MÓRA Ferenc
—9.
—*Song of the Wheatfields.* Translated by George Halász. London, 1930. Allen & Unwin. 283 p.

MÓRICZ Zsigmond
— *Be Faithful unto Death.* Translated from the Hungarian by Susan Körösi-László. Budapest, 1962. Corvina Press. 265 p.
— *The Torch.* Translated from the Hungarian by Emil Lengyel. New York, 1931. Knopf Publ. Co.
see also
—4, 9, 10.

NAGY Lajos
—9.

NÉMETH László
—10.

PAP Károly
—4.

PASSUTH László
— *The Rain God Weeps for Mexico.* Translator unknown. London, 1948. F. Aldor Publ. 397 p.

PETŐFI Sándor
—1, 2, 3, 8.
—*Sixty Poems by A. Petőfi.* Translated by E. B. Pierce and E. Delmár. Budapest, 1948. Published under the auspices of the Petőfi Society. Franklin Press. 78 p.

RÁTH-VÉGH István
—*From the History of Human Folly.* Translated by Zs. Horn. Budapest, 1963. Corvina Press. 290 p.

REVICZKY Gyula
—4.

SÁRKÖZI György
—4.

SOMLYÓ Zoltán
—2.

SZABÓ Lőrinc
—6.

SZABÓ Magda
—*The Fawn.* Translated by Kathleen Szasz. London, 1963. Jonathan Cape. 215 p.
—*Tell Sally...* Translated by Ursula Mclean. Budapest, 1963. Corvina Press. 286 p,

SZABÓ Pál
—10.
—*People of the Plains.* Translated by George Halász. Boston, 1932. Little-Brown. 287 p.

SZÁSZ Károly
—1, 3.

SZÉP Ernő
—*In May—A Play.* Translated by J. Szebenyei. New York, 1925. Samuel French. 31 p.
see also
—3, 4.

SZERB Antal
—4, 10.

SZOMORY Dezső
—4, 10.

TAMÁSI Áron
—4, 10.

TAMÁSI Lajos
—10.

TERSÁNSZKY Józsi Jenő
—4.

TÖMÖRKÉNY István
—9.

TOMPA Mihály
—1, 3, 8.

TÓTH Árpád
—3, 8.

VAJDA János
—1, 3, 8.

VERES Péter
—10.

VÖRÖSMARTY Mihály
—1, 3, 8.

ZELK Zoltán
—10.

ZILAHY Lajos
—*The Dukay.* Translated by Pók. New York, 1949. Prentice Hall Publ.

ZRÍNYI Miklós
—3, 8.

# THE HUNGARIAN LANGUAGE

A few notes on the pronunciation of Hungarian may be useful. Readers may wish to know the correct pronunciation of proper names appearing in the text. A short explanation of the origin and development of the language may also be found interesting.

First, here are a few of the differences from the English pronunciation of vowels and consonants:

*c*   has a special sound, unlike either the hard or soft English *c*. It resembles *ts* pronounced together, as in *tsetse*.

*cs*   like the English *tch*, as in ma*tch*.

*g*   is always hard, as in *g*ood.

*gy*   a soft *d*, as in *due*.

*j*   like the English *y* in *y*ear.

*ly*   rather like *oy* in b*oy* or *ay* in d*ay* according to which vowel precedes it. The *l* is silent.

*ny*   a soft *n*, as in *new*.

*s*   is the same sound as the English *sh*, as in *sh*ort.

*sz*   is the same as the English *s*, as in *s*on.

*ty*   a soft *t*, as in *T*uesday.

*zs*   is the same sound as the English *su*, in plea*su*re, mea*su*re.

Among the vowels we should notice the following differences from English pronunciation:

*á*   long, clear vowel, similar to the *a* in l*a*rge.

*a*   a short, open *o*, as in n*o*t.

*é*   like the *a* in st*a*te.

*e*   like the *e* in m*e*n.

*ó*   closed, long *o* as in h*o*rn.

*ö*   similar to the *er* in bigg*er*.

*ő*   similar to *ö* but longer, as in w*or*d.

*ü*   a sound which does not exist in English, but is like the French *u*. In English the nearest sound is the *u* in fut*u*re.

In Hungarian the stress is *always* on the first syllable.

Hungarian belongs to the Finno-Ugric subfamily of the Ural-Altaic languages, which includes Finnish and Esthonian. It has no relationship to other European languages which are classed as Indo-European. Among the differences is the fact that grammatical gender is unknown in Hungarian. Its original word stock has been added to by borrowing from Turkish, the Slav languages, German, Latin and French among others. Towards the end of the eighteenth and beginning of the nineteenth centuries the language was reformed and made more suitable for modern usage, a great many new words being added. Present-day Hungarian has about a million words, roots and derivatives. Eight to ten thousand of these are used in everyday life.

# INDEX

49496

PH
3012
K513

KLANICZAY, TIBOR
HISTORY OF HUNGARIAN LITERATURE.

## DATE DUE

| | |
|---|---|
| | |
| | |
| | |
| | |
| | |
| | |
| | |
| | |
| | |
| | |
| | |
| | |
| | |
| | |
| | |
| | |
| | |

GAYLORD                                           PRINTED IN U.S.A.